Motocross & Off-Road
Performance Handbook
Third Edition

Motocross & Off-Road
Performance Handbook
Third Edition

Eric Gorr

MOTORBOOKS

First published in 2004 by Motorbooks, an imprint of MBI Publishing Company, Galtier Plaza, Suite 200, 380 Jackson Street, St. Paul, MN 55101-3885 USA

Motorbooks titles are also available at discounts in bulk quantity for industrial or sales-promotional use. For details write to Special Sales Manager at MBI Publishing Company, Galtier Plaza, Suite 200, 380 Jackson Street, St. Paul, MN 55101-3885 USA.

ISBN 0-7603-1975-8

Edited by Lee Klancher and Lindsay Hitch
Designed by Mandy Iverson

Printed in China

On the front cover:
Off-road superhero Scott Summers and his tweaked CRF450 shred a berm. *Joe Bonnello*

Inset:
Talon hubs . . . Drool. *Lee Klancher*

On the back cover:
To check the valve-to-guide clearance, extend the valve out of the seat about 10 mm and try to wiggle it in any direction. Excessive movement means that the guides need to be replaced.

On the title page:
Chad Reed on his No. 22 Yamaha YZ250. *Joe Bonnello*

CONTENTS

ACKNOWLEDGMENTS

So many people have helped with the success of these three editions of the performance handbook. These are the people that deserve special thanks: My dad, John, and my mom, Carolyn, for encouraging my brother Chris and I to learn how things work and giving us the tools and things to take apart. Thanks to Rich Rohrich for all of his scientific and engineering information over the years and help with the improved four-stroke material for this book. Thanks to Bob Vanorden of DirtRider.Net for providing a web forum where information is exchanged and knowledge expands. Jeremy Wilkey of MX-TECH helped me update the suspension information in this book. Jeremy's contributions to the Suspension Forum of DirtRider.Net have empowered thousands of dirt bikers to understand how to make their bikes handle better. Tom Profita provided so much information for the model tuning tips section. Being a race mechanic dad with competitive sons Pat and Casey, he experiences what works and what breaks on a bike first hand. Tom has been a great help for all three editions of this performance handbook.

Thanks to Scott Reath of US Chrome for supplying performance coatings and the information about how they're used on modern racing engines. Tryce Welch helped with Chapter 3 regarding the setup of DTX bike. Steve Johnson of Wiseco has been a resource for all three editions of this book with his support on cylinder power systems.

Congratulations to Lee Klancher for convincing MBI Publishing Company to start this successful series of motocross and off-road performance and riding books nearly ten years ago. Thanks to Lindsay Hitch for editing the text and photos of this book.

And finally, two writers deserve special thanks for influencing in my motorcycling life—Rick "Super Hunky" Sieman and the late Gordon Jennings. Gordon was the premier motorcycle technical writer when I was growing up in the 1970s. In recent years, he was the technical editor for *Motorcyclist* magazine. His tech articles motivated me to run out to the garage and chuck up a burr in a drill and have a go at porting cylinders. Thanks to Rick Sieman for setting an example of how to write technical articles and teach a generation of dirt bikers a crash course in mechanical common sense.

Thank you for purchasing this third edition of the performance handbook. So much has changed since I started writing this book in 1995. Back then, dirt biking was a fringe sport. The flow of information was centralized at the popular dirt bike magazines, where motojournalists often put the needs of the advertisers before the needs of the readers. The Internet was in its infancy, doubling in users every three months. The sport of dirt biking was ready for explosive growth, but the information infrastructure couldn't handle the demand. The first edition of this book featured a foundation of all the basics in caring for a dirt bike, plus inside tips on what breaks and what products work with the model tuning tips. Technology ushered in some huge changes in engine and suspension designs. Back in the first edition, four-stroke dirt bikes were overweight air-cooled trail bikes. Now, the latest thumpers are 1/8 of a Formula 1 engine and just as maintenance demanding. In the first edition, twin-chamber forks and position-damping sensitive shocks were new innovations that looked like they wouldn't catch on. Now, twin-chamber forks are the standard and both designs require a higher level of specialized knowledge and tooling just to service the suspension properly.

In the first edition, we used frequently asked questions (FAQs) and I offered free email support for the readers of my book with their own FAQs. But soon the demand from the readers was growing at rate that couldn't be satisfied by one-on-one email. For this third edition, we were decided to post a master file of 100 pages of FAQs on my Web site, www.ericgorr.com. Over the years, readers have complained that the phone and address information contained in the resource guide goes out of date quickly. So I decided to post and update the resource guide on my Web site also.

In the second edition, I added more tuning information and offered free technical support through a web-based bulletin board named DirtRider.Net in the Mods & Performance forum. Bob Vanorden had a great idea—he created DirtRider.Net to become the first web-based forum that gave dirt bikers a place to ask and answer questions. DRN has become the "Positronic Brain" of dirt biking, with well over a million posts in 30 different forums. I've helped as a moderator of the Mods & Performance forum. This forum's participants helped me with the second and third editions. Answering questions, looking for mechanical trends, reading riders' reviews of products they purchased . . . . it all feeds into this third edition to benefit you, the reader.

Today, dirt biking is moving from the fringe to the mainstream. With television coverage of supercross, freestyle, and supermoto, dirt bikers are becoming sports icons. Sales of dirt bikes grow 25 percent a year, yet the service sector of the industry is shrinking. Dealership mechanics make easy money tuning up street bikes and they can't be bothered with dirt bikes. Dealership labor rates average $75/hour and few dirt bikers can afford those rates. Do-it-yourself is a necessity in dirt biking and there is a huge demand for home-based dirt bike mechanics. This third edition of the performance handbook features more information on four-stroke engines and suspension systems. We've added 25 pages and 50 more photos and switched to color to better communicate the revised information contained in this book. I hope you like it! Looking forward to the fourth edition of the performance handbook; I expect that we'll see the advent of computerized engine management systems, fuel injection, pneumatic valvetrains, and two-wheel fluid drive. Dirt biking has a bright future.

—Eric Gorr, August 2004

Author Eric Gorr is an inventor and performance engine builder from Chicago, Illinois. Eric worked as a contributing technical writer for the biggest dirt bike magazines on three continents and is the moderator of the Mods and Performance forum at www.dirtrider.net. He earned two U.S. patents and has produced innovative designs in motocross since he started working as a motorcycle mechanic in 1971. Eric's mail-order company, Forward Motion, provides dirt bikers with performance machining solutions to maintenance problems.

CHAPTER ONE

GETTING STARTED

TYPES OF DIRT BIKING

There are several types of dirt bike sports and each sport has a bike designed especially for the demands of its application. Off-road sports include enduro, hare scrambles, cross country, dual sport, and desert. Motocross sports include stadium and freestyle. Some of the more off-beat sports include dirt track, grass drag, hillclimb, and trials.

TYPES OF BIKES

Choosing an off-road bike depends on the demands of your local riding areas, including the terrain and laws regarding off-road use. Recent government legislation restricts the use of two-stroke engines in dirt bikes manufactured after December 31, 1997. That means that on government-owned off-road vehicle (ORV) parks, you can't buy a license tag (green sticker) for two-stroke dirt bikes of a 1998 model year and newer. You can ride older bikes in those areas and four-stroke bikes too. In 2006, because of emissions regulations, bikes with two-stroke engines will be banned from ORV parks.

If you're looking for a well-rounded bike that you can ride on the street and the trails, consider a dual-sport bike. The KTM LC, Suzuki DR, Kawasaki KLR, and Honda XRL are street-legal dirt bikes. The bikes aren't designed for serious off-road use, but they can be adapted for competition in enduro, hare scrambles, cross country, or desert racing.

If you're committed to off-road competition, including MX but no street riding, consider an enduro bike. Models like the Honda XR, KTM XC,

These are the different types of dirt bikes.
- A) PeeWee 50-cc automatic with training wheels
- B) Pit bike
- C) Motocross
- D) Off-road
- E) Hillclimber
- F) Supermoto
- G) Side-hack MX
- H) Observed trials
- I) Desert/Rally
- J) DTX

Suzuki DRS, Yamaha WR, and Kawasaki KDX are versatile, strong bikes that hold their value better than a modified dual-sport bike.

For off-beat sports such as dirt track, hillclimb, or freestyle, you'll need to make modifications to adapt the bike and conform to the rules of competition. Sports such as trials require a very specialized and expensive bike. Most trials clubs have a competition class for dual-sport bikes. Overall, a dual-sport bike is a great way to get into dirt biking, and when you get serious about a particular sport, you'll probably want to keep your old dual-sport bike for a spare.

EVALUATING DIRT BIKES

Whether you are figuring out how to modify your own machine or buying a used bike, the best way to start is to use the following simple tests to evaluate the bike. Below is a list of the major components of a dirt bike and tips on evaluating and estimating the cost of repairs. Use Chapter 6's model-specific tuning tips to help focus on the characteristic mechanical problems of the model you are looking to buy. Those sections have subsections on flaws, fixes, and best value modifications. The section on mods can help you evaluate the aftermarket accessories on the bike. Some aftermarket products really give performance value,

but others can actually cause mechanical failures.

Once you've looked over the bike, you can calculate how much it will cost to bring it back to tip-top condition. At that point, you can decide whether or not it's worth fixing the bike and begin to budget. If you are looking at a used bike, you can determine how much you are willing to pay for the bike (see the section on buying a used bike later in this chapter).

SPARK PLUG

A spark plug is a record of the engine's condition. Large globules of aluminum melted to the plug denote that the piston is disintegrating because of a crankcase air leak. A glazed finish on the plug denotes sand that passed through the air filter and has probably ruined the engine. Heavy carbon buildup denotes a leaking crankshaft seal on the clutch side. A bike

with this problem will have white smoke billowing out the exhaust pipe and oil oozing from the exhaust manifold.

COMPRESSION TEST

The correct way to perform a compression test is to thread the gauge into the spark plug hole, hold the throttle wide open, hold the kill button on, and kick the engine over until the gauge needle peaks. An 80-, 125-, 200-, or 500-cc bike should have 150–190 psi. A 250-cc bike should have 170–230 psi (these numbers are for sea level). If the compression gauge reading is far below these numbers, the top end will need to be rebuilt. Four-stroke engines cannot be tested with a compression tester. Instead, you'll need a pressure leak-down tester and compressed air source. These testers can be excellent diagnostic tools, helping you differentiate between piston assembly and valve train problems. Prices for top-end rebuilding vary greatly

Test the top-end condition of a two-stroke dirt bike with a compression tester. Four-stroke bikes can't be tested this way because most bikes use automatic decompressors for easy kick starting.

Check the engine main bearings by trying to shake the flywheel up and down. If you feel any movement, it could mean an expensive overhaul.

grasp the flywheel and try to move it back and forth and up and down. If you feel any movement, the engine's lower end needs to be rebuilt. Normal service intervals for lower ends are once per season on 60-cc to 125-cc engines and every two to three years on 200-cc to 500-cc engines, assuming that the owner services the air filter regularly and always mixes oil in the fuel. The average cost to have a motorcycle shop rebuild the lower end is $300 to $500.

AIR FILTER

You can tell a lot about how a guy maintains his bike just by looking at the air filter. If he neglects the filter, he probably never works on the rest of the bike. Check the filter for tears that could have allowed dirt to enter the engine. On four-stroke engines with crankcase vent hoses, look for crankcase oil residue in the bottom of the air box. That oil residue is from excessive blowby pressure, which could mean that the piston assembly and cylinder bore are worn out.

The condition of a bike's air filter can speak volumes about the owner's maintenance practices. This filter is torn, indicating that the engine may have ingested dirt, causing accelerated wear.

between two- and four-stroke engines and electroplated and iron-lined cylinders. Plated cylinders cost $200 to re-plate, while steel-lined cylinders cost $50 to bore and hone. Piston kits and gasket sets range from $75 to $350.

CRANKSHAFT

Remove the flywheel cover and look for rust or corrosion on the flywheel. Rust

and corrosion indicate that water either entered the side cover or condensation was allowed to occur. Look for an oily residue below the flywheel, which denotes a crankshaft seal leak. A new seal only costs about $15 and can be replaced externally except on KX 80s, 250s, and 500s. On those bikes, the cases must be split, which can be very expensive. To check the main bearings,

FRAME

Lay the bike on its side and inspect the underside of the frame. Look for smashed frame tubes, a cracked shock clevis (common on YZs), and bent link bars. Smashed frame tubes and broken motor mounts look expensive to fix, but a good fabricator can splice in a new tube or weld a mount if you strip down the entire frame. Frame repairs range from $50 to $200. New frames cost from $500 to $800.

SUSPENSION COMPONENTS

Check the rear shock for oil leaks. If the seal is leaking, the gas bladder may be punctured. The average cost of rebuilding a shock is $150 for service alone. Look closely at the shock shaft. If the chrome has peeled, has deep scratches, or is blue from overheating, the shaft will need to be replaced or re-plated. The average cost will be $150 more than standard rebuilding.

Hold the front brake and compress the forks. Does oil ooze out of the seals? Are the forks difficult to compress? Check the fork tubes and the aluminum sliders for rock dents. Rock dents in the tubes can be incredibly expensive to repair. Each of the four fork tubes can retail for as much as $300!

COOLANT SYSTEM

Remove the radiator cap and check the fluid level. A low level means the system has a leak. If the coolant is brown, the head gasket may be leaking internally, meaning combustion pressure has leaked into the coolant system. The worst-case scenario is that the leak has caused erosion on the top edge of the cylinder. It costs $300 to repair, and new cylinders cost from $300 to $850. If the coolant is gray and foaming, that indicates that the water pump seal is blown. The blown seal allows transmission oil to mix with the coolant. Start the engine and rev it in neutral. If coolant flows out of the weep hole at the bottom of the water pump case, the water pump seal and bearings are worn out. If coolant flows out of the overflow tube, the radiator cap is broken or the head gasket is leaking. Check the radiators for crash

damage. Radiators can be welded or sealed with epoxy when minor damage occurs. Check the side of the cylinder head where the head-stay is mounted. Look for white or green residue of leaking coolant. This is common on older CR250s and all KXs and indicates that the head gasket is leaking externally. Cylinder head surfacing costs about $50 and a gasket or O-ring set is about $25. The common cause of external leaks is excessive forces transferring from the top shock mount through the head-stay brackets. Check the rear suspension linkage on a bike with an external leak; chances are the bearings are seized or worn.

SWINGARM AND LINKAGE

Sit on the bike and bounce up and down to compress and rebound the rear suspension. Do you hear a screeching noise? Is the rear suspension seized in an extended or compressed position? This indicates that the bearings, bushings, and seals need to be replaced because they weren't greased. The cost of this repair could vary greatly. The average cost of replacing just the bearings is $125.

Grasp the linkage with your hand and try to move it back and forth to feel for free-play. If the linkage is bent or the bearings have disintegrated and elongated the mounting holes, the linkage will need to be replaced. The average cost of the linkage is $100 without any bearing parts.

WHEELS AND BRAKES

Put the bike on a stand and grasp each wheel with your hands. Try to move the wheel from side to side with the axle held stationary. If you feel any movement, the wheel bearings are worn out. This could cost as little as $30 for new bearings, or the hub could be damaged from riding the bike with the bad bearings. Hubs cost about $180 each.

Check the surface of the brake discs for deep scratches or signs of overheating. Discs can be resurfaced for as little as $25. Bent front discs on enduro bikes are common. New discs cost about $130. All brake pads have wear-indicator

lines scribed into the sides of the pad for quick visual checking. If you can't see the lines, the pads need to be replaced. The average cost is $30 per set.

DRIVETRAIN

The drivetrain consists of the clutch, transmission, chain, and sprockets. The transmission oil can give clues to mechanical problems. Dip a strip of white paper in the trans oil. If the oil sample is gray and bubbly, the water pump seal is blown and the coolant has polluted the trans oil. You can confirm the problem by test riding the bike. The clutch action will be prone to slipping when loaded, and dragging when engaged.

The chain and sprockets can be visually checked for wear. Put the bike on a stand so you can rotate the wheel and check the chain slack at several different points. If the slack varies greatly, the chain is worn out. The average cost of replacing the chain and sprockets is $115.

The cost to replace the water pump shaft, seals, and bearings is about $90 and labor is about 1.5 hours.

TIPS ON TEST RIDING
CLUTCH

Pull in the clutch lever and put the bike in first gear. Rev the engine. Does the bike creep forward? If so, the clutch basket may need to be replaced. When you rev the engine, does the clutch slip? If so, the plates and springs may need to be replaced. That can cost between $55 and $90. The price of clutch baskets varies from $150 to $350.

THROTTLE RESPONSE

Ride the bike in second gear at 1/4 throttle. Snap open the throttle quickly. Does the bike bog or die completely? If so, the engine may have a problem as simple as a clogged pilot jet or as major as a crankcase air leak.

TRANSMISSION

Ride the bike in third gear. Accelerate while gently applying the rear brake. Does the clutch slip? Does the transmission pop out of gear? Third gear is the most abused gear in the transmission. If

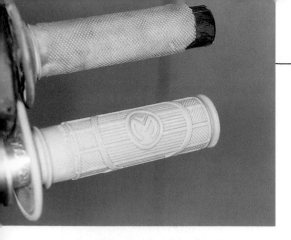

A torn throttle grip could cause a sticky throttle. Good clean grips and an aluminum throttle tube are a worthwhile investment when trying to sell a used bike.

the transmission pops out of gear, the shift forks may be bent or the engagement dogs on the gears may be worn. This is a common problem on RM250s and KX500s. Repair costs range from $300 to $550 if a motorcycle shop performs the repairs.

BRAKES

Apply the brakes separately. Does the lever or pedal pulsate as you apply the brake? This means that the disc is bent or warped and needs to be replaced. Does the front brake have a spongy feeling? If so, the problem could be as simple as trapped air in the system or as major as a worn master cylinder. Check the brake line for leakage. Even if the owner cleaned the leak, brake fluid will damage the plastic cover on the brake hose.

CRANKSHAFT

Put the transmission in neutral. Rev the engine and let off the throttle. Does the bike make a loud shuddering vibration? Do you feel the vibration transfer through the footpegs and handlebars? If so, the engine's lower end may need to be rebuilt. Four-stroke engines have a counter-balancer. Sometimes the keyways can shear, throwing the balance weight out of time.

WHERE TO SPEND YOUR MONEY

The road to better performance is paved with pitfalls. Simply throwing money at your bike won't make it faster. Even if it does, it might become so hard to ride

that you go slower despite the fact that your bike is faster. The key to performance mods is starting with the biggest problem areas, which may turn out to be swingarm and steering head bearings rather than engine or suspension work. Once your bike is working the way it should, you can start to improve the systems that need the most help. When considering any performance products or mods, you have to get the right mix of reliability and performance gain. That way you can spend less money and get the results you're after.

Begin by evaluating your bike (this is the same process you'd go through if you were buying a used bike). Check all the basic systems and figure out what needs help. Then take an inventory of your checkbook and decide how much you can afford to spend in a given time period. Now you can map out a path to better performance.

In order to make your bike perform better, you need a clear understanding of what it's doing well and where it needs help. Certainly, you'll have some basic ideas already: "It needs more low end to get a better drive out of corners," or, "It seems to need more top end because I'm getting passed on long straights and uphills." In order to get more specific, though, start a log and keep notes on your bike. When you notice a problem, make a note of it. When something is working well, write that down too. Keep track of when you service and replace things or if you inspect a component. Use the suspension data log (see Chapter 4) to track what suspension settings you're using and how the suspension works in different conditions. After a while, you'll find you have a very specific idea of what works on your bike and what doesn't.

Perhaps you've looked over the latest models of dirt bikes and decided that those bikes aren't that much better than the bike you're riding. And maybe you're in the market to upgrade your current bike to be competitive with the new bikes. If you are considering investing in rebuilding services or performance mods, use this section as a

guide to determine a budget and priority list of upgrades. The most important thing is to focus your resources on improving the mechanical condition of your bike before spending your money on the "wants." A new pipe won't make up for the horsepower you lose to a worn top end, and a suspension revalving can't cure the instability of a shot steering head or swingarm bearings. Aftermarket accessories such as radiator and tank graphics seat covers and colored plastic are big temptations, but they won't do you any good if the engine is ready to fall apart.

In order to evaluate the condition of your bike, you have to be very objective. Most riders tend to deny certain mechanical problems exist because they don't want to deal with fixing the problem. Make a list of the maintenance tasks that you've been avoiding. Then think about the hidden problems that your bike might have. Review the sections of this book that describe how to inspect and evaluate components such as the crankshaft, transmission, brakes, and shock. In the end, your list should be tiered, starting with maintenance tasks, followed by performance modifications, and ending with cosmetic changes.

If you are considering some performance mods for your bike, ask yourself questions about your riding demands. Are you having problems keeping up with lesser-skilled riders because your bike doesn't handle right? If so, then browse Chapter 4—in particular, read the section on revalving. That chapter also contains a suspension troubleshooting guide to help you determine what changes will be needed for the forks and/or shock.

Regarding engine mods, you also have to ask yourself what type of riding demands you have. Consider things like powerband choices, fuel economy, the type of fuel, the altitude where you ride, noise restrictions, and engine longevity. Chapter 4 contains key information on how changes to engine components affect the powerband. Also, check out the model-specific tuning tips in Chapter 6 for recommendations on the best value mods for your dirt bike.

When preparing to send your engine or suspension parts to a mail-order service company, take care to package the expensive parts to avoid damage. MX-TECH supplies free shipping boxes for a set of forks and a shock.

SHOPPING FOR REBUILDING AND TUNING SERVICES

Mail-order engine rebuilding and tuning services have increased in popularity in recent years. Most people who live in rural areas don't have dirt bike shops near them. Buying by mail order offers them access to experts.

The tasks of rebuilding dirt bike components such as shocks, engines, and forks are fairly complex for the average franchised-dealership mechanic. Sometimes you need to look to specialists. There are companies that specialize in crank rebuilding; porting; cylinder boring, sleeving, and electroplating; suspension; and wheels. There are several specialists in each category to choose from nationwide. Read on for some tips on evaluating the best specialists to suit your needs and budget.

If you have already read Chapter 4's section on suspension component rebuilding, you know how difficult and tedious suspension servicing can be. The average cost of $160 to perform basic service to a set of forks or a shock may not seem very expensive. But buyers beware—not all suspension technicians do the same quality work. The manufacturers don't regulate technicians, and it

doesn't take a big investment in tools to get started in suspension servicing. As a consequence, the motorcycle industry is glutted with suspension service companies. How can you choose a suspension technician you can trust? Here are some tips on screening technicians in order to find the best one to suit your ongoing suspension servicing needs.

SCREENING TIPS FOR REBUILDING AND TUNING SERVICES

1. Make a list of at least five potential service companies, preferably a mixture of local and national mail-order companies.
2. Determine what range of services the technicians offer—suspension oil changing, seal and bushing replacement, shaft chroming, and revalving; engine cylinder repair, crank rebuilding, porting, electrical, and carburetors.
3. Make a survey list of prices for services and ask what is included. Examples: labor, oil, parts, or cleaning supplies. Inquire about a complete breakdown of the costs. Some companies charge extra for rush service, and some charge excessive shipping and handling fees.

4. Ask about technical support. Some companies provide free support materials in the form of booklets and videos; other companies direct technical phone calls to a toll 900 number. These are things that must be considered when comparing costs for services.
5. Ask about turnaround times on services. Consider the time it takes to ship your package there and back.
6. Ask what information you need to supply with your parts. The most important things are your name, address, city, zip or postal code, telephone number, and the best time to call you.

ADDITIONAL INFORMATION

In order for a technician to do a proper job, he may need information about your riding demands and the condition of your bike. If the suspension is being revalved, copy and complete the suspension data log in Chapter 4. The more information you can provide to your suspension technician, the better he can tune your suspension components.

PRICING METHODS

The last thing you should be concerned with is the price. A reputable technician will charge a fair price for high-quality work. Don't make the mistake of rating a technician by price. Often, novice technicians will set high prices because it takes them longer to do a job than an expert. Some companies set their prices based on volume. In the motorcycle business, there is absolutely no connection between price and quality. Prices for mail-order services vary based on several factors, including the average price published in magazines. If a company spends a lot of money on race teams and support programs, their prices are bound to be a little higher.

PACKAGING PARTS FOR MAIL-ORDER SERVICE

If you've made the decision to send your engine or suspension components to a mail-order company, you will need to package the parts carefully. Here is a checklist of how to package your parts for mail-order service:

1. Start by getting a strong cardboard box that is about two times larger than the part you are sending.
2. Leave the engine or suspension component assembled, especially engine parts. Those parts are heavy, and if they bump up against one another they could get damaged. If you are sending a shock, don't bother removing the shock spring. The difference in shipping weight doesn't reflect much in the shipping price. If the shock has a remote reservoir, don't loosen the banjo bolt that connects the hose to the reservoir. The suspension technician won't know where to position the hose when he tightens it to complete his work.
3. Center the part in the box and tightly pack crumpled newspaper on the part. Styrofoam peanuts don't offer good impact resistance and they are difficult to pick out of the part. If you are sending a cylinder, protect the sleeve that protrudes out of the bottom of the cylinder. I recommend using a 4-in. PVC cap fitting to protect the sleeve. They're available in the plumbing department of any hardware store.
4. Put a letter in the box with your name and address information. Include your telephone number and the best time to call in case the technician has any specific questions about your parts.
5. Ship the box and insure the package for the retail value of the parts. Insurance is cheap at about 30 cents per $100.

SPECIAL PACKAGING FOR FORKS AND ENGINES

If you are sending a set of forks for service, you will need a special box that is rectangular and 40 in. long. Look to your local auto parts dealers. Ask for a box used to package parts like mufflers, suspension control arms, or torsion bars. Even if you have to pay $10 for a used box, it's still worth it if the box prevents the forks from being damaged in transit. Companies like MX-TECH supply free suspension boxes that safely house a set of forks and a shock.

This 2002 RM125 was purchased from a pro for $2,000 after only one year. The bike looks like a rat, but it just wasn't taken care of well.

If you are sending an entire engine, put it in a plastic milk crate first, then into a cardboard box. Always drain the engine fluids. It is illegal to knowingly ship flammable liquids without the proper labels. Take the box to a packaging store and they'll place the engine in a bigger box and allow you to insure it.

PERSONAL SUSPENSION TUNERS

When your suspension is tuned properly, it will make you a more competitive racer and your bike safer to ride. Find a suspension technician with whom you can develop a long-term working relationship. Everyone has questions on suspension tuning. Once you develop a rapport with a technician by purchasing his services, you can then ask his advice on tuning. Take care not to abuse this privilege! Suspension tuners spend a lot of time developing their proprietary knowledge without pay. You may think they charge a lot of money for revalving, but consider this—when you call to ask a basic question, the technician has to stop working to answer your free question.

Most technicians work on piecework, so they only earn money when

working, not talking. Try not to waste their time by asking questions that are already answered in this book. Let this book educate you so you can ask important advice from your tuner. To get the most benefit from your tuning questions, keep a log book of all the current settings. A good tuner will need settings data before he can make an informed suggestion as to how to fix a tuning problem. The best type of information that you can provide to a suspension tuner is a videotape of you riding your bike on the sections of terrain where a handling problem occurs. Refer to the section on video suspension tuning in Chapter 4.

BUYING A USED DIRT BIKE

Buying a used dirt bike can be very risky. The most expensive components to repair are the ones that are most difficult to examine. First, use the section earlier in this chapter on evaluating a bike. That section gives you a guide to examining a used dirt bike and estimating the cost of repairs so you can gain bargaining leverage with the seller.

BIKE EVALUATION CHART

Use the following chart to make notes as you evaluate a bike, either your own for your modification plan or a bike you are considering buying. Note if each system is OK, and refer to the text for more specific information on each test.

Spark Plug Condition?
Compression Test: _____ psi
Crankshaft (engine revs smoothly?)
        Oil under flywheel cover?
        Main bearings tight?
Air filter condition?
Frame condition
        Frame tubes?
        Motor mounts?
        Shock mount?
        Linkage mount?
Suspension
        Rear shock oil leaks?
        Rear shock shaft OK?
        Front fork seals?
        Front fork tubes?
Coolant system
        Fluid level?
        Fluid clear-green color?
        Radiators straight?
        Radiators leaking?
Swingarm and Linkage
        Suspension compresses smoothly and
            silently?
        Rear linkage tight?
Wheels and Brakes
        Hubs tight?
        Brake discs smooth?
        Brake pads fresh?
Drivetrain
        Transmission oil clean?
        Chain and sprockets fresh?
Test Ride
        Throttle response smooth?
        Transmission OK?
        Brakes smooth and positive?
        Crankshaft balanced?

APPROXIMATE COSTS TO REPAIR

Note: These costs are average for a Japanese full-size bike. You may find you pay a bit more or less for your particular model, especially if you have a European bike (more) or a mini. Still, this should give you a ballpark figure to use when estimating repair costs or evaluating a used bike. Note that the labor is listed in hours. Call your local shop to get an hourly rate, and you can figure costs.

COMPONENT	PARTS	LABOR (HOURS)
Two-stroke rebuild top end	$100–150	2.0
Four-stroke rebuild top end	$200–400	3.0
Four-stroke valvetrain replacement	$200–500	2.0
Rebuild bottom end	$100–150	4.0
New exhaust pipe	$125–300	0.3
Carburetor rebuild	$25–35	0.5
New radiator	$80–200	0.8
New chain & sprockets	$80–150	1.5
Replace Fork seal	$20–30	1.0
Install new fork tubes	$200–300	1.0
Rear shock rebuild	$125–150	2.0
New rear shock	$400–650	1.0
Replace brake pads (per caliper)	$20–25	0.3
Brake rotors	$150	0.6
New hubs	$150–300	–
New spoke sets (per wheel)	$90	–
Replace and true wheel	–	1.3
New tires	$50–100	0.3

Extreme makeover—with a modest investment of $600, this rat was transformed into a sharp-looking race bike.

RACE BIKES AND RATS

Bikes that are trail ridden are usually used more often than race bikes. Used race bikes purchased from expert riders are normally well maintained and have relatively little running time. Expert riders usually have several sponsors and their bikes may have extra accessories such as suspension or engine modifications, stiffer springs, good tires and brakes, or a special pipe. Don't be afraid of race bikes, they can be a good bargain.

"Rats" are bikes that have been crashed and abused. Normally, they have many serious mechanical problems. If you are mechanically confident, you can do well to repair and resell these bikes. You can usually buy these types of bikes very cheap. Sometimes franchised motorcycle dealers will have dirt bikes that were abandoned by their owners because the repair estimates were too expensive. In most cases, the dealer just wants to get rid of the bikes because they take up space in the service department. Rat bikes can be a bargain for a skilled mechanic who gets a good discount on parts and accessories. Most people buy these types of bikes because they think it's a cheap way to get into dirt bikes, and then later find out that the cost to repair the bike is more than a one-year-old race bike.

WHERE TO FIND USED DIRT BIKES

There are five main places to look for used dirt bikes: motorcycle shops, riding areas, banks, newspapers, and eBay. Here is how each rates in time spent versus the value of the deal.

Few franchised dealers take trades on dirt bikes. However, some motorcycle shops service, buy, and sell used dirt bikes. These are good places to buy your first dirt bike because the shop owner will know some maintenance history on the bike. The independent shop can also answer your questions and supply you with reliable parts and services. Sometimes you can meet other enthusiasts at dirt bike shops and get leads on new places to ride.

Racetracks and riding areas are good places to find used bikes, especially in the summer. In the heat of the summer, dirt bike riders tend to slack off riding and switch to water sports. Some riders get injured and desperately need to sell their bikes. Others may want to sell their bikes in order to buy new bikes when they are released in August. Often, riders will show their bikes at the racetrack. You can also ask racers if they know of anyone who wants to sell their bike. July and August are the best months to find deals on used bikes from private parties.

Banks are great places to buy used dirt bikes! The typical repossession scenario is an 18- to 24-year-old male who was accepted for his first major loan through the aggressive financing programs promoted by the Japanese motorcycle manufacturers during the recession following September 11, 2001. After a year, he found out that "zero down" meant that he'd have zero money down in his pocket for several years to come if he didn't bail out of his loan commitment. Bankers are not in the competitive business of fixing and selling used dirt bikes so repossessed bikes are often open for sealed bid and can be purchased for 25 cents on the dollar. Although dealers are made aware of repossession opportunities, few take advantage of them because there isn't a lot of profit in selling dirt bikes.

The newspapers can be really lame places to look for dirt bikes. Shopping for bikes in a local paper can be frustrating because the advertisers either put a ridiculous asking price on the bike or they have already sold it. The best newspapers for used bikes in America and England are *Cycle News* and *Motorcycle News*. The classified advertisers tend to be serious enthusiasts who price their bikes and parts to sell.

eBay is quickly becoming an excellent venue for buying used dirt bikes and the parts to repair them. Many small dealers are going out of business and frequently liquidate their stock on eBay. There are books on how to work eBay to your advantage. I suggest reading one before you attempt to buy a used dirt bike in an auction format.

NEGOTIATING A FAIR PRICE FOR A DIRT BIKE

Whenever you check out a used bike, try to contain your enthusiasm. Look at the bike objectively, especially all the hidden things that could cost a lot to repair. Copy and use the 0. Chart when you check out a used bike. Also, clip ads from dirt bike magazines that feature discount prices for OEM parts. That's good information to include with the Bike Evaluation Chart. Another excellent tool for negotiating the price of a used bike is a Blue Book guide, which you can get at the library or over the Internet. Although the prices listed for used dirt bikes do not reflect regional market values, they are a good indicator for determining if the seller is way out of line on the price of a bike. Normally, the Blue Book value will be lower than the typical price you would be able to pay for a used bike; motorcycle shops use the guides to negotiate trade-in value.

BUYER BEWARE!

If you are looking for a 1980s-model Japanese or Italian dirt bike, consider that the price of OEM Japanese parts increases over time, and because of the acquisition of Husqvarna by Cagiva, some parts for those bikes aren't even available anymore.

Motorcycles are built with parts from several small subcontractors and assembled by a motorcycle manufacturer. The manufacturers try to order all the parts for the bikes and parts stock up front. If the manufacturer runs out of stock, it has to order a new batch of parts from the subcontractor. Each subcontractor has a minimum order for a parts run, so individual parts orders may accumulate for months before they are fulfilled. Small parts runs mean that the individual part's price will be higher. Generally speaking, parts for older bikes are more expensive than parts for new bikes. Example: a cylinder for a 1986 CR250 is over $400 more expensive than a 2002 cylinder.

When Cagiva bought out Husqvarna in the early 1980s, the OEM-parts-manufacturing network of subcontractors had to be revised. All the blueprints and specs on the parts had to go through a bidding system in Italy before the contracts could be awarded to the small manufacturing firms. There are some models of Huskys that you can't even get parts for. For replacement parts, you would have to look to salvage companies. If you have one of these broken-down bikes sitting in a shed and waiting for a part, your bike is worth more in pieces than together.

EXTREME MAKEOVER FROM RAT TO RACER

A pro-ridden one-year-old 125-cc bike is one of the best bargains on the used dirt bike market. Local experts race for contingency and prize money and are desperate to turn over their bikes. Some riders turn over motorcycles as many as ten times per year. I purchased a 2002 Suzuki RM125 for only $2,000. It was a dealer trade-in. A pro rider needed a new bike in order to earn contingency money. The bike looked trashed but was solid underneath. It had a new top end and the suspension was revalved.

The changes we made were mostly cosmetic with some annual maintenance tasks handled. Basic wear items needed replacement. The plastic was scuffed, the grips torn, chain and sprockets shot, clutch plates smoked, and the brakes were worn to the metal. While repairing crash damage and servicing high wear parts, I selected products that increased the overall reliability of the bike. I started by stripping and cleaning the bike. The brakes were Dunlop pads and Moose Racing brake pins. After a year of hard use, the pads were grooved, and the Moose pins feature a hex-nut rather than an Allen head. The stock plastic throttle tube was cracked from a fall so I chose a Moose closed-end aluminum tube and grips, and I safety-wired the grips in place. The clutch was smoked so I switched to more durable steel plates and new fibers. The frame and pipe were scruffy so I used some PJ-1 original frame paint, taking care to isolate and mask painted areas. The transmission drain bolt is prone to damage on an RM125 because it sticks out below the cases. A CRD glide plate was selected to protect the drain plug, frame rails, and cases. The CRD glide plate is wider than traditional skid plates that fit inside the frame rails. A full set of UFO plastic was covered with Factory Effex graphics to give the bike a fresh look. The suspension components were sent back to the original tuner for fluid changing. Full service and tuning records on the previous owners were collected to establish a maintenance history for the bike.

The total cost of the makeover was about $600. The total price of the bike and makeover was $2,600, a full $2,000 less than a bike one year newer.

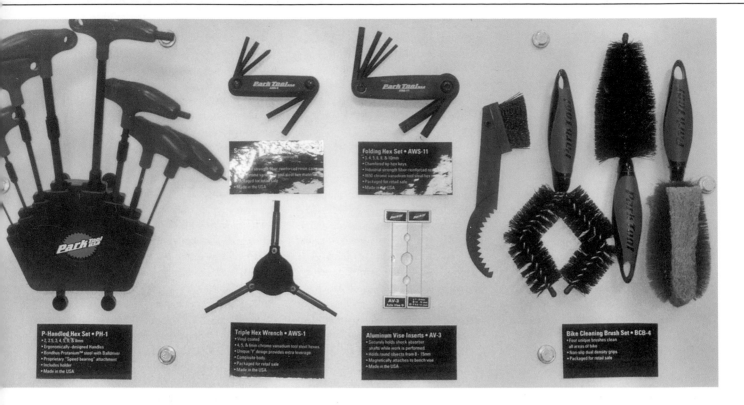

Park Tools makes specialized tools for dirt bikes ranging from cleaning brushes to T-handles and special suspension tools.

SELECTING THE RIGHT TOOLS

If you've made the commitment to spend more time working on your bike, you will need the right tools and workbench setup. This section is a guide to the different types of tools needed to maintain a dirt bike and rebuild the engine or the suspension components. Having the right tools can make a tough job less frustrating and save you money in labor. This performance handbook is not intended to replace the factory service manual for your model bike; it is a supplementary manual that gives you information on the overall operation of the components of a motorcycle. The factory service manual is ideal for quick references on parts wear dimensions and torque specifications. The factory service manual is also an important reference for special tools. These tools are for single-purpose dedicated use and only available through a franchised dealer. For most maintenance tasks the tools described in this chapter will cover your needs. For complex tasks such as rebuilding the suspension components or the lower end of the engine, you'll need to first review the factory service manual and check for the use of special factory tools. Companies such as Kiowa and Motion Pro sell replica factory tools for competitive prices.

TOOL LISTS

You could spend a fortune on good tools or buy a bunch of cheap tools that wear out fast. Then, there is the rip-off factor to consider. If you have expensive tools, people will borrow them and conveniently forget to return them.

I believe in buying inexpensive tools for the weather exposure maintenance jobs and high-quality special tools used in performance tuning. Look to Craftsman (Sears) for routine maintenance tools such as wrenches and screwdrivers. They make good-quality tools for a low price and provide free replacements if the tools break. Harbor Freight company sells T-handle sets for under $10 that are good for use at the track or practice meetings because those activities usually involve harsh use and theft. A Japanese company named Kiowa makes excellent quality T-handle sets. Most factory mechanics use Kiowa tools, and they are available from Pro-Circuit dealers. Race Tools makes black finished T sets that are case-hardened for longevity. Those tools are available from MSR or Tucker Rocky dealers.

LIGHT MAINTENANCE

On Japanese dirt bikes, there are only about five different sizes of bolts, so you don't need a lot of tools to do light maintenance. Here is a list of the basic tools that you need in your tool collection:

- Special wrenches: spark plug, spoke, rear-axle, and carb main jet wrenches
- Combination wrenches in sizes of 8–19 mm
- T-handles in sizes of 8–17 mm
- Screwdrivers: one wide and one narrow flat-blade (10 and 3 mm wide) and #2 and #3 Phillips drivers
- Allen wrench combination set (2.5, 4, 5, 6, 8, 10 mm)
- Miscellaneous tools: feeler gauge, air-pressure gauge, measuring tape, cable-lubing tool, chain brush, pliers, and plastic mallet
- Impact driver with a 3/8-in. drive

INTENSIVE MAINTENANCE

These are the tools you will need to do intensive maintenance on Japanese dirt bikes. Include all the tools listed in the light maintenance list plus the following:

- 3/8-in. ratchet wrench and sockets in six-point shallow socket sizes of 8, 10, 12, 14, 17, 19, 22, 24, 27, 30, and 32 mm; Allen sockets in sizes of 2.5, 4, 5, 6, 8, and 10 mm
- Combination wrenches in sizes of 22, 24, 27, and 32 mm
- Needle-nose and channel-lock pliers, side cutters, chain clamp, and tweezers
- Hand-powered, electric, and pneumatic impact driver
- Torque wrench, 3/8-in.
- Ball-peen hammer
- Rat-tail, big flat fine and triangular files; set of needle files; and a thread file
- Large- and small-diameter round punches and a 1/4-in.-wide flat chisel
- Parts washer
- Miscellaneous tools: flywheel puller, chain breaker, magnet, flashlight, and propane torch

ENGINE REBUILDING

These are the tools you will need to rebuild a two-stroke engine. Include the tools from the light and intensive maintenance lists. You may also need some special tools that are brand and model specific such as case splitters, flywheel pullers, or blind-side bearing removers.

- Bearing and seal driver set
- V-block and dial indicator
- Machinist's square
- Crankcase-splitting tool
- Stud remover
- Flywheel puller
- Dial caliper
- 20-ton press

SUSPENSION REBUILDING

These are the tools you will need to rebuild Showa and Kayaba forks and shocks:

- Scribe set
- Oil level setting tool
- Nitrogen tank
- Pressure regulator
- Bladder cap remover
- Allen socket, 14 mm
- Vise
- Cartridge wrenches
- Seal drivers
- Bleeder rods
- Digital caliper

Dirt bikes require frequent maintenance. Reserve a corner of your garage and outfit it with a toolbox, cabinets, parts washer, and air compressor.

The latest trend in bike haulers is a combination of a box van and a motor home. This rig is made by Fun-Mover in Elkhart, Indiana. It features a workshop in the back and living quarters up front.

Some excellent sources for special tools include Kiowa, Motion Pro, Race Tech, Race Tools, Scott's, White Brothers, and Moose Off-Road dealers.

OUTFITTING YOUR WORKSHOP

It's difficult to work on your bike when you don't have the tools. It's even worse when you don't have a place to work on your bike. Reserving a small place in your garage, shed, basement, or even at a rental storage locker is the most basic need. Making the most of that space and providing a measure of security and organization takes a bit of creativity. Here is an inexpensive solution to the problem of organizing your tools and workshop.

Think about the things you need for a workshop—a solid bench, a vise, a parts washer, and a safe place to store your tools and parts. In previous editions I suggested using a metal

motorcycle crate as a foundation for a workbench, but now there is a much better alternative. Pallet racks used to be exclusive to warehouses but the latest trend in motorcycle dealer service departments is to buy the smaller pallet racks marketed at home improvement stores. These pallet racks are available in kit piece form so you can customize the height, width, and depth to fit the space you have available. For about $120 you can buy a rack that is 72 in. tall, 96 in. wide, and 24 in. deep. The side Z-beams are notched so you can set the shelf and bench heights to your ergonomic needs. There are several other ways to customize a pallet rack, including adding wheels to make it mobile, fitting a power strip in the frame rails, enclosing it for security, fitting a toolbox or cabinets, adding a parts washer to the bench top, fastening a mini air compressor, and even adding a refrigerator.

ENVIRONMENTALLY CONSCIOUS METHODS FOR CLEANING PARTS

Cleaning is a part of dirt biking. Having the right kit can make it easy to maintain your bike. Choosing the right chemicals and cleaning methods can be environmentally conscious and safer for your health. Much of the maintenance tasks that you'll need to perform on your bike revolve around a parts washer. You'll use it to do preliminary cleaning such as degreasing. You can buy the components of the parts washer, the tank and the chemicals, but the disposal of the chemicals can be expensive. Companies such as Safety Kleen offer rental on parts washers, a variety of chemicals, and disposal service. Its services are fair, about $80 for solvent and the disposal. That's about the same amount that it would cost you to either buy the solvent or dispose of it legally. I

A good parts washer is key to maintaining a dirt bike. This unit, rented from Safety Kleen, features a vacuum distillation machine to recycle the mineral spirits solvent so you don't have to deal with the hassle of waste disposal.

rent a Safety Kleen System One parts washer for $145 per month. The machine features a vacuum distillation pump that cleans the solvent and separates the oil and spooge to a collection chamber that can be drained and recycled. Many auto parts stores offer free reclamation of 1-gallon containers of oil and antifreeze. Antifreeze is a dangerous fluid to leave in open containers, especially if you have a dog. Dogs are attracted to the smell of antifreeze and often drink it, causing a slow death from the poison. With free reclamation services available from auto parts stores and most municipal garages, there is no excuse for leaving open containers of toxic fluids lying around.

The cleaning chemicals used in parts washers are either mineral spirits solvents or alkaline detergents. Some areas of the country prohibit mineral spirit solvents because of air pollution or flammable considerations. The alkaline detergents are advertised as biodegradable, but don't be fooled into thinking that you can just pour it down the drain when it's spent. As soon as you clean an oily part in it, it's contaminated and fits into a different waste category. The alka-line detergents tend to be harsher on unprotected skin than mineral spirit solvents. Some solvents have lanolin, a skin moisturizer, mixed in with them. Solvents are also graded in flash points. Generally speaking, the higher the flash point the better the cleaning action. Most local fire departments have the right to inspect your parts washer and specify what type of chemicals you use, the flash point temperature, and the type of fusible link fitted to the tank's lid. Fusible links are used on all dedicated parts washers. They are built into the hinge of the lid and will melt if the solvent catches fire, closing the lid and smothering the fire.

Always use gloves when cleaning parts in solvents or detergents. You don't have to wear big clunky gloves anymore. The latest thing is a nitrile glove; it fits like a second skin. Over the years my skin has become hypersensitive to solvents and detergents, yet the tactile nitrile gloves keep my skin from breaking out in a rash. For mechanical and machining tasks, I use Kevlar reinforced gloves from Ringer Racing. They supply most of the NASCAR teams with gear that offers heat and abrasion protection.

CHAPTER TWO

BASIC MAINTENANCE

The best way to extract maximum performance from your bike is to maintain it well. It's just that simple. Maintenance is generally economical and doesn't require a ton of time. It can, however, make the difference between the front and back of the pack or a great ride and being left stranded in the woods.

This chapter covers the myriad maintenance tasks that you will need to perform on your bike on a frequent basis. In addition to explaining simple maintenance tasks and enabling you to diagnose and repair common problems, this section is packed with tips and techniques not found in factory service manuals or the off-road magazines.

DIRT BIKE CLEANING TECHNIQUES

You're probably thinking, "Why do I need to read this? Cleaning a bike is just blasting the hell out of it with a power washer." Actually, cleaning a dirt bike takes a lot of caution because you can do more damage by cleaning it than by leaving it a muddy mess. Dirt bikes have nooks and crannies that trap dirt and water. Compulsive cleaners tend to chase dirt with the power washer and can sometimes force dirt and water into areas where it can damage expensive engine components.

Here is a step-by-step guide to cleaning a dirt bike. Start by scraping off the big clods of mud under the fenders, on the tires, and around the engine. Next, remove the seat, air filter, and chain. Stuff a rag in the intake air boot or buy a Twin Air filter cover and fasten it in place. Cap the end of the silencer with a rubber plug to prevent water from entering the pipe. Use a

Pressure washers are either electric or gas-powered. Degreasers can be used to break down dirt and oil, but don't use pressurized detergent because it can damage components such as oil seals and brake pads.

strong degreaser like Formula 409 on the oily areas of the bike such as the swingarm and crankcases.

Don't spray these areas with detergent: the brakes, fork and shock seals, electrical connections, chain, or the seat. Strong detergents with alkaline work similar to acids in the way they corrode certain materials. For example, alkaline can break down the bonding agent in the brake pads, causing them to disintegrate quicker. The electrical connections can corrode and cause greater resistance and an increase in voltage that may contribute to the premature failure of these expensive parts. Clean the outside of the seat with a brush because the foam can absorb water like a sponge. The water will cause the seat foam to break down and lose its cushion effect. It's better to wash these components with just water.

Twin Air makes covers for the air boot so you can wash the dirt from inside the air box.

Specialty cleaners and lubricants are needed to operate and maintain dirt bikes. Water-displacing agents such as All-In-One, LPS, or WD-40 are excellent for squeezing out water and providing anti-corrosive lubrication.

Strong detergents can break down the bond in brake pads and damage the rubber seals that protect the bearings in engine and suspension components.

The chain requires special maintenance that is similar to that of servicing air filters. First, place the chain in a container with a mild solvent. Then scrub it with a nylon brush to remove the dirt and debris. Next, let the chain drip dry and lubricate it once dry. The latest product in chain lubrication is chain wax. It doesn't attract dirt or make everything around the chain oily and attractive to dirt.

When washing a bike, a bucket of water and a wise selection of brushes are just as effective as a power washer. If you routinely use a power washer, remember to try and deflect the dirt away from the bike rather than chase it into crevices.

After you clean the bike, spray certain parts with some chemicals. Remove the magneto cover and spray the flywheel and coils with non-chlorinated brake cleaner. Spray the disc brake rotors to remove the dirt and water. Next, spray the steel parts with WD40 or LPS to displace the water. Spray the tires and plastic parts with silicone to protect them from drying out and cracking. The silicone will cover the scratches in the plastic, renewing its

look. The silicone also will reduce the chance of dirt sticking to the plastic, making it easier to clean the bike after your next ride.

FUELS, LUBRICANTS, AND FLUIDS

The harsh conditions in dirt biking require performance fuels, lubricants, and fluids to protect different components of the bike.

FUEL

There are several different forms of fuel available in the United States and some specific types for Europe. In the United States, the popular racing fuel brands are ELF, Klotz, Phillips, Powermist, Sunoco, and VP Racing. In Europe, the racing federation (FIM) only allows unleaded fuels with an octane rating of 100, but many people have access to aviation fuel. Aviation fuel is restricted and regulated in the United States. Racing fuel enables a dirt bike to rev higher before misfiring or popping. Some models of dirt bikes are designed with compression ratios and combustion chamber profiles that require racing fuels to run properly. Racers use racing fuel because it is consistent in quality and blended specifically for certain engine configurations.

It's possible to run super-unleaded pump fuel in a dirt bike if the ignition timing is retarded and the cylinder head modified. Oxygenates are added to pump fuel to reduce emissions. That type of fuel makes a dirt bike run leaner and hotter than normal. Pump fuel is graded seasonally. The boiling point is changed in order to make it easier for cars to start when the temperature changes. If you buy pump fuel for cold temperatures and run it in hotter weather, it will make the engine prone to bogging, pinging, and eventually piston failure. Octane booster additives can be mixed with pump fuel to help reduce pinging, detonation, pre-ignition, and flat spots in the powerband.

Performance Tip: Use a steel container rather than a plastic one. Plastic absorbs the additives that affect the octane rating of the fuel. The best fuel container is called a safety can and is marketed in automotive racing. These steel containers have mesh material inside them that collects vapor, the fuel component that is easiest to ignite.

Safety Tip: Never fill a fuel storage container when it is sitting on the plastic bed liner of a truck. The container will be insulated from ground and prone to static electricity sparks. Always place a fuel storage container on the ground when filling with fuel.

For more information on fuel, check out Rich Rohrich's sidebar on fuel in Chapter 5.

PRE-MIX ENGINE OIL

Two-stroke engines without oil injection require oil to be mixed with the fuel. This oil lubricates the piston and cylinder on the top end and the crankshaft and bearings in the lower end. There are three types of pre-mix oils: petroleum, synthetic, and castor based. Castor oils are the most expensive and best for performance but require mixing just prior to use. Synthetic and castor oils should never be mixed in the same fuel tank. The two oils will quickly separate from the fuel and could cause engine damage through loss of lubrication. Synthetic oils are marketed as smokeless. The pre-mix ratio is based on the oil manufacturer's recommended dilution rate, which can range from 20:1 for castor to 60:1 for synthetic. Every motorcycle is sold with a sticker on the rear fender that says to mix the oil at a ratio of 20:1—that is just a generic recommendation.

CRANKCASE OIL

Some four-stroke engines have an open crankcase. The oil that lubricates the top and lower end moving parts is circulated through the crankcase. This is the most commonly available oil. Designations like SAE 10/40 describe the viscosity. Synthetic oils are not recommended for engines with shared transmissions and crankcases because they could cause clutch slippage.

TRANSMISSION OIL

A two-stroke engine has a separate cavity for the transmission and clutch. A four-stroke engine has two designs, one with a separate cavity for the tranny and one that shares the oil in the crankcase. For engines with separate tranny cavities, you can use three different types of oils. The different oils are used for specific reasons. The oils are crankcase (SAE 10/40), ATF (auto trans fluid), and gear oil. Gear oil is available in hypoid and standard. The designation set by the SAE denotes the number of tons of pressure (psi) that it takes to make metal-to-metal contact with an oil film. SAE 80-weight gear oil is used in the gear cases on autos, and hypoid 80-gear oil is used in the tranny of a dirt bike because it pours thinner than standard gear oil. Standard gear oil available from auto parts stores is too thick to put in the tranny of a dirt bike. It gives good lubrication but it causes too much drag on the tranny. SAE 10/40 oil is inexpensive but requires more frequent service than gear oil. Pros use ATF because it gives good clutch action and poses minimal drag on the tranny, but it is one-ride oil.

SUSPENSION OIL

Modern suspension components require low-viscosity oils with additives that guard against fade, which is the oil's ability to transmit loads when the oil temperature rises. Use only oils designated for use in rear shocks and cartridge forks. Otherwise the damping characteristics could be negatively affected.

AIR FILTER OIL

With the filter being exposed to dirt, it requires frequent service. Air filter oil must be resistant to breakdown from the fuel and trapped dust particles. The best filter oils are those that pour thin and saturate the foam cells of the filter, then dry and become sticky. WD40 should never be used as air filter oil! No-Toil is a brand of biodegradable air filter oil. This type of oil can be cleaned with degreaser detergent and water. It's suitable for municipal sewer systems and it's easier on your skin and sinuses.

CHAIN LUBRICANTS

There are three different types of chain lubricants: petroleum lube, white lithe grease, and chain wax. Petroleum spray lube products are the most popular and easy to use, but the oil tends to sling off and splatter other parts of the bike. Lithe grease can only be used after a chain is degreased and dried. Chain wax is gaining popularity because it stays right on the chain. Petroleum lubes can also be used for cables and chain guides. O-ring chains are sealed with lithe grease so they don't require lubrication from spray lubes. After washing a bike, water-displacing sprays can be used on an O-ring chain, but take care not to soak the links. The water-displacing sprays could penetrate the links and dilute the grease.

GREASE

Grease seals out water and dirt and provides lubrication to components. The most important areas of the bike that require grease are the air filter's sealing edge, swingarm and linkage pivot bolts and bearings, wheel bearings and seals, fork and shock seals, and the steering head bearings. There are three types of greases used for dirt bikes: petroleum, moly, and PTFE-based. Most manufacturers specify the use of moly grease for the swingarm, linkage, and steering

No-Toil is a line of biodegradable lubricants and cleaners. You can clean your dirty air filters along with your riding gear.

head bearings. This grease contains molybdenum disulfide. It offers a low coefficient of friction and holds viscosity with temperature. Petroleum grease is good for all applications of a dirt bike but it requires more frequent service. PTFE-based grease is ideal for suspension components.

BRAKE FLUID

There are two types of brake fluid: denatured alcohol and silicone-based. The designations DOT 3 and 4 are for denatured alcohol fluids; DOT 5 is for silicone fluid. These two types of fluid should never be mixed in the same brake system. DOT 5 is good for brake systems exposed to high temperatures and water. DOT 3 and 4 fluids absorb water, reducing the boiling point of the fluid. Most motorcycle manufacturers recommend DOT 4 for use in dirt bikes.

PC-1 makes special mounting plates and gaskets to improve the seal between the air intake boot, air box, and filter.

AIR INTAKE SYSTEM

The air intake system comprises the air box, boot, air filter, and box drain. A cheap piece of foam and a thin barrier of oil—the filter—is all that protects the expensive engine parts from disintegrating into a pile of melted metal, so if you don't learn the basic maintenance practices for air filters fast, you won't be riding for very long! I remember when I was a service manager at a motorcycle dealership and a guy brought in his kid's bike. The bike was only two weeks old, yet the engine seized because dirt had passed through the filter. The man was outraged and argued that his car went 30,000 miles before it needed a new air filter. Air filter maintenance doesn't seem obvious until your engine chokes to a grinding halt, but by then it's about $500 too late.

CLEAN AND INSPECT

Every time you clean a filter, check the seams for tears. Some filters are sewn together and others are bonded together with adhesives. Filters don't last forever. Over time the seams will split. Professional racing teams only use a filter for one moto. That may be extreme, but the point is to replace the filter often, preferably after about 20 cleanings.

The best way to clean a filter is with two stages of a petroleum degreaser. Gasoline is a bad choice for two reasons—it can ignite causing burns and it disintegrates the filter's seam glue.

Filter oil manufacturers make specific filter cleaner products. The second stage of filter cleaning is with detergent and water. I recommend mixing equal parts of water and Simple Green, a biodegradable detergent made by Gunk that is sold at most hardware and auto parts stores. Let the filter soak for five minutes and then work it with your hands. Whip the filter around to shake off the water rather then wringing it out, which could damage the filter and push the dirt particles deeper into the foam.

OIL AND GREASE

The filter must have special oil for the foam, and grease for the mounting surface. Filter oil is blended with chemicals that keep the oil diluted so it pours and spreads throughout the filter. These chemicals evaporate quickly in the open air, allowing the filter oil to become very tacky. Don't be tempted to use substitutes for filter oil. Filter oil is available from most motorcycle shops. Apply the oil evenly and sparingly across both the inner and outer surfaces of the filter, and squeeze the filter several times, adding oil periodically until the filter foam is lightly saturated with oil.

Apply a thin layer of grease to the flange-mounting surface to help prevent leakage at the mounting surface. I recommend Bel Ray waterproof grease.

MAKING IT EASY

Nobody likes to clean and oil air filters, but there are a couple of things you can do to make air filter maintenance easier. If you can extend the time between cleaning and do three filters at one time, you'll save yourself time, so I recommend that you buy two spare filters. Apply oil to the filters and store them in clear plastic bags. Then, if you have to service the filter at the racetrack or riding area, you don't have to clean it, just replace it with one of the pre-oiled spares. Disposable nitrile gloves are great for keeping the goop off your hands

when changing filters between motos. The gloves come in boxes, typically of 100 for about $15. You can find nitrile gloves at cleaning supply, industrial, and hardware stores.

Filter covers can extend the service interval of air filters. There are two types of filter covers: a cloth sock cover for the filter and a plastic lid cover for the top of the air box. These things shield the filter from dust and mud. Some people think that the plastic air box covers choke off the air flow to the air box and hinder performance, but that's not true; the covers are designed to reduce intake noise. When you remove the cover, the bike makes more noise, and you think it has more power. Leave the plastic cover on the air box. It will save you from cleaning the filter as often.

The latest trend in air filter maintenance is convenient, pre-oiled disposable air filters sold in packs of ten. This is a great idea, but you still have to take care to distribute the oil evenly before installation in the bike.

THE AIR BOX AND BOOT

It's easy to overlook the air boot and box when you don't even want to clean the filter, but consider this: a small leak at the air boot or box flange can allow dirt to bypass the filter and go directly into the engine. Here are some tips to consider when servicing the filter:

- After you remove the filter, look into the air boot from the filter side. Look for dirt that indicates a leak. The chain roller may wear through the boot or sticks and rocks could puncture it.
- Never aim the power-washing wand directly at the boot-to-box flange. There is sealant at that junction, but the high-pressure detergent can easily penetrate the flange and blow out the sealant. It is advisable to power-wash the air box from the top. Twin-Air makes special air boot covers so you can block off the boot and wash the box. This serves to flush the drain located on the bottom of the box.
- Seal the flange-to-box junction with weather-strip adhesive only. Never use silicone sealer because it is fuel soluble.

• When washing the bike, remove the seat and the air filter. Install a Twin-Air filter cap to seal off the carburetor from water, wash the dirt out of the air box, and flush out the drainpipe.

SPARK PLUG BASICS

Spark plugs must operate within a fairly narrow temperature range. At idle, a spark plug must run as hot as possible so it doesn't cold foul, which occurs at about 800 degrees Fahrenheit. At full throttle, a spark plug must dissipate the heat quickly so it doesn't exceed 1,800 degrees Fahrenheit, where pre-ignition occurs. Consequently, many riders often curse spark plugs as they sit stranded on the side of a trail, trying to clean the oily goop off the plug. This section will tell you how a plug problem can be a sign of a more serious mechanical problem.

Examining the spark plug can tell a lot about the condition of the engine. This plug has tiny beads of aluminum. The engine overheated, causing the piston to melt and disintegrate, transferring metal to the spark plug.

This spark plug has a glazed appearance from sand bypassing the air filter and melting onto the spark plug.

The spark plug is black because the carb jetting is too rich. This condition is called wet-fouling.

This spark plug has heavy oil deposits. For a two-stroke engine, the cause could be a blown right-side crankshaft seal. For a four-stroke engine, the cause could be worn piston rings, an overfilled crankcase, or blown valve stem seals.

This spark plug is the perfect color. The insulator is cocoa brown all the way down to the base and the first three threads are black. This bike's carb is jetted close to optimum.

COMMON PROBLEMS

Modern dirt bikes have come a long way from the days when a pocketful of spark plugs was necessary for even a short ride. Some bikes even had two plugs in the head so you could switch when one fouled! Today, if your bike is tuned properly, a spark plug can last an entire season. Even so, two-stroke engines do occasionally foul plugs. If you have chronic troubles, here are a few places to look.

COLD FOULING

This occurs when the bike and engine are still cool. On the extreme, cold fouling occurs when the plug's electrode temperature falls below 800 degrees Fahrenheit. At this point, carbon deposits accumulate on the insulator (the ceramic part of the spark plug that holds the center wire). The voltage will travel the path of least resistance. Deposits such as these are a path for the voltage to follow to ground rather than arcing across to the plug's electrode. Keep in mind that it is more difficult to fire a spark plug under compression pressure than at atmospheric pressure. Just because a plug fires in the open air, doesn't mean it will work inside the engine.

MELTED PLUG

When you find a plug that has melted or is coated with globules of melted metal, something is seriously wrong. Combustion pre-ignition occurs when the spark plug or anything in the combustion chamber reaches a temperature over 1,800 degrees Fahrenheit. At this point, the hot spot could ignite unburned mixture gases before the spark occurs. Hot spots can be caused by everything from too-lean jetting, air leaks, lack of cooling, lack of lubrication, or a sharp burr in the head.

HEAT RANGES

The length of the insulator nose largely determines a plug's heat range of operating temperatures. Colder range plugs have a short heat flow path, which results in a rapid rate of heat transfer. The shorter insulator has a smaller surface area for absorbing combustion heat. Conversely, hotter range plug designs have a longer insulator nose and greater surface area to absorb the heat from combustion. It is most important to install a spark plug of the heat range specified by the manufacturer as a starting point. When tuning racing engines, it is not uncommon to go up or down three heat ranges of plugs to optimize performance. For example, when your jetting is slightly rich but not enough to require a jet change, you could select a plug one range hotter to achieve the target exhaust-gas temperature. Each step in heat range will effect a 50-degree-Fahrenheit change in the exhaust-gas temperature.

TYPES OF SPARK PLUGS
FINE-WIRE PLUGS

Fine-wire electrodes provide easier starts and reduced cold fouling, partly because they require slightly less voltage to fire the plug compared to standard-size-electrode center wire. The fine wires are made of precious-metal alloy and are excellent conductors of voltage. Fine-wire spark plugs produce a more direct and confined spark that is better for igniting the air-fuel mixture.

PROJECTED-INSULATOR PLUGS

Projected insulator refers to the extension of the insulator beyond the end of the shell. This design can only be used if there is sufficient clearance to the piston crown at top dead center (TDC). The advantage of this design is that it benefits from the cooling effect of the incoming fuel charge at high rpm, which provides some pre-ignition protection. At low rpm when cold fouling occurs, the insulator is more exposed to combustion, which helps to burn off deposits on the insulator that can cause cold fouling. Projected-insulator plugs can be used on any 200-cc to 500-cc dirt bike. These types of plugs cannot be used on 125-cc engines with shallow-domed combustion chambers or those with flat-top pistons. These engines do not have enough clearance between the piston and head, and the piston would contact the plug.

MAINTENANCE INTERVAL CHART

The following are recommended intervals for maintaining different components of your bike. Keep in mind that these are averages; if you are riding in extremely dusty, muddy, or wet conditions, times will be shorter.

COMPONENT	RIDING HOURS				
	2	5	10	20	50
Chain	C&I	–	–	–	R
Air filter	C&I	–	–	R	–
Brake pads	C&I	–	–	R	–
Cables	C&I	–	L	–	–
Brake fluid	–	–	R	–	–
Radiator coolant	–	R	–	–	–
Transmission oil	R	–	–	–	–
Top end	–	C&I	RB	–	–
Reed valve	–	C&I	–	–	–
Air boot	–	C&I	–	–	–
Magneto	–	C&I	–	–	–
Crank seals	–	–	–	R	–
Clutch plates	–	–	R	–	–
Bottom end	–	–	–	C&I	–
Shock fluid	–	–	C&I	RF	–
Fork fluid	–	–	–	RF	–
Wheel bearings	–	C&I	R	–	–
Spokes	–	–	C&I	–	–
Steering head bearings	–	–	L	–	–
Swingarm & linkage bearings	L	RB	–	–	–

KEY: Clean & Inspect (C&I) Replace Fluid (RF) Lubricate (L) Rebuild (RB) Replace (R)

RESISTOR PLUGS

Non-resistor spark plugs give off excessive electromagnetic interference (EMI), which can interfere with radio communications. That is the primary reason why the manufacturers recommend resistor spark plugs. In North America, engine manufacturers must install resistor plugs in new engines because many people in rural areas depend on CB radios for their communication needs. In Canada, it's actually a law that you must use resistor plugs in your off-road vehicle. Dirt bikes manufactured after 1996 may have some type of sensitive electronic engine management controls that require the use of resistor plugs.

SPARK PLUGS WITH GIMMICKS

There are many different types of plugs on the market with every possible gimmick. Some manufacturers make ridiculous claims for their plugs, such as resistance to fouling, more power, or better fuel economy. There is an old saying, "Paper accepts all ink in advertising and litigation." That is certainly true with spark plug ads. The sad truth is that if an engine isn't tuned properly, an expensive plug will foul just as fast as a cheap plug. The best spark plug design is one with a precious-metal electrode and ground arm, shaped to a fine point, and a core sealing ring that resists high pressure. Unfortunately, no such plug exists. There are, however, plugs with precious-metal electrodes and excellent core designs. Forget about the funky ground arm shapes because the spark is going to jump from the electrode to the ground arm at the point of least resistance, so specialized ground arm shapes with multiple points offer no real advantage. Worse, the shapes of some ground arms can actually make them susceptible to breaking off. A really good design for a ground arm is the 45-degree (straight arm). This ground arm doesn't have a bend in the middle so it's not susceptible to breaking due to the pressure conditions in the combustion chamber. Suzuki recommends these types of plugs in the

RM85 and 125 models because the ignition maps are so aggressive that they could melt a bent ground arm. Nippon Denso sells these plugs for the most reasonable price, about $10 each. Forget the gimmicks and spend your money testing three or more different heat ranges until you find the plug that best suits your riding demands.

THE THROTTLE

Many top riders are cautious about their throttles. Factory mechanics routinely disassemble and clean throttles between races, and sometimes between motos if the conditions are muddy. Use the following tips to clean a throttle and identify trouble signs.

BASIC CLEANING AND INSPECTION

After removing the throttle's rubber dust cover and plastic housing, examine the throttle pulley and cable for frays in the cable or dirt in the pulley. Examine the plastic guide for cracks, which can cause the cable to fray or catch on a tree branch, pulling the throttle wide open. If this happens to your cable, don't try to fix it with tape, just replace it with an OEM part.

The throttle pulley is made of nylon and doesn't require lube, but the cable does. Use a cable lubing tool to force chain lube down the throttle cable. Remove the carburetor slide and stuff a rag into the top of the carburetor to prevent any dirt from entering the carburetor. Make sure you disconnect the cable from the carburetor slide first, otherwise you will force dirt and lube from the cable down into the slide, and that can cause the throttle to stick open.

Clean the throttle tube and pulley with brake cleaner. Lube the throttle tube and handlebar with penetrating oil.

INSPECTING THE SLIDE AND CARB

Check the corners of Keihin PWK carbs for dents or deep wear marks. Newer model slides are chrome-plated. Older model carbs are anodized or Teflon-coated and can appear a dull gray or black color. The gray PWK slides tend to wear at the corners and

can cock and jam in the carb's slide bore when the throttle is turned wide open. This is a common problem on older KX 250s and 500s. Replace the gray slides with chrome-plated slides when they get worn. The chrome slides are the standard OEM part for 1993-and-later KXs and are available from accessory companies such as Moose Off-Road, Carbs Parts Warehouse, and Sudco in the United States.

REPLACING THE THROTTLE TUBE AND GRIP

The stock throttle grips on modern off-road bikes are molded to the throttle tube. If you damage the grip and need to replace it, it's a very tedious job to remove the old grip. Plastic throttle tubes are susceptible to crash damage and sticky operation. The best setup is to install an aftermarket aluminum throttle tube. There are two types: closed- and open-end. Closed-end tubes are the best for MX applications; open-ended tubes are needed for off-road because of the mounting fixtures used in handguards. Throttle tubes are knurled to improve the bond to the grip. Grip glue is an easy way to bond the rubber grip to the throttle tube and some brands of grips are designed with ridges to accommodate stainless-steel safety wire to help fasten the grip to the throttle tube.

If your bike is so old that aluminum throttle tubes are not available, then here are some tips on removing and replacing the grip:

1. Use a pocketknife to strip off the grip.
2. Use a file, a wire wheel, or a lathe to remove the plastic splines and the remains of the rubber grip.
3. Apply a thin coating of grip cement to the throttle tube and slide the new grip onto the tube and let it dry for 24 hours.
4. As an extra safety precaution, wrap the grip with 0.020-in. or 0.5-mm stainless-steel safety wire. Wrap the grip at two equidistant points and twist the wire end and clip it with 1/4 in. remaining. Position the wire end so it faces on the lower palm side of the grip. This way it won't stick to the rider's glove.

RUNAWAY THROTTLE

It's a riding situation that most riders have experienced—the lack of control that makes riders panic when the engine runs wide open uncontrollably. This is often called stuck throttle condition, or STC.

STUCK THROTTLE CONDITION (STC)

STC means that the engine runs at high rpm without control from the throttle. STC can occur in three different forms: mechanical, air pressure, and auto-ignition.

MECHANICAL

Mechanical STC occurs in the throttle grip, pulley, cable, carb slide, or carb jet needle. Mechanical STC happens when crash damage or normal wear and tear cause one or more of these parts to stick in one position.

Examples: The bike falls on the right side and crushes the grip end, causing it to bind on the handlebar; the cable wears and frays, causing it to stick in the cable housing; the carb's throttle slide and needle are exposed to dirt that passes by the air filter and gets wedged, making the slide and needle inoperable.

AIR PRESSURE (TWO-STROKE ENGINE ONLY)

Air pressure STC occurs when there is an air pressure leak somewhere between the carburetor and the cylinder, including the reed valve and manifold, crankcase, and crankshaft seals. The crankcase of a two-stroke engine is sealed and works like a vacuum pump. Leaks can occur at places such as the rubber intake manifold and gasket surface, dry rotted cracks in the rubber, cracks in the reed valve or cylinder, gasket leaks at the reed valve and cylinder base, cracks or holes in the crankcase, and worn crankshaft seals.

Air leaking into the crankcase can cause the engine to run lean and get hot. This is a common cause of piston seizures.

Examples: The engine idles erratically or won't idle when the throttle is shut; the engine bogs badly when accelerating abruptly; the engine pings in mid range and pops on top end. Air

pressure STC may also occur when the engine runs out of fuel, causing a momentary lean condition followed by the engine shutting off.

AUTO-IGNITION

Auto-ignition STC can occur on two-stroke engines that suffer from pre-ignition, which occurs when there is a point (other than the spark plug) in the combustion chamber with a temperature high enough to ignite the fuel–air mixture. Once this type of STC starts, it can't be controlled with the throttle or kill button. The carburetor's choke mechanism is the only thing that can kill the engine.

Example: Air pressure leaks can lead to auto-ignition STC. Low crankcase pressure causes the engine to run lean and hot. Raw fuel gets trapped in the bottom of the crankcase. If the piston crown hits the melting temperature of 1,100 degrees Fahrenheit, it could form an ignition source. Fuel then gets drawn up from the crankcases and the engine revs until a catastrophic mechanical failure stops the engine.

WHY WON'T THE KILL BUTTON WORK?

If you've ever experienced a bike with STC, your first reaction may have been to push the kill button, and perhaps it worked. But were you ever surprised when it had no effect? It's possible, and here's why: The kill-button interrupts the ground to the igniter box. But when the engine revs high, there is significant energy flowing through the box and electricity arcs to the point of least resistance. Antifreeze spilled where the igniter box meets the frame is a common cause of an alternate ground path. The filler cap and overflow vent tube are located close to the igniter box on most bikes. It's easy for overspill to splash the igniter box and frame.

WAYS TO KILL AN ENGINE

When a bike suffers from STC, there are three ways to kill the engine: spark, fuel, and load. The kill button should end the spark. If that doesn't work, the next easiest thing to do is to lock up the rear

and front brakes in order to apply a load to the engine. On engines with air pressure and auto-ignition STC, engage the carburetor's choke mechanism. It's like the song by David Bowie, "putting out fire with gasoline." A rich mixture will saturate the combustion chamber, lower the temperature, and reduce the available space for air to mix with fuel in order to sustain ignition.

TIPS FOR CHECKING YOUR BIKE'S THROTTLE SLIDE

If you're concerned that the throttle slide in your bike may be sticking, remove the throttle slide from the top of the carb. Visually examine it for dirt or sand. Dirt is the most common cause of a stuck slide. Look for vertical scratches in the slide face. Those scratches are wear patterns from dirt wedged between the slide and slide bore. To examine the slide for chrome peeling, look for jagged spots of discoloration in the surface of the slide. When the chrome chips, the base metal aluminum is more gray and dull than the chrome finish. Some slides are coated with a dry black film lubricant. When the color changes from black to gray, it indicates wear. If any slide has peeling from dirt or chrome damage, replace it rather than trying to repair it. Also, take care to polish and clean the carb's throttle slide bore. If the new slide still binds or rattles with too much clearance, replace the carburetor too.

CHAIN AND SPROCKET BASICS

The condition of the drivetrain has a significant effect on both the handling and the engine performance of a dirt bike. The simple chain-and-sprocket drivetrain is still the most efficient way to transfer power from the engine to the rear wheel, especially on a motor vehicle with 12 in. of travel. The forces transferred through the chain and into the suspension can have a positive effect on handling. During acceleration, the chain forces push the rear wheel into the ground. That's why when you land from a jump with the throttle on, the

This drive sprocket is visibly worn. The teeth become thin and shaped like a wave in the direction of travel.

rear suspension has more resistance to bottoming. Pro racers depend on the chain forces when pre-jumping and landing. If the chain is too tight, too loose, or the wheel is not aligned in the swingarm, a good rider will notice the difference. When the chain and sprockets get packed with mud or corroded from lack of lubrication, they can generate a significant amount of friction to load the engine. A poor set of chain and sprockets could absorb as much as 5 horsepower from the average 250-cc dirt bike. Learning the basics of drivetrain maintenance can improve your riding performance because you'll be able to use the chain forces to your advantage.

CLEAN AND LUBE

After each ride, spray the chain and sprockets with degreaser, rinse the chain with water while scrubbing it with a wire brush, and then spray the chain with a water-displacement chemical such as WD40 or LPS. When you scrub the chain and sprockets, make sure to remove the dirt and oil deposits embedded near the teeth of the sprockets. If you don't clean off the debris, the sprocket will wear faster.

The ideal chain lube is a spray lube with a chemical that penetrates the chain's links but doesn't fly off or attract dirt. There are many different types of chain lube that fit the ideal, to varying degrees—moly, lithe grease, and even chain wax. However, each is designed for a specific use. Chain lube made from moly is good for street bikes because it doesn't make a mess, but it offers little resistance to water. Spray-lithe grease lasts a long time and offers protection against water damage, so it is good for enduro and trail riding. Chain wax was designed for motocross race bikes that are serviced every moto or practice session. Chain wax is a light coating that seals the link and doesn't fly off or attract dirt. This type of lube is easily stripped off when the bike is power-washed.

TIPS ON CHAIN ADJUSTING

The two most important things to know about chain adjusting are to maintain alignment of the sprockets and to correctly set the chain free-play when the swingarm is parallel to the ground.

There are a few ways to set the sprockets in alignment—by adjusting the axle to the stamped marks or using an alignment gauge. All dirt bikes have marks stamped in the swingarm at the axle mounts. The chain adjusters have marks denoting the center of the rear axle. Normally, you would use the marks to keep the rear wheel centered in the swingarm while adjusting the chain's free-play. However, production frames are robot-welded, and there are slight tolerance differences that can put the stamped marks out of alignment. That's why race mechanics prefer to use an alignment gauge, which fits into the centers of the rear axle and swingarm pivot bolt. Race Tools in New York makes a simple alignment bar that fits all dirt bikes. You simply fit it in the center of the axle and pivot while you adjust the wheel position for the proper chain free-play.

No matter how much travel a dirt bike has, the ideal chain free-play is 0.5 in. or 13 mm measured when the swingarm is parallel to the ground. At that point, the rear axle is at the farthest point from the swingarm pivot and the chain free-play will be at its minimum.

Just because the wheel is aligned when the bike is stationary doesn't mean it will stay in alignment when the bike accelerates up a bumpy hill. Whenever you set the chain free-play,

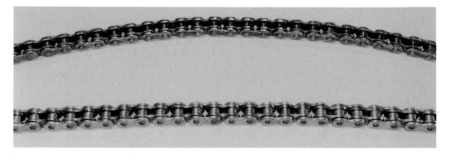

For the bow test, lay the chain on the ground and try to form a bow shape. If it deflects 8 inches over a 3-foot span, the rollers are worn out. The chain on top is used and the one on the bottom is new.

The drive sprocket is fastened with a bolt, nut, or circlip. For circlips, apply a dab of silicone or Yamabond to prevent the clip from vibrating off the shaft. Notice the direction of the master link clip—the closed end should always face the direction of travel, otherwise it will pop off as soon as you hit the gas.

try to wiggle the rear wheel and the swingarm. If any of the bearings are worn, the drivetrain can run out of alignment, causing a big power drain.

TYPES OF CHAINS

There are two types of chain: conventional and O-ring. Conventional chains use steel pins with a press-fit soft metal bushing to form each link. These chains use a mechanical seal to protect the link, meaning that there is minimal clearance between the rollers and links. O-ring chains use the O-ring to seal lubrication in the link and keep dirt and water out. O-ring chains are more durable, more expensive, and heavier. These chains are great for long-distance off-road riding because the chain doesn't require as much maintenance as a conventional chain.

Some chains are advertised as having the ability to resist stretching, but this claim is misleading. No chain really stretches; metal doesn't stretch and stay at a larger size. When you turn the bike's rear wheel and the chain has points where the free-play varies, that is due to chain wear, not stretch. It's normal for a chain to wear at different rates at different points.

The variance of the wear is greatly dependent on sprocket alignment and the chain's free-play.

CHECKING A CHAIN FOR WEAR

There are a few different ways to determine if a chain needs to be replaced. Examine the chain for kinks—points where the link and roller have seized, preventing them from freely rotating—and replace the chain if there are kinks. Also, with the chain installed, cleaned, lubed, and adjusted, rotate the wheel and check the chain's free-play at different points. If the chain needs to be adjusted frequently and has many points where the free-play varies, then the chain needs to be replaced. The sprockets tend to wear twice as fast as the chain, but replace the chain when the sprockets are worn enough to need replacement and vice versa. If you install a new chain on worn sprockets, the chain will wear prematurely.

MASTER LINKS

There are two types of master links: slip-fit and press-fit, but both use a clip. Conventional chains use slip-fit links, and O-ring chains use press-fit links.

Position the clips so that the opening faces opposite the direction of rotation. Press-fit links can be installed by pressing against the link with the end of a hammer handle and pressing the link plate on by placing an 8-mm socket over the link pins and tapping on the socket with another hammer. Tap on the socket alternately until the link plate is pressed on so far that the entire clip notch is exposed. To install slip-fit links, simply push the link together with your fingers and install the locking clip with the closed end facing the direction of rotation.

TYPES OF SPROCKETS

Sprockets or chain rings come in many different colors, patterns, tooth designs, materials, and sizes. Sprockets are made of steel, aluminum, or titanium. Steel is a better material for longevity and cost; aluminum is lighter; and more expensive alloys such as stainless steel and titanium offer advantages in wear and performance. The individual teeth of the sprocket tend to wear in the pattern of a wave. When the profiles of the front and rear sides of the teeth look different, the sprocket is worn out. Once the teeth wear far enough, they allow the chain links to skip over the top of them. Don't allow your sprockets to wear so far that the chain skips. If the chain derails while you're riding it, the bike will stop abruptly and you could be injured. If the chain derails forward and gets jammed between the sprocket and crankcases, it can break the cases or shift shaft. It's best to retain the original front chain guard or buy a suitable aftermarket product. The chain guard prevents the chain from derailing forward and directs it downward.

TIPS FOR CHANGING THE SPROCKETS
COUNTERSHAFT SPROCKET

There are two different types of front-sprocket retaining methods: bolt/nut and circlip. Circlip retainers can be removed with circlip pliers, available at any hardware store. However, the circlips can only be removed a few times

This is the proper way to tighten the rear wheel after adjusting the chain. Insert a T-handle or screwdriver between the chain and sprocket to apply some tension and prevent the axle from pivoting when being tightened. Position the torque wrench so you're driving the wheel into the ground rather than compressing the suspension.

Once you remove the sprocket, clean the inside and outside of the counter-shaft bushing, which is the spacer that fits between the bearing and the sprocket on the countershaft. The bushing is sealed on the outer edge by the counter-shaft seal that fits into the crankcase and by an O-ring on the inside. If the seal and O-ring wear out, water and dirt can enter the countershaft bearing and that is expensive to fix. You'd be surprised how much tranny oil can seep past the seal and O-ring while you're riding! After cleaning, apply a dab of Bel Ray water-proof grease to the inner and outer faces of the bushing to help keep out water and dirt.

REAR SPROCKET

Rear sprockets are bolted to the wheel hub. Normally, a tapered-head bolt with a flanged nut fastens the sprocket to the hub. Sprocket bolts tend to loosen up. That makes mechanics overtighten them, causing the Allen hex head or the nut to strip. Avoid these problems by using blue Loctite on the threads of the bolts. Always use a six-point box wrench on the sprocket nuts, and tighten the bolts in an alternating diagonal pattern.

GEARING TIPS

You'll have to change gearing to suit different tracks. Tracks with steep hills, many tight turns, and long whoops sections require higher final-drive ratios. Fast tracks require a lower ratio. A simple rule of thumb: For more top speed, switch to a countershaft sprocket with one more tooth than stock; for quicker acceleration, switch to a rear sprocket with two more teeth than stock. Use the gearing chart below to find the difference between different combinations of sprockets for your model bike.

FINAL-DRIVE GEAR-RATIO CHART

Match the front and rear sprocket size to determine the final drive ratio. Divide the number of teeth of the rear sprocket by the number of teeth of the front sprocket.

before their shape is distorted. Factory mechanics use a coating of Yamabond 4 or Three-Bond 1104 to prevent the circlips from vibrating off or getting hooked by small rocks.

The bolt/nut retainers use either a cupped spring washer for a bolt or a bend-able retaining clip for a nut to prevent them from loosening. The average torque setting for a large diameter nut is 24 ft-lbs but only 15 ft-lbs for a small diameter bolt. Most cupped washers are marked "OUT" for the part that faces out. If that wears off, install the washer with the highest part of the cup under the bolt head to

provide spring tension for the locking effect. If you don't have an electric or pneumatic impact wrench to remove the sprocket's retaining bolt/nut, you'll need to prevent the sprocket from turning while you loosen the retainer with a hand wrench. Applying the rear brake will cause the chain to prevent the sprocket from turning—assuming, of course, that you did not remove the chain first. Never wedge anything between the chain and sprocket while removing or tightening the front sprocket bolt/nut because the wedge can come out and injure you or damage the chain and sprocket.

GEAR RATIO CHART

REAR SPROCKET SIZES	FRONT SPROCKET SIZES		
	12	13	14
49	4.08	3.76	3.50
50	4.16	3.84	3.57
51	4.25	3.92	3.64
52	4.33	4.00	3.71
53	4.41	4.07	3.78

COOLING SYSTEM

A dirt bike's cooling system is such a compromise of design. Because of the emphasis on low weight and compactness, motorcycle designers are forced to fit aluminum radiators to one small area at the front of the motorcycle chassis, an area that is constantly hammered with sticks, stones, and crashing. At the 1990 500-cc USGP, Rodney Smith collided with another rider. The other bike nailed Rodney's KX500 and crushed three channels of one radiator. I was working as Smith's mechanic, and we had to repair the bike before the next practice session. I applied epoxy to the damaged area of the radiator, and it held for the entire race!

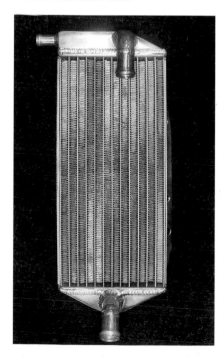

Pro-Circuit sells these aftermarket radiators, which feature thicker cores and greater volume.

Here are some tips on how to maintain a cooling system for maximum performance, and how to do emergency repairs to a punctured radiator.

SOFT TOOLS

Several excellent products are invaluable when you need to repair your coolant system. Duro Master Mend epoxy can make temporary repairs to the outside of the radiator. Alumaseal can make temporary repairs to the inside of the coolant system, and it works great for chronic head-gasket leaks. Use radiator cleaner to flush out the coolant system on a yearly basis because corrosion, debris, and waste products from combustion gases leaking into the coolant system can accumulate in the tiny channels of the radiator and reduce the cooling efficiency.

Enginekool, Moose Juice, Engine Ice, or Spectro coolant products are surfactants that enable better flow through the water jackets of the engine. These products are available from most auto parts stores or your local dirt bike shop.

BASIC CLEANING AND INSPECTION

A dirt bike's cooling system should be flushed and changed once a year. Before you drain the cooling system, add 4 ounces of an aluminum radiator flushing fluid. Several companies make the product, and it is available from any auto parts store. Run the engine for about ten minutes and then drain the cooling system. Take care when disposing of the old coolant. Some states have strict EPA regulations regarding the disposal of used coolant. Call your local auto repair garage and ask if they have a recycling drum for used coolant. Now there are non-toxic, biodegradable coolants available.

Remove the water pump cover and check for corrosion and debris. Check the water pump's bearings by grasping the water impeller with your fingers and trying to move it up and down. If you feel any movement, the water pump bearings and seals need to be replaced. If you see oil leaking into the water pump housing, it is a sign that the seals and bearings are worn too. Sometimes, the bearings will be so worn that they cut a groove in the water pump shaft. In most cases, when the water pump seals and bearings are worn, so is the shaft. It's best to replace the parts as a set because they aren't that expensive. The water pump is gear-driven by the crankshaft. Some bikes use gears made of plastic; other bikes use metal gears. Metal gears are more durable but are very noisy. Plastic gears are vulnerable to melting, especially when the gearbox oil is low and at very high temperatures.

FILLING AND BLEEDING TIPS

Some bikes have bolts on top of the cylinder head or water spigot that are used to bleed trapped air in the coolant system. If the air isn't bled from the system, the air pocket will prevent the coolant from circulating and the temperature will rise until the radiator cap releases. The proper way to bleed the trapped air is to fill the system to the top of the radiator, leave the cap off, and loosen the bolt until coolant streams out. Then top off the radiator, install the cap, and run the engine for ten minutes before checking the coolant level.

CAUTION: Let the engine cool down before releasing the radiator cap; otherwise, the hot coolant could rush out and burn your hand.

Boyesen Engineering offers aftermarket kits such as high-flow aluminum impellers and housings. Some OEM impellers are made of plastic and can melt if the engine overheats.

High-pressure radiator caps can raise the boiling point of the coolant. Most bikes don't use thermostats, but they can actually be beneficial in preventing piston seizures when riding in cold weather.

Here are new and worn water pump impeller shafts for a Honda CRF450. Notice the lines in the shaft. Even if the seal is replaced, this water pump will leak coolant out of the weep hole at the bottom of the water pump housing. Whenever the water pump leaks, always replace the shaft, bearings, and seals as a set. CRFs wear out the water pump parts frequently because only one side of the shaft is supported on a bearing.

DAMAGE CONTROL

The radiators of dirt bikes seem to mysteriously attract rocks and branches. Crashing a bike can damage the radiators too. Radiators and exhaust pipes are like bumpers for dirt bikes, so chances are you will have to perform emergency repairs on your bike's cooling system. It may be at a race, on the trail, or in the wilderness several miles from any roads. Every trail rider should carry epoxy in a tool bag.

Any type of quick-setting epoxy works great for radiator repairs. Epoxy isn't an adhesive in that it isn't sticky. Epoxy bonds when it can wrap around the edges of surfaces. It's easy to get epoxy to bond on a radiator because there are so many edges on the cores and the surrounding fins, but the area affected must be cleaned before the epoxy is applied. Quick-setting epoxies need only about 30 minutes drying time when air temperatures are over 75 degrees Fahrenheit, longer in colder weather.

Epoxy radiator repairs should be regarded only as temporary fixes. When you get your bike home, replace the damaged radiator or have it heli-arc welded by one of the many companies that specialize in radiator repair, such as Myler's in Utah and Fontana Radiator Works in California.

PROTECTION FOR RADIATORS

Radiators can be protected on the front and the sides. Aluminum bars protect the sides of the radiator from damage if the bike is dropped on its side. Screens are used in place of the plastic louvers in front to protect the radiator cores from being punctured by tree branches. This protection comes at a cost, however, because the cooling system will not work as efficiently when the louvers are removed and replaced with screens. The louvers serve to collect and channel air at high velocity into the cores. DeVol Racing makes guards for radiators, and they may have models to fit your machine.

IMPROVING THE COOLING SYSTEM

There are three things that you can do to improve the efficiency of the cooling system: raise the pressure, improve the flow, and add capacity. Switching to a radiator cap marked 1.6 will raise the pop-off pressure point in the radiator and prevent the coolant from boiling until a higher temperature. Installing a Boyesen Engineering aluminum impeller and water pump spigot will improve the flow. Most stock impellers are made of plastic and can actually melt. The Boyesen product features vanes with a cup shape to increase the coolant flow. The outer spigots are designed with a shape to accommodate the larger, more efficient impellers. Lengthening the hoses or installing a larger aftermarket radiator can increase the capacity of the cooling system.

TROUBLESHOOTING

SYMPTOM: Coolant flows out of the overflow tubes

PROBLEM: Leaking head gasket, trapped air in system, or stripped water pump gear

SYMPTOM: Engine overheats quickly

PROBLEM: Coolant is low or radiator is clogged

SYMPTOM: Grinding noise from the right side of the engine increases with rpm

PROBLEM: Water pump bearings and seals are worn

SYMPTOM: Clutch slipping, water in transmission oil

PROBLEM: Water pump bearings and seals are worn

SYMPTOM: Coolant leaks from rear of the cylinder head

PROBLEM: Chronic head gasket leaks are usually due to frame problems

Look at the depth of the serration to visually inspect the fiber plates. You can also measure the thickness of the plates with a caliper.

CLUTCH REPAIR

A motorcycle's clutch has a significant effect on power delivery and handling. If the clutch doesn't engage and disengage smoothly, the bike's rear wheel could break loose and compromise traction or, worse, cause the rider to crash.

Does your bike lurch when you fan the clutch? Do the clutch plates break or burn out fast? Does the clutch make a grinding noise when the engine is idling in neutral? This section provides insight into the problems that affect clutches, and some tips on how to permanently fix clutch problems.

COMMON CLUTCH PROBLEMS

Too many riders replace their clutch plates before they are worn out. They don't measure the plate thickness, plate warpage, or the spring free length. One guy called me, complaining that he had spent over $600 on clutch plates in one riding season. He said his bike burned up clutch plates on every ride. I asked him to send me the entire clutch and all the old plates and springs. The problem was that the springs were sacked out and didn't exert adequate spring tension on the plates. That allowed the plates to slip, causing them to burn. All his clutch plates were the standard thickness and none of the plates were warped. The plates all had a minor surface glazing problem that was easily fixed using medium-grit sandpaper. The

average cost of replacing a set of clutch plates is about $100, which brings up the moral of this story: Spend some time looking for the cause of a clutch problem rather than just throwing money at it.

MEASURING TOOLS

There are three inexpensive tools that you need to perform basic measuring of clutch parts. A flat surface, such as a piece of glass or preferably a thick piece of steel, will give you a surface to check plate warping and deglaze the plates. A feeler gauge will enable you to measure plate warping. A dial caliper will enable you to measure the free length of the clutch springs and the plate thickness. Dial calipers are available from Sears, auto parts stores, or Enco.

HOW TO MEASURE THE PARTS

Before you attempt to measure the clutch parts, you will need the manufacturers' recommended dimensions for the parts. The factory service manual lists this information, or you can call your local motorcycle dealership. Dimensions such as the clutch plate thickness or the spring free length will be listed as standard and minimum. The standard dimension refers to the dimension of a new part, while the minimum dimension refers to the worn-out dimension of the part.

Measuring the Plates

Clutch plates wear thinner with use and can warp if they become overheated. Use the caliper to measure the thickness of the face of the plates. If the plate thickness is within spec, place it on a flat surface such as glass or steel. Press the plate down evenly and try to insert a 0.020-in. feeler gauge between the plate and the flat surface. If the feeler gauge can be inserted under the plate, the plate is warped and cannot be repaired.

Measuring the Springs

Clutch springs sack out with use, meaning that they become shorter in length. Measuring the free length of the spring is the best way to determine if the springs should be replaced. Use the

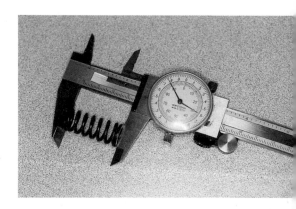

Clutch springs sack out and become shorter. Replace them every other time that you change the fiber plates. Worn springs make the clutch plates slip.

caliper to measure the free length of the spring and compare the dimension to the minimum length spec listed by the manufacturer. Sacked-out clutch springs will cause the plates to become glazed and the clutch to slip.

TROUBLESHOOTING CLUTCH PROBLEMS

The previous section covered basic clutch service, but what happens when you have a serious clutch problem such as a grinding noise or a combination of both dragging and slipping? This section provides some insight into troubleshooting common and serious clutch problems.

Grinding Noises

Warm up your engine, put the transmission in neutral, and turn the throttle so the engine runs steadily, just over idle. Slightly pull in the clutch lever. Check for a significant reduction in vibration and the grinding noise. If the noise is reduced, then the needle bearing and bushing that fit between the clutch basket and main transmission shaft are slightly worn. This is very common on KX250s, but it isn't a serious problem. There is no way to measure the needle bearing, but the service manual will list a dimension for the bushing diameter. Always replace the needle bearing and bushing as a set.

If the grinding noise isn't affected by engaging the clutch, then the problem may be more serious. Check the bolt that retains the primary gear to the crankshaft and the nut that retains the clutch hub. If the nut and bolt are tight, then the crankshaft main bearings may be worn out. The 1991 and 1992 Suzuki RM125s and 250s had a characteristic problem with bad primary gear bolts. Suzuki has corrected the problem, and new bolts are available from any Suzuki dealer. There is no implied warranty from Suzuki, but I suggest replacing the bolt just for safety's sake.

wear caused by the splined teeth of the clutch plates. Eventually, the notch marks become so deep that the plates just stick in one place and resist engaging or disengaging. If the notch marks are less than 0.020 in. deep, it's possible to draw-file down the high spots of the notches. Be careful—if you file too much aluminum from the clutch basket or inner hub, then the clutch will be prone to dragging. A common symptom of dragging is the bike creeping forward when you put it in gear.

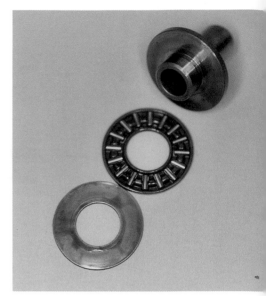

The typical throwout bearing consists of a pushrod cup, radial thrust bearing, and a shim. The bearing wears and can cause a grinding noise when you engage the clutch. If the clutch makes a grinding noise in neutral and becomes quieter when you engage the clutch, the needle bearing that supports the clutch basket is worn.

This is a close-up view of the chatter marks that form in the fingers of the outer clutch basket. When this occurs, the clutch suffers from chronic fiber plate breakage, drag, and jerky clutch feel at the hand lever. This clutch basket needs to be replaced with a high-quality aftermarket part.

Dragging or Lurching Problems

Dragging and lurching problems are primarily caused by deep notch marks that form in the clutch basket and inner hub. The notch marks are the result of

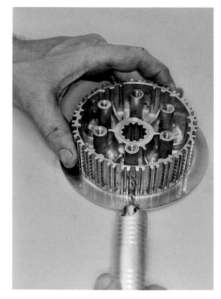

The inner clutch hub can be improved by drilling two small holes in the undercut splines, spaced equidistant. The holes enable better oil flow to lubricate the driven plates. Brands such as KTM and most aftermarket clutch hubs have either oil holes or dry film lubricants to increase longevity.

Draw-filing refers to a filing method whereby you stroke the file in one direction, evenly along the length of a surface. This enables you to file down only the high spots of the notches equally. You will need two types of files—a flat file for the clutch basket and a triangulated file for the inner hub. You'll also need a file card to clean the aluminum debris from the file; otherwise, the file grooves will become clogged with aluminum and prevent the file from cutting.

Before you attempt to draw-file the notches from your clutch basket, you must check the basket for hairline fractures at the base of each of the fingers. If you find any cracks, replace the basket. If the fingers break off, the debris will cause catastrophic engine damage. If you draw-file a basket with fracture cracks, it will fail much faster. Late-model KX125s (pre-1993) and 1992 RM250s have characteristic problems with clutch baskets. The manufacturers have redesigned the clutch baskets, and they are available from your local dealer.

Aftermarket Clutch Baskets

Four aftermarket manufacturers offer replacement clutch baskets: Hinson Racing, Wiseco, Vortex, and Moose Racing. Most of these products are machined from billet aluminum and hard-anodized for wear resistance. Hinson products are hard-anodized and coated with Teflon to reduce friction. The Wiseco clutch baskets are forged from billet slugs. Hinson offers

This is the procedure for removing the kick start gear. Using a hydraulic press with a capacity of at least 5 tons, support the back side of the basket with a sleeve; use a large socket or tube to press the gear.

Hinson Racing makes a full line of aftermarket clutch parts, including baskets, hubs, pressure plates, and aluminum clutch plates. The Hinson products are machined from billet aluminum and feature hard anodizing with Teflon impregnation. The Hinson aluminum plates feature a coarse, hard coating that produces more friction and protects the plates from wear.

replacement rubber bushings because they tend to wear out on 250-cc bikes. Hinson also offers a wide variety of performance clutch parts such as inner hubs, pressure plates, and hard-anodized, aluminum-driven plates that are lightweight and have a rough surface finish for more friction.

All the aftermarket clutch baskets require you to remove the original primary gear, kick-start gear, and rubber bushings from the clutch basket. That sounds difficult but it isn't. Here is an overview of installing any aftermarket clutch basket. You will need access to a drill press and a hydraulic press.

1. Start by cleaning the oil residue from the old clutch basket.

2. Use a drill press and a 0.250-in. drill bit to bore out the stock mild steel rivets that retain the primary gear. Drill off the head of the rivets deep enough to remove the thin sheet-metal retaining plate.

3. Strip off the retaining plate, rubber bushings, and primary gear. Take care to remove the parts in order because it's possible to install the gear upside down.

There are several manufacturers of aftermarket clutch baskets, including Hinson, Moose, Wiseco, and Vortex. The installation procedure is essentially the same. Since none of the aftermarket baskets include the primary and kick start gear, the original gears must be removed from the old basket and installed on the new basket. Use a drill press to drill the head from the rivets. Remove the backing plate and then the primary gear and dampers.

Before you attempt to install the kick start gear, apply some assembly lube or anti-seize to the splines of the gear to prevent gauling. Make sure you have your setup straight and level or the gear will cock and seize, ruining the new expensive clutch basket.

4. Use a hydraulic press and a bushing driver or large diameter socket to press out the kick-start gear. Don't try to hammer the gear out because you'll fracture the hardened gear and you can't buy a replacement, only a complete new clutch basket.

5. Aftermarket clutch baskets use tapered panhead Allen screws to retain the primary gear. Always use Red Loctite on the threads of the bolts for the gear and tighten them with a hand-impact driver. Wiseco clutch baskets use Plasti-Lok screws so you don't need a thread-locking agent like Loctite.

6. Wipe a dab of anti-seize compound on the kick-start gear before you try to press it into the new clutch basket. Take care to press it all the way on but don't bottom it too hard or the basket may crack.

The auto clutch is the latest innovation in clutch technology. This is the Rekluse Z-Start, which replaces the stock pressure plate. This is essentially a centrifugal clutch that expands at a certain rpm to apply pressure to the clutch plates. It sells for about $300.

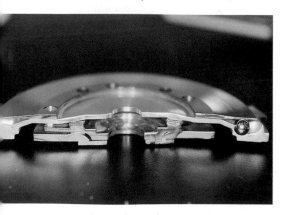

AUTOMATIC CLUTCHES GROW UP

The biggest innovation in dirt bike clutches is automatic, or "slipper," clutches. For the past decade, clutch pressure plates such as these were used on 50-cc bikes and now they've grown up and are becoming popular in

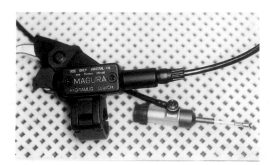

This is an aftermarket hydraulic clutch lever kit made by Magura.

enduro, DTX, and supermoto. The automatic clutch is essentially a pressure plate with a set of centrifugal weights (steel balls), a wave washer spring, and a channeled ramp. Put the bike in gear and rev the engine until the centrifugal force of the spinning balls causes the balls to roll up the channel ramp far enough to overcome the spring force of the wave washer. I first rode a CRF450 with the Rekluse brand of auto clutch. I found that I could start in fifth gear from a dead stop and the clutch would engage smoothly. The other advantage to an auto clutch is that it's nearly impossible to stall the bike. However, the downside is that the fiber clutch plates wear faster.

ELECTRICAL AND IGNITION SYSTEMS

Electrical systems fail for the stupidest reasons. Water, heat, and vibration are the three main causes of electrical component failure. Simple preventative maintenance can save you hundreds of dollars in electrical parts. Simple tasks such as cleaning the dirt and condensation from the flywheel and stator to prevent corrosion, applying dielectric grease to the connectors, and periodically checking the spark plug cap for tightness may save you from pushing your bike rather than riding it. This section shows you how to care for your motorcycle's ignition and electrical systems and what can go wrong if you neglect a problem. It also provides a troubleshooting guide for detecting fluke electrical problems.

IGNITION SYSTEM

Modern ignition systems are designed with specific timing curves. The typical Japanese ignition system fires at about 6 degrees before top dead center (BTDC) at idle, and then advances to 20 degrees BTDC at the rpm of peak torque. At high rpm, the timing changes back to the retarded position of 6 BTDC. This serves to reduce the heat in the cylinder and shift it into the pipe to prevent the engine from overheating and seizing. The "black box," or "igniter," controls the timing curve. That is the small plastic box located under the fuel tank on most dirt bikes.

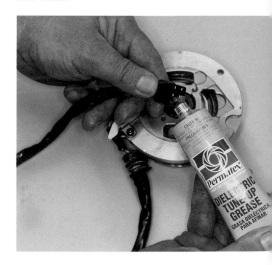

Apply dielectric grease to the wire fittings to prevent corrosion and water penetration.

The black box has either analog or digital circuitry. Analog circuitry uses a series of zener diodes to trigger the spark based on the amount of voltage generated by the rotor magnets and stator coils. Analog black boxes produce and are vulnerable to heat. Digital ignition systems use chips that sense rpm and adjust the ignition timing to suit. It isn't possible for us to change the timing curves of digital or analog black boxes, but it is possible to change ignition timing by adjusting the position of the stator plate.

Dirt bike flywheels and coils are prone to corrosion so you need to clean them at least twice a year. Use a flywheel puller tool to extract the flywheel from the crankshaft. If the flywheel puller doesn't work on the first try, use a propane torch to heat the area around the shaft and spray it with penetrating oil.

Some four-strokes, like the CRF, route the oil through the crankshaft so a protective cap must be used in conjunction with a flywheel puller to protect the oil jet.

BASIC IGNITION SYSTEM MAINTENANCE

Apply Dielectric Grease to Connectors
Auto parts stores sell dielectric grease. If you apply it to the wire connectors, they will never corrode. Clean the connectors with brake or contact cleaner, let the connectors dry, then apply a light coating of the grease. Wipe the plastic covers of the connectors to seal out water. Take care to route the wires and connectors clear of the exhaust system and away from the rider's boots. Use electrical tape to route the wires, not zip ties, which can pinch or sever the wires and then ground them to the frame.

Cleaning and Checking the Magneto
The magneto of a dirt bike consists of the stator plate for mounting the generator and signal coils and the flywheel rotor that houses the magnets. Most two-stroke dirt bikes have plastic magneto covers that are flexible and prone to leaking. That can allow water and dirt to enter the magneto and cause corrosion. If you want to protect the magneto on your dirt bike, I suggest installing a Boyesen Factory Racing side cover. With four-stroke dirt bikes this isn't a problem because the magneto covers are made of aluminum and are well sealed due to the crankcase oil flowing through the system.

To clean the magneto properly, you'll need a flywheel puller (K&N and Motion Pro sell flywheel pullers for under $20). First, remove the flywheel nut and thread the puller into the flywheel in the counterclockwise direction. Most flywheel pullers use left-hand threads on the main bolt that threads on to the flywheel. The center bolt has right-hand threads. This bolt pushes up against the crankshaft end, forcing the flywheel off the crankshaft's tapered end. It's best to apply a dab of grease to the crankshaft end so the puller's bolt doesn't damage the end of the crankshaft. Special precautions must be taken when attempting to remove the flywheels from four-stroke dirt bikes. The end of the crankshaft may be part of the lubrication system as it is on the Honda CRF450. Trying to use the wrong puller may cause the end of the crankshaft to become mushroom-shaped and could lead to loss of oil pressure. The factory Honda flywheel puller features a protective end cap to use with a traditional bolt-type puller.

With the stator plate removed from the engine, you can use fine-grit sandpaper to remove the corrosion from the coil pickups. Clean the stator plate coils with brake cleaner. Check the coils for dark spots that would indicate a shorted wire and a heat buildup. In previous years, when the stator plate coils shorted out, you had to replace the whole generator assembly. But now, Electrex makes primary and lighting coils for most late-model dirt bikes. These kits require you to solder the wire connections with a simple soldering iron and rosin-core silver solder.

How to Adjust the Ignition Timing
Rotating the stator plate relative to the crankcases changes the timing. Most manufacturers stamp the stator plate with three marks near the plate's mounting holes. The center mark is the standard timing. If you loosen the plate mounting bolts and rotate the stator plate clockwise to the flywheel's direction of rotation, that

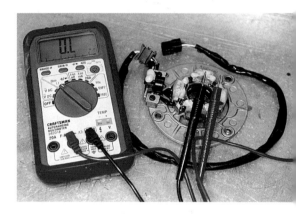

A multi-meter is required to test electrical components. Ohm resistance is the most common test. Look to your factory service manual for exact specs on electrical testing.

will advance the ignition timing. If you rotate the stator plate counterclockwise to the flywheel's direction of rotation, that will retard the ignition timing. Never rotate the stator plate more than 0.040 in. or 1.0 mm past the original standard timing mark. Kawasaki and Yamaha stator plates are marked with standard, full-advance, and full-retard timing marks. Honda stators have a sheetmetal plate riveted to one of the mount holes. This plate ensures that the stator can only be installed in one position. If you want to adjust the ignition timing on a Honda CR, you'll have to file the sheetmetal plate with a 1/4-in. rat-tail file.

Electrex makes inexpensive replacement primary coils that even include lighting coils. However, the wires need to be carefully spliced and soldered to the original wiring loom.

Aftermarket Ignition Systems

Two popular aftermarket ignition systems are marketed in the motorcycle industry: PVL and Vortex. PVL makes high-quality, inexpensive replacement systems that include the generator assembly, igniter, and secondary coil. These systems also offer a performance gain on most minis because they feature an internal rotor-type flywheel. The smaller diameter flywheel enables the engine to rev quicker. Vortex makes a variety of igniter boxes that feature things like performance curves, a handlebar-mounted switch that enables a rider to change ignition maps on-the-fly, and a complete custom programming setup for tuners.

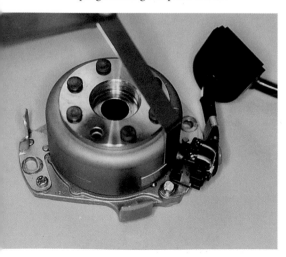

Some generators use signal coils positioned outside of the flywheel. If the engine main bearings fail, the flywheel might knock the signal coil out of adjustment. The proper air gap between the raised nub on the flywheel and the signal coil is 0.025 inch.

DIAGNOSING ELECTRICAL PROBLEMS

The Kill Switch

A faulty kill switch is the most common electrical problem. The kill button can easily be checked with either a continuity light or a multi-meter. Link the two test leads between the two wires from the kill switch. When the switch is depressed, the circuit will be continuous. Neither wire should ever be grounded to the handlebar.

Spark Plug Caps

Spark plug caps can break loose from the coil wire after repeated removal of the cap. Most caps thread in to the wire. Whenever you reinstall a cap, cut 1/4 in. from the end of the wire to ensure that the cap threads bite into fresh wire. Nology is the only company that sells an aftermarket wire and cap. It's a high-quality item that requires you to thread on and glue the wire into the coil. Spark plugs can also be faulty. Refer to the section on spark plugs for more information.

This is a PVL aftermarket ignition. It features an internal flywheel with less inertia than a standard external flywheel.

Wire Connections

Poor wire connections or faulty ground eyelets are also a common cause of electrical problems. Check the wires from the magneto for burn marks or cuts. Often, the wires will be routed too close to the pipe and melt. Flying rocks can also hit the wire, causing it to break or fray. If the wire connectors aren't insulated properly, they could corrode or short out from moisture. Clean the connectors with contact cleaner and apply a thin coating of dielectric grease to protect the connectors from corrosion. Check the ground wires too. They are colored solid black and may have a white stripe. These wires have eyelets that fasten to bolts like those on the coil or black box mounts.

Magneto

The magneto consists of a flywheel with magnets (rotor), and a stator plate with a few types of coils mounted to it. The two basic coils are the generating coil and the signal coil. The generating coil is also known as a primary coil, and the signal coil is also known as a pickup coil. The generating coil produces the primary AC voltage, and the signal coil is the trigger that releases the voltage to the igniter/black box. The additional coils mounted to the stator plate are charging coils for a lighting system. Some manufacturers put all the coils under the flywheel rotor, and some mount the signal coil outside of the flywheel.

The individual coils of the magneto can be tested for resistance (ohms) and AC voltage output. The resistance is measured with an ohmmeter. The manufacturers publish resistance testing specs in their factory service manuals. They specify which two wires to connect to the ohmmeter and the correct ohms reading. The output of the generating coil can be tested with a multi-meter set to AC volts. At the average kick-starting speed (spark plug removed), the AC voltage output of the generating coil should be at least 45 volts.

Igniter Box

The igniter box, or black box, contains sensitive electronic circuitry that controls the ignition timing in accordance with changes in engine rpm. All sorts of things can cause a black box to fail, and it is very difficult to test for anything but complete failure. Heat and vibration are the main causes of black box failure. The electronic circuitry is encased in an epoxy material

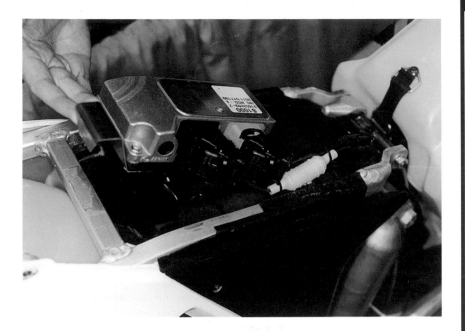

Aftermarket igniter boxes such as the Optimum GP Control and Vortex products feature at least two different digital ignition-timing maps and a handlebar-mounted switch. In the near future, small computers will replace igniter boxes. These computers will assume a higher level of engine management tasks, including controlling the exhaust valves and carb solenoid pumps.

PROBLEM: The engine is hard to start and dies periodically.

SOLUTION: *Unplug the kill switch. If it cures the problem, replace the switch with an OEM part.*

PROBLEM: The engine coughs under hard midrange acceleration and misfires at high rpm.

SOLUTION: *The stator coils are probably deteriorating. Use a multi-meter on the ohm setting to check the coils. Ohm specs for the coils are listed in the service manual. Sometimes the coils become corroded from condensation and just need to be cleaned. Stator coils can be rebuilt for about $125.*

PROBLEM: The engine runs fine on flat ground but misfires when riding over a series of whoops or braking bumps.

SOLUTION: *Check the top coil mounted under the fuel tank. Make sure the ground wire, coil mounts, and spark plug cap are tight and clean. There is also a slim possibility that the black box is faulty. These units are potted with epoxy to hold the fragile circuits from breaking apart. Sometimes the epoxy material breaks down, allowing the circuits to vibrate and short out when you ride over rough terrain. Unfortunately, there is no reliable way to test an intermittently faulty black box, but an ohm test can determine if the unit has completely failed. See your factory service manual for testing procedures.*

PROBLEM: The engine overheats, the pipe turns blue in color, and the piston is melting in the front center of the dome.

SOLUTION: *The ignition timing is too far advanced at the stator plate or the black box is faulty and doesn't retard the ignition timing curve at high rpm. This is simple to check with the aid of an inductive pickup timing light. See your local franchised dealer and a service technician can run a test for you.*

to insulate the components from the heat and vibration of the motorcycle.

Black boxes are usually mounted in areas of free airflow, such as the frame neck, under the tank, or under the seat. Sometimes water gets into the black box or the epoxy cracks and causes damage to the circuitry. There are some simple ways to test a black box for complete failure using an ohmmeter. The manufacturers publish wire connection and Ohms specs for their black boxes.

The black box can also be tested dynamically with an inductive pickup timing light (plastic body). Remove the magneto cover, start the engine, and point the timing light at the flywheel. Look for timing marks to appear at one side of the flywheel and focus the strobe light at that area. You should see a "T" and "F" and "|" marks. The T means TDC (top dead center), the F means fire at low and high rpm, and the | line means full advance. The F mark should line up with a fixed point on the crankcase at idle. When the engine is revved to mid-throttle, the timing mark will advance to the | line. When the

engine is revved higher, the timing mark will jump back to the F mark. If the spark occurs after TDC, the engine may idle roughly. If the ignition timing doesn't go to the F mark at high rpm, then the piston may seize from too much cylinder pressure and heat.

Externally Mounted Signal Coils
Some stator plates have the signal coil mounted outside of the flywheel. The signal coil looks like a small black box. When a raised nub on the flywheel passes the signal coil's pickup, it discharges the energy from the primary coil up to the igniter box. The signal coil can be damaged when the crankshaft main bearings fail and allow the flywheel to wallow around and strike the signal coil. A common complaint is that a bike loses spark after a low end failure. Most of the time the signal coil isn't permanently damaged and it just needs to be readjusted for an air gap of 0.020 in./0.5 mm. The signal coil is fastened to the stator plate by two screws and is easily adjusted for air gap over the raised flywheel nub.

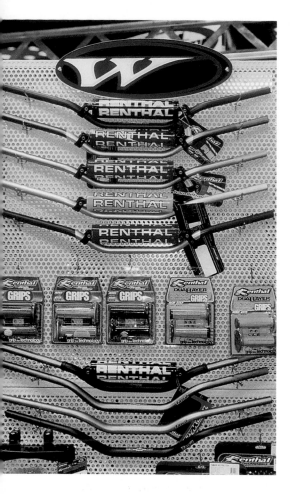

Handlebars are available in all sorts of configurations. Handlebars are rated for rise height and sweep-back distance. Handlebars are made of steel or aluminum. Thick-walled aluminum bars without crossbars are designed to flex a bit and absorb vibration.

FITTING ALUMINUM HANDLEBARS

There is nothing worse than the sinking feeling you get when you land from a big downhill jump and the bars fall to the tank, preventing you from steering. This section provides tips on how to custom-fit aluminum handlebars and keep them tight in the clamps. First, determine the optimum width of the handlebars, based on your body positioning and riding needs. For example, if you are tall with wide shoulders, leave your bars at the maximum width. If you ride enduros through tight woods sections, cut the bars down so the bike fits between trees.

CUTTING AND POLISHING

In general, cut the bars to a width that matches the width of your shoulders. You may want the bar a bit wider or narrower than this to suit your personal taste and riding conditions. Motocross riders tend to use wider bars for a bit more leverage, and enduro riders tend to cut them narrower (down to about 28 in.) for maneuvering through tight trees.

Measure and mark the area of the bar that you need to cut and wrap a piece of black tape around the bar. This will help guide your hack saw and enable a smooth, straight cut. After cutting the bar with a hack saw, wrap a piece of medium-grit emery cloth around the rough edge and polish it smooth. The rough edge of the saw cut could gouge the inside of the rubber grip or plastic throttle grip and cause the throttle to stick wide open! Remember to install the end plug in the bar after you have finished sawing and polishing. Some aluminum handlebars do not have diamond-shaped knurling for the handlebar clamps. It may be difficult to keep these bars tight, especially if the clamp and bar surfaces have deformities. It may be necessary to lap these surfaces together to increase the clamping surface area.

LAPPING AND FITTING THE BARS AND CLAMPS

Factory mechanics in Europe recommend using medium-grit valve lapping compound ($3 at auto parts stores) to lap the surfaces of the bars and clamps so the clamps can get a tighter grip on the bars. To begin the process, apply the compound between the handlebar and clamps. Then snug the clamps down and rotate the handlebars back and forth. This procedure polishes the high spots off the surfaces of the bar and clamp and effectively increases the clamping surface area. After lapping, the handlebars will stay tight in the clamps, eliminating any chance of slipping. This method of clamp-to-bar lapping is also recommended for the crossbar clamps. Normally, they have a locking agent applied to the clamp from the manufacturer, but a couple of hard

landings cause the locking agent to break bond with the bar. The lapping method is a reliable way to keep the crossbar tight.

HANDLEBAR TIGHTENING WARNINGS

Pay attention to the manufacturer's recommendation on how to tighten your handlebar clamps and to what torque specification. Some handlebar clamps are designed for equal-distance gaps on each side of the bar and some are designed for zero gaps on one side. For example, Honda stamps one side of the clamp with a dot mark. That indicates that the dot should face the front of the bike and that clamp bolt should be tightened until the clamp has zero gap. This is a common clamping system used on late-model Japanese motorcycles. Honda uses this system on all the front-end clamps from the handlebars to the controls and the front-axle clamp. Some other manufacturers use arrows to denote directions of forward or up. If you are ever unsure of which direction a clamp should face, refer to your factory service manual or call your local franchised motorcycle dealer.

VIBRATION IN HANDLEBARS

If vibration in the handlebars is making your hands go numb, then you may want to consider some options. You can fill the inside of the bars with liquid foam to isolate vibration. These products are sold at home improvement stores under the category of spray-on insulation. There is a product specifically designed for handlebars called the Bar-Snake. It is a solid piece of rubber that can be threaded through the bars. Another option is to use a tapered wall tubing bar without a crossbar. On some models you can adapt top triple clamps that use the rubber-mounted bar clamps. Rubber-mounted bar clamps tend to get damaged easily in a crash but offer a lot of insulation protection from vibration.

NOTES ON TAPERED WALL TUBING BARS

Aftermarket handlebars such as the Answer Pro-Taper and the Magura Bulge Bar are tapered wall tubing bars designed for a bit of flex. These handlebars do not use crossbars. The extra flex is intended to absorb some of the vibration and shock of impacts transferred up the forks. These types of handlebars may require different top clamps and handlebar clamps. Check with the manufacturer as to the availability of clamping kits for your model bike before purchasing these products.

FITTING RADIATOR GUARD AND TANK STICKERS

Are you a little nervous about trying to apply expensive radiator and tank stickers on your bike? Here are some tips on how to reduce the chances of misaligning the stickers, making bubbles, or having them peel off the first time you ride your bike. Robert and Matt Davis of Throttle Jockey provide a demonstration on how to apply stickers and staple seat covers.

CLEAN AND PREP

If the plastic panels are scratched, consider replacing them. If your bike has an exposed fuel tank and it is deeply scratched, you can repair it by sanding down the scratches with 220-grit sandpaper. Clean all the plastic parts with

Align the graphics over the bolt holes. Then, peel back the wrapper from one side and rub out the trapped air bubbles evenly.

contact or brake cleaner and wipe dry with a clean cloth. When applying stickers to an exposed fuel tank, it's best to drain the fuel first because the fuel vapors seep through the plastic and deteriorate the adhesive.

Some sticker manufacturers include an acetone-soaked swatch so you can clean the outside of the plastic. The acetone actually dissolves the substrate of the plastic, sealing it from leaking fuel vapors while the stickers are applied.

KEEP IT STRAIGHT!

The best way to keep the stickers straight while applying them is to remove a small section of the backing paper and align the covered part of the sticker on the plastic. Then press down the exposed part of the sticker. Now carefully peel off the backing while pressing down the sticker. This ensures that no air bubbles get trapped between the sticker and the plastic. If some air bubbles get trapped under the sticker, you can remove them by popping them with a pin and pressing out the air. Popping the bubble results in a slight distortion in the sticker but nothing compared to what would happen if you tried to press the air bubble across the sticker to bleed it out at the edge.

You can also install radiator and tank stickers by coating the plastic with a light film of water and dishwashing liquid. Then remove the backing from the entire sticker. Now apply the sticker to the plastic and slide it into position. You'll need a plastic scraper to force out all the water and air bubbles.

Prior to installing tank graphics, clean the surface of the gas tank with acetone.

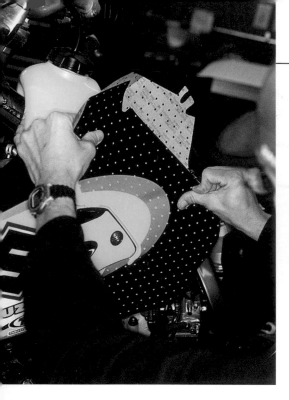

Most graphics that are applied to gas tanks have perforations that allow the fumes to escape without causing unsightly bubbles in the graphics.

The latest in graphics are special textures that enable riders to grip their bikes with their legs.

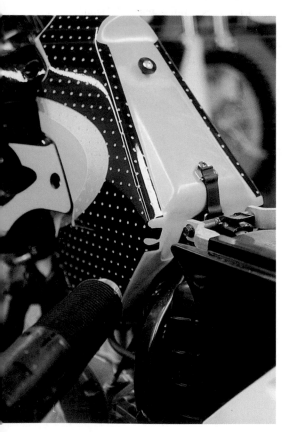

The final step in applying graphics is to cure the adhesive with a hair dryer or heat gun.

CARE FOR NEW STICKERS

Stickers eventually start to peel at the edges. To reduce the wear and tear on stickers, don't pressure-wash the stickers directly at the edges. Also, be careful not to use harsh detergents meant to strip grease from metal parts. These detergents deteriorate the adhesives in the stickers. The best way to clean the stickers is with a sponge and water. If the edges of the sticker start peeling, use a razor knife to remove the peeled part of the sticker.

FITTING SEAT COVERS AND FOAM

Have you ever spent $50 on a seat cover and botched the installation, leaving it looking like the ruffled trousers of a wobbly old man?

There are two different opinions on how seat covers should be installed. Some people believe you should remove the old cover first. Others believe you should install the new seat cover over the top of the old cover. That may work on a cheap seat cover, but not on one that is designed to fit properly. One important thing to consider when installing a new cover is the foam. Seat foam deteriorates when you power-wash the seat with detergent. When you strip off the old cover, you may find that pieces of foam have crumbled off. This is an indication that the foam has gone bad, and that the foam must be replaced too.

AFTERMARKET SEAT FOAM

Aftermarket companies offer many different types of seat foam. You have the option of stiffer foam in two degrees or foam both shorter and taller than stock. Before you buy a new seat cover and foam, consider your height, weight, and riding style. A very tall, heavy rider needs the tallest, stiffest foam possible. Stiffer foam makes the seat seem taller.

Gutz Racing specializes in making tall, stiff foam for riders over 74 in. in height. The foam is stiffer than stock foam and more resilient over time and is available in two heights. If you are not a tall rider and want to lower the stock seat foam, you may want to trim the foam. This enables you to rest your foot flat on the ground when coming to a stop or waiting at the starting line. Trimming the foam lower is accomplished with a "hot wire." Most upholstery shops can handle this task. Afterward, you will need to stretch the seat cover tighter and reposition it on the seat base.

Use a pneumatic staple gun to secure the seat cover.

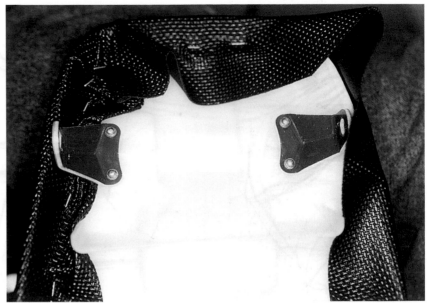

Install the staples at least 1/2 inch from the edge so they don't protrude out the sides.

FITTING THE SEAT COVER

You will need a staple remover, razor knife, and staple gun to fit the seat cover correctly. A pneumatic staple gun is best because it uses significant force to inject the staple into the plastic seat base. If you try to do it with a hand-squeeze stapler it will be difficult to get the staple to bite into the base while keeping the cover taut. If the staple doesn't seat into the base, the cover will just tear apart and the staples will fall out. If you doubt your abilities, take the seat and cover to an upholstery shop and make a copy of this section on seat cover installation tips to guide the person doing the work.

1. Remove the old seat cover by extracting the old staples with a hooked staple remover. You can also use a flat-blade screwdriver and side-cutter pliers.
2. Hook the seat cover to the front of the seat and pull it tight at the back. Remove all the wrinkles along the length of the seat before you staple it.
3. Start stapling the seat at the back. Just put four staples in to begin.
4. Staple the seat at the front corners. Pull the cover tight and put two staples on each side.
5. Now take a razor knife and cut the cover to accommodate the seat mounting tabs. Cut two vertical lines on each side of the tabs. Pull the cover tight on each side equally and put a staple on each side of the tabs. Take care in aligning the seat equally on each side. Now that the cover is set into position, you can staple it every 1/2 in. around the perimeter.

RACE DAY PREPARATIONS

Every time I go to the races, I see racers fumbling around with their bikes for hours between motos; later, they push their bikes back from the second moto because the bikes broke down for silly reasons. It only takes about 20 minutes to thoroughly inspect and service a bike between motos. Servicing a bike can give a rider confidence and peace of mind. It's also a great way to channel "nervous energy." Many talented professional riders share some of the maintenance duties with their mechanics as a way of preparing for the next moto. Paul Cooper cleans his throttle, Jeff Stanton adjusts his bars and levers, and Danny "Magoo" Chandler used to change his own tires just to psyche out other racers. Too many riders and mechanics are unorganized when performing between-moto maintenance. This section is a guide to help you become more organized and build your mechanical confidence.

START DURING THE RACE

A good mechanic prepares during the race for the tasks he will need to do between motos. For example, if the rider gets involved in a crash but continues the race, the mechanic will think of what parts were damaged in the crash. If the mechanic hears that the engine is detonating at the end of a long straight, he'll know that he must increase the carburetor's main jet size between motos. If the first race starts muddy but the sun begins to shine and the wind starts blowing, he'll know that in the next moto the track will dry out. This will require him to change the suspension settings and perhaps even the tires in order for his rider to have a competitive advantage in the next race. Here is a checklist for moto maintenance, listed by priority order.

Arenacross star Tommy "Sleepwalker" Hoffmaster practices with a Powerstart timing system so he and his mechanic dad, Dean, can accurately evaluate performance changes to his bike.

WASHING THE BIKE

This seems like a very simple thing, but washing a bike incorrectly can cause more damage than racing. Start by scraping the majority of the mud from the bike to reduce the amount of water needed to wash the bike and keep your pit area clean. Remove the seat and air filter, and then cap the silencer end and the air boot. Seat foam manufacturers warn not to power-wash seats because the foam acts like a sponge to absorb water (added weight) and the water and detergent can break down the seat foam to make it "mushy." Never point the power-washing wand directly at rubber seals (forks, shock, sprocket, wheel bearings). Never spray detergent on the brake pads or disc to clean them. The detergent bonds to the disc and glazes the first time you use the brakes, rendering the pads useless. The best way to wash the bike between races is with a stiff brush, sponge, and a bucket of water.

At the 1993 USGP, a factory mechanic criticized my bike for not being perfectly clean. He spent a lot of time making his bikes perfectly clean, but that reduced the amount of time he could spend doing maintenance. This mechanic was later made famous for forgetting to put gas in his bike, costing his rider valuable points at a national championship race. However, the bike was clean when the rider pushed it back to the pits!

After you wash the bike, you need to do some things immediately. Drain the carb's float bowl just in case water seeped past the air filter cover. Dry the air box and boot with a towel. Grease the air filter flange and install a clean filter to prevent anything from accidentally falling into the exposed air boot. Finally, use a wire brush on the chain and spray it with chain lube to prevent it from corroding.

For race days when the dust and water are minimal, you can use a thin disposable sock over the filter. Rather than changing your filter between motos, you can simply pull off the sock and have a clean filter. Some systems allow you to pull off the sock without even removing your seat. Several companies sell them in the United States and Europe.

FUEL PRECAUTIONS

If you use petroleum or synthetic pre-mix oil, you should immediately top up the tank with fuel-oil mix after washing the bike so you don't forget. If you use castor-based pre-mix oil, dump the fuel from the previous moto and mix your fresh batch of fuel just prior to staging. Castor-based oils separate quickly from fuel and that can cause either spark plug fouling or piston seizures. On very hot days, place a wet white towel over the fuel tank so the sun doesn't heat the fuel. Cool fuel gives a definite advantage on the start of a race.

QUICK CHECK

Grab a set of T-handles and check all the bolts on the bike. This will force you to look over the entire bike, enabling you to find problems such as worn, bent, or broken parts. Check the wear-indicator lines scribed on the sides of the brake pads after every moto because muddy races can wear out a set of pads in one moto. Check the chain adjustment. Look for oil leaks at the suspension components. Adjust the clutch cable if the lever has too much free-play.

WHEELS AND TIRES

Check the tire pressure and make corrections based on track conditions. Muddy conditions: front 8 psi, rear 6 psi. Dry conditions: front 14 psi, rear 12 psi. Always use heavy-duty inner tubes because they allow you to run lower tire pressure without the threat of a puncture.

If you can't afford a new rear tire for every moto, use a hack saw to cut the rounded edge from the knobs. Don't ignore the braking edge of the knobs (back side) because it's just as important to stop as to go. There are some good tools available for the purpose of restoring the edges on the knobs between motos.

The best way to tighten the spokes is to start at the valve stem and tighten every third spoke 1/8 turn. When you get to the stem again, start with the next spoke and repeat the procedure. Once you have tightened three spokes from the stem, you will have tightened every spoke equally. Check the spokes for loose ones and tighten them to the same tension as all the others. Don't use the "tap the spoke and listen to the pitch of the sound" method. It doesn't work. You have to develop a sense of feel for spoke tension. If the spoke is too tight, you'll hear stress relief sounds.

Ex-Grand Prix mechanic and current suspension tuner Mark Hammond goes through an organized, disciplined routine at the races, including the most important task, filling the tank with fuel.

INVOLVE THE RIDER

I make it a practice to always involve the rider in the final sequence of between-moto maintenance. Have the rider sit on the bike and check the rear spring sag, handlebar and lever positions, and brake- and clutch-lever adjustments. Ask him how the bike worked in the race and if there is anything he wants you to check or change. This is mainly done for psychological reasons, showing the rider that you care about what he thinks and proving to him that the bike is in great working order. This will give him confidence and also prevent him from making up some bogus mechanical problem as a reason for quitting during the next moto.

THE RIDER-MECHANIC RELATIONSHIP

I place a lot of emphasis on being willing to do whatever it takes to give the rider an advantage. I've been able to get better-than-normal results out of riders just by being an empathetic listener between motos. I like to finish the bike maintenance as quickly as possible so I can talk to the rider and help him prepare for the next moto by doing things together—walking the track, watching the start of other races, observing how the track develops. Your respect and confidence can help the rider boost results in a race. The simple truth is a good mechanic has to be able to respond to the rider's needs in an organized manner.

CHAPTER THREE

TRANSFORMING YOUR MX BIKE

CONVERTING YOUR MX BIKE OR DUAL-SPORT BIKE FOR OFF-ROAD RIDING
TWO PERSPECTIVES

Off-road riding consists of everything from enduro, cross country, hare scrambles, desert, and rally. This versatile form of motorcycle riding usually requires some modifications to the typical MX or dual-sport (street) bike.

In the early 1970s, street-legal dual-sport bikes were entry-level bikes for many motorcyclists. The bikes were far from off-road-worthy and required modifications such as bigger front wheels, gearing changes, knobby tires, plastic fenders, serrated foot pegs, and wider handlebars. The bikes were also heavy and required stripping down the non-essential street kit-like gauges, turn signals, horns, reflectors, and mirrors.

Modern dual-sport bikes come with most of the basics, but they still need

modifications based on the degree of challenging terrain.

Late-model MX bikes often need to be de-tuned and built stronger in order to handle the long rides off-road. Components such as crash guards, narrower handlebars, bigger fuel tanks, and spark arrestor tailpipes are some of the basic parts needed to make your MX bike off-road reliable. Depending on how serious you are, more complex changes may need to be made to the engine and suspension.

This chapter provides a guide to the types of modifications needed to make your bike more fun to ride and reliable for off-road adventures.

GOING ON A DIET
Dual-Sport Bikes

The reasons for removing unnecessary parts from your bike are twofold; unnecessary weight, and protrusions could

injure you in a crash. Remove the passenger pegs and brackets, chain guard, luggage rack, reflectors, and electrical switches. These original parts are expensive to replace and you might as well pack them in a safe place to maintain the resale price of your dual-sport bike. Exchange the bulky mirrors, turn signals, and taillight for parts designed for off-road use. Companies such as Acerbis, Moose, and UFO make rubber-mounted miniature mirrors, turn signals, and taillights to reduce the chance of damage if you fall.

Dual-Sport Tires and Wheels

Selecting tires requires careful consideration. If you ride on roads to get to areas where the terrain is hard-packed and dry, consider the DOT knobbies. You'll get better traction than with a full knobby tire. If you ride strictly off-road and you're looking for maximum traction, use the chapter on tires to select the right tire for your needs. Don't ignore the inside of the tire—most dual-sport bikes aren't equipped with rim locks to prevent the tire from rotating on the rim. You'll need to fit one rim lock to the front wheel and two rim locks to the rear wheel. Regarding inner tubes, heavy-duty tubes are a must. If you ride on terrain with sharp rocks, then you might consider fitting mousse in place of the inner tubes. Mousse is heavier and affects the wheel balance so it's not suitable for prolonged periods of high-speed street riding, but you'll never get a flat while riding off-road.

Some dual-sport bikes have steel rims as standard equipment. Steel rims bend easily when hitting rocks or big jumps. Tallon, Excell, and Sun

This Honda XR650L street bike was modified for off-road use by toughening it up with bash guards, stiffer suspension, heavy-duty tubes, and knobby tires. All the street bike "pork" was stripped off to save weight.

This Honda CR500 was converted to a street-legal, dual-sport bike with electrical and lighting systems supplied by E-Line and Baja Designs.

manufacture strong aftermarket alloy rims. Companies such as Tallon in England make complete wheels designed for heavy-duty off-road use.

LIGHTING KITS

A street-legal dirt bike must have a 12-volt battery to provide lights when the engine is shut off. Several battery manufacturers make units that can endure being tipped upside down in a crash and the constant vibration of riding off-road.

If you just want to fit lights to your MX bike to make it enduro legal, all you need is a functional head and taillight and a mirror. Companies such as Acerbis

E-Line makes high-output generating systems capable of running huge lighting systems.

and UFO make headlight number plates and taillights built into a rear fender. These lights can be powered either by 12V DC or AC volts. The 12V DC setup requires a NiCad battery, a simple switch, and a wiring harness connecting the head and taillights. This is a total-loss charging system. The battery is only good for about one hour, and then it has to be recharged.

An AC lighting system involves generating coils mounted near the flywheel magnets, a voltage limiter, a switch, and a wiring harness. There are two types of kits available for most late-model MX bikes. One setup is a simple coil that bolts on to the stator plate. The other is a more powerful system for greater headlight wattage. CRE is one company that distributes the high wattage system. The kit has an alloy side cover with a ring of several coils positioned around the outside of the flywheel magnets.

The simple lighting coil kits sell for about $80 and the deluxe kits sell for over $300. Companies such as Moose and Pro Racing sell the less expensive bolt-on coils along with other components, including wiring harnesses, voltage limiters, and switches.

FUEL TANKS

The typical range of an MX bike's fuel tank is about 30 minutes. If you intend to ride long distances you may want to consider getting a larger fuel tank. Aftermarket companies such as Acerbis and Clarke make fuel tanks with capacities of 3.5 gallons, or about 1.5 gallons more than stock. You can also buy smaller auxiliary fuel tanks that clamp to the crossbar or fit in place of the front number plate.

DAMAGE CONTROL

If Murphy had a law for off-road riding it would be that you will hit things, fall down, and break a component of your bike that makes it necessary for you to push it for several miles over harsh terrain. Zen law infers that if you spend the money on protection, you'll never need it.

Whether you are converting a dual-sport or MX bike for serious off-road use, you'll need to give it a shield of armor. Starting with the top of the bike and working down, the handlebars and controls are the most important area to concentrate on because that's where your hands are. Stronger handlebars are available, made with tapered wall tubing or stronger crossbraces. The standard width of an off-road handlebar is 28 in. The Answer Pro-Taper and Magura Bulge-Bar are made of tapered alloy tubing that allows a certain

The stock plastic disc guard won't survive logs and boulders. IMS and Moose Off-Road make aluminum disc protectors and caliper holders.

amount of flex to prevent permanent bending upon impact. These bars also absorb some of the vibration transferred through the forks and into the bars.

If you use a traditional handlebar, you might consider filling the inside of the bar with an energy absorbing rubber like the "Bar Snake." It's a rubber rod that can be inserted through the handlebar to help absorb vibration.

Fastening guards to the ends of the handlebars is very important to protect your hands from impacts such as trees and rocks. Hand guards come in a variety of designs. The two main types are aluminum flat-stock and injection-molded plastic. Fredette Racing, Moose, and Summers Racing Components make the aluminum hand guards. The Summers guard features bushings at the mounts to enable a bit of movement. Acerbis and UFO make plastic guards that are very lightweight and feature shrouds for added protection against rock roost.

Moving down to the radiators, companies such as DeVol Racing and Works Connection make aluminum guards that reduce the chance of the radiators being crushed in a fall. DeVol

CRD makes wraparound engine guards, and DeVol makes radiator guards that protect the radiator from branches and trees.

also makes a front guard to prevent branches from poking holes in the radiator. However, this type of guard replaces the standard louver and reduces the cooling efficiency of the radiator.

The exhaust pipe of most two-stroke dirt bikes is prone to damage from rocks, ruts, trees, and even casing the bike in deep whoops. A couple of different types of guards are effective against flying debris but don't really offer protection during crashes. The second-skin-type aluminum and composite pipe guards also have an added feature of insulating the pipe from big changes in temperature that could affect the tuning. A few new pipes on the market are designed with protection in mind. The Extreme aluminum pipe and FMF Burley pipe are made of thick-gauge material. The Extreme pipe is made of aluminum for light weight and the FMF is made of steel. Considering the replacement cost of a pipe, weight isn't that big of an issue. It is easier to remove the dents from steel pipes, using heat and pressure tools.

The bottom of the bike has some key areas that need extra protection. The frame tubes, crankcases, engine side covers, and brake and shift levers all need protection against rocks and trees. Guards for the bottom of the engine range from lightweight to heavy-duty. The lightweight guards designed for MX are usually made of aluminum or carbon fiber and are designed to streamline the bottom of the engine and make the bike less prone to grounding out on the peaks of jumps. The heavy-duty guards are huge aluminum pans that cover the bottom frame rails and extend up on the edges to protect the side covers. These guards are designed for use in conditions where there are a lot of big rocks and fallen trees. IMS specializes in heavy-duty guards because they serve the desert racing market. If you are a handy fabricator, you might want to make your own skid plate. If your bike has a steel frame, get a sheet of 1/8-in. mild steel and cut it to encompass the outer frame tubes and the bracket for the shock linkage. For more information, see the section on frame maintenance in Chapter 4.

Works Connection side cover guards are also popular. These guards fasten to the engine mounting bolts and protect the side covers and the foot levers. You can also use a steel cable connected to the front edge of the levers and attached to the frame to protect the foot levers from being torn loose by ruts and trees. Buy the raw materials at the hardware store or buy cable guards from companies such as Moose, White Bros., WER, and Works Connection.

WATERPROOFING

The electrical and intake systems are two major areas of a dirt bike that need to be waterproofed. An extreme off-road adventure might require that you submerge the bike in a river all the way up to the tailpipe.

Starting with the electrical system, two materials are needed to seal wire connections: dielectric grease and electrical tape. Dielectric grease seals out water, prevents corrosion, and enables a good electrical connection. Wrap electrical tape around connectors for added assurance against moisture.

The intake system needs attention at the inlet and bottom drain of the air box and the carburetor vents. Most dual-sport bikes have constricted air boxes and the drainpipes are usually routed to a one-way check valve chamber that allows outward flow only. MX bikes use a short rubber tube with slots that restrict airflow and enable free fluid flow out the bottom of the air box. The Honda XR250 uses an excellent check valve that can be adapted to the air box of most dirt bikes. The key is to enable outward flow in case water runs down the fuel tank or from the sides and seeps into the air box. If the air box has seams on the sides, then you need to seal them with weather-strip adhesive. All carbs use vent tubes to allow air to flow in and apply atmospheric pressure to the fuel floats. The vent tubes also enable fuel to flow out of the carb when the bike is tipped over. Normally, the vent tubes exit from the bottom of the carburetor, which makes them vulnerable to drawing in water when crossing a stream. The best way to waterproof the carb's vent system is to buy 5 feet of 1/8-in.-inner-diameter tubing and replace the original vent tubes. Route the new vent tubes up into the top of the air box. That way, if the bike falls over, the fuel will spill into the air box where it can be safely collected by the bottom drain valve.

ENGINE MODIFICATIONS
Dual-Sport Bikes
Street bikes are normally plugged up because of noise and emission considerations. There are baffles in the exhaust pipe, louvers and shrouds around the air box, and the carburetors are jetted lean. It's not a simple matter of removing the obstructions to flow; the carb jetting may need to be compensated richer in order to get any power gains. Some aftermarket companies sell tailpipes and jetting kits as a set. These items will yield the biggest performance gains for

the money, plus the aftermarket tailpipes are usually lighter in weight.

Changing the gearing usually requires a complete set of sprockets and chain. Get an O-ring chain for less maintenance. Expect to set the final drive at about 4:1, which equates to a 12-tooth sprocket on the engine and a 48-tooth sprocket on the rear wheel.

MX Bikes
Dirt bikes need to be de-tuned for off-road riding. Most MX bikes have high compression ratios, which require expensive fuel. The powerbands are also designed for aggressive, high-rpm racing. Off-road riding conditions vary in terrain and available traction, and it's implied that there is a lot more slow-speed riding. Off-road riding generally requires a powerband that is centered in low- to mid-range rpm. In the case of an MX bike, the term de-tuning means that the powerband is shifted down the

rpm range and the compression ratio is lowered to reduce the hit in the power-band. That way, the bike will be easier to control while riding over rocks and tree roots. A typical list of engine mods for a two-stroke engine would include a cylinder head modification to reduce the compression ratio, a switch to dual-stage or thinner single-stage reeds, a flywheel weight, steel clutch plates, a spark arrestor tailpipe, and advancing the ignition timing. For more specifics on changing the engine's powerband for more low-end power, check out Chapter 8 on two-stroke tuning.

The transmissions on MX bikes have closely spaced gear ratios that limit the bike's top speed. It is possible to install wide-ratio gear sets for the two top gears. Companies such as A-Loop and IMS sell kits for popular 250-cc and 500-cc MX bikes.

The carburetion on MX bikes needs some attention too. Because most trail

Grand National Cross Country superstar Rodney Smith uses an RM250 MX bike and outfits it with a larger gas tank, hand guards, and an FMF Gnarly pipe to make the bike survive the grueling 100-mile off-road races.

Mike Harlow Jr.'s Schaumburg Honda/4&6 Cycle-sponsored CRF450 supermoto bike features lowered suspension, 17-inch White Bros. wheels, Braking oversize discs, and all supermoto styling from an Acerbis plastic kit.

riding is done at low throttle openings, it's important to fine-tune the jetting of the pilot/slow jet, air screw, throttle slide, and jet needle. Sometimes you need to jet leaner or use a hotter spark plug just to prevent wet-fouling while riding on and off the throttle through tight trails. Most MX bikes have carburetors that aren't designed to idle. The Keihin PJ and Mikuni TM carbs don't have an idle circuit. Instead, these carburetors bleed raw fuel through the choke system or the needle jet, which just makes the spark plug wet-foul quicker. The Keihin PWK Air-Strike is a good choice for an aftermarket carb. It has an efficient idle circuit and two airfoils positioned in the air inlet of the carb to boost the velocity and direct the flow for quicker throttle response.

SUSPENSION MODIFICATIONS

Dual-Sport Bikes

Street bikes are usually sprung too soft for off-road riding. The heavy weight of the bike requires much stiffer springs than normally used on an MX bike. Modifying the suspension components of a dual-sport bike isn't as easy as just changing the springs. The valving must be changed to suit the harsh conditions and the stiffer springs. It's necessary to increase the damping on the compression and rebound circuits. Some of the shocks on dual-sport bikes are sealed units and cannot even be serviced, let alone revalved.

MX Bikes

Dirt bikes are designed with suspension valving that works best on the high end of the damping scale, meaning big jumps and square-edged bumps. That usually requires a sacrifice in damping performance for other riding conditions. You may read motorcycle magazine articles that refer to the "mid-stroke harshness" of a bike's forks or shock. That term best describes how an MX bike handles when you don't ride it hard enough. For riding off-road, you may want suspension that rides plush because you will spend more time sitting on the seat than standing in an aggressive position. You may also want the suspension to be sprung softer so you can easily shift the bike's weight and carry the front end over small obstacles. Softer springs enable the bike to sag more, which makes it easier to handle tight turns without the front end pushing to the outside of the turn.

Hand guards protect the rider in case of a crash and enable the bike to slide on the pavement. The Magura in-board reservoirs protect fluid from spilling on the pavement during a crash.

The Acerbis supermoto styling package makes the bike more aerodynamic for attaining speeds up to 100 miles per hour.

CONVERTING YOUR MX BIKE FOR DTX OR SUPERMOTO RACING

Supermoto and dirt track racing are distinctly American sports with strong roots tracing back to the 1970s. Both motorcycle sports are on the rebound, with a sharp increase in promoted events. Supermoto races are being held on kart tracks and parking lots. Dirt track racing is popular on horse tracks at county fairgrounds. The modern motocross bike is an ideal platform for a custom supermoto or DTX bike. Although an MX bike is legal to race with changes to the tires and brakes, there is a standard profile of component changes to make a bike more competitive in supermoto and DTX.

Tryce Welch was an innovative developer of the DTX bike during its inception by the AMA. Welch worked closely with Jeremy Wilkey on suspension valving changes such as spring force, damping, and travel bias as well as tires and wheels, gearing, and steering damping. Welch was the driving force in the development of the modern DTX bike and has built bikes ranging from 50 to 505 cc, raced by generations of racers in the AMA Amateur Nationals.

The growing sport of supermoto is thick with dirt track racers. DTX bikes are ideal for conversion to supermoto. Here are some tips from Welch on customizing an MX bike into a DTX or supermoto racer.

CHASSIS MODS

Modifying the chassis for better handling starts by lowering the center of gravity. Options for accomplishing a lower CG include reducing the travel of the forks and shocks with spacers, an aftermarket triple clamp with adjustable offset and rake angle, and linkage bars.

HANDLEBARS AND CONTROLS

AFAM offers a special set of swept-back handlebars for DTX bikes. Many pro riders are switching to MX-style bars.

WHEELBASE

Wheelbases for the SM and DTX bikes vary with the brand but end up between 55 and 56.5 in. There are some modifications possible, but the linkage systems restrict how short you can go.

SWINGARM ANGLE

Track conditions dictate the perfect swingarm angle, but 5 degrees is a good starting point. Adjustable links to fine-tune the angle are starting to become popular.

FORK RAKE AND TRAIL

The best steering head angle is between 24 and 25 degrees. There really isn't any need to modify the frame to achieve this angle as it is very close to a stock MX bike and can be dialed in by the front ride height. Offset triple clamps are useful in fine-tuning a DTX bike. Stock MX bikes run 50 to 52 mm off true offset, not triple clamp offset. The DTX bike will push in the fast corners unless the front end is pushed out about 10 mm. Baer aftermarket DTX triple

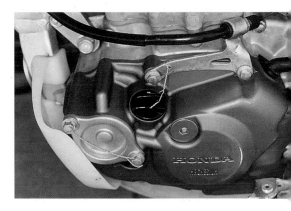

Supermoto racing rules require that all engine oil filler and drain plugs are safety-wired. Also, a spill reservoir, or "catch can," must be fitted to the bike to collect spills from the coolant, lubrication, and fuel systems. Traditional coolant must be replaced with distilled water.

clamps are perfect for the DTX conversion, as they allow offset and fork angle with a simple adjustment knob.

STEERING DAMPERS

Due to space limitations caused by the radiators, steering damper selection is space restricted. WER, Ohlins, and Scott make rotary-style dampers that work well for DTX and supermoto. WER offers a special damping profile for DTX bikes that concentrates the damping effect just over center since these bikes have limited steering movement.

LINKAGE SYSTEMS

Aftermarket linkage systems are great for changing the rear ride height. They should not be used to actually lower the rear. Lowering the center of gravity by limiting the travel needs to be done by modifying the internals of the shock and fork.

SUSPENSION SYSTEMS

Valving

The changes in valving of the suspension components are as important as the spacing to limit travel. Supermoto and DTX bikes need both stiffer compression and rebound damping as compared to an MX bike.

Springs

It's possible to shorten the springs with the travel and make the spring rate stiffer, which is also better suited to supermoto and DTX. Traditionally, a suspension tuner will shorten the travel with aluminum spacers, stiffen the damping (LSC and LSR), and then install a shorter, stiffer spring to complement the valving changes.

Titanium springs are lightweight and starting to gain popularity. Otherwise, steel springs are readily available. Some tuners choose to shorten stock springs, which compensates for the lesser travel in two ways: It makes the spring shorter to fit the shock and stiffens the spring rate.

WHEELS AND TIRES

The only restrictions on MX bikes are the tires. Supermoto and DTX events won't allow knobby tires because of limited traction, braking, and the possibility of erosion to the track. Dual-sport tires are the only alternative for the stock MX wheels, but smaller diameter wheels and wider rims are the most competitive choice. Companies such as Buchanan and FTM sell rims and custom spoke kits for the do-it-yourselfer. White Bros. sells complete wheel kits based on Tallon hubs and Akront and Excell rims. KTM sells complete supermoto wheels in its accessory catalog.

Supermoto wheels are 17 in. because that size has the best quality tires. DTX wheels are 19 in. and there are several tires used for hard-packed and cushioned tracks. Typical rim sizes are: Minis 2.75x17-in. (front and rear), 125-cc bikes 2.15x2.5-in., and 250 to 500-cc bikes 2.5x2.75-in.

BRAKES

DTX bikes do not use front brakes, and the lever and caliper must be removed for competition. Supermoto bikes need oversized front brakes. Kits available from Braking and Gaffer use a larger disc with a longer caliper mounting bracket.

AUTOMATIC CLUTCHES

SM and DTX place similar demands on the clutch, requiring smooth power

Supermoto racing bikes need big front brakes. This is the Braking oversize disc, which requires an extended caliper bracket and a four-piston Brembo caliper.

delivery and resistance to stalling during braking and cornering. Both slipper clutches and auto clutches are popular for different reasons. Slipper clutches are used in DTX for smooth traction on acceleration. Auto clutches are great for supermoto because they reduce rear wheel chatter on braking and the need to shift in the tight, twisty turns.

Z-Start and Rekluse are the two most popular brands of auto clutches for late-model dirt bikes. The Z-Start is a complete unit that replaces the clutch basket and pressure plate; it sells for about $800. The Rekluse auto clutch is just the pressure plate. It costs $300 and can be installed in 20 minutes.

DTX bikes are often lowered and fitted with 19-inch wheels and wider rims. Front brakes are not allowed in DTX. Engine mods typically include a slipper clutch, flywheel weight, and high-rev valvetrain.

CHAPTER FOUR

SUSPENSION AND CHASSIS

Jeremy Wilkey of MX-TECH helped us with this chapter on suspension. Jeremy is the moderator of the Suspension Tuning forum at www.dirtrider.net, where he answers questions.

rear spring sag, the compression and rebound clickers, the fork tube overlap, the tire pressure, and even the torque settings for the steering head, triple clamp bolts, and swingarm pivot bolt. In many cases, the suspension components only need to be rebuilt and sprung correctly for the rider's weight and riding demands.

MEASURING SAG

Measure and set the rear sag before measuring the front sag. If the rear sag is too little and is corrected, more weight will then be placed on the front end and it will sag more than normal. Here are some guidelines for measuring the sag:

1. First, measure the distance of the front and rear ends while fully extended on a bike stand. Measure the rear from the axle to the base of

Your bike's handling is critical to your riding experience. If your bike handles poorly, it destroys your confidence and can make your body ache for days after riding. The information presented in the later part of this chapter is targeted to the needs of veteran riders and race mechanics who want to gain control over suspension servicing and revalving. Novice riders and mechanics can benefit from this information too, because it will make them a more informed consumer when shopping for suspension tuning services.

BASELINE SETTINGS

Every day, I see people sending out their suspensions for expensive revalving before they ever attempt to adjust and record the baseline settings—settings such as the front and

Basic settings start with checking the race sag. Measure the fully extended distance of the back end with the bike on the stand.

With a person holding the bike straight up and the rider centering his weight on the foot pegs, measure the sag. Add 10 mm to the measurement if the rider isn't wearing riding gear.

the back of the seat. Measure the front from the axle to the triple clamp. Be sure to measure from the same point each time. Use a metric tape measure and record the extended lengths of the front and rear ends. A metric tape measure's small increments are easier to work with than fractions of an in.

2. Set the sag after practice and refuel the bike with the normal amount of fuel that you race with. If it's a mud race, don't scrape the mud off the bike.

3. The rider should be fully dressed in racing clothing.

4. The rider should get on the bike and bounce up and down while the mechanic pushes the bike. This will help work out the stiction from the suspension to allow for an accurate measurement. Coast the bike to a stop. Tapping the brake will shift the bike's weight and give you a false measurement.

5. The rider should sit in normal racing position while someone holds the bike vertical. The bike should be on flat ground for best accuracy. The mechanic should measure the compressed distance on the rear suspension at the same two points where he measured the extended distance.

6. Increase or decrease shock spring preload to set the rear sag at 90 to 105 mm.

7. Measure the front fork sag the same way and, if necessary, adjust the sag to 35 to 50 mm with 5 to 15 mm of fork spring preload (measured internally).

8. Finally, measure the unladen sag of the rear shock. Be sure to measure this *after* you have the sag adjusted with the rider aboard. Let the bike sink under its own weight and measure the sag. It should sag 15 to 25 mm if the spring rate is correct. If

the sag is less than 15 mm, the spring is too soft for your weight. If the sag is greater than 25 mm, the spring is too stiff for your weight. It sounds backward, but think of it like this: If the sag is too little, then you had to preload the spring too much in order to get it to the correct race sag for your weight.

DETERMINING SPRING RATES

Measuring the unladen sag of the rear shock, after you have set the race sag, is a good guide for the rear spring rate. The front is more difficult; measure the fork sag and then compare the internal fork spring preload. Expert riders may choose stiffer forks springs than the sag and preload indicate because they use the front brake hard and transfer more weight to the front end. One of the main causes of headshake is a fork spring rate that is too soft or an oil level in the forks that is too low.

Spring force and valving work hand in hand. Good suspension tuners measure the spring rate before attempting revalving.

This bike's low-speed compression damping is too soft. Even with a relatively lightweight rider, the bike is bottomed out on the face of a jump.

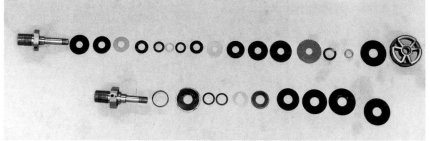

This is a view of the typical mid-valve located on the top of the piston rod in a twin-chamber fork. The mid-valve controls the active damping of the fork and is critical to many riding situations. The mid-valve on the bottom is stock, and the unit on top is the new MX-TECH fixed-post mid-valve with inverted valving. It enables the forks to initially compress and absorb small bumps and extends the range of damping over stock.

DAMPING CIRCUITS AND ADJUSTERS

The suspension circuits of the forks and shock are the HSC (high-speed compression), HSR (high-speed rebound), MVC (mid-valve compression), LSC (low-speed compression), and LSR (low-speed rebound). The compression adjuster for the shock is located on the reservoir, and the rebound adjuster is on the clevis (bottom shock mount). The compression adjuster for the forks is located on the bottom of the cartridge forks and on the top of twin chamber forks. The rebound adjuster is located on the fork cap of cartridge forks and on the bottom of twin chamber forks. Not all forks have rebound adjusters. Kayaba first used rebound adjusters on production cartridge forks in 1989.

LSR and LSC Circuits

The low-speed circuits work in two common track sections: landing on the back sides of jumps, G-outs, and accelerating on a straight with far-spaced, shallow whoops. All Japanese dirt bikes have suspension adjusting screws that affect the low-speed circuits only. Turning the adjusting screws clockwise will increase the damping and slow/stiffen the low-speed circuit. Turning the screws counterclockwise will decrease the damping and speed up/soften the low-speed circuit.

HSC and HSR Circuits

The high-speed circuits work in two common track sections: landing from big jumps and accelerating on a straight with tightly spaced, sharp-edged whoops. In 1996, Honda was the first to introduce HSC adjusters on the rear shock of the CR models. The adjuster has an inner screw for the LSC circuit and an outer ring for the HSC circuit. This adjuster can only make a slight difference in the high-speed damping. White Power shock and fork adjusters are high-speed-only adjusters.

SPRING RATE/RIDER WEIGHT CHART

This chart will give you a starting point when trying to determine the proper spring rate for your weight.

Rider Weight (pounds)	SHOCK-SPRING RATE (KG)		FORK-SPRING RATE (KG)	
	125cc	250cc	125cc	250cc
130–140	4.6	4.8	0.36	0.38
140–150	4.6	4.8	0.36	0.38
150–160	4.8	5.0	0.38	0.39
160–170	5.0	5.2	0.39	0.40
170–180	5.2	5.4	0.40	0.41
180–190	5.4	5.6	0.41	0.42
190–200	5.6	5.8	0.42	0.43
200–210	5.8	6.0	0.43	0.43
210–220	6.0	6.3	0.43	0.44
220–230	6.3	6.7	0.44	0.45

MVC

The mid-valve compression circuit works in three common track sections: landing from big jumps; braking bumps at the end of fast straights; and accelerating on a straight with tightly spaced, sharp-edged whoops. In 1996, Honda introduced HSC adjusters on the rear shock of the CR models. The adjuster has an inner screw for the LSC circuit and an outer ring for the HSC circuit. This adjuster can only make a slight difference in the high-speed damping.

BASIC TORQUE SETTINGS

There are some basic torque settings that have a dramatic effect on the handling of a bike. The torque settings of the rear end are covered later in this chapter, so we'll focus on the front end.

The rebound adjuster for the rear shock is located on the right side of the clevis, underneath the bike. Turn the adjuster in to zero (fully closed) and then turn it out 10 clicks for a baseline setting.

The critical torque settings on the front end include the steering head, triple clamps, and axle clamps. Modern dirt bikes have tapered steering head bearings that require a balance to torque. Too much torque makes it difficult to steer. Too little torque allows the forks to rock fore and aft during braking or when hitting bumps. Improper torque on the bearings can also contribute to premature wear.

A generic way to adjust the steering head tension goes like this:
1. Put the bike on a stand and elevate the front wheel.

The compression adjuster is located on the top right side of the shock. Turn the adjuster in to zero (fully closed) and then turn it out 10 clicks for a baseline setting.

The rebound adjuster for twin-chamber forks is located on the bottom of the fork, which is opposite of a traditional cartridge fork. The setting is performed just like the rear shock—turn the adjuster clockwise to zero and then turn it out 10 clicks.

The adjusters for the forks can be confusing because traditional cartridge and twin-chamber are opposite. This twin-chamber fork has the compression adjuster on the top of the fork, labeled with a "C."

2. Loosen the top clamp bolts and the large center nut of the steering stem's bolt.

3. Use a steel punch and hammer to tighten the spanner nut located just below the top clamp. Turn the spanner nut 1/8 of a turn at a time and check the steering tension by turning the handlebars. Remember that when you tighten the large center nut on the steering stem, the steering tension will increase.

Steering tension is largely based on rider preference. Some mechanics use the flop test. They turn the handlebars slightly off center and the front end flops to the steering stop. Keep in mind that the steering tension will decrease with use and require periodic maintenance. When a bike is new, the tension changes quickly because the bearings and races (half of a tapered roller bearing) are still in the process of seating on the frame and steering stem.

Triple clamp bolts must be loosened and retightened periodically to reduce the stress on the forks' internals and realign the forks in the triple clamps. If the clamp bolts are too tight, the forks will be constricted, causing binding in the fork travel. Another important aspect of the triple clamps is the fork tube overlap. Measure the overlap distance of the tubes and make sure they are equal. Then torque the clamp bolts to the specification listed in your bike's service manual.

Measure the fork tube overlap distance from the triple clamp. The baseline setting is 5 mm. A depth caliper is a handy tool for measuring the overlap distance.

This is a WER steering damper. These devices are popular in off-road applications because the forks can be revalved for slow-speed trail riding and the steering damper prevents head shaking at high speeds.

Front axle clamps on telescopic forks are critical to a fork's performance. If the fork tubes are not running parallel from top to bottom, the forks will have excessive stiction ("stiction" is a popular motorcycle slang term, a merge of sticking-friction), which will cause binding and premature wear of the bushings. This is a generic procedure for ensuring that the fork tubes are parallel before you tighten the axle clamps:

1. Place the bike on a stand and elevate the front wheel.
2. Torque the axle to factory specs, but leave the fork-to-axle clamps loose.
3. Spin the front wheel with your hand and quickly grab the front brake. Repeat this procedure at least three times to help align the forks parallel.
4. Make sure the arrows on the axle clamps are pointing up and tighten the top bolts until the clamp bottoms out. Then torque the bottom bolts to factory torque specs.

Torquing the swingarm pivot bolt requires a torque wrench rated in foot-pounds since the torque value is in the 50-plus range.

SUSPENSION DATA LOG

Keep a log of suspension adjustments and settings to help you in tuning. The log should track the following data for the fork: oil level, spring rate, spring preload, oil weight, fork tube overlap, compression adjuster setting, rebound adjuster setting, tire type, and tire pressure. Keep similar logs for the shock with the following data: spring rate, spring sag, oil weight, compression adjuster setting, rebound adjuster setting, tire type, and tire pressure. You'll find a handy blank data log in this chapter in the section on video suspension tuning.

SUSPENSION DATA LOG

Make some spare copies of this data log and record all of the pertinent data about your suspension, ideally at every track. This information is also vital for having work done on your suspension.

PERSONAL DATA
Rider's weight (with gear): _____ (lbs.)
Height _____
Skill Level _____
Type of riding
(circle those you do regularly)

motocross	enduro	DTX	supercross
desert	hillclimb	dual-sport	

TERRAIN DATA
(circle conditions you encounter frequently)

Soil content: sand   mud   rocks
tree roots   loam   hard clay
Elevation: big hills   off-camber   many jumps
square-edged bumps   sand
whoops

MOTORCYCLE DATA
Brand _____ Model _____ Year _____

FORK DATA
Spring rate _____ kg
Spring sag _____ mm
Unladen sag _____ mm
Spring pre-load _____ mm
Fork tube overlap _____ mm
Steering head tension set? _____
Compression adjuster: _____ clicks out
Rebound adjuster _____ clicks out/number

Maintenance history of the forks, including any crash damage _____
_____
_____
_____
_____
_____
_____
_____

Handling problems with the front end, including terrain condition and riding circumstances
_____
_____
_____
_____
_____
_____
_____
_____

SHOCK DATA
Spring rate _____ kg
Spring sag _____ mm
Unladen sag _____ mm
Oil brand and weight _____
Compression adjuster _____ clicks out
Rebound adjuster _____ clicks out

Maintenance history of the shock, including frequency of link lubrication and bearing replacement
_____
_____
_____
_____
_____
_____
_____
_____

Handling problems with the rear end, including terrain condition and riding circumstances
_____
_____
_____
_____
_____
_____
_____
_____

TIRE DATA
FRONT Brand _____
Model _____
Pressure _____ psi

REAR Brand _____
Model _____
Pressure _____ psi

FINAL TIPS ON BASIC TUNING

Remember to do the tasks that are listed earlier in this section for the best results. Record the race sag and adjuster positions in a race logbook. Check the sag every four races because shock springs loosen up and break in. Fork springs tend to sack out in about one season. Try setting your race sag first and install the correct springs for your weight and riding demands before you spend $600 on revalving.

CARTRIDGE FORK SERVICE AND TUNING

More than likely your bike uses cartridge forks. They were introduced in 1986 on Kawasakis and were used by most bikes starting in 1987.

This section has some tips for getting better performance out of any cartridge-type fork. Some tips involve just replacing worn bushings, while other tips are difficult to perform and require specialized knowledge and tools. Some parts of the cartridge are easily damaged and expensive to replace. Before you attempt to service your bike's cartridge forks, purchase the factory service manual for details on assembly and tightening torque specs.

HOW A CARTRIDGE FORK WORKS

The cartridge consists of two tubes with damping valves. The tubes slide together. The large tube is the damper rod and it houses the compression valves. The small tube is the piston rod and it houses the rebound valves. Cartridge forks rely on several plastic and metallic bushings to keep the telescopic rods from binding as they slide back and forth.

Cartridge fork valving consists of thin washers and cylindrical pistons with tiny bleed passages and slightly larger ports for the fluid to flow through. Damping is accomplished by restricting the fluid flow. An inherent problem with cartridge forks is that the debris from the bushings gets trapped between the valve washers and in the piston, thereby ruining the damping effect. This is the main reason why cartridge forks need to be cleaned and have the oil changed often (every 10–15 hours of riding). The twin tube design features improvements to extend the service time between cartridge servicing and improve the high-speed tuning (resistance to hard bottoming).

EVOLUTION OF THE FRONT FORK

The need for better front suspension developed when front fork travel went from 6 to 12 in. in 1975. Factory teams were scrambling to find forks that were soft enough for slow-speed, bumpy off-camber turns yet stiff enough for hard landings from big jumps. Yamaha turned to a partnership with Steve Simons to try and make the long-travel suspension work. This alliance signaled the start of the best innovations in front forks.

In 1977, Yamaha adapted the accumulator from its monoshock to each fork cap on the front forks of the YZ250. It consisted of a cylindrical chamber with a free-floating piston that separated two nitrogen gas–charged, spring-backed chambers. These accumulators worked as a pneumatic high-speed compression damping control. Modern cartridge forks use hydraulic damping controls (pistons and washers). Yamaha was bold to include this innovation on production bikes, but it was doomed to suffer the same fate as the Yamaha B.A.S.S. system for rear shocks from the mid-1980s. The average mechanic had no tuning or service information so the accumulators weren't maintained properly. During the same era, Roger DeCoster worked with a Brazilian inventor named Ribi. Their fork design was a radical departure from standard telescopic forks. The Ribi fork featured beams, linkage, and a rear shock to control the damping. The forks were rigid but top-heavy.

In 1978, Steve Simons invented and patented a hydraulic bottoming cone and cup design that is used in all Kayaba cartridge forks. In the mid 1990s, several companies started selling aftermarket bottoming cones for cartridge forks. The products were based on the original Simons design but were slightly different than OEM parts. The forks still have a hydraulic lock but it occurs more progressively than the stock part.

Terry Davis' Two-Stage Reservoir product was popular with desert riders in the early 1980s. It was designed for non-cartridge forks and was a hydraulic/pneumatic version of Yamaha's accumulator fork cap. The main difference was that Terry Davis' design linked the fork tubes together with balance tubes and connected them to one giant aluminum-finned reservoir. It looked like you were riding with a beer keg clamped to your crossbar. Despite the horrendous looks, it worked great if you had the patience to tune it.

This technology was used on Honda factory bikes in 1989 and nearly appeared on the 1990 CR250. These 1989 Showa factory forks were actually more advanced than the 1994 RM fork! Instead of using a floating piston and a spring, the design used a nitrogen-charged gas bladder (same as a rear shock). The gas pressure was increased if more resistance to bottoming was needed. These forks were the factory riders' favorites for supercross because they were specially developed for front wheel landings. This fork design was scheduled for the 1990 CR250, but Honda switched at the last moment because they didn't feel the average guy could service the forks and was more likely to ruin something. They were right—better to have bad damping than no damping.

1994 Twin Chamber Showa RM Forks

In 1994, one of the Japanese manufacturers finally had the bullocks to select the Showa forks. The fork cap houses the compression valve at the top of a semi-sealed cartridge, so debris can't clog the valve. The fork cap also houses a free-floating piston-backed spring. The spring is used only during very high compression and full bottoming of the forks. This system offers trackside quick-change of the compression-damping circuit.

This damper rod has a worn bushing that supports the piston rod. Stake marks are in the damper rod head. Here, a milling machine is used to bore out the stake marks so the head of the damper rod can be unthreaded to expose the bushing.

1995

That was the year for aftermarket fork innovations. Bottoming cones became the rage. Products such as these replaced the stock OEM hydraulic bottoming cones that fit on the piston rod of cartridge forks. The aftermarket cones are longer than the OEM cones and have more progressive angles that enable the forks to hydraulically lock at an earlier point in the travel. Later designs incorporated elastomer foam bumpers. Terry Davis of Terry Products designed another innovative product. The Double Pumper kit also enables the cartridge to be replenished with oil during a series of high-speed compression impacts.

1996

That was the year that signaled the return of conventional cartridge forks that featured innovations similar to the Double Pumper. Two of these fork designs were the RM Suzuki Showa and the WP fork made in Holland.

FMF licensed a patent from a European inventor that returns the forks and shock to the sag point of the suspension. The sag point for the shock is about 95 mm and 55 mm for the forks. The device is basically a spring-backed cartridge that enables a tuner to adjust the point to where the suspension components top out in travel, eliminating some inherent problems associated with rear end kicking during braking or head shaking of the forks. Apparently a rider must adjust his pre-jumping skills because the suspension won't top out completely. Ohlins experimented with a similar device in the early 1990s but abandoned it.

2000

Kawasaki fitted a rubber sleeve to the cartridge of its Kayaba forks to effectively make it like a twin tube fork, preventing circulation between the oil in the cartridge and outer tubes.

Special Tools for Servicing the Cartridge

It takes more special tools to service cartridge forks than to rebuild the motorcycle's engine. The basic tools include a damper rod holder, a bleeder rod, and a seal driver. Race-Tech offers the widest selection of suspension rebuilding tools, besides the motorcycle manufacturers. A tape measure can be used to set and measure the oil level, but a suction-type level-setting tool is more convenient.

Damper rod holding tools are used to prevent the rod from spinning when the base valve bolt is unthreaded. These holding tools are not universal in size and flange shape because the flange shape on top of the damper rod varies by brand and model.

Bleeder rod tools thread on to the top of the piston rod. During the final air-bleeding procedure, it's necessary to stroke the piston rod through its travel to facilitate bleeding of the cartridge. Four different sizes of bleeder rods are made to service cartridge forks made from 1986–1996.

Seal drivers are metal slugs machined to fit the outer diameter of the fork tube. There are two types of seal drivers—solid and split. Split drivers are needed for upside-down forks because those types of fork tubes have axle clamps. Conventional cartridge forks can use solid seal drivers because the driver is installed from the top of the tube.

Servicing twin chamber forks does not require a holding tool or a bleeder rod; you will need two special wrenches. One wrench holds the fork cap and the other holds the damping rod. However, you still need a seal driver to install the fork seals.

There are some general tools that you'll need as well, including a vise with soft jaws, an assortment of large-diameter six-point sockets, a plastic mallet, a flat-blade screwdriver, an oil pan, and cleaning solvents.

If you are interested in revalving the fork valves, you'll need some very special tools such as digital calipers for measuring the shims and drivers to remove the peened tab on the bottoming cone. The bottoming cone is located in the middle of the piston rod. By removing the bottoming cone, you can separate the piston rod from the damper rod.

CHANGING FORK OIL

I strongly recommend that you completely disassemble and clean your cartridge forks every 20 riding hours. However, if you are sure that the forks are in good condition and you just want to change the oil, here is a simple method.

1. Remove the forks from the bike.
2. Unscrew the jam nut on the fork cap.
3. Unscrew the fork cap.
4. Remove the plastic spacer.
5. Slide out the spring.
6. Turn the fork upside down and drain the oil.
7. Stroke the piston rod to pump the oil out of the cartridge while draining the forks.

8. Add about 4 ounces of fork oil to each tube and use it to flush out the tubes.

9. After you have drained out the flushing oil, follow the procedure listed later in this section for filling the oil and bleeding air from the cartridge.

10. Reassemble the forks and put them back on your bike, being careful to torque the pinch bolts to recommended settings.

DISASSEMBLING FORKS

Simply changing the oil is fine for periodic maintenance, but if your forks haven't been serviced in a season or more, you'll have to disassemble and clean the cartridge. Cartridge forks are especially susceptible to dirty oil, as gook tends to accumulate around the cartridge and the fork loses damping.

1. Remove the forks and drain the oil (see above).

2. Take the nut off the very bottom of the fork, either with an air impact wrench or by holding the damper rod in place with a damper rod holding tool.

3. Pull the cartridge out of the bottom of the fork.

4. Lay out all the parts and clean thoroughly with contact cleaner (note that at this point, the fork tube can be pulled from the fork slider to replace fork seals, etc.).

5. Replace any worn seals or bushings (see below).

6. Install the cartridge.

This bushing should be replaced every two years. If the bushing wears out, rebound damping will be reduced.

7. Tighten the nut on the bottom of the fork, using the special tool or an air impact wrench (be *very* careful with the impact wrench; you can blow the O-ring off of the cartridge and lose all damping).

8. Install the spring and spacer.

9. Follow the procedure listed later in this section for filling the forks with oil and bleeding air from the cartridge.

10. Reassemble the forks and put them back on your bike, being careful to torque the pinch bolts to recommended settings.

REPLACING BUSHINGS

The seals, wipers, and bushings should be replaced at least once a year. If you are looking for the highest level of performance, replace the bushing that fits in the head of the damper rod and supports the piston rod. The standard bushing has excess clearance that can cause the piston rod to go off-center and produce more stiction in the forks. After you have spent the time to polish the bearing surfaces of the damper and piston rods, replace the standard bushing with an accessory bushing that has tighter clearances and a low coefficient of friction.

When your forks lose rebound damping, the main cause is worn piston rod bushings. When these bushings are worn out, they allow the cartridge fluid to bypass the bushing and piston rod, thereby losing the damping effect. If your bike's cartridge forks make a clunking sound when they extend, the piston rod bushing is worn out.

The piston rod bushing can be replaced by unthreading the head from the damper rod, where the bushing is housed. Heating the steel head to break the bond of the locking agent on the threads does this procedure. Then, use a chain clamp wrench to grasp the steel head and unthread it from the aluminum damper rod. After the bushing is replaced, the threads of the damper rod and head must be carefully cleaned and a permanent locking agent applied. Then, tighten them with the chain clamp wrench. Warning: This procedure is very

difficult and should only be entrusted to a professional suspension technician. The Teflon bushings support the fork tube to the slider. You can tell when they are worn because there will be discoloration on the load-bearing surface. These bushings are easy to replace and should be changed once a year. The slider bushing (large-diameter bushing) falls out when you separate the two tubes. The fork tube bushing (small diameter) is under spring tension, so it must be removed using a straight-blade screwdriver to spread the bushing at the side slit and slide it off the end of the fork tube. When you install the large-diameter bushings, take care to seat them properly in the slider before trying to install the fork seals. You do not need to use any special oil or grease on these bushings because they are Teflon coated.

REPLACING FORK SEALS

Once you have the forks disassembled and the fork slider and tube separated (see previous section), the fork seals can be removed. When installing the new seals, you must be very careful not to tear them when sliding them over the fork tube. Some grease and a plastic bag are key to getting your new seals installed without tearing.

1. Apply Teflon grease to the wiper and seal.

2. Place a plastic bag over the end of the fork tube.

Place a plastic bag over the end of the fork tube to protect the seal lip from being damaged by the bushing recess upon installation of a new seal.

This is a seal driver. There are several different types based on the diameter of the seal and fork tube. The driver is split in two pieces to fit tightly around the tube. Race-Tech makes the largest selection of fork tools and seal drivers.

3. Slide the seal over the plastic bag and onto the fork tube. The plastic bag covers the bushing grooves and prevents the seal from tearing as it slides over the sharp edges of the bushing grooves.

Now you can reassemble your forks and be confident that your new seals will hold.

FILLING WITH OIL AND BLEEDING AIR FROM THE CARTRIDGE

Here are some tips for filling Showa or Kayaba cartridge forks with oil and bleeding out the air:

1. During the initial filling and bleeding sequence, compress the fork tube and fill the fork to within 2 in. of the top.

2. Extend the fork, cap your hand over the end of the tube, and compress the fork. You'll feel air pressure building up under your hand. The oil is under pressure and that will help force tiny air bubbles through the shims of the compression valve and also displace the air that gets trapped between the fork tube and slider. Repeat this procedure at least four times, adding oil each time.

3. Use a stroker rod to grasp the piston rod and stroke the rod up and down until the tension through the stroke is equal. Equal tension is an indication that the air is bled from the cartridge.

4. To set the oil level, remove the spring and compress the fork. Use a thin ruler (preferably metric) to measure the distance between the top of the tube and the top of the oil. An oil level setting tool (or a large syringe with a bit of hose attached) is the quickest way to set your oil level. Make sure there is an excess amount of oil in the fork so the oil level setting tool can suck out oil to set the proper level.

5. The oil level should be set with the spring removed and the fork tube bottomed. Kawasaki recommends setting the oil level 10 mm higher than the spec to compensate for the small amount of air trapped between the slider and tube. That bit of air works its way out when the bike is ridden.

TWIN TUBE MAINTENANCE AND TUNING

The twin tube cartridge forks are essentially cartridges that don't re-circulate the oil into the outer tubes. The twin tube fork doesn't require as much maintenance because the internal cartridge is sealed from the outer tubes, and the sliding interface between the two outer forks tubes is the source of the metallic contamination that ruins the performance of a cartridge fork. Twin tube forks also don't require special tools to service the cartridge. Some companies such as Motion Pro and Race Tech make dedicated wrench sets for the top cap and the cartridge rod; you can use standard wrenches to do the same job. This is a generic procedure for servicing a twin tube fork.

1. Loosen the fork cap with a six-point box wrench. It's best to hold the fork tube in the bike's triple clamp; just be sure to loosen the top clamp bolts. If the forks are separate from the bike, you can use soft jaws in a vise; take care not to clamp the vise so tight that you crush the fork tube.

2. Loosen the bolt at the bottom of the fork until it separates from the bottom fork tube.

3. Depress the fork cap until the cartridge rod extends out the bottom of the fork far enough to expose the wrench flats. Use an open-end wrench to hold the cartridge rod and unthread the bottom bolt completely. Take care when removing the bolt because the telescopic rebound adjuster tube will fall out of the bottom of the cartridge.

4. Remove the cartridge from the fork tubes by pulling it out from the top.

5. Use a straight-bladed screwdriver to remove the wiper, and then remove the circlip that retains the fork seal.

6. Use a propane torch to heat the area around the seal to break the bond of the bushing.

7. Grasp the fork tubes with both hands and yank them apart several times rapidly until the tubes separate.

8. Carefully inspect the bushings inside and outside to look for wear marks. Normally, you should replace the bushings and seals every time you change the fork oil, or about every 50 riding hours. That will ensure that the expensive aluminum fork slider doesn't wear out prematurely. Installing new bushings and seals is the same for normal cartridge forks. See the photos in this chapter for examples.

9. Disassemble the compression valve and clean any debris from the piston ports and between the shims by spraying brake cleaner on the parts.

10. To assemble the forks, start by filling the inside of the cartridge to the level specified by the manufacturer. Usually that is a ledge where the compression valve fits.

These are some of the tools needed to repair twin tube forks.

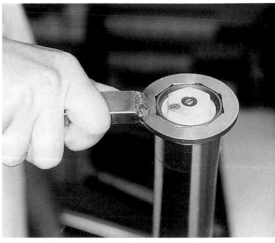

Start by removing the fork cap. Don't squeeze the tube in a vise; try to loosen the cap with the forks in the triple clamps or hold the tube with a strap wrench.

These two wrenches are essential. The large wrench is for the fork cap and the small shouldered wrench is for the bottom of the cartridge. Race-Tech sells these tools.

Extend the cartridge out the bottom of the forks and use the small shouldered wrench to hold it while you loosen the base bolt with a six-point socket.

11. Bleed the cartridge of air in the normal way by slowly stroking the cartridge rod through its full travel. Do this until the rod moves smoothly. Smooth travel indicates that the air is bled to the top of the cartridge.

12. Put the cartridge in the top of the forks, insert the telescopic rebound rod, and tighten the bottom bolt.

13. Fill the outer tubes with a measured volume of oil based on the manufacturer's specification.

14. Thread in the top cap and compression valve.

The fork tubes are held together with a circlip that is located below the wiper.

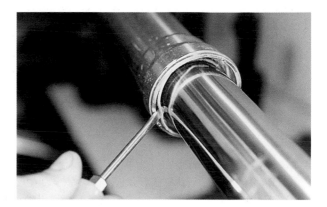

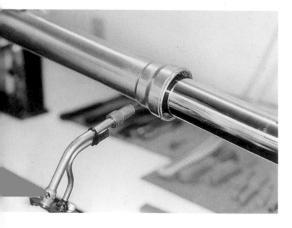

Before attempting to separate the tubes, use a propane torch to heat the area where the bushings fit. This will reduce the chafing between the bushings.

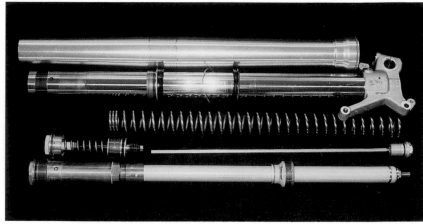

This is a disassembled twin-tube cartridge fork. From top down and left to right: fork slider, fork tube, spring, fork cap with compression valve, telescopic rebound rod and base bolt rebound adjuster, and main cartridge.

To disassemble the cartridge, clamp the wrench flats of the upper part of the cartridge in a vise with soft jaws.

BASIC FORK REVALVING

The latest design rage for cartridge forks is to increase the diameter of the compression and rebound pistons and separate the compression valving into low-, medium-, and high-speed damping modes. For our tuning tips discussion, we refer to the two states of compression valving as passive (slow speed) and active (mid speed). All 1996 and later models of 125-cc and 250-cc Japanese MX bikes use the new design. Expect other models of forks to evolve to this type of design in the near future.

Circulating Controversy

The main difference between the popular models of cartridge forks is the circulation paths of the oil. Twin tube forks are non-circulating whereas most other cartridge forks are circulating. Twin tube forks utilize the oil in a sealed cartridge. The theory is that the main sources of contamination in a fork are the wear between the spring, interface of the fork tube and slider, and the bushings. The metallic debris generated from these moving parts contaminates the oil and forms deposits in critical areas like the pistons and valve stacks. Aftermarket tuning companies such as Pro-Circuit offer services to convert circulating cartridge forks to non-circulating types. They don't convert it to a twin tube fork, but rather a hybrid design. Other tuners

such as Terry Davis of Terry-Cable manufacture aftermarket fork kits that increase circulation in non-twin tube forks. The theory is that in desert racing the vehicle speeds are so fast that when you ride over a section of washboard terrain, the cartridge doesn't have the ability to replenish with oil. The oil is pumped into the outer tubes and the damping fails because of air lock. Generally speaking, the Pro-Circuit modification is intended for stadium motocross and the Terry-Cable kit is designed for desert racing.

Passive and Active Valving

On a twin chamber cartridge fork, the piston mounted on the cartridge rod is bi-directional and controls the rebound and active compression damping. The compression adjusting screw located in the fork cap controls the passive damping. Different types of pistons and shim valves can separate the compression damping circuits. The compression valve and adjusting screw are mounted on one end of the forks, usually at the top of the forks on twin tube forks or to the bottom of re-circulating cartridge forks. The rebound adjuster is mounted in the bottom of the forks on twin tube forks and to the fork caps on re-circulating forks. It doubles as the bolt that fastens the cartridge tube to the lower fork leg, thereby holding the forks together.

The compression valve is mounted in a column of fluid (fork oil) inside the cartridge. The type of damping that the compression valve absorbs is passive in nature, because the valve doesn't move through the oil. The oil is forced through the compression valve by the displacement action of the moving rebound piston.

The shim valves mounted on the top side of the cartridge rod piston are called the mid-valves and control the active damping of compression. When the forks compress, the cartridge rod and piston accelerate through the column of fluid inside the cartridge. The mid-valves have a huge effect on the damping of the fork for most riding situations. The mid-valves are like the jet needle in a carburetor. In order to modify the mid-valve, you have to disassemble the cartridge, including removing the head from the damper rod. That is a difficult procedure and should be entrusted only to a professional suspension technician.

PROBLEMS THAT MIMIC POOR TUNING

Mechanical problems, such as worn parts, can cause your forks to act as if they are poorly tuned when they are not. Before you spend a lot of money on revalving or other fork tuning, make sure there is not a mechanical cause for your forks' problems. The following is a list of potential trouble spots to check on your forks:

1. Oil breakdown can make the damping seem too fast or soft, especially when the fork oil gets hot. Debris can also accumulate in the valving to hinder the damping. Fix by cleaning the forks and changing the fork oil.
2. Blown oil seals cause a lack of damping and a number of other catastrophic problems such as worn bushings. Replace the seals.
3. Worn rebound piston rings. Most bikes use a plastic seamless band for a rebound piston ring. If your forks seem to rebound too quickly, the oil may be bypassing the rebound piston and shim valving. Unfortunately,

this seal band cannot be replaced; you must buy the entire piston rod assembly.
4. Sacked fork springs. Fork springs become shorter in length with use, which can cause headshake or wobbling at high speeds. Plan on replacing fork springs every season. Check to make sure they are even in length as a set.
5. Dented aluminum sliders. The sliders are made from thin-walled aluminum tubing, so the rocky roost from other bikes can easily dent the sliders. These dents can cause the forks to bind, making the fork damping harsh. Replace the sliders when they get dented, and install plastic rock guards to prevent rock dents.
6. Worn bushing for the piston rod to damper rod. This bushing is located in the head of the damper rod and supports the piston rod. If your forks appear to have lost rebound damping, this bushing is probably worn and must be replaced.

TUNING WITH OIL VISCOSITY

There are two ways to rate suspension fluids: the Society of Automotive Engineers (SAE) weight and the viscosity index number. The SAE determines the weight number with a standard test that measures oil flow through a fixed orifice at a certain temperature in a 30-minute period. The viscosity index number is a measurement of the oil's flow rate through a fixed orifice over a specific temperature range in a set time period. The fluid velocities through the tiny steel shim valving and pistons of the cartridge forks are much greater than in the old-style forks, which used drilled jet passages.

Be sure to use cartridge fork oil when you replace the oil, and the weight, in reality, is not that important. Cartridge fork oil is available from about 2 1/2 to 7 weight and any of those work well. In general, as the weight gets higher, you'll get an incremental increase in compression and rebound damping, but most riders wouldn't be able to notice the difference.

The latest rage in fork tuning is an air tank. This device threads into the fork cap and provides an extra measure of tuning to the "air spring" of the fork.

In general, raise the oil level when you're bottoming hard. Increased oil will help the last third of the stroke only.

FORK OIL BREAKDOWN

The fork oil breaks down when its additives are depleted and it is contaminated with aluminum and bronze debris. The additives that enable the oil to have a low flow resistance are polymer particles, and they eventually accumulate as a varnish-like coating on the inside of the fork tubes. Consequently, the oil in new-style cartridge forks should be changed every 15 or 20 rides to maintain the best performance.

The main source of debris in the oil is spring flaking. Eibach aftermarket springs are coated with a flexible polymer that resists flaking. The aluminum damper rods and sliders, along with the plastic and bronze high-wear bearing parts, also slowly break down during use and contaminate the oil. Further debris is produced when steel preload rubs against the springs. Pro-Action sells aluminum preload cones of an updated design for the early 1990s Japanese dirt bikes. These cones greatly reduce the amount of debris produced by the cones rubbing on the springs.

FORK SPRING PRELOAD TUNING

Before you try to measure and set the preload, measure the length of both springs and compare the measurements to the manufacturer's spec for minimum length. If the springs are too short, it means they are sacked out and need to be replaced. When you purchase new springs, make sure you get the proper spring rate for your bike and rider weight. The Japanese manufacturers have recommendations listed in the service manual for the best spring rate based on rider weight. If you are an expert rider and use the front brake hard or ride on tracks with big jumps, you should select the next stiffer spring rate from the one recommended in the service manual.

Here is how to measure and set the spring preload: Disassemble the fork. Let the fork tube bottom and extend the piston rod. Slide the spring over the piston rod. With the rod extended, measure the distance between the end of the spring and the point where the spring retaining collet clips into the rod. That gives you the preload measurement. Normally, the preload should be 5 to 15 mm. The only way for you to vary the preload is to adjust the jam nut height on the piston rod to set the correct preload.

White Power and Ohlins fork springs are available in a wide variety of spring rates and are the proper length to replace extra-long Japanese springs that have too much preload. True-Tech sells aftermarket fork caps for 1990s models of Japanese dirt bikes. These fork caps feature an adjusting screw to vary the spring preload. This is an excellent product but requires frequent maintenance. If you purchase a set of these fork caps, be sure to pick up a spare set of seals for the caps.

SHOCK DAMPING MODES

Rebound Damping

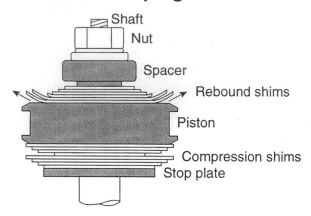

Compression Damping

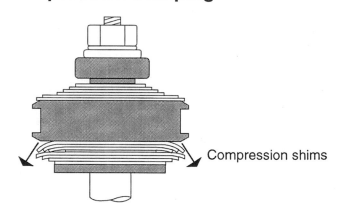

Arrows show flow path

This is a diagram of the typical bi-directional shock piston. A series of steel shim washers provide resistance to oil flowing through the shock piston.

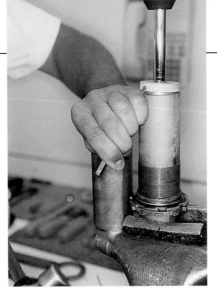

Use a clothespin to hold the cap out of your way, and use two punches to depress the seal pack so you can remove the circlip.

On Japanese shocks, the cover for the seal pack is wedged into place. Remove it with a punch and hammer by tapping on the indentations machined in opposing sides of the cap.

Clamp the clevis in soft jaws and a vise to hold it while you gently tap on the shock body with a plastic mallet to separate the body from the shaft assembly.

REAR SHOCK SERVICING

This section is a general overview for single shock servicing. You'll see what you can clean and inspect yourself and how a professional service technician would service a shock. This section is also intended to give a thorough understanding of how suspension works and tell you all the things they leave out of the service manual. You can become a more informed consumer by learning when to have your shock serviced and how to shop for suspension services.

Total shock service with cleaning and oil changing should be performed every 15 to 20 riding hours. Servicing suspension components is a specialized task that requires knowledge, experience, and access to special tools and replacement parts. If you lack any of these important things, don't attempt to service your suspension components yourself. Trust revalving to a suspension technician.

Also, you should regularly clean, inspect, and grease your rear linkage. See the section on "Servicing Rear Suspension Linkage" later in this chapter for more details.

Your bike's shock is constantly subjected to internal and external torture. Inside the shock, the bronze piston ring scrapes up against the hard-anodized aluminum shock body walls in oil that reaches temperatures of 450 degrees Fahrenheit. The bronze and aluminum particles quickly contaminate the small volume of shock oil, causing the oil to break down.

To make matters worse, the outside of the shock is constantly subjected to dirt particles being rammed into the shock seal by the foam bumper and the high-strength detergents from the spray of a pressure washer.

COMMON PROBLEMS

The external elements cause the wiper and seal to fail. Small quantities of oil flow past the seal and you hardly notice until most of the oil is lost and the shock shaft turns blue from overheating. It's easy to forget about the shock because it's bolted into the center of the bike, but it's hard to forget about the replacement cost of a shock if it fails.

BASIC CLEANING

This procedure should be performed every 5 riding hours:

1. Power-wash the shock. You want the dirt off the outside of the shock before you do the detail cleaning. Take care not to spray directly at the shock seal. Also, be sure to spray clean the fine threads on the shock body.
2. Spray penetrating oil on the threads and wait 15 minutes before you try to unthread the spring retaining nut. Unthread the nut to remove the spring collet and the spring so you can remove the seal cap. There are two types of spring collets. One has an open slot and the other is a solid disc with a circlip. The circlip must be removed before you can remove the spring.
3. Use a plastic mallet and punch to rock the seal cap back and forth until the cap pops loose from the shock body. Notice how much dirt and debris is under the seal cap, jammed up against the seal wiper. It's very important to carefully clean under the foam bumper and the seal cap with detergent and water.
4. Check the seal wiper for oil seepage. Seepage indicates that the seal is worn and needs to be replaced.
5. Check the shock shaft for deep scratches and a blue color. The blue indicates that the shock severely overheated, probably from the loss of oil at the seal. The shaft can be re-plated or replaced if it is discolored or deeply scored.
6. Your factory service manual lists a minimum free length for the shock spring. Measure it to make sure it hasn't sacked out.
7. Remove the seals from the top shock mount and clean the dirt and old grease from the seals and spherical bearing. The bearing doesn't require lube but you should pack the seals

Late-model Showa shocks use additional stake marks to prevent the compression bolt from unthreading. These stake marks must be drilled before attempting to remove the compression bolt. Otherwise, the fine threads on the bolt will be stripped as it is unthreaded.

Japanese shocks have a standardized method for retaining the parts on the shaft. A nut is threaded onto the shaft and then peened over. In order to do any service tasks to the shaft, such as seal changes or revalving, the nut must be removed. The easiest way is to grind the nut on a 45-degree angle until the peened edge is gone. Then the nut can be unthreaded. A bench grinder and a steady hand are needed to do this task.

with grease to prevent dirt and water from reaching the bearing.

8. Check the lower shock mount clevis for cracks at the bolt hole. Cracks are common on late 1980s and early 1990s YZ shocks because the bottom shock mount protrudes below the frame tubes and is prone to damage when casing the bike on whoops or jumps.

SHOCK DISASSEMBLY

The following is a typical disassembly procedure that a professional service technician would follow when servicing a shock:

1. Depressurize the gas bladder, noting any oil mist escaping with the gas, which would indicate a perforated bladder that needs to be replaced.

2. Remove the compression adjuster bolt and let the oil drain. Take care when removing the compression adjuster bolt. You must use a tiny drill bit to drill down the center of the three center-punch points, where the threads of the shock body and the compression adjuster are threaded together. Drill into center-punch points about 0.030 in.—just enough to drill through the points. The compression adjuster can then be unthreaded without the threat of damaging the fine threads.

3. Use a bladder-cap-removing T-handle to depress the bladder cap enough to remove the circlip. Now, the bladder cap can be removed.

4. Remove the shock shaft by popping up the seal cap, depressing the seal pack assembly with two drift rods and removing the circlip that holds the seal pack in place. Use a scraper to remove the burr left by the circlip because this burr could prevent the seal pack from lifting out of the shock body. Remove the shaft assembly from the shock body.

5. Clean all the shock parts thoroughly in mineral spirits solvent, but never in fuel. Fuels are explosive and will damage the rubber seal and foam bumper.

6. Smart technicians measure the inside bore of the shock body for excessive out-of-round wear. Although the shock bodies are hard-anodized, they can still wear out and let oil bypass the piston and shim valves, thereby reducing the damping effect. Those shock bodies wear out in a few seasons of riding. Some manufacturers don't offer the bodies through spare parts, but there is a way to repair worn-out shock bodies. The body is rebuilt by

This is an example of a worn shock shaft. Because the shock is mounted on an angle, one side of the shaft will wear out quicker. If the shaft isn't bent, it can be re-chromed.

honing it straight and electroplating it with nickel silicon carbide and then diamond-honing to size. The service costs about $125.

7. Other high-wear parts of the shock include the seal pack and piston ring. The seal pack has a bushing built inside, along with the seal and wiper. When the wiper fails, the seal and bushing wear out quickly. They should be replaced as a set. Average replacement cost of a seal pack is $50. The best way to install the seal packs on the shock shaft without damaging the seal is to wrap a piece of Teflon tape over the end of the shaft threads. Piston rings are made of either bronze or plastic. The bronze ones wear fast and should be replaced every time you have the oil changed.

8. If the shock shaft is bent, blue, or deeply scratched, repair or replace it. European shock manufacturers offer replacement shafts, but some Japanese manufacturers don't offer any replacement parts for their shocks. Some companies offer re-chroming and polishing services for shock shafts. The best method of shaft plating is hard chrome. Companies such as Race Tech and Pro-Action offer these services, but turnaround time is about three weeks. Works Performance offers complete shaft assemblies for late-model Japanese dirt bikes. These items come with the shaft, clevis, seal pack, and bumper. You have to swap over your piston and valve stack. The Works Performance product is an inexpensive alternative to buying a new shock.

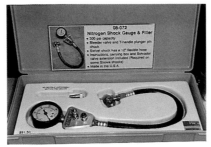

This is a Motion Pro shock-charging regulator. It's used to set the nitrogen gas pressure in the shock bladder.

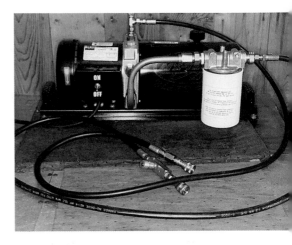

PDS shocks require an oil-bleed pump to force out trapped air bubbles from the dual-stage piston in the shock.

This is what the shaft assembly looks like when it is disassembled. The washers (shims) on the right side control the compression damping, and the washers on the left control the rebound damping. Starting from the top, the larger diameter shims control the low-speed damping. The small shims in the middle of the shim stack are called transition shims. The diameter and thickness of these shims are critical because the low-speed shims flex over the transition shim to contact the high-speed shims.

ASSEMBLING THE SHOCK AND BLEEDING AIR

While reassembling the shock, it is critical for good damping performance that you make sure that no air is trapped in the shock. If air is trapped in the shock, the oil will become aerated and break down faster. Also, the air travels through the piston and shim valves, reducing the damping effect. That can be dangerous because the shock will rebound faster and cause the rear end of the bike to kick. The following is a general procedure that technicians use when reassembling shocks:

1. Pour shock oil into a cup and set the compression adjuster bolt and the piston side of the shock shaft assembly in the oil for at least 30 minutes before assembling the shock. This will reduce the chances of air becoming trapped between the tiny shim-valve washers.

2. Pour oil into both the shock body and reservoir, and install the compression bolt. Clamp the top shock mount in a vise, and pour shock oil in both the reservoir and shaft sides of the shock body.

3. Pour oil to within 1/2 in. of the top of the reservoir. Apply Denicol or Noleen seal grease to the top edge of the bladder. Install the bladder and its retaining circlip.

4. Pressurize the bladder with 10 psi of nitrogen gas. This will make the bladder inflate to full size and force oil through the reservoir, past the compression bolt, and into the shaft side of the shock body. This also helps to force tiny air bubbles out of the shock. Let the air flow up out of the shock for at least 30 minutes.

5. Pour oil to within 1 in. of the top of the shock body and install the shaft assembly. It will be difficult to depress the seal pack in order to install the circlip because you are compressing the inflated bladder. The shock is now overfilled with oil. This is done to facilitate the final air bleeding procedure.

6. Some shocks, such as those built by Kayaba, have a 5-mm Allen bolt on the top shock mount of the body that is used for bleeding air from the shock. Others, such as older Showa shocks, do not. These shocks must be bled though the compression adjuster bolt. In either case, position the top shock mount in the vise so the bleeder bolt or the compression adjuster is at the highest point to ensure that no air enters into the shock during the final bleeding procedure.

7. Compress and extend the shock shaft several times so the trapped air congregates at the highest point on the shock, near the bleeder bolt. Lightly tap on the shock body and reservoir with a hammer. This will help tiny air bubbles to break loose from the sides of the body. If you feel any tight and loose spots during the shaft's travel, then there must be a lot of air trapped in the shock and you must start completely over.

8. If the shaft travels smoothly, you can extend the shaft and slowly remove the bleeder bolt. The excess oil and air will flow out of the shock.

9. Set the bladder pressure to the factory-recommended spec; normally that is 150 psi of nitrogen. Never use air to pressurize the bladder.

This is the new Progressive brand of PDS shock absorber. PDS shocks are used on bikes without rising rate linkage systems. PDS shocks require special tools and setup; you can't fix one of these babies in your garage!

Notes on White Power and Ohlins PDS Shocks

PDS is an acronym for position damping sensitive and is the type of rear shock used on modern motorcycles that are mounted directly to the swingarm without a rising rate linkage setup. PDS shocks are extremely difficult to rebuild unless you have a bevy of special tools, including a bleeder-pump machine.

Installation Tips

Check the shock linkage and steering head bearings for wear and grease. Also, be sure to reset the race sag on the back end. On full-size bikes, the rear race sag should be 90 to 105 mm with unladen sag of 17 to 25 mm. Always check race sag with your full riding gear on, the fuel tank at race volume, and your feet on the pegs. If you go to a mud race, set the rear race sag after the bike gets muddy in practice. You'll be surprised how much it varies from when the bike is clean.

VIDEO SUSPENSION TUNING

Suspension tuning can be a mystery for both the rider and mechanic. As a rider on race day, you go out for your practice session and your suspension nearly kills you. You come back to the pits and your mechanic asks you if the high-speed

rebound feels too fast? You haven't got a clue because for the last 20 minutes you struggled to keep your motorcycle on two wheels. After riding and tuning motorcycles for years, I still cannot diagnose suspension problems by riding or watching the bike on a racetrack.

The best suspension tuners in the world have a well-developed sense of high-speed vision. They can watch a bike and rider on various sections of the track to determine how well the four different suspension circuits are working. Some suspension tuners are starting to encourage riders to make video samples for review.

You can acquire that same sense of high-speed vision with the help of a video camera. After videotaping the rider attacking various sections of the track, you can replay the tape one frame at a time and see exactly how the four different suspension circuits damp the impacts of jumps, whoops, and other track irregularities.

This section tells you how to use videotape to tune your suspension. First,

you'll learn the four suspension circuits and the track sections that help isolate each circuit. At the end of this section is a troubleshooting chart that will help you to identify problems with each circuit. A suspension data log sheet is also provided so you can record all the pertinent information on your bike and have the data reviewed by a suspension tuning expert. The data log will help you to develop a mental framework for setting up your suspension properly. Finally, you'll learn what changes suspension tuners make during revalving. A warning though: Do not try to revalve your own suspension. One small mistake can put you over the bars. First, set up your suspension with the proper springs, settings, oil heights, and so on. If you still need revalving performed, at least then you will know exactly what your suspension needs are. Too many people have their suspension parts revalved without first trying to set up the bike properly.

TUNING WITH THE DAMPING CIRCUITS

As previously mentioned, the four suspension circuits of the forks and shock are the high-speed compression

This rider is experiencing kicking while entering a turn. The rear suspension can't absorb the bump because the compression and rebound damping are too soft.

Dutch sand master Pedro Tragter skips the whoops in perfect form with the wheels hugging the terrain and the suspension handling the impacts.

High-Speed Compression (HSC) and High-Speed Rebound (HSR) Tuning
The high-speed circuits work in two common track sections, landing from big jumps and accelerating on a straight with tightly spaced, sharp-edged whoops. Video a rider as he lands from a big jump and for about 15 yards after he lands. That is important because there are usually many small bumps in the landing path after a big jump. Replay the tape one frame at a time and watch to see how equally both the front and rear suspension compress and rebound. If the rear shock rebounds too fast, the rear end may spring up so fast that it loads the forks. If both ends rebound too fast, the whole bike may spring up off the ground. That can be hazardous if there is a turn after the jump.

When taping in whoop sections, try to pan the rider in as much of the section as possible. Watch how the suspension reacts to the sharp-edged whoops at speed. The rear wheel shouldn't pack up. Packing is caused when the HSC and HSR are too slow to react to the terrain.

(HSC), high-speed rebound (HSR), low-speed compression (LSC), and low-speed rebound (LSR). Your main objective in video suspension tuning is to make video samples of the rider on sections of the track that best isolate two of these circuits at a time. Before you start riding and taping, change the suspension fluids, grease the linkage, and have the proper spring rates and sag settings on the shock and forks.

Low-Speed Compression (LSC) and Low-Speed Rebound (LSR) Tuning
The low-speed circuits work in two common track sections, braking for tight turns and accelerating on a straight with far-spaced, shallow whoops. When taping a rider, be sure to have the whole bike and part of the ground in the film frame. Stand far enough back from the track section and pan with the rider for at least 25 yards. Replay the tape one frame at a time and pay attention to how the wheel follows the ground as the bike hits the bumps. The wheel shouldn't compress quickly or rebound abruptly. All Japanese dirt bikes have suspension adjusting screws that affect the low-speed circuits only. Turning the adjusting screws clockwise will increase the damping and

slow/stiffen the low-speed circuit. Turning the screws counterclockwise will decrease damping and speed up/soften the low-speed circuit.

These are the forces acting on the bike when accelerating out of a turn. The chain force drives the rear wheel down; the resultant force extends up the swingarm, causing the front end to wheelie.

The wheel will stay compressed as it hits the next whoop. Eventually, the rider loses control and must slow down. Taping in whoops also helps the rider; if the bike is reacting properly, he may gain enough confidence to go faster through the section.

If the videotape indicates that you need to change the high-speed circuits, you must take the suspension to an expert in revalving because there are no external adjustments that you can make to the high-speed circuits.

SUSPENSION REVALVING

How Damping Works

Suspension fluid (oil) flows through the ports of the piston and up against the shims. The shims pose a resistance to the oil flow, which provides a damping effect. The damping effect is directly related to the diameter and the thickness of the shim. The shims act as a series of tiny springs, flexing to increase the flow area for the oil. The greater the flow area, the greater the oil flow and the less the damping effect. The first shims that the oil encounters are the ones that affect the low-speed damping. These shims are large in diameter and thin in thickness. The oil deflects these shims easily because of their large surface area, and the relatively thin steel poses low spring tension. The shim stack or valving is arranged in a taper shape. The large-diameter low-speed shims are positioned closest to the piston, and the small-diameter high-speed shims are positioned farthest away from the piston. The low-, mid-, and high-speed circuit shims are separated by transition shims. Think of the valve stack as gears in a transmission, and the transition shims as shift forks. The more tapered the valve stacks, and the thinner the transition shim, the plusher the suspension becomes in its handling. Less plush suspension is typically too stiff to absorb the small bumps on acceleration and too soft for square-edged bumps at speed. Much of the problem has to do with a mismatch between the piston's port arrangement and the overall valve stack.

Why Revalve?

The term revalving is often tossed around in the dirt bike magazines, but have you ever wondered what suspension tuners do to revalve a set of forks or a shock? The answer ranges from not much to a whole lot. Some unscrupulous tuners just power-wash the outside of the components, turn the clickers, and charge you a lot of money. Other tuners replace the pistons and valve stacks, carefully crafting the arrangement of the valve shims to suit your riding demands and compensate for the idiosyncrasies of your model bike. Tuners need information about you and the way you ride in order to revalve your suspension. If they don't give you a survey form or interview you, be suspicious about the work they are asking to be paid to perform. Revalving can be defined as the removal, repositioning, or replacement of shims in the valve stacks of the compression and rebound pistons of a cartridge fork or rear shock. Revalving should be performed when you've exhausted the basics such as setting the sag; making sure your bike has the right springs; and checking that the forks and shock have fresh oil, seals, and bushings. Only then can you determine whether your bike needs revalving to make it handle better. The main reasons why you need good handling suspension on a dirt bike are:

• To keep the wheels in contact with the ground to provide traction and drive for the rear wheel and steering for the front wheel;

• To minimize the impacts and vibration on the motorcycle;

• To minimize the stress loads on the rider and prevent fatigue and injuries.

The rear wheel must stay in contact with the ground to provide driving force. The front wheel needs to stay in contact with the ground to provide steering control. Impacts on the motorcycle can cause all sorts of problems, including loose bolts, foaming of the fuel in the carb's float bowl, long-term damage to the bearings that support the suspension components, and long-term damage to the electrical components.

Curt McMillen takes a leap of faith over Englishtown's big triple jump. Having confidence in your bike's suspension enables you to push it to the limit.

The chronic problems caused to a rider by a poor handling bike are much more obvious. Forearm pump-up is probably the most common. Long-term damage to a rider's neck and spine may take years to manifest but some people might be immediately sensitive to pain. Having a professional suspension tuner revalve your suspension might seem expensive (average cost of total rework with parts is $600), but what price do you put on pain?

The main things that affect a suspension system are changes in the sprung mass from moving up and down and changes in motion such as acceleration, braking, and turning.

The sprung mass of a moving dirt bike can be hard to define because the entire motorcycle leaves the ground. Technically, the sprung mass includes

This is a layout for the Pro-Action three-stage incremental valving setup.

This is the MX-TECH aftermarket piston. The compression and rebound ports have been modified for a specific flow characteristic. The dark coating is DLC (diamond-like carbon). The DLC coating is very low friction and prevents the piston from micro-seizing.

everything but the wheels, swingarm, lower fork tubes, and rear shock. Those parts are considered unsprung mass. Because dirt bikes are capable of jumping, gravity and the weight of the rider affect the sprung mass. The movement of a motorcycle's suspension going up is termed rebound and the movement down is compression.

Changes in the motion of a motorcycle can cause it to roll, pitch, yaw, or any combination thereof. When a motorcycle accelerates, the bike pitches backward. The driving chain forces try to wrap the swingarm underneath the bike. That cannot occur because the shock is a finite length and connects the swingarm to the frame, but it causes a transfer of force. The rear wheel pushes down into the ground, transferring force up the swingarm and causing the front end to lift. The natural tendency of the rear wheel is to hop because the damping isn't enough to compensate for the spring force. When a motorcycle brakes for a turn, the bike pitches forward, shifting the weight to the front. The rear end tends to kick because of the torque reaction of the brake caliper on the swingarm and the weight shift.

When a motorcycle is turned, it rolls, pitches, and yaws at the apex of the turn—complicated motion! The front

end is forced to either compress or change the fork angle or extend and plow out of the turn. Meanwhile, the rear end tries to make a radial motion without losing traction and spinning out.

INTERNAL AND EXTERNAL ADJUSTMENTS

Suspension dampers can be adjusted internally and externally. External adjustments are limited to the riding circumstances and the adjustment range on the compression and rebound clickers. Internal adjustments are virtually unlimited because they encompass revalving and re-porting the damper piston and valve shim stack.

The external adjusters, low-speed compression and rebound, can only effect minor changes in handling. Typical low-speed compression or rebound riding situations might include far-spaced shallow whoops, tabletop jumps, and braking and accelerating around tight turns. All compression and rebound clicker adjusters are marked S and H, meaning soft and hard. That can also be interpreted as soft–fast and hard–stiff.

A professional suspension tuner's work revolves around internal adjustments. When a suspension component is revalved, it is also rebuilt, meaning that the bushings and seals are checked for replacement and the oil is changed.

Revalving is the discipline of repositioning, removing, or replacing valve shims in such an order as to effect a change in the damper's performance.

AFTERMARKET PISTON KITS

The latest trend is to combine a piston design with a valve shim pack so as to effect a greater change. There are three main types of piston/shim systems. The manufacturers are MX-TECH, Race Tech (Gold Valve), and Pro-Action (3-Stage Incremental). The main difference between the three is the port design of the piston. The Race Tech setup relies on a high-flow piston with a large series of shims that can be rearranged in set patterns to adapt to the needs of a set number of rider profiles. The Pro-Action setup relies on a piston with smaller ports and a multi-stage shim arrangement that separates the circuits of passive and active to give the damper a wider tuning range. The piston works at the edge of the spectrum and provides a hydraulic lock capability during riding situations where all the suspension travel is used quickly. The MX-TECH design uses a unique piston port

Force vs. Displacement

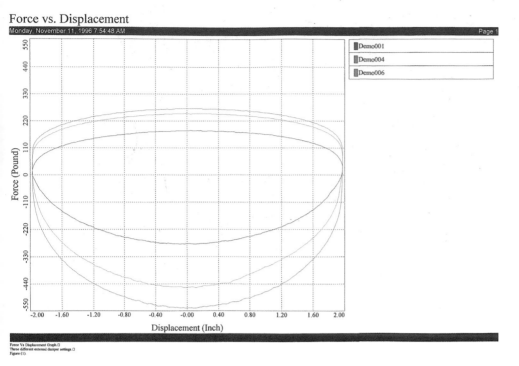

Force Vs Displacement Graph.
Three different external damper settings.
Figure (1).

This is a printout from a shock dyno run. Shock dynos are used mainly to bench test shocks to identify problems such as stiction and trapped air. There are only a few shock dynos in the world capable of simulating the rigors seen in professional motocross.

arrangement and a DLC (diamond-like coating) to prevent the piston ring from seizing and premature failure of sealing.

The Race Tech Gold Valve is simple and can be installed by inexperienced technicians. The support provided by Race Tech is excellent. The kits come with detailed instructions, an optional video, and training seminars geared toward amateur race tuners and home-based mechanics. The MX-TECH and Pro-Action 3-Stage Incremental valve aren't available over the counter. Only company technicians can install them. The reason is that the valving must be set up for the individual, and there is a wide variety of valving patterns to suit virtually any rider profile. The Pro-Action approach also relies on matching the proper spring to the valving. MX-TECH and Pro-Action's setups are more expensive than a typical revalving job, but they are more comprehensive and produce a truly custom result.

HOW INCREMENTAL VALVING WORKS

The rear shock valve stack is comprised of a series of steel washers with a variety of outer diameters and thicknesses, mounted on two sides of a piston. This is called a bi-directional valve. One side handles the compression damping and the other handles the rebound damping. The valve shim stacks have different arrangement patterns because the compression stack aids the spring and the rebound stack controls the stored energy release of the spring. With regards to the sizes of the shims, the larger the diameter and the thinner the thickness, the more easily the shim will bend and increase oil flow through the piston. The faster the oil flow, the less the damping. Stock Japanese dampers use high-flow pistons with a complicated series of shims that aren't very sensitive at slow shaft speeds. The shims don't open at slow shaft speeds and the clickers primarily control the damping. However, that can

cause potential handling problems when accelerating out of turns. The bike is riding at a point on the rear spring where the clickers don't provide enough damping and the piston valving isn't in the response range, so the bike chatters. The incremental valving concept separates the three main damping phases of low, mid, and high. They do this by using a special piston and a valve stack with transition shims to separate the three circuits. The incremental valve stack is more sensitive at low shaft speeds so the clickers don't have to carry the damping load. The mid-speed valve helps make the transition from low- to high-speed damping modes to give a plush ride especially under an acceleration load. The piston has smaller ports, which provide a hydraulic lock effect at high shaft speeds, which reduces the load on the nitrogen-charged gas bladder and the elastomer foam bumper.

THE SHOCK DYNO

A shock dyno is a computer-controlled, electro-hydraulic machine that simulates and measures the damping characteristics of dampers (rear shock or front fork). A shock dyno is comprised of an electric motor, a hydraulic ram, a mounting guide, and a load cell (pressure transducer). A shock dyno quantifies how much resistance (force in pounds) the damper produces at different shaft speeds (velocity in inches/second) and stroke lengths (displacement/travel in inches).

The load cell is connected to a PC program that plots the damping of the compression and rebound over a range of shaft speeds. The two basic types of graphic plots that a shock dyno provides are force versus velocity and force versus displacement. There is an optimum profile for the plots, so a suspension technician can use the results of the plots to see if there is an obvious problem with a shock or fork. The force versus displacement plots can show how smoothly valve shims are opening, if there is air trapped in the shock, the condition of the seals and bushings, and the condition of the oil with regards to fading over time. The shock dyno can

Rich Rohrich made his YZF and CRF motorcycles easier to manage by having MX-TECH perform the typical super-moto suspension setup, including limiting the travel and lowering the ride height, stiffening the spring rate, and adding more rebound damping. The result is a lower center of gravity and a bike that hugs the inside line on turns.

Limiting the travel with spacers between the stop plate and seal pack serves to shorten suspension components.

also test the condition of the adjusters, the gas bladder, and the bearing on the top mount. In auto sports, it's routine to test shocks before and after servicing. It enables the professional suspension technician to test and verify his work.

SUSPENSION TUNING FOR UNIQUELY SIZED PEOPLE

The thing that most frustrates me about dirt bikes is that they're all the same size. Riders are made in all different sizes but dirt bikes are made for skinny guys who are 5 feet 10 in. Over the years, my website has been posed questions from every shape of dirt biker imaginable. The questions can be divided into two categories: too big or not tall enough to touch the ground. Here are some setup tips from experimentation by real dirt bikers.

This photo compares the reduced-travel bike next to a standard MX bike. A bit of ground clearance is sacrificed for a ride height that makes the bike easier to control for most riders. A lower center of gravity makes the bike easier to turn. Lowered bikes are ideal for woods riding, DTX, or supermoto.

Shortening Suspension for Rider Comfort
Ever wonder why dirt bikes are built with 12 in. of travel when 4 in. of it is sag? Why don't the manufacturers offer an option of providing a kit to give a bike 8 good in. of travel? Perhaps they will after they read this book! Suspension

tuners have the capability of modifying forks and shocks for shortened lengths. FMF's contractive suspension was basically a suspension whereby springs were fitted to the rebound side of the shock shaft or fork damper rods. When the bike topped out its suspension, it would

rely on the springs to contract to the point the bike normally sags to (8 in.). The magazine tested some prototype bikes and raved about the handling through turns but criticized the bike for its vulnerability at getting grounded in deep ruts.

Average giant Fritz Huebner modified his KTM540 for his unique ergonomics. Huebner installed the Barry Hawk replica tall handlebars, a GUTZ Racing extra-tall seat, and Fastway offset adjustable foot pegs.

Jeremy Wilkey of MX-TECH (www.mx-tech.com), a suspension tuner outside Chicago, specializes in all sorts of suspension tuning but especially shortening suspension for DTX (dirt track) and other off-road applications. When performing such modifications, many factors have to be considered. When you make one change to a suspension component, it affects several other things. A suspension component can be shortened a few different ways. For a rear shock, a spacer can be turned on a lathe and fitted between the rebound stop washer and the seal pack. A 1-in.-long spacer will shorten the rear travel by 4 in. because of the linkage system. Most shocks have enough threads on the shock body to accommodate adjustment of the spring. If they don't, the spring must be shortened. When a spring is shortened, it becomes effectively stiffer. When the spring is stiffer, the rebound damping must be increased to compensate for the additional potential stored energy of the stiffer spring. Generally speaking, if you are a heavy person, shortening the travel will adjust the spring to your weight but the shock will still need to be revalved. If

you are a lightweight person, you may need to switch to a progressive shock spring. Obviously, by changing the ride height of the bike, the rising rate of the linkage system is going to be narrowed. One product that is available to adjust the linkage ratio is the DeVol Link. The mounts of this product are fitted with adjustable lugs. For modifications to the front forks, it may be possible to just shorten the spring and place the cutoff section of spring on the rebound rod in place of the top-out spring. I did that on my XR600 to make contractive suspension. Some types of cartridge forks don't have the space for a spring but a plastic or elastomer foam rubber spacer can be made to shorten the fork travel. Like the rear shock, the spring rate is the biggest factor. You don't have to shorten the front travel as much as the rear because you can still adjust the forks at the triple clamps. Normally, a bike with shortened travel will be better suited for low-speed riding. Consideration will need to be given when jumping or riding through deep ruts because the lowered ground clearance will make the bike more prone to grounding out.

Ergonomics for Big Guys

Big guys face the same problems as the vertically challenged. Dirt bikes just aren't designed for them either. A lot of big guys adjust their bikes by revalving the suspension and installing a stiffer set of springs. Tall guys have the added problem of leverage. When they stand up and lean forward or backward they can easily change the pitch of the bike and drastically affect the handling. That's why stiff springs are important. Some popular mods that big guys perform to customize dirt bikes are a taller seat using special seat foam and covers manufactured by GUTZ, handlebars with a high rise, forward offset handlebar clamps, extended shift and brake levers, and wider foot pegs by Fastway. These mods are done to adjust the ergonomics of the bike but may compromise the handling.

Engineering students and suspension tuners e-mail all the time with questions about other books on suspension tuning and motorcycle engineering topics. Check out the sidebar titled "The Technogeek's Library" for suggestions on more advanced books.

FRAME CARE

Most people think of the frame as the thing that all the rest of the motorcycle parts bolt to. That is true in a sense, but a frame can be a tunable component of the suspension system. The stiffness of the frame is one thing that distinguishes a new bike from an old bike. A stiff frame gives you confidence when you ride, the confidence of knowing that you can bottom the bike from jumps or stuff it into a berm without losing control.

Let's think about what makes a frame feel worn out and twitchy. The front forks, shock linkage, and swingarm are fastened to the frame with large bolts that pivot on bearings. When the bolts loosen up, the bearings lose the side tension needed to keep the components in alignment. If the bearings are worn on the linkage, dangerous side forces will be applied to the shock as it compresses, increasing rear stiction,

Strengthen the frame with a gusset plate over the area where the bottom of the frame tubes butt to the linkage bracket.

causing a handling problem or, worse, a bent shock shaft. Also, the tapered roller bearings that support the triple clamp assembly loosen up over time, and too little tension will allow the fork assembly to rock back and forth when the bike hits bumps and when braking for turns. Slop in the steering head bearings is the major reason for side-to-side shaking of the front end.

This section is a guide to inspecting and protecting a frame and its attached components. You'll read tips on how to care for the bearings and tension pivot bolts, and how the factory race teams gusset frames for greater strength.

INSPECTING THE FRAME

Most dirt bike frames are made of mild steel with only 2 percent chrome-moly.

Metal fatigue can occur when the engine mount bolts or pivot bolts get loose. Excessive vibration from the engine and flex forces from the swingarm and steering head can cause frame cracks. Check for frame cracks where the neck is welded to the top and down tubes. Also check the engine mount sleeve flanges that are welded on each side of the tube because cracks can form around the circumference of the tube. This is a common failure on early model KX perimeter frames. Some bikes have thin plates for engine mounts. The manufacturer doesn't weld along the entire seam of the plate and frame tube; they only spot-weld the plate at key places. Look for cracks on the spot welds. The frame can crack at both the motor mounts and the top shock mounting plate. Also, if the bottom frame tubes aren't covered with a skid plate, they may be susceptible to water corrosion, so inspect the bottom of the frame too.

Frames become sprung with use, the most common evidence of which is a "spreading apart" at the engine cradle. That's why you often hear a cracking noise and see gaps open up between the mounts and the engine when you loosen the engine mounts.

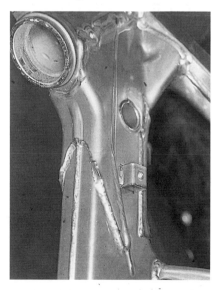

This is a view of the neck of the frame. Japanese frames are spot-welded. Pros have their frames welded along all the seams and mount plates. It's a lot of work but worth it to have a stiff frame.

The trend in modern dirt bikes is going toward aluminum frames. This bike is Marnicq Bervoets' factory YZF from the 2000 season. Yamaha tested the frame for five years before making it production. It is a combination of cast and billet sections TIG-welded together.

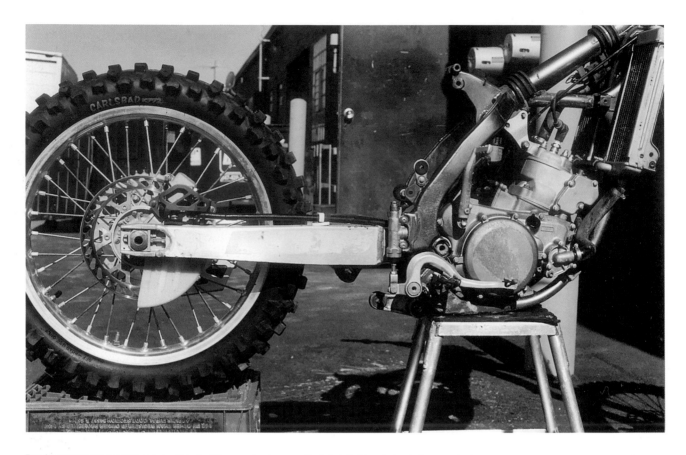

To gain access to the linkage bearings, place the bike on a stand, remove the linkage bolts, and elevate the rear wheel.

To service the linkage, start with the most over-looked part—the spherical bearing of the top shock mount. Removing the shock makes it easier to service the linkage.

The basic linkage setup: two pull rods, three pivot bolts, and a link.

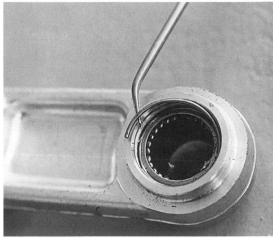

Some linkage bearings are retained by circlips. Remove the clips before attempting to remove the bearing races or you could break the linkage.

Place the parts in a container and wash off the dirt and grease in mineral spirits solvent. Linkage bearings are full-complement, meaning that they don't have retaining cages. Be aware that all the individual needle bearings will fall out when you clean the linkage.

TIGHTENING PIVOT BOLTS

The torque on the pivot bolts is critical. If it is too high, the swingarm and linkage will bind. If the torque is too low, the swingarm and linkage will twist when the suspension is bottomed, making the bike handle twitchy. See your service manual for correct torque figures.

Shimming the mounts is as important as tightening the bolts to the proper torque. As mentioned earlier, frames tend to spread out near the engine cradle, which results in gaps between the mounts and the engine, swingarm, or top shock mounting plate that bolts to the mounts. If you tighten the bolts on perimeter frames without shimming these gaps, you put the frame under considerable stress, and the stress may cause the frame to crack faster than normal. Kawasaki makes thin engine mount shims (8 mm and 10 mm inside diameter) that can be inserted between the engine and frame to take up the excess clearance and reduce the stress on the frame. These shims fit the motor mounts of any Japanese dirt bike.

LINKAGE SERVICE
SERVICING REAR SUSPENSION LINKAGE

Remove the link bolt that fastens the linkage to the swingarm and elevate the rear wheel with the 10-in. block. This allows greater access to the shock bolt and other link pivot bolts. Take care when removing the links because some bikes use thin shim washers between the linkages. The linkage consists of two main parts: the frame-mounted link arms and the swingarm-mounted link bar.

Remove the rubber seals from the ends of the pivot bushings. Push the bushings halfway out and use degreaser and a shop towel to remove the old grease and dirt buildup. If the needle bearings are dry or corroded, the seals are leaking and the bearings and seals should be replaced. If the bearings still have grease on them, use a small brush to apply new grease to the bearings. Take care not to displace any of the needle bearings because they don't have a race-cage to hold them in place. Repeat this procedure for the bearings on the other side of the linkage.

If you have to change the bearing races, use a hydraulic press and a couple of sockets—one with a diameter bigger than the bearing on the bottom and one socket with a slightly smaller diameter than the race to press down from the top.

To grease the swingarm pivots, you'll have to remove the swingarm pivot bolt. You may have to remove the brake pedal to remove the pivot bolt, and you should grease the brake pivot too. Remove the chain or you won't be able to extend the swingarm back far enough to reach the pivot bearings. The pivot bolt may be difficult to remove, so use a brass drift rod and a hammer to drive the bolt out. The brass rod is softer than the pivot bolt and won't damage the threads. If the bolt is still very difficult to remove, loosen the engine mounting bolts. Clean and grease the bearings and bushings the same way you did for the linkage parts.

QUICK LINK LUBING

Follow these steps to quickly lubricate the rear suspension link:

1. Place the bike on a stand and remove the linkage pivot bolt that goes through the swingarm.
2. Elevate the rear wheel with a 6-in.-tall block.
3. Unbolt the link stay bars from the frame.
4. Clean the old grease and dirt from the seals and bearings with a rag and re-grease the bearings with wheel bearing grease.
5. Reinstall the parts and torque the linkage pivots to factory specs.

DeVol makes these trick linkage systems that feature eccentric inserts to change the rising rate ratio.

Use a good grade of grease and apply it deep into the bearings with a small brush.

SUSPENSION TROUBLESHOOTING

FRONT FORKS: PROBLEM (P), CAUSE (C), AND ACTION (A) SUGGESTIONS

P) *Front end bottoms after big jumps.*
C) Fork springs too soft; fork oil level too low; mid-valve compression damping too soft.
A) Install stiffer springs; raise fork oil level 10 mm; revalve HSC for more damping.

P) *Forks make clunking sound on bottoming.*
C) Fork oil level too low; bottoming cone needs more aggressive angle or length.
A) Raise oil level; install aftermarket bottoming cone or air tanks.

P) *Forks make clunking sound when topping out.*
C) Forks rebound too fast.
A) Check bushing in the top of damper rod head; check top-out spring or stop.

P) *Forks shudder when riding downhill over bumps.*
C) Fork tubes unbalanced; spring rate, oil level, and height in triple clamps or torque.
A) Service forks; check spring lengths, carefully set axle clamp, and triple clamp torque.

P) *Headshaking occurs on deceleration.*
C) Front tire pressure too low or sidewalls are shot; fork springs too soft or not enough preload; fork oil level too low; fork compressed reducing trail and loss of self-steering.
A) Increase tire pressure to 15 psi, check for cracks in tire's sidewall; change to stiffer springs or add preload spacers; raise fork oil level 5 mm; install a steering damper.

P) *Forks dive during braking.*
C) Fork springs too soft or worn out; fork oil level too low, fork oil contaminated, compression valve stuck open from trapped debris, damper bushing worn out; LSC too soft.
A) Replace fork springs with the correct rate; service forks; turn LSC adjuster in three clicks.

P) *Front end climbs out of ruts.*
C) LSC too stiff; springs have too much preload.
A) Turn compression clicker out three clicks; set spring preload to 5 to 10 mm.

P) *Front end oversteers and washes out in turns.*
C) Fork springs too stiff; LSC too stiff; fork tubes do not overlap enough.
A) Install softer springs; turn out compression adjuster three clicks; increase fork tube overlap 5 mm.

P) *Front end understeers and high sides in turns.*
C) Fork tube to clamp overlap too great; fork springs too soft; LSC too soft.
A) Reduce fork tube overlap; install stiffer springs; turn in compression adjuster three clicks.

P) *Forks compress with inconsistent feel.*
C) Fork clamps at axle out of alignment; lower triple clamp bolts too tight.
A) Realign front axle clamps; loosen and re-torque triple clamp bolts.

P) *Forks lock when riding up the face of a steep jump at speed or when landing into the face of a jump.*
C) Mid-speed valves are too stiff.
A) Revalve mid-valve for softer damping.

P) *Fork sag reduced after riding in hot weather.*
C) Fork bushings worn, allowing aeration and pressure buildup in forks; fork oil contaminated.
A) Service forks; let forks cool down, fully extend and bleed off air pressure through fork caps.

P) *Front end rattles and shakes fore and aft when riding or braking over bumps.*
C) Steering head bearings loose or worn.
A) Check steering head bearings and preload torque.

P) *Front end self-centers and steering feels knotchy.*
C) Steering head bearings worn.
A) Replace steering head bearings and races.

P) *Race sag more than 2 in.*
C) Fork springs worn out or too soft of a spring rate.
A) Install stiffer springs.

P) *Fork seals are chronic leakers.*
C) Fork tubes scratched; bushings worn out; seals not installed properly.
A) Check tube for scratches; replace bushings seals and wipers; wrap a plastic bag around seals on installation and use Teflon grease on the seals and wipers.

REAR SHOCK: PROBLEM, CAUSE, AND ACTION SUGGESTIONS

P) *Bike has too much sag.*
C) Spring needs more preload.
A) Tighten the spanner ring on the shock to reduce sag, tighten jam nut.

P) *Bike has too little sag.*
C) Spring needs less preload.
A) Loosen the spanner ring on the shock to increase sag, tighten jam nut.

P) *Bike has too much unladen sag when the race sag is correct.*
C) Spring rate is too stiff for the rider's weight.
A) Install the next lower rate spring.

P) *Bike has too little unladen sag when the race sag is correct.*
C) Spring rate is too soft for the rider's weight.
A) Install the next higher rate spring.

P) *Rear end kicks over braking bumps.*
C) LSR is too soft/fast.
A) Turn in the LSR adjuster three clicks.

P) *Rear end chatters under acceleration out of turns.*
C) LSC too soft; LSR too stiff.
A) Turn in LSC adjuster three clicks; turn LSR adjuster in two clicks.

P) *Rear end packs while riding over whoops.*
C) LSC too stiff; LSR too soft.
A) Turn out LSC adjuster two clicks; turn in LSR adjuster two clicks.

P) *Rear end pogos when hitting small square-edged bumps.*
C) Mid-speed rebound valving too soft/fast.
A) Revalve shock or increase rear sag and turn in LSR adjuster three clicks.

P) *Rear end bottoms out hard when landing from big jumps.*
C) HSC too soft.
A) Reduce rear sag, increase spring rate, and revalve shock.

P) *Rear end hardly compresses when landing from big jumps.*
C) HSC too stiff.
A) Revalve shock.

P) *Damping performance becomes noticeably softer after riding for 20 minutes.*
C) Oil is contaminated.
A) Service shock.

P) *Rear end wants to swing around when cornering.*
C) Wheel alignment incorrect; rear axle loose; over-steering.
A) Check wheel alignment; reduce fork tube overlap.

P) *Bike pitches back as if in a wheelie.*
C) Spring bias incorrect.
A) Check front versus rear spring sag, reduce rear sag, and increase LSC.

P) *Bike pitches forward as if in an endo.*
C) Spring bias incorrect.
A) Check front versus rear sag, increase rear sag, increase LSC, increase fork spring preload.

P) *No unladen sag after shock gets hot.*
C) Air trapped in shock, gas bladder punctured.
A) Service shock and check bladder.

P) *Shock leaks oil.*
C) Seal pack worn, perforated bladder, shaft's chrome worn down, shaft scratched.
A) Rebuild shock and examine shaft for wear.

SUSPENSION TERMINOLOGY

Have you ever read a magazine test on a new bike and been confused by the words used to describe the bike's handling? Suspension terminology is a mixture of engineering and slang words. Read this section before you read any of the sections on suspension servicing.

ANGULAR MOTIONS

Pitch—A motion fore or aft, when the front end dives or when the rear end squats.

Roll—A motion where the motorcycle leans left or right from straight-up riding.

Yaw—A motion that veers left or right from the motorcycle's heading angle.

GENERAL TERMS

Active damping—When a piston and shim valve accelerate through the column of fluid in a fork or shock.

Air spring—The volume of the air space at the top of the fork, working with the suspension fluid, provides cushion effect when the forks are bottomed out.

Air tanks—A closed-end cylinder with a connection line to the fork cap, and controlled with an adjustable needle valve. Air tanks give a wider range of operation to the air spring.

Anti-squat ratio—A formula that calculates the relation between the drive sprocket, rear tire contact patch, swingarm pivot height, and the chain force lines to determine the rear suspension's resistance to squatting under acceleration.

Arm pump—When the muscles in a rider's forearms tense up to the point that handgrip is weakened or uncontrollable.

Axle—The axis about which a wheel spins.

Baseline settings—A series of standard settings performed to the chassis in order to establish a known base of information. Settings items include race sag, unladen sag, compression and rebound clicker positions, tire pressure, and chain tension.

Base valve—The compression piston and valving that fits onto the compression bolt assembly.

Bladder—A closed-end, thick rubber, cylindrical-shaped piece that contains the nitrogen gas in a rear shock.

Bottoming—A riding situation in which all the suspension travel is used.

Bumper—A tapered, dense foam piece that fits on the shock shaft and provides last-ditch resistance to bottoming.

Bushing—A bronze or plastic ring used as a load-bearing surface in forks or shocks.

Center of gravity/mass center—The center point of the motorcycle's mass, normally located somewhere behind the cylinder and below the carburetor of a dirt bike.

Chassis—The frame, swingarm, suspension, and wheels of a motorcycle.

Clevis—A fork-shaped piece of aluminum used as the bottom mount for most shocks.

Clickers—The screws or knobs used to fine-tune the low-speed damping on forks or shocks.

Compression bolt assembly—A large-diameter bolt that houses the LSC adjusting screw and the compression valve assembly.

Compression damping—The damping circuit that absorbs the energy of compression forces on the damper.

Countersteering—When the rider applies steering pressure in the opposite direction of the turn.

Damper—A fluid chamber with a means of regulating the fluid flow to restrain the speed of the moving end of the damper during the compression or rebound strokes. A set of forks and a rear shock are considered dampers.

Damper assembly—The parts of a shock comprised of the clevis, shaft, bumper, piston, and shims.

Damper rod—The large-diameter aluminum tube in the lower leg of telescopic forks.

Damper speed—The relative speed at which the moving end of a damper compresses or rebounds. The two different speeds are high and low.

Damping—The process of absorbing the energy of impacts transmitted through the forks or rear shock on the compression stroke, and the process of absorbing the energy of the spring on the rebound stroke.

Damping circuits—There are normally four damping circuits that affect the damper's speed: low-speed compression (LSC), high-speed compression (HSC), low-speed rebound (LSR), and high-speed rebound (HSR).

Flicking—The action of putting the bike into a full lean position quickly.

Front-end diving—This is what happens when the front forks compress quickly. It usually occurs when braking for turns.

Handling—The quality of response from the chassis of a motorcycle while riding through turns, jumps, hills, whoops, and bumps.

Harshness—An undesirable quality of the damping that results in sharp shocks being transferred through the suspension to the chassis.

Headshaking—The high-speed oscillation of the forks as a result of losing self-steering. Headshaking occurs on acceleration when the front end starts to wheelie and there isn't enough downward pressure from the forks to make it self-steer. Headshaking occurs when decelerating with the front brake, compressing the forks and changing the pitch of the bike. The fork angle changes to produce less trail, causing a loss of self-steering.

High side—The outside of a turn.

Hopping—When the tire bounces up off the ground due to a reaction from a bump.

HSC—The high-speed compression circuit is affected most when riding fast over square-edged bumps.

HSR—The high-speed rebound circuit is affected in the same riding circumstances as HSC.

Kicking—Describes both "pogoing" and "packing."

Low side—The inside of a turn.

LSC—The low-speed compression circuit is affected most when riding through turns.

LSR—The low-speed rebound circuit is affected in the same riding circumstances as LSC.

Mid-turn wobble—When the bike wobbles or weaves near the apex of a turn.

Mid-valves—On a twin chamber fork, at the top of the cartridge rod, a piston-port and shim valve control the active compression damping.

Nitrogen—An inert gas used to pressurize the bladder or reservoir of shocks.

Packing—When the rear shock is compressed by the wheel hitting one bump and cannot rebound quickly enough to absorb the impact of the second or third bump.

Passive damping—A piston and shim valve mounted with a displacement volume of suspension fluid flowing through it.

PDS—Position damping sensitive is the type of rear shock design that is used on modern dirt bikes where one end of the shock is mounted directly to the swingarm. PDS is a long tapered needle that fits in a series of pistons.

Piston—A cylindrical piece of steel with several ports arranged around the periphery so as to direct oil toward the face of shocks.

Piston ring—A ring that fits around the piston and prevents oil from bypassing the piston and shims.

Piston rod—A small-diameter steel rod that fits into the upper legs of cartridge forks. It fastens to the fork cap on one end and holds the rebound piston and shims on the other end.

Pivot—A fixed point about which a lever rotates. Examples: swingarm or suspension linkage.

Pogoing—When the rear shock rebounds so quickly that the rear wheel leaves the ground.

Preload—Preload is applied to the fork and shock springs to bring the bike to the proper ride height or race sag dimension. The preload can be biased to change the bike's steering geometry. For example, high preload/less sag in the front forks will make the steering heavy/slow and more stable at high speed.

Race sag—The number of mm that the forks or shock sag with the rider on the bike in full riding gear. This is essential to proper suspension tuning but is often overlooked or adjusted incorrectly.

Rake—The angle between the steering axis and a vertical line.

Rear end squatting—When you accelerate, the chain forces push down on the rear wheel and the resultant forces are transferred up the swingarm into the main frame, causing a lifting force that extends the front end and shifts the weight backwards.

Rebound damping—The damping circuit that restrains the release of the stored energy in the compressed spring to reduce the rebounding speed of the damper.

Reservoir—A cylindrical device that contains suspension fluid and nitrogen gas with a floating piston separating the fluid from the gas.

Revalving—Altering the compression and rebound shims in order to fine-tune damping characteristics.

Seal—A rubber or plastic cylindrical piece that prevents oil from being lost from the damper.

Shaft—The chrome-plated rod on the rear shock that has a clevis on one end and the piston and shims fastened to the other end.

Shim—A circular flat washer of thin steel, used to exert resistance on the oil flow through a piston. A series of shims (valve stack or valving) with varying outer diameters and thicknesses arranged in sequence to provide a damping effect.

Shock body—The aluminum cylinder that contains the damper assembly.

Shock dyno—A machine that cycles a shock absorber at different damper speeds and measures the resistance posed by the four damping circuits.

Shock fade—When the shock oil becomes so hot that the damping effect is reduced, so the shock compresses easily and rebounds quickly.

Speed wobble—When a motorcycle wavers back and forth rapidly at high speeds.

Spiking—How the forks work when the damping is too stiff/slow. This is also associated with arm pump.

Spring—A steel wire that is wound into a coil shape and tempered to provide resistance to compression forces and store energy for expansion to the extended position.

Steering angle—The angle of the handlebars as you rotate them left or right about the steering axis.

Steering axis—The axis about which the forks rotate.

Stiction—A combination of the words "static" and "friction" used to describe the drag exerted on the moving damper parts by the stationary parts such as the bushings, seals, and wipers. Low stiction is desirable because it results in more responsive suspension.

Stiff/slow or soft/fast—The damping characteristics of the forks or shock. With regard to the clickers, these words refer to the direction of rotation that you will turn the clickers in order to improve the damping. Turning the clickers clockwise will make the damping stiff/slow. Turning the clickers counterclockwise will make the damping soft/fast.

Stinkbug—A term that refers to a dirt bike's pitch forward and the damping characteristics front to back.

Swapping—When the rear end of the bike skips from side to side very quickly.

Swingarm—The rear fork that connects the rear wheel to the frame.

Swingarm angle—The angle of rotational motion about the swingarm pivot axis.

Swingarm pivot axis—The point where the swingarm mounts to the frame and about which the swingarm rotates.

Tank slapper—When the forks rotate from stop to stop rapidly and the rider's arms and body slap back and forth against the motorcycle's gas tank.

Trail—On the front end, the horizontal distance between the point where the steering axis reaches the road surface and the center of the front tire's contact patch. Generally, forks with offset axles have more trail than forks with straight-through axles.

Transition shims—These are shims with very small outer diameters used to separate the normal shims of the low- and high-speed valve stacks.

Transmitability—The suspension oil's ability to transmit shock loads. As the oil's temperature rises, the transmitability falls. For example, with every increase in temperature of 18 degrees Fahrenheit, the transmitability of the oil falls 50 percent.

Trapped air space—The height of the air space that forms in the top of the fork tube between the fork cap and the oil.

Triple clamp assembly—Includes the steering stem, bottom clamp, and top clamp. The triple clamp assembly connects the forks to the frame.

Unladen sag—The number of mm that the bike sags under its own weight without a rider.

Unsprung/sprung weight—The unsprung weight of the motorcycle comprises many parts, including the wheels, brakes, swingarm and suspension linkage, and the lower front fork legs, the weight of which does not bear down on the fork and shock springs. The sprung weight is all the parts of the motorcycle that are supported by the suspension.

Valves—Refers to a series of shims either for the compression or the rebound damping.

Viscosity—A rating system for oil that measures the oil's flow rate through a fixed orifice at a certain temperature. Also known as the oil's weight, as in 30-weight oil.

Viscosity index (VI)—The flow rate characteristic of the oil over a range of temperatures. The VI rating of an oil is directly linked to the oil's transmitability. Cartridge fork oil has a VI number of 115. Shock oil normally has a much higher average operating temperature so its VI number is 300.

Washout—A term used to describe what happens when the bike's tires lose traction and slide to the outside of a turn, causing the bike and rider to fall to the inside of a turn.

Weight bias—The amount of weight on each wheel of the motorcycle; also called weight distribution.

Wheelbase—The distance between the front and rear axle centers.

Wheelie—A motorcycle in motion with the front wheel off the ground.

CHAPTER FIVE

CARBURETOR TUNING

Carburetor tuning has the greatest effect on engine performance. When motorcycle manufacturers build bikes, they usually install jets in the carb that are too rich. The manufacturers sell the same model worldwide, so they couldn't afford to install different jets in the carburetor to suit all the different climates and types of fuel. In addition to the climate and fuel, the manufacturer would also have to consider factors such as the terrain and type of riding. And then there is the most important jetting consideration: the rider.

When I worked as a mechanic, I was in charge of jetting the bike over the course of the day. During morning practice sessions, the track was usually muddy and the air temperature was at its lowest point. I had to jet the bike rich for practice because the air density was greater and the mud put more of a load on the engine. Then I had to watch the rider and the bike perform on different sections of the track. I would go to the obstacle on the track that presented the greatest load on the bike, typically an uphill straight section. I'd listen to my engine and watch the rider. I'd listen for pinging or knocking noises or excessive smoke from the pipe. I would watch to see if the rider had to fan the clutch a lot and how my bike pulled in comparison to others. Getting feedback from the rider is difficult because they are concentrating on riding, not the bike's performance. At a pro national there is one practice session, followed by a series of qualifiers and eventually two race motos. The time spacing of the riding sessions over the course of the day was such that I had to compensate the jetting two or three times. Otherwise, the bike would either seize from being too lean in the morning or running too rich for the second moto.

Race mechanics have different techniques for carb jetting. The techniques range from asking other mechanics what jets they are running to using precise measuring gauges to monitor the engine performance. In motocross races, where most of the riders are of equal skill, a hole shot in the start can mean the difference between a place on the podium and 30 minutes of roost in your face! The difference in horsepower between the bike that gets the hole shot and the bike that brings up the back of the pack may only be a few ponies. The race mechanic can give his rider an awesome advantage if he carefully monitors the carb jetting.

This section will give you insight into the carb tuning process, from diagnosing mechanical problems that mimic poor jetting to tuning tools like gauges. It will also provide tips on a jetting method that I've developed called the "ride and feel" method, which I consider to be the best method. It's a technique that I teach to all the riders I've worked with. You don't need any fancy tools, just the ability to make observations while you ride.

THE DIFFERENCE BETWEEN TWO-STROKE AND FOUR-STROKE CARBURETORS

The difference between a two-stroke and four-stroke engine is intake velocity. Two-stroke engines have lower velocity so the needle jet has a half-moon-shaped hood protruding into the venturi to produce a low-pressure area that aids in drawing the fuel up through the needle jet. Four-stroke carbs need to atomize the fuel more than a two-stroke carb because so much of the fuel shears along the intake port and separates from the mixture stream. Four-stroke carbs have more jets and finer adjustment screws, plus they usually are equipped with an accelerator pump. The Keihin CR is a typical state-of-the-art, four-stroke carb.

The latest trend in two-stroke carbs features a pump that sprays fuel into the venturi from 1/4 to 3/4 throttles. In the past, carburetor manufacturers made jet needles that attempted to compensate for the natural lean condition of the midrange but that compromised the jetting at full throttle. The auxiliary pumps are powered by electricity supplied by the alternator (about 5 watts) and controlled by either a throttle position or an rpm sensor.

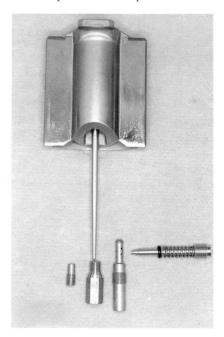

This is a breakdown of the jets of a Keihin PWK carburetor. The crescent slide and needle are on top. The jets starting from the left are the power jet, main jet, slow jet, and on the right is the pilot air screw.

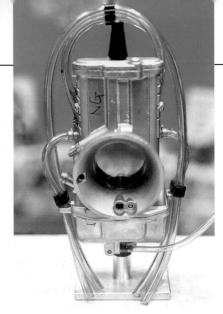

This is the Mikuni VM round slide used on most two-stroke dirt bikes from 1970 to 1986. It is common for the soldered seams to leak on the brass floats. People routinely assemble the carburetor incorrectly, covering the bleed hole in the slide with the needle retaining plate, which can cause bogging and sticky throttle. Also, the brass washer under the main jet is often lost, causing the engine to run overly rich.

This is the Mikuni TMX flat slide, one of the most reliable carburetors ever made. It was introduced in 1987 and used on many models of Yamaha YZ and Suzuki RM motorcycles. The carb bowl and jets are easy to remove and service, but removing the top and accessing the needle requires a college degree in anger management.

This is the Mikuni PM oval slide, introduced in 2000 and used on Yamaha YZ and Honda CR motorcycles. It is a short-body carb for quick-throttle response with a chrome-plated oval slide design that resists sticking. It has the same ridiculous needle retaining clip as the TMX.

CARBURETOR ID GUIDE

Keihin and Mikuni carburetors are used on nearly every two-stroke dirt bike.

Keihin has several different models. The most popular ones are the PJ, PWK, and PWM. The PJ is used on Honda CR125, 250, and 500 models from 1985–1997. The slide is oval-shaped and there are no additional pumps; it's just a simple carburetor. In fact, it's so simple that the choke and idle screw share the same jet. The PWK is the next step up from the PJ. The PWK has a crescent-shaped slide and a separate idle circuit from the choke. The PWK is used on Kawasaki KX125, 250, and 500 models from 1990–97. The latest version of the PWK features a pump to supply extra fuel in the mid-range. The PWM is similar to the older PWK (no pump) and the overall length is shorter.

Mikuni has several different model carbs too. The original model VM had a round slide. There are many different parts available, including needle jets of different diameters and jet needles with different taper angles and diameters. The next model was the TMX, which became available in 1987. It was a flat-slide carb

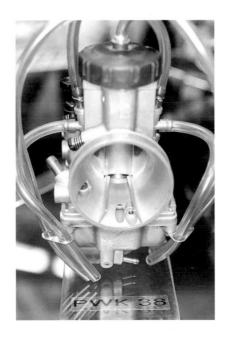

Keihin makes two carburetors for dirt bikes: the PJ and PWK. The PJ has an oval slide, and the choke and idle circuit are one and the same. The PWK, pictured here, has a crescent-shaped slide and excellent features like an independent idle circuit, a threaded needle retainer, and a set of wings to straighten the air entering the venture. Overall, it is an excellent carburetor. The PJ series was used on Honda CRs from 1985 to 1999. The PWK is used on Kawasaki KXs from 1988 to present day.

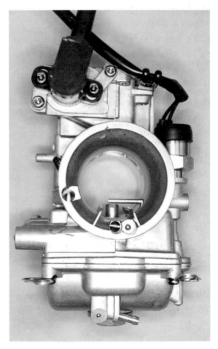

This is the electronic version of the Keihin PWK. It features a throttle position sensor mounted on top of the slide and a solenoid pump mounted on the right side. This carburetor lends itself to engine management, taking input from the TPS and engine rpm to regulate the fuel flow through the solenoid. The solenoid pumps fuel in during the midrange via the brass tube entering the venturi from the right.

and offered a greater peak flow rate. The TMX was revised several times, becoming smaller with fewer parts. The TMS carb, introduced in 1992, had no main or pilot jet. The slide and jet needle handled all the jetting. That carb worked great on 250-cc bikes but never became popular. The PM is the latest Mikuni model. It features an oval, crescent-shaped slide and a very short body. That carburetor comes standard on Yamaha YZ125 and 250 1998-and-newer models.

CARBURETOR PARTS AND FUNCTION

A carburetor is a device that enables fuel to mix with air in a precise ratio while being throttled over a wide range. Jets are calibrated orifices that take the form of parts such as pilot/slow jets, pilot air screw, throttle valve/slide, jet needle, needle jet/spray bar, air jet, and main jet. Fuel jets have matching air jets, and these jets are available in many sizes to fine-tune the air–fuel mixture to the optimum ratio for a two-stroke engine, which is 12.5:1.

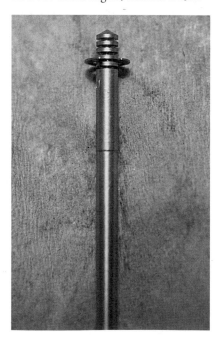

When you raise the clip, the jetting from 1/3 to full throttle becomes leaner because the needle lowers into the needle jet thereby decreasing the area of the needle jet. When you lower the clip, it makes the jetting richer.

FUEL JETS, AIR JETS, AND THROTTLE POSITIONS

Three circuits control the air: the air screw, the throttle slide, and the air jet. Four circuits control the fuel: the pilot/slow jet, the spray bar/needle jet, the jet needle, and the main jet. The different air and fuel circuits affect the carb jetting for the different throttle-opening positions as follows:

Closed to 1/8 throttle—air screw and pilot/slow jet

1/8 to 1/4 throttle—air screw, pilot/slow jet, and throttle slide

1/4 to 1/2 throttle—throttle slide and jet needle

1/2 to full open—jet needle, spray bar/needle jet, main jet, and air jet

(Note: On many modern carburetors, the spray bar/needle jet and air jets are fixed-diameter passages in the carburetor body and cannot be altered.)

BASIC CARB SERVICE

Nobody likes to fiddle with a carb if they don't have to. Wedged between the engine and frame with tubes, cables, and wires sprouting out like spaghetti, carburetors are a pain to work on. But they require cleaning just like anything else, and some careful observations can save you big money in the long run. Start by pressure-washing the bike, especially around the bottom of the carburetor where roost from the tires and oil from the chain accumulate. Take care when removing the carb—it's easy to damage the cable. It's better to remove the subframe so as to enable unrestricted access to the carb. This will also make it easier to route the vent hoses in their proper positions.

When you remove the carburetor, look at the vent hoses. Are they melted from heat or clogged with mud? If so, that can cause a vapor-locking problem in the float bowl and make the engine bog. Remove the top of the carb and disconnect the cable from the slide. Is the cable frayed or kinked? Is the rubber dust cover missing? If so, replace the cable. Now remove the float bowl, jet baffle (white plastic shroud around main jet), float and fuel inlet needle,

This is the procedure for adjusting the float level of a Mikuni VM, PM, TM, and the Keihin PJ and PWK carburetors. Set the carb on a flat bench upside down. Pivot the float lever up, and slowly set it down to the plunger tip of the inlet needle. Observe the seam line or float lever in relation to the float bowl gasket surface—it should be parallel.

and the air screw. Shake the floats and listen for fluid that may have seeped inside. Replace the floats if there is fluid present or the engine might suffer from constant fuel flooding. Check the fuel inlet needle. It has a Viton rubber tip and occasionally fuel additives and dirt damage the tip. Also check the spring-loaded plunger on the opposite end of the tip. Replace the spring if it doesn't push the plunger all the way out. Check the air screw; there should be a spring and O-ring on the end of the needle. The spring provides tension to keep the air screw from vibrating outward, and the O-ring seals out dirt and water from entering the pilot circuit. Next, check the bell mouth of the carburetor. Look for the two holes at the bottom of the bell mouth. The one in the center is the air passage for the needle jet and the other hole offset from center is the air passage for the pilot circuit. It's typical for those passages to get clogged with dirt and air filter oil. That would cause the engine to run rough because without a steady stream of air to mix with and atomize the fuel, raw fuel droplets make the jetting seem rich.

Once the carb is stripped down (pilot/slow and main jet still in place), you can flush the passages. Get an aerosol can of brake or carb cleaner from

This is a front view of the Keihin FCR carburetor used on most modern four-stroke dirt bikes. This carburetor has more moving parts than any previous model. With a TPS, accelerator pump, and a series of jets and tapered needles, it is imperative that the air filter is serviced frequently.

The FCR has a slow-speed fuel adjustment screw that makes a huge difference in throttle response in most riding situations. Here, a Pro-Tec thumb-driver is used to make an adjustment. This jet is prone to vibrating out, causing a lean bog condition. Ty Davis makes an extended adjusting screw that is easy to tune and holds the jet in place.

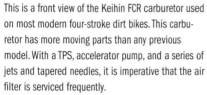

This is a side view of the FCR carburetor.

an auto parts store. Make sure you get the type with the small-diameter plastic tube that attaches to the spray tip. Direct the tip into the air screw passage. When you spray the cleaner, you should see it flow out the pilot/slow jet and the air passage in the bell mouth. Next, spray through the pilot/slow jet, look for flow through a tiny passage located between the venturi and the intake spigot. Spraying cleaner through these passages ensures that the low-speed air and fuel circuits are open and free-flowing.

The last areas to flush with the carb cleaner are the slide bore and slide. Dirt tends to get trapped there, causing the mating surfaces to develop scratches that could cause the throttle to stick. Just a small amount of water and dirt trapped in the tiny passages of the carb can cause havoc with jetting or even engine damage. How often should you service the carb? Whenever it gets dirty. For example, if you ride in muddy, wet conditions, you should check the vent hose after each ride. If the riding conditions are dusty and your air filter is covered with dirt, then it's a good idea to do a basic carb servicing.

This is a view of the FCR carburetor with the float bowl removed. At the top, you can see the slow-speed fuel screw. The three jets clustered around the center are, from left to right: slow jet, main jet, and power jet.

Damaged reeds can make a bike hard to start and run rich in the low to midrange.

MECHANICAL PROBLEMS

The process of jetting—changing air or fuel jets in order to fine-tune engine performance—is very simple. Jetting becomes complicated because mechanical problems sometimes mimic improper jetting. This causes you to waste time and money trying to correct the problem with expensive carburetor jets.

Before you ever attempt to jet a carb, make sure the engine doesn't have any of the problems in the following list. If you are in the process of jetting a carb and are stumped with a chronic problem, use this section as a guide to enlightenment.

Crankcase air leaks—Air leaks can occur at the cylinder base, reed valve, or the magneto seal. Air leaks make the throttle response sluggish and may produce a pinging sound. That sound occurs when the air–fuel mixture is too lean.

Crankcase oil leaks—The right-side crankcase seal is submerged in the transmission oil. When the seal wears out, oil can leak into the crankcase. The oil is transferred up to the combustion chamber and burned with the air–fuel mixture. The oil causes the spark plug to carbon-foul. This mechanical problem makes the jetting seem to be too rich.

Coolant-system leaks—Coolant systems leaks commonly occur at the cylinder-head gasket. When the coolant leaks into the combustion chamber, it pollutes the air–fuel mixture and causes a

misfire or popping sound at the exhaust pipe. Check the engine's coolant level frequently. Hondas and Kawasakis have characteristic coolant leaks because they use steel head gaskets. Yamahas and Suzukis use O-rings to seal the head and cylinder. Coolant-system leaks lower the engine's peak horsepower. They make the engine run as if the air–fuel mixture is too rich.

Carbon-seized exhaust valves—The exhaust valves sometimes become carbon-seized in the full-open position. This mechanical problem can make the engine run flat at low rpm and make the slow-speed jetting seem lean. The carbon can be removed from the exhaust valves with oven cleaner. Clean the exhaust valves whenever you replace the piston and rings.

Blown silencer—When the fiberglass packing material blows out of the silencer, excess turbulence forms in the silencer and the turbulence causes a restriction in the exhaust system. This restriction makes the engine run flat at high rpm.

Broken reed valve petals—The petals of the reed valve can crack or shatter

Two-stroke engines have sealed crankcases to pump the fuel–air mixture through the cylinder and into the combustion chamber. The magneto side seal is prone to failure because it doesn't run in a bath of oil. You can see the seal leaking with oil and dirt clustered around the seal and dripping down the case. A blown magneto seal makes a bike bog and run flat, eventually causing a piston seizure. If the tranny side seal blows out, the crankcase will ingest and burn oil. The spark plug will show heavy oil deposits, and the pipe will blow heavy, white smoke.

This is a four-stroke YZF engine. Notice the heavy oil deposits on the piston crown. Bad piston rings have made the engine's carb jetting seem too rich.

A relative air density gauge (RAD) is a convenient way to monitor and tune the carb jetting for constantly changing weather conditions. RAD gauges are available from automotive performance shops and suppliers such as Longacre Automotive in Washington and Pegasus Racing in Wisconsin.

when the engine is revved too high. This mechanical problem makes the engine difficult to start and can also cause a loss of torque. Expert riders should switch to carbon fiber reed petals because they resist breaking at high rpm. Novice riders should use dual-stage fiberglass reeds (Aktive or Boyesen). These types of reed petals provide an increase in torque.

Weak spark—When the ignition coils deteriorate, the engine performance will become erratic. Normally, the engine will develop a high-rpm misfire problem. Check the condition of the coils with a multi-meter.

Clogged carburetor vent hoses— When the carburetor vent hoses get clogged with dirt or pinched closed, the jetting will seem to be too lean and the engine will be sluggish. Always check the condition of your carburetor vent hoses. Make sure there is no mud in the hoses and that the hoses are not pinched between the suspension linkage.

Carburetor float level—When the float level is too low, the jetting will seem to be too lean, so the engine performance will be sluggish. When the float level is too high, the jetting will seem to be too rich.

Worn carburetor fuel-inlet needle— When the fuel-inlet needle wears out, excess fuel enters the float bowl and travels up the slow jet and into the engine. This makes the carb jetting seem to be too rich. Replace the fuel-inlet needle and seat every two years.

JETTING SHOULDN'T BE SCARY!
Jetting is the process of making adjustments to the air and fuel jet sizes in order to fine-tune the carburetion to suit the load demands on the engine and make the power delivery consistent and optimal. Too much anxiety is spent on jetting. Most people just want to call me on the phone and ask what jets they should put in their carb. That's an impossible question that the big dirt bike magazines attempt to answer just to increase readership. People get confused because they read jetting specs in a magazine, put those jets in their bike, and seize the engine. Any quoted jetting in this book is just a baseline. Most magazines don't list parameters for jetting specs such as: Brand-new bike running with VP C-12 fuel with Silkolene oil mixed at 30:1 and an NGK 8 spark plug, ridden by a really slow lard-ass editor twisting the throttle on a hard-packed track.

Some part numbers and jet sizes are given in this book for models that definitely need certain jets in order to get the bike near the baseline. There is an old saying that you can fish for a man and feed him for a day or teach him to fish and enable him to feed himself for life. Here is a quick lesson on how to jet your dirt bike.

THE RIDE AND FEEL METHOD
The most basic method of determining correct carburetor jetting is "ride and feel." This method requires you to determine if the carburetor tuning is too rich or too lean by the sound and feel of the engine. The first step is to mark the throttle body in 1/4-throttle increments, from closed to full open. Then, this method requires that you ride the motorcycle on a flat, circular course. To check the carb jetting for throttle positions up to 1/2 throttle, ride the motorcycle in second or third gear. Roll on the throttle slowly from 1/4 to 1/2 open. If the engine is slow to respond and bogs (engine makes a *boooooowah* sound), then the carb jetting is too lean. You can verify lean jetting by engaging the carb's choke to the halfway position. This will make the air-—fuel mixture richer and the engine should respond better. If the carb jetting is too rich, then the engine will make a crackling sound; the exhaust smoke will be excessive and the engine will run as if the choke is engaged. Careful engagement of the choke can help you determine if the jetting is rich or lean. Change the jets one increment at a time, either rich or lean, until the engine runs better. Most people are afraid to change a jet because they think that the engine will be in danger of seizing. Believe me, one jet size won't make the engine seize, but it could be the difference between running poorly and running acceptably.

To check the jetting for throttle positions from 1/2 to full open, ride the

This photo shows a Lamda sensor (oxygen) fitted to the tailpipe. The wires lead to an air/fuel ratio meter mounted to the handlebars. This setup works well for four-strokes, but exhaust gas temperature (EGT) works best for tuning the jetting of two-stroke engines.

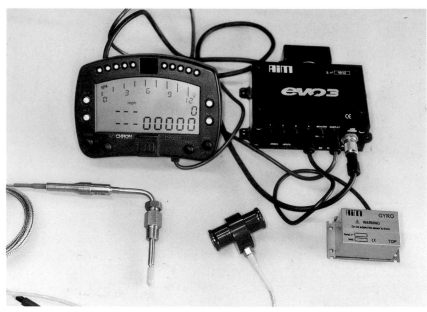

Data acquisition systems are popular in auto racing and are just starting to be used on dirt bikes. This system, made by AIM Motorsports, is the Drack Evolution 3. It is a compact unit that includes a display, six-channel controller, and a variety of sensors, ranging from rpm, water temperature, EGT, TPS, and an accelerometer (gyro).

motorcycle in third and fourth gear. (You may need to increase the diameter of the circular riding course for riding in the higher gears.) Check the jetting in the same manner as listed above. The carb jets that affect the jetting from 1/2 to full throttle are the jet-needle, main jet, power jet (electronic carbs), and the air jet (on four-strokes).

If you want to take this technique out to the racetrack, you can test the pilot/slow jet when accelerating out of tight hairpin turns, the needle clip position on sweeper turns and short straights, and the main jet on the big uphill or long straights. Of course, be careful if you try to use the choke technique because you could lose control when riding one-handed.

JETTING FOR RIDING TECHNIQUES
Certain types of riders require jetting to complement their technique. For example, beginner mini bike riders will need slightly richer jetting on the pilot/slow jet and the needle clip position to mellow the powerband and make it easier to ride. Conversely, desert racers who hold the throttle wide open for long periods of time need rich main jets to compensate for the high load.

THE WEATHER MAKES THE BIGGEST DIFFERENCE!
The weather can have a profound effect on the carb jetting because of the changes in air density. When the air density increases, you will need to richen the air–fuel mixture to compen-

sate. When the air density decreases, you will need to make the air–fuel mixture leaner to compensate. Use the following as a guide to correcting your jetting when the weather changes.

Air temperature—When the air temperature increases, the air density becomes lower. This will make the air–fuel mixture richer. You must select jet sizes with a lower number to compensate for the lower air density. When the barometric pressure decreases, the opposite effect occurs.

Humidity—When the percentage of humidity in the air increases, the engine draws in a lower percentage of oxygen during each revolution because the water molecules (humidity) take the place of oxygen molecules in a given volume of air. High humidity will make the air–fuel mixture richer, so you should change to smaller jets.

Altitude—In general, the higher the altitude, the lower the air density. When riding at racetracks that are at high altitude, you should change to smaller jets and increase the engine's compression ratio to compensate for the lower air density.

TRACK CONDITIONS AND LOAD
The conditions of the terrain and the soil have a great effect on jetting because of the load on the engine. Obstacles such as big hills, sand, and mud place a greater load on the engine, which then requires more fuel and typically richer jetting. In motocross, track conditions tend to change over the course of the day. Typically, in the morning the air temperature is cooler and the soil wetter, requiring richer jetting. In the afternoon, when the temperature rises and the track dries out, leaner jetting is needed in order to keep the engine running at peak performance.

Other changes for mud and sand riding might include changing to a lower final-drive ratio (rear sprocket with more teeth) to reduce the load on the engine and help prevent overheating. Advancing the ignition timing will make the engine more responsive at low to middle rpm.

FUEL AND OIL MIXTURE RATIOS
When we talk about the "fuel" in the air–fuel mixture for a two-stroke

engine, we are really talking about a mixture of fuel and oil. If you richen the pre-mix ratio (20:1 as opposed to 30.1), there is more oil and less fuel in the same volume of liquid, which effectively leans the air–fuel ratio. This fact gives the clever tuner one more tool to use when the correct jet is not available or when none of the standard jets are exactly right. You can richen the jetting by slightly reducing the pre-mix ratio (less oil). You can lean the jetting by increasing the pre-mix ratio (more oil). Changes in the pre-mix ratio affect the jetting over the entire throttle-opening range, but the changes in ratio must be small to prevent excess wear from lack of lubricating oil or fouled plugs from too much oil.

Pre-mix oils are formulated for a fairly narrow range of pre-mix ratios. You should examine the oil bottle for the oil manufacturer's suggestion on the pre-mix ratio. All production two-stroke dirt bikes have a sticker on the rear fender suggesting that you set the pre-mix ratio to 20:1. That sticker is put there for legal purposes. Always refer to the oil manufacturer's suggestion on pre-mix ratios. In general, small-displacement engines require a richer pre-mix ratio than do large-displacement engines because smaller engines have a higher peak rpm than larger engines. The higher the engine revs, the more lubrication it requires.

TUNING GAUGES

There are three types of gauges that professional tuners use to aid carb jetting:
1. Relative-air-density (RAD) gauge
2. Air–fuel (AF) ratio meter
3. Exhaust-gas-temperature (EGT) gauge

The following is a description of how each gauge functions and its advantages.

RAD Gauge—A RAD gauge is the best choice for dirt bikes because of the convenience, but the gauge is no good unless you get the jetting perfect. The RAD gauge provides you with an indication of how much the air density changes, helping you compensate for the effects of changes in the air temperature, altitude, and barometric pressure.

The gauge is calibrated in percentage points. Once you set the jetting with the ride and feel method, you can set the calibration screw on the gauge so the needle is pointing to 100 percent. When the air density changes, the RAD gauge will show the relative percent of change. Using a calculator, you can multiply the percentage change shown on the RAD gauge by the jet size and determine the corrected jet size for the air density. The pilot/slow and main jet have number sizes that correlate with the RAD gauge, but the needle clip position can only be estimated. Normally for every two main jet increments, the needle clip must be adjusted one notch.

AF Ratio Meter—The AF meter measures the percentage of oxygen in the exhaust gases and displays the approximate air–fuel ratio of the carb. The gauge displays AF ratios from 10:1 to 16:1. The optimum AF ratio for a two-stroke engine is 12:1. The AF gauge utilizes a lambda sensor that is inserted into the center of the exhaust stream, approximately 6 in. from the piston in the header pipe of a four-stroke and in

The number one cause of stuck throttle condition is a bad throttle cable. Improper routing caused this cable to fray above the carburetor. The cable should route through the center of the head-stay brackets.

the baffle cone of a two-stroke engine. A permanent female pipe fitting (1/4 in.) must be welded to the side of the exhaust pipe in order to fasten the sensor. The weld-on fitting setup is also used on the temperature gauges, and the fitting can be plugged with a 1/4-in. male pipe fitting when the gauge is not in use. This gauge is ideal for four-stroke engines.

EGT Gauge—The EGT gauge measures the temperature of the gases in the exhaust pipe by means of a temperature probe fastened into the exhaust pipe, 6 in. from the piston. This type of gauge enables you to tune the carb jetting and the pipe together, taking advantage of the fact that exhaust pipes are designed with a precise temperature in mind.

An exhaust pipe is designed to return a compression wave to the combustion chamber just before the exhaust port closes. Most pipes are designed for a peak temperature of 1,200 degrees Fahrenheit. Most dirt bikes are jetted too rich, which prevents the exhaust gases from reaching their design temperature, so power output suffers. Sometimes just leaning the main jet and the needle-clip position makes a dramatic difference.

Digitron is the most popular brand of EGT gauge. It measures both EGT and rpm. The gauge is designed for kart racing and is not suited for wet weather conditions. It is designed to mount on the handlebars so the rider can focus in on it. Once you perform the baseline jetting, send the rider out on the bike with the EGT. The rider observes the EGT to give you feedback on the necessary jetting changes. Once the jetting is dialed, use the tachometer to check the peak rpm of the engine on the longest straight of the racetrack. For example, if the peak rpm exceeds the point of the engine's power-peak rpm, change the rear sprocket to a higher final-drive ratio (rear sprocket with fewer teeth) until the rpm drops into the target range. An EGT gauge is ideal for dirt track bikes and karts, where peak rpm temperature is critical.

CHAPTER SIX

TWO-STROKE TOP-END REBUILDING

Top-end rebuilding is the most frequent and costly service routine on two-stroke dirt bikes. Every year, dirt bike riders waste loads of money on top-end parts that didn't need to be replaced, or they make costly mistakes while performing repairs. This section provides the dos and don'ts to easy top-end rebuilding, plus some tips that aren't printed in your factory service manual.

BEFORE YOU START

Thoroughly wash your bike because dirt stuck to the underside of the top frame tube could break loose when servicing and fall into the engine. Use a stiff plastic brush and hot soapy water to clean off the grit and grime around the base of the cylinder, on the carburetor and intake boot, and especially underneath the top frame rail. Degreaser can be used on metal surfaces, but take care not to leave it on rubber or gasket surfaces.

TOOLS

You'll need at least some 3/8-in.-drive metric sockets and box wrenches (open-end wrenches will round off the edges on the cylinder or head nuts and shouldn't be used for top-end rebuilding), needle-nose pliers for removing circlips, and a gasket tool to scrape the old gaskets away. For soft tools, get some shop towels, aerosol oven cleaner, a Scotch-Brite pad, a locking agent such as Loctite, a gasket scraper, a brush, and a bucket of soapy water. You'll also need a compression tester, a feeler gauge, and a digital vernier caliper.

COMPRESSION TESTING

A compression tester is a useful diagnostic tool, readily available from Sears or auto parts stores. Buy the threaded type, and make sure the kit comes with an adapter that matches the spark plug threads of your engine.

Performing a compression test is simple. Start by removing the spark plug, threading in the adapter, and holding the throttle wide open with the kill button on. This prevents any spark and enables the engine to draw in maximum airflow. Then kick-start the engine several times until the needle on the pressure gauge peaks. The pressure reading depends on two main factors: the compression ratio and the altitude at which the engine is tested. The compression ratio will also depend on whether or not the engine is equipped with exhaust valves and the condition of the valves. When the exhaust valves are in the closed position, the compression ratio will be greater than if the valves are carbon-seized in the open position. The difference may yield a pressure reading of 25 psi. The quality of compression testers varies greatly. The main thing that a compression tester can identify is a change in condition. Whenever you rebuild the top end, take a compression pressure reading and mark it down. When the pressure changes 20 percent, check the condition of the piston and rings. Pistons usually last twice as long as rings.

CRANKCASE PRESSURE TESTING

The crankcase of a two-stroke engine is sealed off from the tranny. It's important that the two crankshaft seals are in optimum condition. One side of the crankshaft uses a dry seal and the other a wet seal. The dry seal runs on the magneto side and the wet seal runs in oil on the tranny side. When the dry seal wears, the crankcase sucks in hot air, causing the mixture to run lean and overheat the engine. When the wet seal wears, the crankcase sucks in tranny oil, causing the engine to run rich and eventually wet-foul the spark plug.

A crankcase pressure test involves the use of a vacuum pump with spark plug adapter and rubber plugs to block off the intake and exhaust manifolds of the cylinder. The piston must be positioned at BDC to allow the transfer ports to be wide open, linking the bore and the crankcase. The hand pump produces vacuum pressure up to a standard setting of 5 psi. The normal bleed-down pressure loss is 1 psi per minute. Cylinders with complicated exhaust valve systems can be difficult to block off air leaks and harder to test. Crankcase pressure testing kits are available from Motion Pro.

If I suspect that an engine has an air leak in the crankcases, I do a visual test. Start by power-washing the engine clean. Then remove the magneto cover. Spray the magneto clean with an aerosol can of brake cleaner. Make sure to use a non-chlorinated cleaner. Sprinkle baby powder on all the suspect areas of the engine. Sprinkle the powder on the crankcase around the magneto, at the crankcase seam line, the cylinder base, and the reed valve. Run the engine for a while; the white baby powder will highlight any fluid or air leaks on the engine. The baby powder test is much better than the alternative test of blowing raw propane gas at different areas of a running engine and listening for a change in the idle rpm. That is dangerous because it involves flammable gas and a hot engine with random electrical shorts.

DISPLACEMENT	80 cc	125 cc	250 cc	500 cc
TEAR DOWN AFTER	5 hours	10 hours	20 hours	40 hours

When you do a top-end job, check the condition of the cylinder head. The top-end bearing of this bike started to break apart, and the needle bearings smashed between the piston and head, causing damage to both. The head was refinished on a lathe.

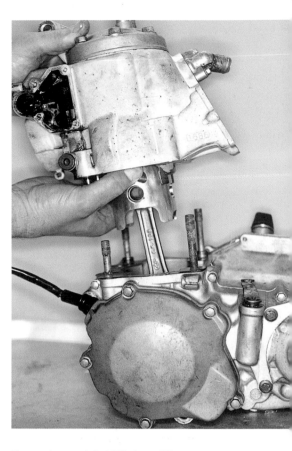

MAINTENANCE AND INSPECTION

A thorough top-end rebuild requires removing the reed valve, cylinder head, and cylinder. You should tear down your top end periodically and inspect the reed valve, cylinder head, cylinder, piston, and so on. Use the following chart to determine when you should tear down your bike:

Note that air-cooled bikes should be inspected more frequently. Also, you may want to inspect more often if you are riding in fine sand or lots of mud. When you tear down the engine, inspect each system and look for the following trouble signs.

REED VALVE

Check the reed petals for open gaps between the sealing surfaces. In time, the reed petals lose their spring tension, and the backflow can cause a flat spot in the throttle response. Stock nylon reeds tend to split at the edges on bikes that are constantly over-revved. Expert riders find that carbon fiber reeds last much longer.

Most cylinders use alignment pins to locate the cylinder on the crankcase. If those pins get tweaked or rusty, it may be difficult to bolt the cylinder to the cases. Sometimes, stress fractures will occur on the cylinder or the case. Check out this hairline crack in the cases below the cylinder bolt.

CYLINDER HEAD

Check the head at the edge of the chamber for erosion marks—a sign that the head gasket is leaking. If the head or top edge of the cylinder is eroded, it must be turned on a lathe to be resurfaced.

CYLINDER

All cylinder bases use aligning dowel pins around two of the cylinder base studs. The pins are made of steel, and after heavy power-washing, they get corroded. That makes it difficult to remove the cylinder from the crankcases. Never use a pry bar. That will damage the cylinder. Instead, use a plastic mallet to hit upward on the sides of the cylinder at a 45-degree

There are two ways to install the top end. You can install the piston assembly into the cylinder, and then lower the piston and cylinder onto the connecting rod to pin it. The conventional way is to install the piston assembly on the rod and lower the cylinder onto the piston. Never twist the cylinder or rings when sliding the cylinder and piston together. The ring ends can get trapped in the ports and be prone to cracking.

angle. Alternate from left to right sides to lift the cylinder up evenly. After you remove the cylinder, stuff a shop towel into the open crankcases to prevent debris from entering the engine.

THE DIFFERENT TYPES OF STEEL-LINED AND PLATED CYLINDERS

There are two types of cylinder bores used on dirt bikes: steel or cast-iron sleeves or those with plating on the aluminum. Most dirt bikes made after 1989 have plated cylinders. You can check the cylinder type with a magnet. If the magnet sticks to the bore, it is a sleeve. If it doesn't stick, it is plated.

This is a view looking down the exhaust pipe. Notice how carbon buildup has reduced the diameter of the pipe, which can make the bike lose power and run hotter. If your bike ever breaks a piston, power-wash the pipe to flush out the debris.

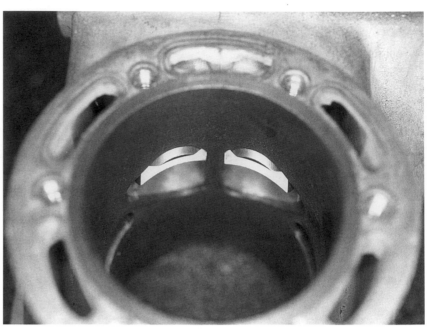

Whenever the cylinder is overbored, check the exhaust valve clearance to the bore. These valves protrude too far into the bore and need to be ground for a piston clearance of 1 mm.

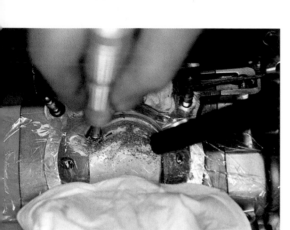

Some big bore kits have pistons larger than the hole in the crankcases. Clearance grinding is necessary and can be performed with careful taping and the aid of a vacuum cleaner.

There are three types of plated cylinders: Kawasaki Electrofusion, hard chrome, and nickel silicon carbide. There are several variations of the nickel silicon carbide process, but the most common trade name is Nikasil. The nickel-based processes have many advantages over hard chrome, Electrofusion, and sleeving. Nickel attracts oil and is an excellent carrier material for silicon carbide particles, a wear-resistant material that carries the load of the piston. The material is electro-plated right on to the aluminum cylinder for the optimum thermal efficiency. Nickel can be honed with diamond stones, which leave distinctive peak-and-valley scratches in the cylinder wall that retain oil and provide a certain bearing ratio between the running surfaces of the bore.

It's possible to rebuild a plated cylinder by fitting it with a sleeve. However, you can expect to pay more for bore maintenance over the life of the bike and lose thermal efficiency and horsepower. Plated cylinders are harder and last longer than sleeved cylinders. Kawasaki cylinders with the original Electrofusion coating or hard-chromed cylinders can be repaired with nickel plating or sleeving. Steel or cast-iron sleeves cannot be nickel-plated unless they are separated from the aluminum cylinder. The pretreatment for the plating would disintegrate the aluminum. There are four companies that re-plate cylinders in the United States. The average cost to re-plate a cylinder is about $200.

THE PISTON

Some unfortunate guys do more damage replacing the piston than the actual wear on the piston. Remove the circlips with small needle-nose pliers and throw them away. It is a common mistake to reuse circlips, but the cheap spring-steel wire clips will fatigue and break if you install them for a second time.

After removing the circlips, you have to remove the piston pin. Never use a hammer and punch to remove the pin. That will damage the connecting rod and needle bearings. Instead, use one of the pin-extractor tools available from your local franchised motorcycle shop. You can also grasp the piston with one hand and use a 3/8-in. socket extension to push the pin out with your other hand.

Too many people replace their pistons too often. The exact service interval for your bike depends on how hard the bike was run, for how many hours, the quality of the lubrication, and the amount of dirt or other debris in the intake air. Bikes that are run hard with dirty air filters may wear out pistons in only six hours, while bikes that are ridden easy with clean filters and adequate fuel octane may last 60 hours.

This Motion Pro piston pin extractor saves you from hammering on the rod to remove the piston.

Never use a chisel to break the cylinder loose from the crankcase.

MEASURING THE PISTON

It is best to measure the piston with a caliper. Digital calipers cost about $100 at industrial tool companies such as Enco or Harbor Freight. A digital caliper is easy to use and gives accurate measurements on the piston diameter and cylinder bore. Measure the widths of the piston (front to back) just above the intake cutaway—this is the widest point of the piston. Check the maximum wear specs in your service manual. Check the piston for detonation marks in the crown, cracks in the skirt, or seizure marks. Look at the underside of the piston crown for a large black spot. The spot is burnt oil deposits that adhered to the piston because the piston crown temperature was too hot. This is an indication that the carb's main jet needs to be richer.

LETTER DESIGNATIONS ON CYLINDERS AND PISTONS

The Japanese manufacturers use a letter designation system for plated cylinders. They intend for you to order replacement pistons based on the letter designation printed or stamped on the cylinder. In mass production, you can't guarantee that all parts will be exactly the same size. The size variance is based on an acceptable level of quality. Tool bits become dull, temperatures of machine tools change through production runs, and machine operators have inconsistent performance. The Japanese manufacturers have two to four different-sized pistons and cylinders, normally labeled A, B, C, and D. If they only had one size, the piston-to-cylinder wall clearance would vary between 0.001

Use a plastic mallet to rock the cylinder up evenly. Damage to the cylinder gasket surface might cause it to leak.

and 0.006 in. In the standard Japanese alpha-labeling system, "A" denotes the smallest bore or piston size, and every letter after that is slightly larger, usually in increments of 0.0015 in. If you try to put a D piston in an A cylinder, the piston-to-cylinder wall clearance will be so tight that a seizure might occur.

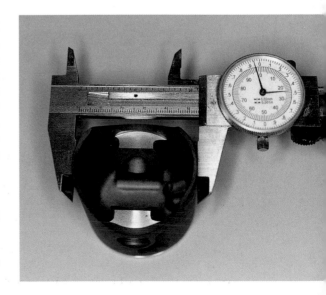

Measure the piston at the bottom, from front to back. Pistons are cam ground and tapered specially for engine running conditions. A $30 caliper is good enough to get an accurate measurement of the piston.

Pro-X piston kits come in increments of 0.0005 inch for most modern Japanese dirt bikes. LA Sleeve distributes Pro-X and more individual top-end engine components than any company in the world.

PRO-X OVERSIZE PISTON KITS

Pro-X is a marketing company that sells surplus pistons from the Japanese company ART, which makes all the cast pistons for the Japanese motorcycle manufacturers. These pistons are the same quality as the OEM pistons, and they are available in sizes larger than the alpha pistons available from franchised dealers. The Pro-X pistons are usually priced lower than OEM pistons. If the cylinder bore is slightly worn (up to 0.005 in.) with only a small area of bare aluminum exposed, you can install a Pro-X oversize piston. The Pro-X pistons are graded oversize in smaller increments than Wiseco pistons, but a wider range than the OEM pistons. For example, Wiseco pistons are sized in 0.010-in. increments and Pro-X pistons are sized in 0.001-in. increments. Before attempting to order a Pro-X piston, you must measure the cylinder bore at the smallest point and allow 0.002-in. clearance between the piston and cylinder.

Wiseco pistons are ideal for overboring and electroplating. The Wiseco rings are compatible with all types of nickel coatings.

MEASURING THE RING GAP

Measure the ring end gap to determine if the rings are worn. Place the ring in the cylinder and use the piston to push it down about 1/2 in. from the top, evenly spaced. Now use a feeler gauge to measure the width of the ring gap. Normally, the maximum gap is 0.018 to 0.025 in.

CYLINDER AND EXHAUST VALVE CLEANING TIPS

Does your cylinder have burnt-on mud on the outside, heavy brown oil glazing on the cylinder bore, or gooey oil on the exhaust valves? If so, there is a way to clean those parts without flammable cleaners. Go to the grocery store and get a can of aerosol oven cleaner. This stuff is great for cleaning the carbon from the exhaust valves without completely disas-

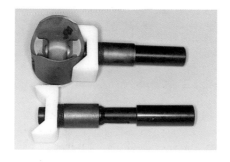

Boyesen Precision Porting makes trick circlip installation tools for 125- and 250-cc dirt bikes. The device has a plunger that installs circlips without the stress caused by pliers.

sembling them. Caution: Oven cleaner attacks aluminum; don't leave it on the cylinder for more than 20 minutes. Oven cleaner can be used on both steel and plated bores.

The oven cleaner will help loosen the oil glazing on the cylinder walls. Then, you can use a Scotch-Brite pad to hone the cylinder walls in a criss-cross pattern. Wear rubber gloves when you use oven cleaner and flush the cylinder afterward with soapy water to neutralize the acid in the oven cleaner and break the molecular bond of the oil, so the debris can be rinsed away. Sleeved cylinders (especially Kawasaki cylinder bores with Electrofusion coating) are vulnerable to corrosion after cleaning. Spray some penetrating oil on the cylinder bore to prevent it from rusting.

Caution: Certain types of cylinders corrode quickly after the cleaning process, so spray the bore area with penetrating oil to displace the water.

HONING THE CYLINDER BORE

Many people e-mail me with questions regarding honing cylinder bores. If you want to buy a hone to deglaze bores or polish off small scratches, a ball hone is the best choice. Ball hones are manufactured by Brush Research in Los Angeles, under the brand name Flex-Hone. These hones are available under different labels and are most easily available from auto parts stores. Buy a size that fits in the range of the actual bore size. Hones are available in several different materials and grits, but the profile that best suits both steel and plated cylinders is aluminum oxide or silicon carbide 240 to 360 grit.

A ball hone cannot remove material from the cylinder bore, especially on hard, nickel-plated bores. However, a ball hone can polish down the peaks of the original hone scratches and increase the bearing ratio. In other words, the piston will be touching a greater percentage of the bore. Sometimes that

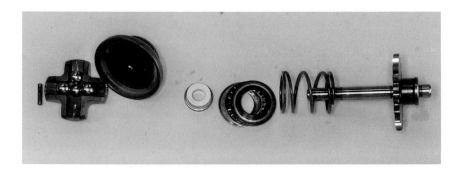

A centrifugal governor mechanism converts rotary motion from the crankshaft and turns it into linear motion to vary the exhaust port's effective stroke matched to rpm. The four steel balls travel in channels on a ramp. The higher the rpm, the farther the balls travel up the ramp, overcoming the force of the spring.

makes the piston wear quicker, but if you have to ball hone the bore to remove scratches, it's a compromise. Never use a spring-loaded finger hone on a two-stroke cylinder. The sharp edges of the stone will snag the port edges and most likely damage the hone and the cylinder.

TOP-END ASSEMBLY

1. Install one of the circlips in the piston with the opening facing away in the 6 or 12 o'clock position.
2. Grease the cylinder-base alignment pins.
3. Set the exhaust valves in the closed position.
4. On cylinders with reed valves, leave the intake port open because you will need to reach in through the port to push the piston-ring ends back in place.
5. The best way to slip the piston into the bottom of the cylinder is to rotate the rings toward one side of the locating pins and squeeze the rings with your middle finger and thumb. That will leave your other hand free to position the cylinder.
6. There are two methods used to assemble the top end. The first method is to attach the piston to the connecting rod and lower the cylinder on to the piston assembly. The second method is to install the piston assembly into the cylinder and lower the cylinder and piston on to the connecting rod. The second method

is easier but involves pinning the piston and installing one circlip with a minimum amount of free space.

7. Take care to align the exhaust valve control mechanism as the cylinder is bolted to the crankcases.

GASKET HYGIENE

The oven cleaner you used to clean the cylinders will help loosen the old gasket material enough to remove it. Carefully scrape the gasket off with a gasket scraper. Never use a flat screwdriver to remove the old gaskets because the aluminum surfaces of the head, cylinder, and crankcases are easily gouged. If these surfaces are gouged on your engine, they should be draw-filed flat to prevent air or coolant leaks.

Never reuse paper gaskets; always replace them with new gaskets, and spray sealer on the paper gaskets, so they will seal better and will be easier to remove the next time. The new-style steel gaskets can be cleaned and reused a few times, but you'll need to spray the gasket with a sealer such as Permatex Spray-A-Gasket or copper-coat.

KEEP A LOGBOOK

Keep a logbook that tracks the number of riding days and the periodic maintenance. From reviewing the log, you will learn how often you need to service the top end if you record the measurements of the ring gap and the piston diameter. A logbook also gives you greater leverage when you try to sell your used bike for a premium price.

BIG BORE KITS

One of the best ways to increase horsepower is to increase displacement by overboring the cylinder. This can be ideal for play or vet-class riders, where the increased displacement won't be illegal for your race class. When done right, a big bore kit can give you more power everywhere rather than an increase in only the top or the bottom of the powerband. Such increases are typically more usable and give you more power where you need it.

Piston manufacturers such as Wiseco make oversize piston kits for popular model bikes. These kits boost the displacement of the cylinder to the limit of a racing class or to a larger displacement class, for example: 80 cc to 100 cc, 125 cc to 145 cc, 250 cc to 265 cc or 300 cc, and 495 cc to 550 cc.

Riders competing in the AMA veteran class can ride a bike with any displacement. Riders competing in hare scrambles and enduro can race the 200 cc class with a 125 converted to any displacement. AMA motocross and enduro racers can make the 250 cc bikes legal for open class by increasing the displacement a minimum of 15 percent (to 286 cc). Also, you should at least consult with an expert before tackling a big bore kit. To get the most from an overbored engine, you need to make sure the carburetion, exhaust, porting, and timing are all adjusted to suit the larger bore. There are several companies specializing in alternative displacement kits involving both overbores and crankshaft stroking.

PORT TIME-AREA

Port time-area refers to the size and flow range of the intake and exhaust ports, relative to rpm. The ports enter the cylinder bore at angles. When the cylinder is overbored, the transfer ports become lower and wider. The same thing happens to the exhaust port. This effectively retards the port timing and reduces the total degrees of duration. When the displacement of the engine increases, so does the demand for more port time-area.

If you just overbored and plated a cylinder, it would have much more low-end power than stock, but the top-end power would suffer. Normally, tuners have to adjust the ports to suit the demands of the larger engine displacement. The proper dimensions for the ports can be calculated using a computer program from Two-Stroke Racing (TSR). The program, "Port Time," enables tuners with limited math skills to run strings of formulas for determining the optimum dimensions of the ports. Generally speaking, if the ports in the overbored cylinder were raised to the same heights as the stock cylinder, it would make the port timing sufficient to run with stock or aftermarket exhaust systems.

CYLINDER HEAD

After overboring the cylinder, the head's dimensions must be changed to suit the larger piston. First, the head's bore must be enlarged to the finished bore size. Then, the squish band deck height must be set to the proper installed squish clearance. The larger bore size will increase the squish turbulence, so the head's squish band may have to be narrowed. The volume of the head must be increased to suit the change in cylinder displacement. Otherwise, the engine will run flat at high rpm or ping in the midrange from detonation.

EXHAUST VALVES

When the bore size is increased, the exhaust valve-to-piston clearance must be checked and adjusted. This pertains to the types of exhaust valves that operate within close proximity of the piston. If the exhaust valves aren't modified, the piston could strike the valves and cause serious engine damage. The normal clearance between the exhaust valves and the piston should be at least 0.030 in. or 0.75 mm.

CARBURETOR

The larger the ratio between the piston's diameter and the carb's size, the higher the intake velocity. Overbored cylinders produce higher intake velocity, which

draws more fuel through the carb. Of course, a larger engine will need more fuel. Normally, when you overbore an engine 15 to 20 percent, the slow jet will need to be richened and the main jet will need to be leaned. Start with the stock jetting and make adjustments after you ride the bike.

IGNITION TIMING

The ignition timing has a minimal effect on the powerband. Retarding the timing reduces the hit of the powerband in the midrange and extends the top-end overrev. ("Overrev" is a slang term that describes the useable length of the powerband at high rpm.)

The scientific reason for the shift of the powerband to extremely high rpm, is because the temperature in the pipe increases with the retarded timing, and that enables the pipe's tuned length to be more synchronous with the piston speed and port timing of the cylinder.

Advancing the timing increases the midrange hit of the powerband, but makes the power flatten out at high rpm. The relatively long spark lead time enables a greater pressure rise in the cylinder before the piston reaches TDC. This produces more torque in the midrange, but the high pressure contributes to pumping losses at extremely high rpm.

PIPE AND SILENCER

Because only the bore size is changed, you won't need a longer pipe, only one with a larger center section. FMF's Fatty pipes work great on engines that have been overbored.

HEAD GASKET

Increase the bore diameter of the head gasket to the dimension of the new piston. If the head gasket overlaps into the cylinder bore more than 1 mm on each side, it could contact the piston or be susceptible to pressure blowouts.

11 TIPS FOR REBUILDING A TWO-STROKE TOP-END

1. Before you begin, power-wash the engine and the rest of the vehicle to

reduce the risk of dirt and debris falling into the engine. Once you remove the cylinder, stuff a clean rag down into the crankcases.

2. The cylinder and head use alignment pins to hold them straight in position from the crankcases on up. The pins make it difficult to remove the cylinder from the cases and the head from the cylinder. Sometimes the steel alignment pins corrode into the aluminum engine components. Try spraying penetrating oil down the mounting studs before attempting to remove the cylinder and head. Never use a flat-blade screwdriver, chisel, or metal hammer to remove the cylinder. Instead, use this technique: buy a lead-shot plastic mallet, swing it at a 45-degree angle upward against the sides of the cylinder. Alternate from left to right, hitting the sides of the cylinder to separate it from the cases evenly. Clean the steel alignment pins with steel wool and penetrating oil. Examine the pins closely. If they are deformed, they won't allow the engine parts to bolt together tightly, which can cause a dangerous air leak or a coolant leak. The pins are about $2 each. Replace them if they're rusty or deformed.

3. Never reuse old gaskets. Remove them with a razor blade or gasket scraper. Don't use a drill-driven steel wool pad to remove old gaskets because the wool pad can remove aluminum from the cylinder and head, which will cause a gasket to leak.

4. Always check the ring end gap on a new ring by placing it in the cylinder between the head gasket surface and the exhaust port. The gap should be 0.012 to 0.024 in.

5. Always install the circlips with the opening facing straight up or down; that way inertia will hold it tight into the clip groove. Place one clip in the groove before installing the piston on the connecting rod. It's easier to install a clip with the piston in your hand than on the rod. There is also less chance that you'll drop the circlip in the crankcases.

6. Always install the rings on the piston with the markings facing up. Coat the rings with pre-mix oil so they slide in the groove when trying to install the piston in the cylinder.

7. Always install the piston on the connecting rod with the arrow on the piston crown facing toward the exhaust port.

8. The traditional way to assemble the top end is to install the piston assembly on the connecting rod, compress the rings, and slide the cylinder over the piston. That can be difficult with larger bore cylinders or if you're working by yourself. Try this method instead: Install one circlip in the piston, place the piston in the cylinder with the pin hole exposed, install the piston pin through one side of the piston, position the cylinder over the connecting rod, push the piston pin through until it bottoms against the circlip, and install the other circlip. It only takes two hands to install the top end this way, and there is less chance that you'll damage the rings by twisting the cylinder upon installation.

9. On cylinders with reed valves and large oval intake ports, take care when installing the piston assembly in the cylinder. The rings are likely to squeeze out of the ring grooves. Use a flat-blade screwdriver to gently push the rings back in the grooves so the piston assembly can pass by the intake port.

10. For steel head gaskets, place the round side of the "bump" facing up. Don't use liquid gasket sealer; use aerosol spray adhesive sealer instead. For hybrid fiber/steel ring head gaskets, place the wide side of the steel rings facing down.

11. When you initially start the engine after a rebuild, manipulate the choke to keep the engine rpm relatively low. Once the engine is warm enough to take it off choke, drive the vehicle around on flat, hard ground. Keep it under 2/3 throttle for the first 30 minutes. Two common myths for proper engine break-in are: A) Set the engine at a fast idle, stationary on a stand. B) Add extra pre-mix oil to the fuel. When the engine is on a stand, it doesn't have any air passing through the radiator and can run too hot. When you add extra oil to the fuel, you are effectively leaning the carb jetting. This can make the engine run hotter and seize.

TROUBLESHOOTING PISTON FAILURES

Examining a used piston can give a mechanic helpful information on the condition of a two-stroke engine. When engine failure occurs, the piston is likely to take the brunt of the damage. Careful examination of the piston can help a mechanic trace the source of a mechanical or tuning problem. This is a guide for the most common mechanical problems.

1. Perfect Brown Crown
The crown of this piston shows an ideal carbon pattern. The transfer ports of this two-stroke engine are flowing equally and the color of the carbon pattern is chocolate brown. That indicates that this engine's carb is jetted correctly.

2. Black Spot Hot
The underside of this piston has a black spot. The black spot is a carbon deposit that resulted from pre-mix oil burning onto the piston because the piston's crown was too hot. The main reasons for this problem are overheating due to lean carb jetting or coolant system failure.

3. Ash Trash
This piston crown has an ash color, which shows that the engine has run hot. The ash color is actually piston material that has started to flash (melt) and turn to tiny flakes. If this engine had been run any longer, it probably would've developed a hot spot and hole near the exhaust side and failed. The main causes of this problem are too-lean carb jetting, too-hot spark plug range, too-far-advanced ignition timing, too much compression for the fuel's octane, or a general overheating problem.

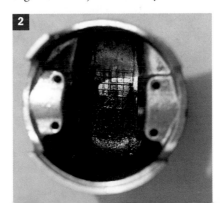

4. Smashed Debris

This piston crown was damaged when debris entered the combustion chamber and was crushed between the piston and the cylinder head. This engine had a corresponding damage pattern on the head's squish band. The common causes of this problem are broken needle bearings from the small- or big-end bearings of the connecting rod, broken ring ends, or a dislodged ring centering pin. When a problem like this occurs, it's important to locate where the debris originated. Also, the crankcases must be flushed out to remove any leftover debris that could cause the same damage again. If the debris originated from the big end of the connecting rod, the crankshaft should be replaced along with the main bearings and seals.

5. Chipped Crown Drowned

This piston crown chipped at the top ring groove because of a head gasket leak. The coolant is drawn into the combustion chamber on the downstroke of the piston. When the coolant hits the piston crown, it makes the aluminum brittle and eventually cracks. In extreme cases, the head gasket leak can cause erosion at the top edge of the cylinder and the corresponding area of the head. Minor leaks of the gasket or O-ring appear as black spots across the gasket surface. When an engine suffers from coolant being pressurized and forced out of the radiator cap's vent tube, it is a strong indication of a head

gasket leak. In most cases, the top of the cylinder and the face of the cylinder head must be resurfaced when a leak occurs. Most MX bikes have head-stays mounting the head to the frame. Over time, the head can warp near the head-stay mounting tab because of the forces transferred through the frame from the top shock mount. It's important to check for warpage of the head every time you rebuild the top end.

6. Shattered Skirt

The skirts of this piston shattered because the piston-to-cylinder clearance was too great. When the piston is allowed to rattle in the cylinder bore, it develops stress cracks and eventually shatters.

7. Snapped Rod

The connecting rod of this engine snapped in half because the clearance between the rod and the thrust washers of the big end was too great. When the big-end bearing wears out, the radial deflection of the rod becomes excessive and the rod suffers from torsion vibration. This leads to connecting rod breakage and catastrophic engine damage. The big-end clearance should be checked every time you rebuild the top end. To check the side clearance of the connecting rod, insert a feeler gauge between the rod and a thrust washer. Check the maximum wear limits in your engine's factory service manual.

8. Four-Corner Seizure

This piston has vertical seizure marks at four equally spaced points around the circumference. A four-corner seizure occurs when the piston expands faster than the cylinder and the clearance between the piston and cylinder is reduced. Also common, a single-point seizure on the center of the exhaust side of the piston occurs only on cylinders with bridged exhaust ports. The main causes of single-point seizure are too-quick warm-up, too-lean carb jetting (main jet), or too-hot spark plug range.

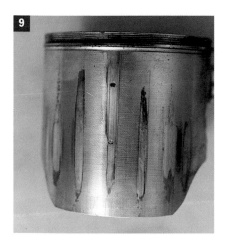

9. Multi-Point Seizure

This piston has multiple vertical seizure marks around the circumference. This cylinder was bored to a diameter that was too small for the piston. As soon as the engine started and the piston started its thermal expansion, the piston pressed up against the cylinder walls and seized. The optimum piston-to-cylinder wall clearances for different types of cylinders vary greatly. For example, a 50-cc composite plated cylinder can use a piston-to-cylinder wall clearance of 0.0015 in., whereas a 1200-cc steel-sleeved cylinder snowmobile set up for grass drags will need 0.0055 to 0.0075 in. For the best recommendation on the optimum piston-to-cylinder clearance for your engine, look to the specs that come packaged with the piston or consult your factory service manual.

10. Intake Side Seizure

This piston seized on the intake side. This is very uncommon and is caused by only one thing—loss of lubrication. There are three possible causes for loss of lubrication: no pre-mix oil, separation of the fuel and pre-mix oil in the fuel tank, water passing through the air filter and washing the oil film off the piston skirt.

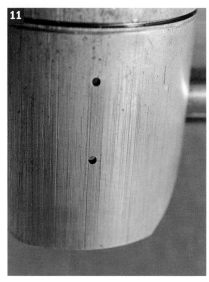

11. Composite Flaking

Most two-stroke cylinders used on motorcycles and snowmobiles have composite plated cylinders. The composite material is made of tiny silicon carbide particles. The electro-plating process enables the silicon carbide particles to bond to the cylinder wall. The particles are very hard and sharp; they don't bond to the ports so the manufacturer or reconditioning specialist must thoroughly clean the cylinder. Sometimes the silicon carbide "flashing" breaks loose from the ports and wedges between the cylinder and the piston. This causes tiny vertical scratches in the piston. This problem isn't necessarily dangerous and doesn't cause catastrophic piston failure, but it should be addressed by thoroughly flushing the cylinder and ball honing the bore to redefine the crosshatching marks.

This type of problem can also be caused by a leak in the air intake system. Debris such as sand or dirt can cause the same type of tiny vertical scratches in the piston skirt and cylinder wall.

However, the main difference is the color of the piston crown and spark plug. Dirt will leave a dark stain on the piston and sand will make it look shiny, like glass. That's because melted sand is essentially glass. Normally, you will need to replace the piston kit because the scratches will reduce the piston's diameter beyond the wear spec.

12. Burnt-Out Blow-Hole

This piston overheated so badly that a hole melted through the crown and collapsed the ring grooves on the exhaust side. Normally, the piston temperature is higher on the exhaust side so catastrophic problems will appear there first. There are several reasons for a failure like this. Here are the most common: air leak at the magneto-side crankshaft seal, too-lean carb jetting, too-far-advanced ignition timing or faulty igniter box, too-hot spark plug range, too-high compression ratio, or too-low-octane fuel.

13. Blowby

This piston didn't fail in operation, but it does show the most common problem, blowby. The rings were worn past the maximum end-gap specification, allowing combustion pressure to seep past the rings and down the piston skirt, causing a distinct carbon pattern. It's possible that the cylinder wall's crosshatched honing pattern is partly to blame. If the cylinder walls are glazed or worn too far, even new rings won't seal properly to prevent a blowby problem. Flex-Hones are available at most auto parts stores. They can remove oil glazing and restore crosshatch honing marks that enable the rings to wear to the cylinder and form a good seal. If you purchase a Flex-Hone for your cylinder, the proper grit is 240 and the size should be 10 percent smaller than the bore diameter.

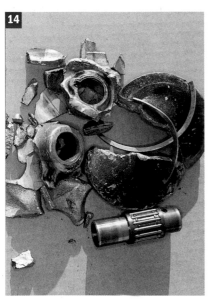

14. Shattered and Scattered

This piston was allowed to run way past its service life. Too much clearance between the piston and cylinder wall caused stress cracks to form at several points. Amazingly enough, this piston shattered and the engine quit without causing any significant damage. Most of the debris was deposited in the exhaust pipe. I flushed the crankcase, replaced the crank seals, bored the cylinder, and fitted a new piston.

15. Bridge Point

This piston has a deep wear mark in line with the exhaust bridge. Two different things can cause a problem like this. The most common problem is that the right-side crankshaft seal is leaking, causing tranny oil to enter the bore. The ionic charge of the friction present at the exhaust bridge and the oily debris cause an attraction. The oily debris works like an abrasive media to accelerate the wear at the exhaust bridge. Another common problem is a lack of proper relief clearance on the exhaust bridge. When a cylinder is re-plated or overbored, the exhaust bridge must be ground for extra clearance over the bore size because the exhaust bridge gets hotter than other areas of the cylinder. The extra relief clearance compensates for expansion. The normal relief clearance is 0.001 to 0.003 in. Generally speaking, the wider the exhaust port in relation to the bore size and the narrower the bridge, the less relief needed. Too much bridge relief will cause the rings to flex the exhaust port and break.

16. Piston Bounce

Do you notice the distinct circular line located near the outside of the piston? It was caused by contact between the piston and the cylinder head's squish band at TDC (top dead center). There are several causes for this problem, ranging from worn connecting rod bearings to an improperly modified cylinder head. The optimum clearance between the piston and head at TDC is 0.040 to 0.080 in., depending on the displacement of the engine. The larger the displacement, the greater the clearance required.

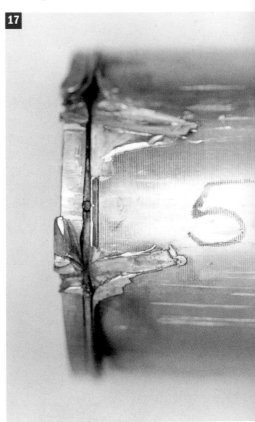

17. Arrow Forward!

This piston was installed backward, meaning that the arrow on the piston crown was pointing to the rear of the bike. The ring end gap was aligned with the exhaust port and the rings expanded out of the groove into the exhaust port, causing them to shear off in the exhaust port. This engine suffered catastrophic damage and required a new cylinder and piston.

Piston manufacturers use the standard of stamping an arrow on the crown that points toward the front of the bike or the exhaust port. Another indication of the correct piston position is to have the ring centering pins facing the intake side of the cylinder. There is only one motorcycle I've ever known that opposes this rule—the early model Kawasaki KDX 175. That model has a piston with ring centering pins aligned on both sides of the exhaust port.

18. Four-Stroke Contact
This piston is from a modern big bore thumper. The cam chain tensioner failed, allowing the cam chain to jump a few teeth on the camshaft which allowed the exhaust valves to contact the piston. This can also be caused by any other problem that allows for valve float or a slack cam chain. For example, the chain guides can wear out, the chain can wear, the cam or crank sprockets can wear, and automatic cam chain tensioners can fail abruptly. Valve float can occur when the engine is over-revved or the valve springs break. Most times this happens when an aggressive camshaft is installed without stiffer valve springs.

19. Reading Piston Burn Patterns
Reading the burn patterns that naturally form on the crowns of pistons can give a tuner insight into several aspects of the engine's performance and condition.

The color and arrangement of the burn patterns and the location with regards to the different types of ports provide insight into what types of changes will make the engine run its best.

The piston shown here is from an RM125. The bike was running a bit weak throughout the rpm range. These are some of the observations of the burn patterns and how they relate to the engine's condition and carb jetting.

1. Outer edge: The light gray color indicates lean carb jetting. Mocha brown is the optimum color, but some oils, such as Yamalube R, have additives that prevent carbon from forming on the piston crown.
2. Front edge: The two black spots align with the sub-exhaust ports and indicate exhaust blowback when the sub-exhaust port valves are closed. If the exhaust valves were carbon-seized and stuck closed, the carbon patterns would be much larger.
3. Rear edge: The two small black spots are above the ring alignment pins. The black spots show pressure leakage, possibly from excessive ring-end gap, which enables the combustion gas to escape past the ring gap and leave a carbon trail in its wake.
4. Rear band: The intake side of the squish band has some light brown patterns. That is the appropriate color for the center pattern when the carb jetting is right. If the color were dark brown, it would mean that the engine is running on the rich side or that the engine doesn't run at the right temperature.
5 Center: The center pattern shape can explain how the engine is running. This pattern is shaped like a heart, showing the flow patterns through the transfer ports. Notice the left side is slightly larger, which indicates that the flow rate of the right-side transfers is greater than the left side. That means that the area and timing

of the left-side transfer ports need to be adjusted to match the right side.

TWO-STROKE EXHAUST VALVES

Three words sum up exhaust valve maintenance: spoogey, gooey, and grungy. If two-stroke exhaust valves didn't have such a dramatic effect on the engine's powerband, I'm sure mechanics would remove them and beat them to bits with a hammer in frustration. There is little information given by the manufacturers on how to diagnose and repair the exhaust valve systems on well-used dirt bikes. This section provides a guide to characteristic mechanical problems that occur in exhaust valve systems of dirt bikes and covers tips on how to re-time exhaust valve systems.

How Exhaust Valves Work
An exhaust valve system is designed to increase the engine's low-end and midrange power. There are three different designs of exhaust valve systems. The first-generation design uses a variable-volume chamber mounted to the head pipe to change the tuned length of the head pipe. A butterfly valve separates the surge chamber and the head pipe. At low rpm, the valve is open to allow the pressure waves in the pipe to travel into the surge chamber, effectively lengthening the pipe and reducing the pressure wave's magnitude when it returns to the exhaust port. This design was primitive and not very effective on 125-cc dirt bikes. Honda and Suzuki used this type of exhaust valve system in the mid- to late-1980s.

The second-generation design features valves that control the effective stroke and the time area of the exhaust port. These valves are fitted to the sub-exhaust ports and the main exhaust port. The main exhaust-port valves operate within close proximity to the piston to control the effective stroke of the engine. The effective stroke is defined as the time from TDC to when the exhaust port opens. At low rpm, the engine needs a long effective stroke, which results in a high compression ratio. At high rpm, the engine needs a shorter effective stroke, longer exhaust duration, greater time-area, and a lower compression ratio. Yamaha used this system starting in 1982 on the YZ250. Honda's HPP system is similar and was used on the 1986 to 1991 CR250 and 1990 to current-model CR125.

The third-generation design of exhaust valve systems attempts to change the exhaust-port velocity, effective stroke, exhaust-gas temperature, and compression wave pressure. Yamaha and Suzuki started using these systems on their 125s in 1995. Both companies employed a venting system to the outside atmosphere. This is very complex because they are attempting to affect the temperature and pressure of the returning compression wave to synchronize it with the piston speed. Two oval wedge valves that enter the exhaust port at a 45-degree angle control the exhaust-gas velocity and the effective stroke. The wedge valves partially block the exhaust port, thereby boosting the gas velocity. Kawasaki's KIPS system uses wedge valves in the main exhaust port to control the effective stroke, drum valves in the sub-exhaust ports to control the time area, and a surge chamber to absorb the excess compression-wave pressure at low rpm.

A centrifugal governor mechanism opens and closes the exhaust valves. The governor is mounted under the right side cover and is gear-driven by the crankshaft. As the engine rpm increases, the governor spins, increasing the angular momentum of the four steel balls encased in the governor. The steel balls fit into an angled ramp-and-cup arrangement. A spring places tension on the steel balls. When the momentum of the steel balls overcomes the spring's tension, the balls force their way up the angled ramp. A spool attached to the ramp enables it to change its linear position with changes in rpm, and the spool is attached to a linkage system that operates the exhaust valves in the cylinder. Factory race teams have different combinations of springs, ramps, and balls to tune the exhaust valve operation and enhance the powerband.

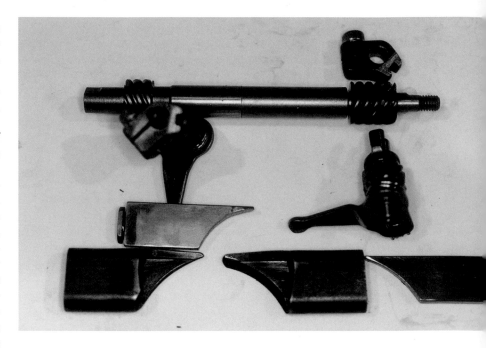

This is a layout of the CR125 HPP 1990 to 1999. Rectangular guides position the exhaust valves that slide in and out to vary the exhaust port. If the clips come off the ends of the valves, the valves could fall into the bore and hit the piston. The 1998 model uses an L-shaped guide that prevents the valves from wearing and contacting the piston. The 1998 model valves are less expensive than previous models and fit back to model year 1990.

EXHAUST VALVE TIPS AND TUNING

Although exhaust valves use the same essential principles, the implementation is different with each manufacturer and each type has its own flaws and fixes. The list below gives you tips on how to install and service the most common exhaust valves, as well as some tuning tips.

HONDA HPP

Honda's HPP system started as a butterfly-operated canister mounted between the cylinder and pipe. It served to control the volume and length of the exhaust pipe. It had little effect on the power, and most aftermarket pipes eliminated the canister. The butterfly was prone to carbon seizure and required frequent maintenance. The next-generation HPP was used on the 1986 to 1991 CR250. This system featured two sliding valves that operated within close proximity of the piston and effectively varied the exhaust port time-area in accordance with rpm. The square valves moved horizontally through a valve guide. The system was plagued with a mixture of design problems and misinformation on how to service and re-time the complicated exhaust valve arrangement. This section lists some common problems and some tips for timing the system, installing the cylinder, and engaging the HPP mechanism.

Common HPP Problems

Two main problems plague the HPP system: carbon fouling and rack-and-cam-spindle damage. The square shape of the valves contributes to the accumulation of carbon in the corner of the valve guide (stationary part) that is directly in the exhaust gas stream and this causes the valve to become carbon-seized. Chamfering the corresponding edge (1 mm) of the valve will eliminate this problem. The rack-and-cam spindles are easily damaged when the cylinder is installed incorrectly or the HPP mechanism is engaged incorrectly. See the photos for examples of damaged rack-and-cam spindle parts.

This is the CR125 2000 exhaust valve system. It's similar to the design proven on Honda's line of road racers and two-stroke sport bikes in Japan. Two main valves are actuated from a single pivot to accurately vary the exhaust port's width and effective stroke. This system has a chronic problem of carbon seizing, so you can't remove the shaft from the valves to service them.

This is the late-model CR250 1992 to 2000. Unlike earlier models, there is no manual engagement bolt. However, there is still an actuating rod in the cases and cylinder, which must align properly.

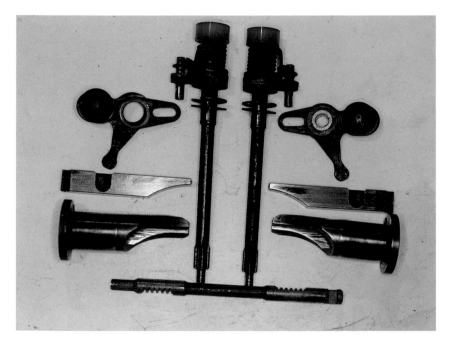

This is a layout of the CR250 HPP 1986 to 1991. This system uses a complicated rack-and-pinion linkage to control the rectangular valves of the left and right exhaust ports. The cylinder and crankcase actuating joint have to be engaged simultaneously with controls on the cylinder.

This is the correct position of the 1988 to 1991 Honda CR250 HPP pinion shafts when the cylinder is seated on the cases correctly.

This is a view of the forked actuating rod from the bottom of the cylinder. Notice that it is cracked. That happened because the cylinder was tightened down with the actuating rods out of alignment. This part needs to be replaced.

You can quickly check the operation of the HPP system of a late-model CR250 (1992 to 2000). Remove the 17-mm cap bolt from the left side of the cylinder. The L and H marks stamped on the cylinder indicate the low- and high-rpm positions of the valves. The line carved in the center rod is the left HPP valve's. You can run the engine with this cover removed to check the valves, but don't let it get exposed to dirt.

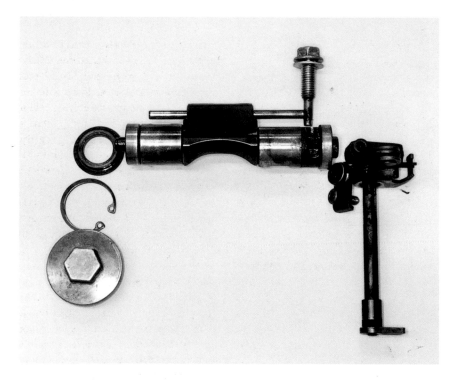

This is a layout of the CR250 1992 to 2000 HPP system. The center valve pivots from one end, and a rod through the front center of the valve links the two sub-exhaust valves. The center valve tends to get caked with carbon, hindering its operation. Clean the valve with a wire brush, and pay special attention to the center of the valve that controls the full open and full closed position of the side sub-exhaust valves. You can use a small-diameter round file to remove the carbon from the center valve.

HPP Timing Procedure

Use the following procedure to time the HPP system.

1. Install the HPP valves and levers, and tighten the pivot nuts. Place the washer on the stud first, then the lever (marked left and right), and then the flanged center bushing with the flange side facing up.

2. Turn the cylinder upside down. To position the rack correctly, slide it to the left until it stops; then move it right 2 mm. Rotate the rack so the square notch faces you. Now the rack is in the correct position to install the pinion shafts. Carefully turn the cylinder right-side-up without changing the position of the rack.

3. Close the valves and install the left pinion shaft with the screwdriver slot facing the 1 o'clock position. Install the right pinion shaft with the screwdriver slot facing the 11 o'clock position (see photo for correct positions). A simple way to determine if the pinions are mistimed to the rack is to look at the screwdriver slots. The wrong position is with both slots facing 12 o'clock.

Installing the Cylinder and Engaging the HPP Drive

After timing the HPP mechanism, the cylinder is ready to be installed on the crankcases. Here are some tips for installing the cylinder and engaging the HPP drive mechanism.

1. Make sure the reed valve is removed from the cylinder. CR250s have such large intake ports that the rings tend to slip out of the ring grooves during installation of the cylinder. This takes the spring pressure off the cam spindle. Turn the engagement bolt 1/4 turn clockwise. You should feel it positively lock into a groove and stop. Remember that the HPP engagement bolt is a spring-loaded detent not a threaded bolt. Slide the cylinder down onto the piston and rings; use a screwdriver to push the rings back in the grooves until the rings clear the intake port.

2. The HPP mechanism should be engaged while the cylinder is being installed, just to keep the cam spindle in position. The cylinder will stop about 3 mm from the crankcases because the cam spindle and the rack are misaligned. Disengage the HPP mechanism by turning the engagement bolt 1/4 turn counterclockwise. Grasp the right-side valve lever and wiggle it; the cylinder should then drop evenly onto the crankcases.

3. Bolt the cylinder down tight. The best way to engage the HPP mechanism is to insert a screwdriver in the right-side pinion shaft and turn it counterclockwise. Now turn the engagement bolt clockwise. You should feel the engagement bolt lock positively in position. If you try to rotate it too far, you will bend the cam spindle and the system won't work at all, so don't be a hammerhead. The best way to check the HPP system is to remove the left-side valve cover from the cylinder, start the engine and warm it up, and then rev the engine. The valves should be fully closed at idle and fully open when the engine is revved.

In 1992, Honda introduced the HPP system currently used on the CR250. The system features a center valve for the main exhaust port and two rotating drum valves to control the flow of the sub-exhaust ports. The system also features a return of the old resonator as used on the mid-1980s model. The resonator improves the throttle response and mellows the powerband at low rpm. A thin rod links the valves together, and the whole system is mostly self-scraping to prevent carbon buildup. The inside of the center valve has an elongated passage where the tie rod travels. This elongated passage is prone to carbon buildup over time (one to two years). The carbon limits the range of movement in the valves. The carbon is easily removed by using a small-diameter rat-tail file. The sides of the center valve and the drum valves interface, and that area is prone to

carbon buildup as well. A wire brush or file is an effective tool in cleaning the exhaust valves. Here is a simple way to check the operation of this system: On the left side of the cylinder there is a 17-mm cap bolt that exposes a straight-line mark in the left drum valve. There is a corresponding mark on the cylinder. The "L" mark denotes the low-speed position of the valve, and the "H" denotes the high-speed position. To check the HPP, start the engine. At idle, the valve should align with the "L" mark. Then rev the engine; the valve should align with the "H" mark. If the angle of the mark on the valve is slightly off, the valve probably needs to be de-carboned. The system is very easy to disassemble and can only fit together one obvious way so I won't waste space on that procedure.

There are some aftermarket parts to adjust the performance of this system for different types of dirt biking. Pro-Racing in England makes a spacer for the right-side valve cover. It serves to add volume and length to the resonator part of the system. This is especially suited for enduro riding where a smooth transition to the midrange is important for better traction. ESR (Eddie Sanders Racing) in California makes a replacement HPP system that holds the valves wide open. The center exhaust valve is thinner, which enables tuners to raise the exhaust port. The ESR system is primarily used for dirt track or kart applications where low-end power is of no consequence.

Whenever the cylinder is installed on the bottom end after top-end rebuilding, the valves need to be put in the closed position. Otherwise, the HPP cam spindle that connects the actuator in the cases to the cylinder will get damaged when you tighten down the cylinder. That will also make the valves inoperable. Always check the HPP valve operation after you assemble the top end by using the inspection cap on the left side of the cylinder.

The CR125 HPP system was redesigned in 1990. Honda chose to use a system similar to the 1986 to 1991

CR250, featuring horizontally sliding valves. This system has been plagued with problems over the years. The valves are prone to carbon seizure because the critical square edges face the exhaust stream. If the clips that fit on the ends of the valves vibrate off, or if the valve wears too much, then the valve can tilt on an angle and strike the piston. Another common related problem happens when tuners widen the exhaust port during porting and neglect to grind the valves at the outer corners for piston clearance. There again, the valves strike the piston because they protrude into the bore.

In 1998, Honda made a modification to the valves; they added an L-shaped rib that prevents the valves from angling in and contacting the piston. The problem of clearance between the top of the valve and the guide was eliminated, and the new-style valves provide more low-end power. The valve and guide sets from the 1998 to 1999 models fit the CR125 models back to 1990.

In 2000, Honda redesigned the CR125 engine and adapted the exhaust valve system used on the RS250 road racer. Honda also used this system on several dual-sport and street bikes sold in Asia and Europe. The new system is simple and effective. It is a wedge-shaped valve that pivots at one end, similar to the CR250. The valve is much thicker and can vary the exhaust port's effective stroke, time-area, and duration over a wider rpm range. It's a self-scraping setup, so maintenance should be greatly reduced over previous models.

KAWASAKI KIPS

Kawasaki's KIPS exhaust valve system has gone through steady design refinement. Kawasaki uses a different system to suit the needs of the different model bikes. The earliest KIPS design used two drum-shaped valves to control the flow of the sub-exhaust ports. Opening the ports gave the exhaust port more time-area. The main exhaust port was relatively small with modest timing and duration. A rack-and-pinion setup

This is a common problem for all KX and KDX models that use aluminum drum valves—the gear teeth tend to shear when the valves become carbon-seized.

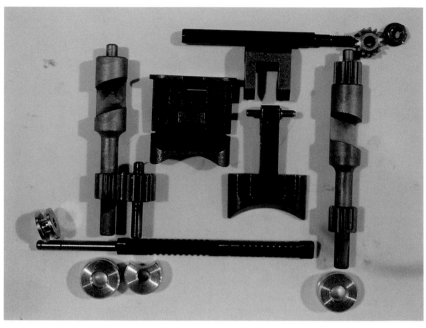

This is a typical KIPS system for the following models: 1992 to 1997 KX125, 1995 to 2000 KDX200, and 1993 to 2000 KX250. As you can see, there are a lot of moving parts. The two racks must be timed with gears to link the main center valves and the drum valves. This valve system performs well, but it requires a lot of maintenance.

All KX250s use a yoke lever like this to transfer the linear motion of the centrifugal governor into the actuator rod. If your bike starts running poorly, unbolt the plastic cover on the lower right side of the cylinder and make sure that the actuator rod is moving in accordance with rpm. If not, the yoke lever is probably broken.

controlled the drum valves, opening them at about 6,000 rpm. Kawasaki used the rack-and-pinion design in all of its KIPS systems except the 1998 and later KX80-cc and 125-cc models. The 1992 KX125 and KDX used the next-generation KIPS, which featured a center-wedge valve with two side-drum valves engaged to a rack-and-gear actuating system. The system is very complicated with all its moving parts. The top and bottom racks have to be synchronized through the left drum valve, which has two drive gears molded in it. The drum valves are made of aluminum. When the drum valve becomes carbon-seized, the steel teeth on the rack shear off the aluminum teeth on the drum valve, rendering the drum valve inoperable. Check the condition of the gear teeth every time you do a top-end service, because if one gear fails the whole system runs out of sync. On the late-model 80-cc and 125-cc KXs, the KIPS is relatively simple, relying on a wedge valve and flapper. The system is self-scraping, so it requires little maintenance.

In the first year of operation (1998), the KIPS system was plagued with failures such as the pin breaking on the flapper, the valve receding into the cylinder and contacting the piston, and over-extension of the valve causing cock and jam. Pro-Circuit made an aftermarket valve cover with a full stop that prevented over-extension and, in 1999, Kawasaki changed the wedge valve and flapper design for more rigidity, which solved all the reliability problems.

The drum valves on the 1988–1992 KX250 and 1990–2000 KX500 are aluminum but have a hard-anodized coating that resists wear. However, the drum valves eventually wear at the drive channels for the center wedge valve, and the sloppy fit between the wedge and drum valves prevents the center valve from fully opening. That is why the bikes get noticeably slower as they get older. There is no preventive cure or aftermarket fix. You just need to replace the drum valves when the drive channels wear out.

The 1993 KX250 was the first year for the KIPS system used through present-day models. The system uses a single wedge and flapper valve for the main exhaust port and two drum-shaped valves for the sub-exhaust ports. The valves are linked together with two rack-and-pinion units on the right drum valve and a steel gear on the upper rack linking the wedge valve. A left-hand-thread nut retains the gear to the rod that actuates the wedge valve. Check the

The 1998 to 2005 KX80, 85, and 100 use this clumsy pinion lever to actuate the KIPS valves. The easiest way to service the top end is to start by removing the bolt that retains the pinion shaft and lift the shaft off with the cylinder. To install the cylinder, close the valves and align the dot on the shaft with the open bolt hole or the valves won't work because they won't be timed correctly.

This is the new-generation KIPS system used on the 1998-and-newer KX80, 100, and 1998 to 2002 125 models. There are three pieces: a stationary guide, a sliding valve, and a pivoting flapper. This design is mostly self-cleaning and should be checked every time you service the top end. It's normal for a large amount of sludge to accumulate under the valve cover.

nut periodically; if the nut loosens, the wedge valves become inoperable. The KX250 KIPS also features two large cavities to allow for dissipation of the compression wave that travels back up the exhaust pipe at low- to mid-rpm. It's important that the two valve covers on the cylinder are sealed with gaskets, and it is normal for large amounts of black sludge to accumulate under those valve covers. It takes years for the sludge to accumulate to the point of adversely affecting performance. The only way to clean out the sludge is to have the cylinder hot tank cleaned at an automotive rebuilding store.

The 1993–2000 KX250 wedge valve tends to form burrs at the outer edges that face the piston. The burrs prevent the wedge valve from opening fully, and the thin flap that comprises the exhaust-port roof hangs out into the exhaust–gas stream, producing a shock wave that closes off the exhaust port. File the burrs until smooth and check the wedge valve through the full range of movement. The valve pocket in the cylinder gets worn too. Aftermarket cylinder rebuilders such as Max Power Cylinders apply a hard coating to that area to reduce wear and build up areas that have worn down from the moving wedge valve.

Another characteristic problem of the KX250 KIPS is broken governor levers. The lever that transmits the movement from the centrifugal governor to the right-side case lever tends to break in half. The piece is located under the right-side cover. If your KX250 suddenly loses top-end power, it's probably due to a broken actuating lever or the carbon-seizure of the KIPS valves.

1988–1992 KX250 and 1990–2000 KX500 KIPS Timing Procedure

The explanation of this procedure, as written in the Kawasaki service manual, is confusing. It requires you to time the upper and lower racks at the same instant. My method of timing the exhaust valves uses simple steps that enable you to check your work as you go. The 1988–1992 KX250 and KX500 use the drive-channel system to actuate the center valve. Here is the best way to time the KIPS on these models.

1. Set the cylinder upside down on a bench.
2. Install the center valve but don't bolt it in.
3. Install the side drum valves and align the drive channels on the drum

valves with the center valve, but don't bolt it in.

4. Lift up the drum valves so the bottoms of the gears are flush with the cylinder base. Take care not to disengage the center valve.

5. Slide in the rack from either side of the cylinder. Position the rack by installing the seal pack and pulling the rack out until it bottoms against the seal pack. This is the full-open position.

6. Drop the drum valves onto the rack so the valves are in the full-open position. Don't pay attention to alignment dots or marks on the valve or rack; just remember that the valves should be open when the rack is pulled out and closed when the rack is pushed in.

1992–1997 KX125 and 1993–2004 KX250 KIPS Timing Procedure

The system on the KX125 and KX250 uses both wedge and drum valves with racks. This is the best exhaust valve system for performance but the most difficult to maintain. Here are some tips for retiming this KIPS system.

1. Install the wedge valves in the cylinder and the actuating rod and lever. Squirt some pre-mix oil on the parts.

2. Pull the wedge valve into the full-open position, place the gear on the end of the rod, and rotate the gear counterclockwise until the rack butts against the stop plate. Thread the nut on the rod and tighten it counterclockwise; it is a left-hand-thread nut.

3. Place the drum valves into their respective cavities until the top of the gears are level with the cylinder base. Now, push the lower rack into place and bolt the seal pack on the rack into the cylinder.

4. Pull the rack out until it stops and push it in 1 mm; now it is in the correct position to install the drum valve. Before you push the drum valves down, make sure the wedge valve and drum valves are in the full-open position.

5. Push the drum valve down with the two gears first; it must engage the

The most common problem with Suzuki exhaust valve systems has to do with the actuating lever spring. On the top right side of the cylinder, there is a shaft that the valves are linked to. If you remove the actuating lever, the spring may snap loose and cross ends. The spring ends should always be parallel in order for the valves to move.

upper rack and lower rack simultaneously. Take care and be patient. You may have to wiggle the wedge valve yoke to get everything to fall into place. Never hammer the drum valves! Push down the right drum valve and

install the idler gear. Now install the bushings and check the system. The valves will bind and stick if you try to move the valves without the bushings installed or if the cylinder is facing upside down. Test the KIPS in this way: pull the rack outward until it stops, and then look through the exhaust port from the pipe side. The valves should be in the full-open position. On cylinders where the base has been turned down more than 0.010 in., the drum valve bushings will also need to be turned down to prevent the valves from binding when the cylinder is tightened.

SUZUKI ATEV

Suzuki first used exhaust valves in 1985, using a drum valve that uncovered a cavity in the head or cylinder to add volume and length to the exhaust pipe, strictly at low rpm. In 1987, they employed a system that featured two large valves that had multiple functions. The system was used on the 1989–2000 RM80, 1987–2000 RM125, and 1987–95 RM250. The wedge-shaped valve was positioned at about a 45-degree angle over the exhaust port. The ATEV system is designed to regulate the effective stroke exhaust–gas velocity through the exhaust port, and on 1995 and later models, it controls the exhaust–gas temperature. The ATEV system is self-cleaning in that carbon is scraped off the valves every time they move. Some of the early RM models suffered from broken exhaust valves when the stem would detach from the cylindrical wedge. That problem was cured in 1991 when the radius between the stem and valve was increased. The two common problems that occur with the ATEV are caused by two errors in assembling the system.

1. Too much preload on the spring. On the left side of the cylinder there is a dial that controls the spring preload for the exhaust valve system. The preload doesn't have a great effect on the engine's powerband, but too much preload will prevent the valves from opening, which causes a lack of top-end power.
2. Crisscrossed spring. A centering spring on the right side of the cylinder, located on the rod, actuates the valves. This spring is commonly installed incorrectly. The spring tabs

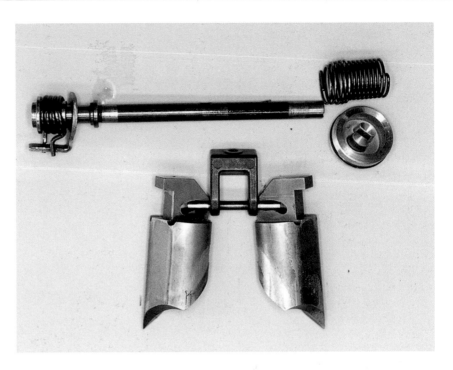

This is a typical layout of the valves used on the following models: 1989 to 2005 RM80 and 85, 1988 to 2003 RM125, 1989 to 1995 RM250, and all RMX models. The cylindrical valves are comprised of a stationary guide and a sliding valve. A knob mounted on the top left side of the cylinder provides spring tension. It's common for the left spring to get twisted in half from turning the knob too much or in the opposite direction (counterclockwise).

Starting in 2001, Suzuki changed its exhaust valve system every year until 2004 on the RM250, fiddling around with everything from electronic solenoids to cam levers and other components. Finally, in 2003, Suzuki settled on a copy of Yamaha that sidestepped its patent. My advice is: If the valves move through their operation, don't attempt to disassemble and clean them.

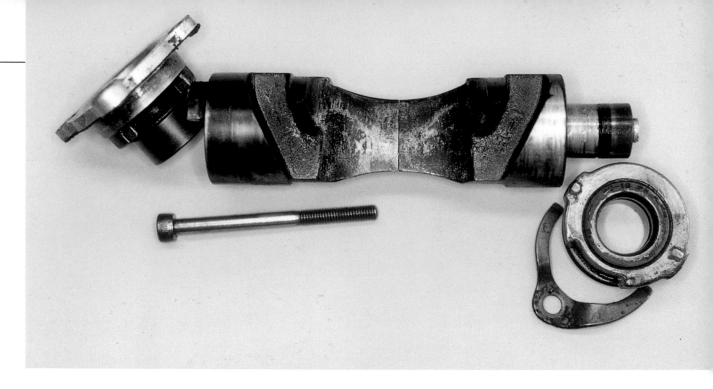

This is the original power valve design that Yamaha patented in 1972. The system is used on YZ125s from 1982 to 1993 and YZ/WR250s from 1981 to 1998. In the early years, Yamaha designed the valve with plenty of clearance from the piston. In 1990, Yamaha added a stop plate on the left side of the cylinder and positioned the valve closer to the piston for better performance. The problem is that the stop plate and valve wear, and the valve eventually contacts the piston, causing a total top-end failure. The best remedy is to grind the valve face for more clearance to the piston in the closed position. You lose a little power but save $500 or more in the long run.

should be parallel when coupled to the lever and rod. If the spring tabs are crisscrossed, the valve travel will be limited and won't open fully.

In 1996, Suzuki redesigned the RM250 engine, going back to a design reminiscent of the 1987 model RM250. For this model, Suzuki modified the Honda HPP design used on the late-model CR250. However, a problem plagued this system. Instead of pivoting the center valve, Suzuki chose to slide it in a passageway of the cylinder. The added mechanical friction made the system prone to binding in one position: half-open. This causes the engine to run flat. The shape of the valve was also a problem. The leading edge that faced the piston was too square and sharp. Even when the valve was in the full-open position it caused a shock wave that impeded the outgoing exhaust flow. Grinding the edge smooth reduced the low-end power but helped improve top end. In 1997, Suzuki redesigned the center valve, choosing steel and splitting the valve into two sections, a major and minor valve. Suzuki also added a two-stage spring

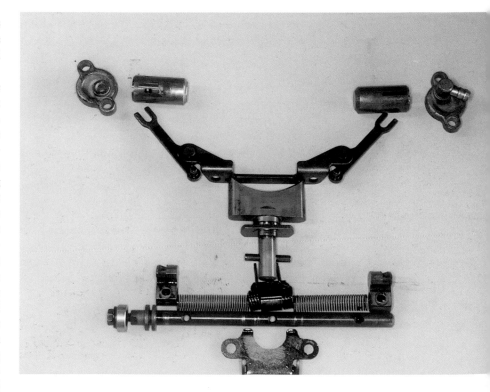

This is the power valve from the 1999 to 2005 YZ250. It's a two-stage system mounted to a single drive shaft where the center valve opens first and the sub-exhaust valves open later, based on the ramp angle of the drive lug. The sub-exhaust valve cam levers aren't marked left and right, so it's common for people to install them backward, which makes the powerband run flat. It's also common for the mounting plate for the center valve to crack, allowing the valve to contact the piston.

system. With some simple grinding to match the valve to the exhaust port when fully open, this setup was a winner. Suzuki chose to redesign the 1997 system design for the 1998–2000 models. The thought was that the steel valve damaged the valve pocket in the cylinder, although simply extending the nickel silicon carbide bore material into the valve pocket would have solved the problem. In 2001–2004 models, Suzuki added many more successive designs of moving parts such as linkages and pins. It's a very difficult system to assemble and requires a factory service manual.

YAMAHA POWERVALVE

Yamaha was the first motorcycle manufacturer to adapt exhaust valves to two-stroke motorcycle engines. Yamaha's simple design uses a cylindrical valve that rotates 1/4 turn to vary the height of the exhaust port and requires little maintenance. The system was used on the YZ250 from 1982 to 1998 and on the YZ125 from 1983 to 1993. Occasionally, you'll need to replace the seals and O-rings to prevent exhaust oil from drooling out of the side of the cylinder. In 1989, Yamaha added a stop plate to limit the travel of the power valve, primarily so mechanics couldn't install the valve in the wrong position. The stop plate is located on the left side of the cylinder. The valve has a small tab that bumps up against the stop plate to limit the fully opened and closed positions of the valve. This design enabled Yamaha to position the valve closer to the piston to make it more effective at varying the exhaust-port timing. Unfortunately, the soft aluminum tab on the valve gets worn, allowing the valve to rotate farther in the fully closed position. Eventually (after about three years' use), the tab wears enough that the valve strikes the piston, causing damage to the piston. Yamaha's exhaust valve is cheap to replace. I recommend replacing the valve when the tab wears more than 0.030 in. (0.7 mm).

In 1994, Yamaha changed the engine design of the YZ125 and included the next generation of exhaust valves. This

This is a view from the left side of the cylinder of the KTM exhaust valve system used on the 1986 to 1997 125s and on all 250s, 300s, 360s, and 380s. The main shaft has a gear plate that turns the side drum valves. Scribe marks show timing alignment. The stop plate with the two Allen bolts controls how far the main exhaust valve closes in distance from TDC. In the KTM manual, the stop plate is referred to as the "Z" dimension. If you turn it too far, the main valve will contact the piston and damage it. The stop plate loosens and the valve breaks the rings and piston crown, causing catastrophic engine damage. Whenever I service a KTM cylinder, I grind the valve face 1 mm to prevent this problem.

system used two oval-shaped wedge valves, positioned at a 45-degree angle over the exhaust port. The system is similar to the one employed by Suzuki. Yamaha experimented with resonator cavity volume and vents for pressure bleed-off and temperature control. Overall, this is a very reliable system. Occasionally, the pins that fit through the ends of the valve to interface with the actuator lever vibrate out, causing the valve to strike the piston. Those pins are a press fit but you can add some Loctite Instant Adhesive to the pins for added protection. Yamaha has added springs to the valves to control high-rpm valve flutter, but future innovations could include a positive seal between the valve and the cylinders' valve pocket.

In 1999, Yamaha redesigned the YZ250 engine and exhaust valve system. The model features a power valve that marks a significant design change from the company that pioneered the use of exhaust valves on two-stroke engines. Looking more like a Rube Goldberg device, the new power valve has separate valves for the main (center) and sub-exhaust ports (sides). The whole assembly is controlled by one actuating rod, but the side valves open after the main exhaust valve. The side valves are controlled by two wedge-shaped ramps that resemble the shift drum from a transmission. The ramp design offers versatility in tuning. By changing the shape of the ramp, the duration and timing of the sub-exhaust ports can be changed to match a rider's ability or the demands of the terrain. So far there are no aftermarket companies making these ramps but you can

Use RTV Ultra Copper silicone sealant on the front exhaust plate of the KTMs.

bet that the factory teams are experimenting with them.

The stop plate of the center valve tends to crack, allowing the valve to contact the piston. Look for cracks in the plate right around the two retaining bolts.

KTM 250, 300, 360, 380 1990–2004

KTM uses two distinct designs of exhaust valve systems. The earlier model uses one large center valve with the actuating rod cast together. Two drum valves control the sub-exhaust ports, and steel gears interface the main and minor valves. The effective stroke can be adjusted by altering a stop plate on the left side of the cylinder. The governor control in the right-side case has an inspection cap that allows tuners to add thin washers and increase the spring preload to effect a change in engagement rpm. The system is prone to carbon-seizure of the steel valves (sub-exhaust

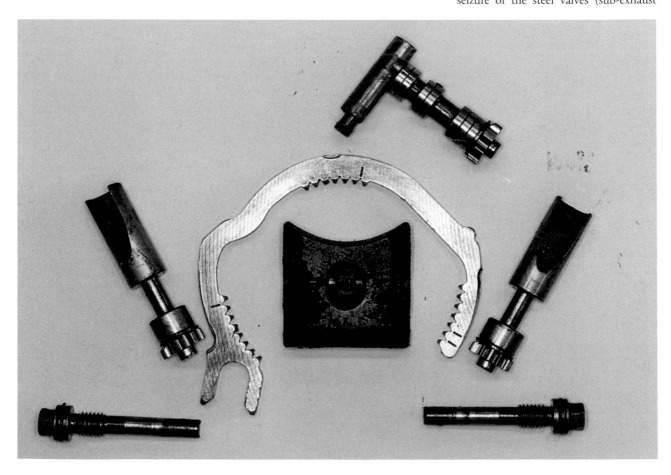

This is the exhaust valve system for the 1998 to 2005 KTM125 and 200 models. Overall, the system is very reliable and performs well.

The KTM system is easy to align, with dots on the valves aligning with lines on the rack.

ports). Also, there are rubber O-rings that prevent oil from leaking out the sides of the actuating rod that eventually wear out. In order to service this exhaust valve system, you need to remove the cylinder. The main valve and all its hardware can remain bolted together. There is an access cover on the front of the cylinder, and four bolts fasten the cover to the cylinder. There is no gasket for the cover; it seals with a non-drying liquid gasket like RTV silicone. The main valve pulls straight out.

The drum valves are held in place by two plates with two tapered, panhead Phillips screws. There is a specific procedure for removing these screws. Start by heating the screw heads for two minutes with a propane torch to break down the locking agent on the threads. Then use a hand impact with a No. 2 Phillips tip. If you strip the heads of the screws (most people do, including me!), use a tapered-point punch to spin the screws out. It will destroy the screw, but you should replace the Phillips with a tapered-panhead Allen bolt. Take care when handling the stop lever on the left side of the main valve. Before you loosen the two Allen bolts, scribe a line to reference the position of the plate relative to the gear plate. It is possible to adjust the stop plate so far that the valve rotates past the fully closed position and contacts the piston. That will destroy the piston.

The 1998 and newer KTMs have an exhaust valve system that makes use of the resonator concept. The system is so complex that you would need the factory service manual in order to service it.

CHAPTER SEVEN

TWO-STROKE LOWER-END REBUILDING

Rebuilding the lower end of a two-stroke engine is the procedure that is most often put off until next race/month/season. When you start hearing the engine make a strange knocking sound, it's time to shut it off and tear it down. Don't pin the throttle wide open and hope it will just go away! The normal service interval for lower-end rebuilding is once a year on engines under 200 cc and once every two to three years for 250 and larger engines. While rebuilding the lower end, you should replace the ball bearings that support the crankshaft and the transmission shafts, plus the rubber seals. In most cases, the crankshaft will need to have a new connecting rod, pin, bearing, and thrust washers installed. Some manufacturers (Honda) don't sell parts for their crankshafts, only the entire part. However, there are companies that offer high-quality replacement parts (Hot Rods) to rebuild modern Japanese cranks and vintage Spanish cranks. Although some aspects of lower-end rebuilding are very specific to a particular model engine, this section gives you an overview of the general process.

THE RIGHT TOOLS

Engine rebuilding is nearly impossible without the right tools. Some guys try to use the "caveman" method—big hammers and chisels. They usually end up doing some stupid thing that ruins expensive engine components.

To properly rebuild the lower end, you will need the following tools from the manufacturer: a service manual for torque specs and disassembly/assembly techniques specific to your model engine, a flywheel puller, a clutch-hub holder, a crankcase splitting tool, and a crankshaft installation tool—but I'll show

you techniques for removing the clutch and installing the crank so you can save money on those tools. You will also need: an air- or electric-powered impact wrench to remove the nuts that retain the flywheel, clutch, countershaft sprocket, and primary gear; a parts washer with solvent to clean the engine parts; a hydraulic press to remove and install the bearings (a hammer will only damage them); a propane torch to heat and expand the aluminum crankcases to remove or install the bearings because they have an interference fit (meaning that the bearing is a slightly larger diameter than the hole that it fits into); a digital caliper to measure certain engine

parts and compare them to the minimum wear specs listed in the service manual; a variety of wrenches and sockets; and soft tools such as brake cleaner, thread-locking agent, penetrating oil, seal grease, and gasket sealer. To hold the engine while you work on it, make an open square box from wood blocks. A universal box for any engine can be made from 2x4-in. blocks with the dimensions of the box being 5x10 in. CC Specialty makes a ball vise for $100 that is convenient if you plan to rebuild engines frequently. To permanently remove the temptation to use steel hammers when rebuilding engines, buy a plastic mallet. Snap-on makes a

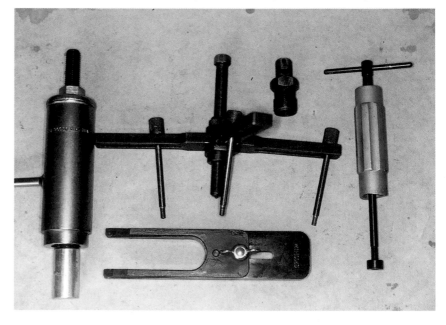

These are the basic tools that you'll need to rebuild the lower end of a typical dirt bike engine. Starting from the left, this is a crankshaft installation tool that draws the crankshaft into the left case half. The three-point tool in the top center is a crankcase splitting tool. Just below that is a wedge tool that prevents the crankshaft from slipping out of parallel alignment when pressed into the right case half. The tools are available from Kawasaki and fit all two- and four-stroke dirt bikes. The small device in the top right is a flywheel extractor. The long T-shaped tool is a piston pin extractor.

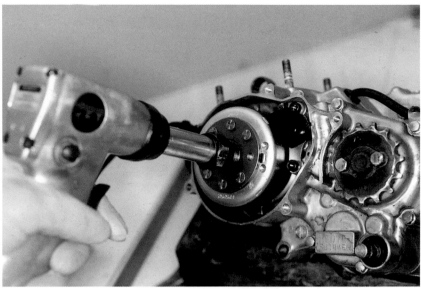

Once the flywheel nut is removed, this is how a flywheel extractor is used. The standard tool has two sets of threads: coarse and fine. The fine threads of the tool are left-hand threads; turn it counterclockwise to thread it onto the flywheel. Thread it on until it stops. Then hold the flywheel side of the tool with a large crescent wrench. Thread in (clockwise) the center bolt with a socket and ratchet. Always use grease on the extractor tool's crank bolt, and apply heat and penetrating oil to a stuck flywheel before you resort to using a hammer.

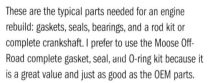

These are the typical parts needed for an engine rebuild: gaskets, seals, bearings, and a rod kit or complete crankshaft. I prefer to use the Moose Off-Road complete gasket, seal, and O-ring kit because it is a great value and just as good as the OEM parts.

lead-filled plastic mallet that works well. Finally, you'll need several parts storage bins to facilitate the engine rebuild. I prefer to separate the engine's components into separate bins—top-end parts, electrical parts, clutch parts, shifter parts, transmission, and crankcase bolts. This enables me to keep the parts organized for quick assembly. I also puncture small holes in the bottom of the bin so I can pour parts cleaning solvent into the bins to clean the parts. Then there isn't any chance of the parts getting lost in the bottom of the parts-washing tank.

TOP-END DISASSEMBLY AND INSPECTION

Refer to the sections on top-end rebuilding and exhaust valve servicing for more information on top-end disassembly and inspection.

ELECTRICAL SYSTEM DISASSEMBLY AND INSPECTION

First, refer to the sections on top-end rebuilding and exhaust valve servicing (Chapter 6) for more information on top-end disassembly and inspection. Then follow the electrical system disassembly and inspection below.

Use an impact wrench to remove the flywheel nut. Don't be tempted to jam a screwdriver in through one of the holes in the flywheel to prevent it from spinning. That will damage the coils under the flywheel. K&N makes a threaded flywheel puller that has left-hand threads to fasten to the flywheel and a right-hand-threaded bolt to push on the crankshaft. Put a dab of grease on the flywheel end to prevent the bolt from galling and damaging the machined center on the crankshaft end (if the center is damaged, it is much more difficult for a technician to true the crank). It's okay to tap on the end of the tightly threaded puller with a plastic mallet.

Here is a tip for removing stuck flywheels: Use a propane torch to heat the center hub of the flywheel. Take care not to shoot the flame through the holes in the flywheel. Then spray penetrating oil between the crankshaft end and the flywheel. This should loosen the flywheel enough to pop it off with the puller.

When the flywheel comes off, inspect the center-hub rivets and look for tiny cracks in the hub around the rivets. Replace the flywheel if there are any cracks. Big-bore bikes may have problems with shearing flywheel Woodruff keys, especially on the KX500 and YZ490. The flywheel is not matched to the crank at the taper, but that can be corrected using the following procedure: Remove the Woodruff key and apply grinding paste to the crank's taper. Hand-press the flywheel onto the crank and turn it back and forth for five minutes. This will hone down the high spots on the surfaces of each part so the flywheel won't ever loosen up and shear the Woodruff key. After matching, clean the parts thoroughly with contact cleaner.

CLUTCH DISASSEMBLY AND INSPECTION

There are a number of things to check on the clutch, and you will need a factory service manual for specifications on the wear limit of the clutch parts. Some of the things you want to inspect include the clutch springs for free length, the clutch plates for thickness, clutch plates for any broken plates, the outer pressure plate for a sizable ridge that would indicate that the plate is too thin, the inner hub and outer basket for chatter marks, the clutch basket's aluminum housing and the primary gear for excessive free-play between the two, and the center bushing diameter. A worn bushing will cause a variety of problems, including broken clutch plates. See the section on clutch rebuilding for more details.

SHIFTER, KICK STARTER, AND PRIMARY GEAR DISASSEMBLY AND INSPECTION

You will have to remove the shift shaft, power valve governor cartridge, and the primary gear that is bolted to the end of the crankshaft. The best way to remove the primary gear bolt is with an impact wrench. There is no factory holding tool for this gear; it's an accepted practice to use an impact wrench. If you are only going to change the main bearings, you don't need to remove the kick-start cartridge or the shift drum and spring-loaded shifting mechanism.

SPLITTING THE CRANKCASES

Remove all the case bolts, and install the case-splitting tool on to the left-side crankcase. The puller's two bolts thread into the stator-plate mounts. The center bolt of the puller will thread up against the crankshaft end. Apply some grease to the end of the crankshaft so the puller's tapered bolt doesn't gall the end of the crankshaft. Slowly tighten the puller bolt and tap around the outside of the cases with a plastic mallet. This will help break the bond of the case alignment pins. If the cases start to split apart with an uneven gap from front to rear, tap on a part of the right-side

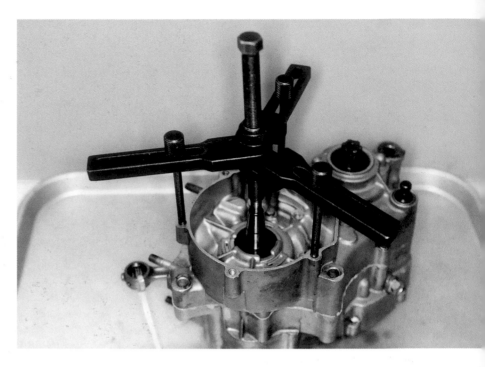

This is a crankcase splitting tool. The long outer bolts thread in the stator plate mounts. The center bolt presses on the end of the crankshaft and separates the case half from the crank. Motion Pro makes a professional kit for motorcycles that is universal and inexpensive. I prefer to use the tool made by Kawasaki and supplied through dealers—it's double the price, but if you use it often, you'll appreciate the difference in quality.

crankcase with a plastic mallet. You may also have to tap on the countershaft, but be careful not to break the bearing support ring that is cast into the case.

To remove the transmission shafts, you need to first remove the shift forks. Pull the rods that hold the forks, and then pull out the forks. Place the forks onto the rods, and set them in a parts bin in the order that they fit in the engine. The rod with the outside of the right countershaft bearing is very vulnerable on Hondas. Pay attention to the placement of shims on the ends of the transmission shafts; sometimes they will stick to the bearings and fall out later when you are washing the cases.

TRANSMISSION DISASSEMBLY AND INSPECTION

There are three shift forks in the transmission, and they are marked "L" for left and "R" for right. They each have a different radius, so you can't install them in the wrong position. Visually check the sides of the shift forks for blue marks that

would indicate that the forks are bent and need to be replaced (RM250s and KX500s are notorious for bending shift forks). Now remove the transmission shafts, paying close attention to shims that may be stuck to the case bearings. Visually inspect the gear engagement dogs for wear. The female and male dogs will have shiny spots on the corners if they are worn. Also, the bike will tend to jump out of gear during acceleration. The best way to keep the gears and shims on the transmission shafts is with rubber bands.

CRANKSHAFT REMOVAL AND INSPECTION

Sometimes, the crank will be difficult to remove from the right-side main bearing (on all engines except Suzukis). Never strike the end of the crank will a metal hammer; try a plastic mallet first. If that doesn't work, thread on the primary-gear nut to protect the threads and use a hydraulic press to remove the crank. Measure the rod clearance to determine if it needs to be rebuilt. Check the

If you don't have a source for crankshaft rebuilding, consider installing a new Hot Rod crankshaft. The part is better quality than stock and priced competitively with the parts and labor associated with rebuilding the old crankshaft.

This steel slug is being heated with a propane torch to transfer heat to the inner race of the main bearing, causing it to expand. The process takes about five minutes. If you don't have the special tools to install the crank and cases, you can always use physics.

This is a crankshaft installation tool for the left-side case. Once the crankshaft is pressed into the right-side case using the wedge tool to hold it parallel, the left side case can be installed, using this tool to bolt to the crank threads and draw the case onto the crank journal. It's really important to install the crank and cases without any impact trauma that could stress the main bearings or knock the crank out of alignment.

crankshaft runout and true it if necessary before installation. See the section on crankshaft repair if your inspection reveals a problem.

BEARING REMOVAL AND INSTALLATION

The best way to remove or install bearings is to heat the aluminum crankcases with a propane torch, and then use a hydraulic press to gently push them out. Never pound the bearings out with a hammer and punch. The outer race of the bearing is the only part where a press slug should be placed. Large sockets or discs work well as press slugs. Placing the new bearings in the freezer for two hours and heating the cases with the torch will enable you to install the bearings without a press. Fit the bearings into position with as little stress as possible exerted on the crank ends. Some manufacturers (Kawasaki) make special tools that wedge in between the flyweights so you can press the crank into place. Other manufacturers use a threaded tool that draws the crank into the bearing.

CRANKSHAFT INSTALLATION

Here is a simple way to install the crank. Place the crank in a freezer for two hours so it contracts in size. Get a cylindrical piece of aluminum with the same diameter as the inner bearing race. Heat and expand the bearing's inner race by heating the aluminum slug with a propane torch for five minutes while it rests on the inner race of the right-side main bearing. Drop the cold crank into the hot right main bearing. Repeat the procedure for the left main bearing, and prepare to assemble the cases.

Yamaha and Kawasaki dirt bikes do not use center crankcase gaskets. You must use a thick, non-drying sealer such as Yamabond 4 or Three Bond 1104. Smear it on evenly with a business card or a clean finger.

This gear has serious damage—the engagement dogs have snapped off. Visually check the male and female engagement dogs for rounding, which will appear as a polish mark on the normally sharp edge.

This is a typical kick-start cartridge. Alignment marks are on the ratchet and the shaft. Take care to align the marks during assembly or your kick-start lever won't fold into place. When kick starters slip, it is usually due to worn ratchet and engagement gear teeth. If a kick-start lever doesn't return properly or hangs, replace the spring.

ASSEMBLING THE CRANKCASES

With the crank and transmission fitted into the right crankcase, you're ready to assemble the cases. Kawasaki and Yamaha use non-drying sealer as a center gasket between the crankcases. Apply the sealer to one side of the case. Spread it evenly with a business card and let it set up for about 10 minutes.

Next, place the left case over the crank and transmission cases, press the cases toward each other to within 5 mm of sealing, install the bolts that fasten the cases together, and slowly tighten them while maintaining an equal gap between the cases. You may need to tap the case lightly because you are trying to align eight different cylindrical pieces together (crank, transmission shafts, shift-fork rods, shift drum, and case alignment pins). Once the case bolts are snugly tightened, try to turn the crankshaft and the transmission shafts. The transmission should turn easily, and the crankshaft should turn with some resistance. Using the plastic mallet, tap lightly on the transmission shafts while spinning them. Do the same with the crankshaft, tapping on both ends. The crankshaft may make a sharp cracking sound that means it has centered between the main bearings. Now torque the bolts on the cases.

BENCH TESTING

When you get the lower end together and the cases are sealed tight, install the shifting mechanism and turn the clutch shaft while clicking through the gears. The transmission is your main consideration when bench testing.

Take care when pressing the main bearings in the cases. This bearing was hammered in place and driven straight through, breaking off the seal housing. The case was repaired with TIG-welding. Crankcases are extremely expensive and often only available as a set. TIG-welding is the only serious method for repairing crankcases.

FINAL ASSEMBLY

Assemble the rest of the engine components, mount the engine in the frame, and hook up all electrical wires, control cables, and linkages. Torque all the mounting bolts, and then you're ready to break in your rebuilt engine.

BREAKING IN A NEW BOTTOM END

The new lower end will need some patient break-in time. The best way is to let the engine idle for three separate 10-minute sessions with a 20-minute rest period between sessions. You don't need any extra pre-mix oil because the engine load is minimal when the engine is idling.

CRANKSHAFT REPAIR

Crankshaft-related problems can cause the most expensive engine damage. Consider that at 10,000 rpm the piston moves up and down in the cylinder 166 times per second. The rod bearing and the crankcase main bearings support the reciprocating mass of the piston and rod. If you don't keep your air filter clean, the dirt will wear out the bear-

ings, causing the crank and piston to whip around unsupported and destroy the inside of the engine. All of this can happen in a matter of seconds in a 125-cc engine. There are several ways to check the condition of the engine bearings, and you should do so frequently to prevent catastrophic engine damage. Here are some tips for monitoring the condition of the crankshaft.

CHECKING FOR CRANKSHAFT AND BEARING DAMAGE

Use these techniques to check the condition of lower-end parts such as the connecting-rod bearing, main bearings, and flywheel rotor.

FLYWHEEL MOVEMENT

Grasp the flywheel with your hand and try to move it up and down and in and out. If you feel any movement, the main bearings are worn out. Remove the flywheel and the stator plate. Check the left crank seal for fuel leakage. If this seal is blown, dirt was drawn into the engine past the seal. Usually a bike will bog at low speed or heat-seize the

piston on the exhaust skirt when the left crank seal leaks.

CONNECTING-ROD MOVEMENT

Grasp the connecting rod and try to pull it straight up and push it down. It is normal to feel some radial play because the rod bearing is a needle bearing, but you shouldn't feel any up and down play. If you do, rebuild the crank. The side clearance between the rod and the thrust washers is a good indicator of rod bearing wear. Use a feeler gauge to measure the side clearance. The factory service manual lists the maximum side-clearance specification for your model of bike.

SHATTERED FLYWHEEL

Flywheels can occasionally come apart. The reason for this is worn main bearings. The crank is supported by the primary drive gear on the right side of the engine. When the main bearings wear, the crank deflects more on the left side where the electrical components are mounted. When the flywheel is allowed to gyrate, the flywheel rivets will eventually shear.

CRANKSHAFT REBUILDING TECHNIQUES

Before you decide to have your crankshaft rebuilt, do a survey on the exact cost of buying a new crank assembly as opposed to the parts and labor for rebuilding. Check the crankshaft ends for hammer marks or peening. When the machined centers of the crankshaft ends are distorted or marred, the crank cannot be set in a truing jig and is nearly impossible to align. If the ends of your crank are marred, you should buy a new crank. You must also evaluate the technician who will perform the rebuilding service. If he doesn't have the proper training or special tools, he can't do the job. Use this section as a guide to evaluating the quality of a crankshaft rebuilding company. If you have a Suzuki or Yamaha, you will find that it is much cheaper to rebuild the crank than to buy a new one. In contrast, Kawasaki and Honda crankshaft assemblies are relatively inexpensive.

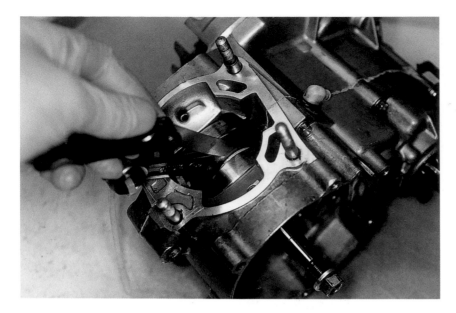

Measure the connecting rod's side clearance by inserting a feeler gauge between the flywheel weights and the side of the rod. Compare the feeler gauge measurement with factory dimension specs.

Grasp the rod and try to pull it up and down. You shouldn't feel any up-and-down play in the rod. Don't be too concerned with the radial movement—the rod is supported on needle bearings.

The Right Tools

To rebuild a crankshaft, you need special tools. The two most important and expensive tools are a 30-ton hydraulic press (about $500) and a truing jig (about $750). It is possible to use a lathe as a truing jig but only when the crank is set between two live centers. You cannot clamp one side of the crank in the chuck and one end in the center and expect to get an accurate deflection measurement; the deflection of the crank is redirected, and the crank reads true when it is far out of true. Other tools needed are a small square, a scribe, a dial indicator and stand, a brass hammer, a steel wedge such as a chisel, and a variety of rectangular steel blocks and pins so you can secure the crank in the press during assembly. Mud Creek Engineering in Michigan makes a great tool that allows you to assemble the crankshaft in perfect alignment; no additional truing is needed. The tool uses bushings to align the crank journals as the crank is pressed together.

Honda CR Crankshafts

Honda cranks have thin, bell-shaped sheetmetal covers pressed onto flyweights. About 1/3 of the crank periphery (around the crank pin) is hollow, so you cannot use the impact method to align a Honda crank. You must use the RCE tool to align the crank. Honda doesn't offer OEM replacement connecting rods, but Hot Rods are an aftermarket rod kit available for late-model Japanese dirt bikes, including Honda CRs.

Step-by-Step Crank Rebuilding

The following step-by-step procedure tells how a technician would rebuild a crank using conventional jigs and a truing stand.

1. Before disassembling the crank, the technician places a square against the side of the flyweights and scribes two parallel lines, 180 degrees apart, across the face of the flyweight. These alignment marks will help the technician align the crank upon assembly. Now the crankpin can be pressed out of the flyweights and all the old parts should be discarded. Never reuse the connecting rod, bearing, pin, or thrust washers.

2. The technician then applies a thin layer of assembly grease to the bearing surfaces of the crankpin, bearing, thrust washers, and rod. After the grease is applied, the crankpin can be pressed into one of the flyweights. The washers, bearing, and rod are then placed onto the crankpin.

3. The technician heats the other flyweight's pinhole with a propane torch for about three minutes. This expands the diameter of the pinhole and reduces the need for excessive

This is the RCE crankshaft assembly jig. This excellent tool features a sturdy jig frame and bushings to align the crank halves and press the crankshaft together true.

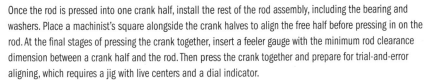

Once the rod is pressed into one crank half, install the rest of the rod assembly, including the bearing and washers. Place a machinist's square alongside the crank halves to align the free half before pressing in on the rod. At the final stages of pressing the crank together, insert a feeler gauge with the minimum rod clearance dimension between a crank half and the rod. Then press the crank together and prepare for trial-and-error aligning, which requires a jig with live centers and a dial indicator.

pressure to assemble the crank. He then uses the square to align the scribe lines on each flyweight so the crank is assembled very close to true.

4. As the crank is pressed together, the technician uses a feeler gauge to monitor the clearance between the connecting rod and the thrust washer. The proper clearance is listed in the service manual. The manual also lists an overall crank width spec that can be measured with a caliper.

Truing the Crank
1. During the truing process, the technician supports the crank between live centers.
2. Knife-edged bearings must be used if the machined centers of the crank ends are damaged. Dial indicators are used to measure the runout of each crank end and the side runout of the flyweights.
3. If the crank has side runout, the flyweights aren't parallel and must be adjusted before the crank ends can be

trued. This is accomplished by hitting the wide side of the flyweights with a large brass hammer and then wedging the flyweights apart at the narrow side with a large tapered chisel and hammer. It sounds very caveman-like, but this is the way the pros do it. Of course, the crank must be removed from the jig before the runout can be adjusted; otherwise the dial indicators and jig centers will be damaged. The crank ends have runout because the flyweights aren't parallel and must be rotated about the crankpin. This is accomplished by striking the flyweight at the exact point of the greatest runout with a brass hammer, while holding the opposite flyweight in hand. It doesn't take much force to rotate the flyweight into true.

Now you can understand why we must be careful how the crank is installed into the crankcases during engine assembly. It is very easy to throw the crank out of true if you beat the hell out of it and the cases during assembly!

CHAPTER EIGHT

TWO-STROKE ENGINES

Changing the powerband of your dirt bike engine is simple when you know the basics. A myriad of aftermarket accessories is available to tune your bike to better suit your needs. The most common mistake is to choose the wrong combination of engine components, making the engine run worse than a stock engine. Use this section as a guide to inform yourself on how changes in engine components can alter the powerband of your bike's engine. Use the "Tuning Guide to Performance Modifications" section to map out a strategy for changing engine components to create the perfect powerband.

TWO-STROKE PRINCIPLES

Although a two-stroke engine has fewer moving parts than a four-stroke engine, a two-stroke is a complex engine with different phases taking place in the crankcase and in the cylinder bore at the same time. A two-stroke engine completes a power cycle in only 360 degrees of crankshaft rotation, compared to a four-stroke engine, which requires 720 degrees of crankshaft rotation to complete one power cycle. Two-stroke engines aren't as efficient as four-stroke engines, meaning that they don't retain as much air as they draw in through the intake. Some of the air is lost out the exhaust pipe. If a two-stroke engine could retain the same percentage of air, it would be twice as powerful as a four-stroke engine because it produces twice as many power strokes in the same number of crankshaft revolutions.

The following explains the basic operation of the two-stroke engine:

1. Starting with the piston at top dead center (TDC, 0 degrees), ignition occurs and the gases in the combus-

This is a view inside a cylinder. A right-angle grinding tool machines the timing edges of the transfer and exhaust ports—this is real porting. Straight tools are used to texture surfaces and polish a port, which is considered metal finishing and doesn't make much of a difference in power.

tion chamber expand and push down the piston. This pressurizes the crankcase, causing the reed valve to close. At about 90 degrees after TDC, the exhaust port opens, ending the power stroke. A pressure wave of hot expanding gases flows down the exhaust pipe. The blow-down phase starts and will end when the transfer ports open. The pressure in the cylinder must blow down to below the pressure in the crankcase in order for the unburned mixture gases to flow out the transfer ports during the scavenging phase.

2. Now the transfer ports are uncovered at about 120 degrees after TDC. The scavenging phase has begun, meaning that the unburned mixture gases are flowing out of the transfers and

merging together to form a loop. The gases travel up the back side of the cylinder and loop around in the cylinder head to scavenge out the burnt mixture gases from the previous power stroke. It is critical that the burnt gases are scavenged from the combustion chamber, to make room for as much unburned gas as possible. The more unburned gases you can squeeze into the combustion chamber, the more power the engine will produce. Now the loop of unburned mixture gases has traveled into the exhaust pipe's header section.

3. Now the crankshaft has rotated past bottom dead center (BDC, 180 degrees) and the piston is on the upstroke. The compression wave reflected from the exhaust

Case-reed engines can benefit from crankcase porting and cylinder matching more so than cylinder-reed engines. Case porting is a metal finishing task that serves to match the crankcase and cylinder transfer ports and polish surface imperfections.

pipe packs the unburned gases back in through the exhaust port as the piston closes off the port to start the compression phase. In the crankcase, the pressure is below atmospheric producing a vacuum, and a fresh charge of unburned mixture gases flows through the reed valve into the crankcase.

4. The unburned mixture gases are compressed and, just before the piston reaches TDC, the ignition system discharges a spark, causing the gases to ignite and start the process all over again.

HOW TO CHOOSE A POWERBAND

By making changes in engine components, nearly every Japanese dirt bike has the potential for two types of power. The engine can be tuned for midrange and high-rpm power or for low-end and midrange power. The midrange and high-rpm bike will have little or no low end, hit explosively in the midrange, and have an abundance of top-end power that can be over-revved. This kind of power can put you out front in the straights, but it is harder to control and will tire out the rider more quickly.

Expert outdoor riders tend to use engines tuned for high-rpm power.

An engine tuned for low-end and midrange power will have plenty of power down low, a beefy midrange, and a flat top end. Supercross and enduro riders favor this kind of power. It is easy to use and gives the rider confidence. Most riders can see faster times and have more fun with more low end and midrange.

With tuning, you can change your motorcycle's powerband to somewhere between one of these extremes. Only a few riders use the extremes. Professionals on outdoor tracks—especially 125-cc European Grand Prix bikes—use engines that are almost all high-rpm power. These machines are extremely fast and require highly talented professionals to make the most of them. Enduro riders in extremely slippery, technical conditions use bikes tuned for lots of low end. Trials riders use bikes that are tuned for nothing but low end.

Generally speaking, the higher the powerband peak (both in horsepower and rpm), the narrower the powerband. Conversely, the lower the power peak, the wider the powerband. Sometimes you can get the best of both worlds. Exhaust valves systems have made the biggest

difference in widening the powerband. Innovations in exhaust pipe design and ignition systems have also contributed to making two-stroke engines as tractable as four-stroke engines.

Riders should choose a powerband according to their skill levels, terrain obstacles, and maintenance practices. Here are some tips on how to select the right powerband.

SKILL LEVEL

Generally speaking, beginning riders need low to midrange powerbands, while expert riders can benefit from top-end powerbands. There are exceptions, though. Supercross bikes have low to midrange powerbands because the steep, far-spaced jumps are positioned so close to the turns. Keep in mind that low-end to midrange powerbands are typically easier to use. In conditions where traction is minimal and the terrain is particularly technical, low-end power will allow you to keep the bike under control and ultimately go faster. Also, "torquey" bikes are more fun to ride casually. Expert and top-level riders need high-end power to be competitive, but the extra juice can slow down lesser riders even in good conditions and is a handicap in slippery, difficult conditions.

TERRAIN OBSTACLES

This term describes a variety of things ranging from the soil content to elevation changes and the frequency of jumps and turns on a racetrack. Low to midrange powerbands work well on soils such as mud and sand. Tight tracks with lots of off-camber or difficult corners will favor low-end to midrange power. Smoother, broader powerbands work well for enduro or trail riding over a variety of terrain and soil conditions. Midrange to top-end powerbands work best on terrain with loamy soil, long fast uphills, and fast sweeping turns.

MAINTENANCE PRACTICES

Generally speaking, powerbands designed for low to midrange require less engine maintenance than powerbands designed

TUNING FOR SPECIFIC POWERBANDS

This chart is designed to give you some general guidelines on different powerbands and the changes required to the individual engine components. For specific recommendations on your model bike, refer to the chapters on tuning tips.

COMPONENT: Cylinder Head

LOW TO MIDRANGE: 9.5:1 compression ratio, squish band 60 percent of bore area

MIDRANGE AND HIGH RPM: 8:1 compression ratio, 40 percent squish

COMPONENT: Cylinder Ports

LOW TO MIDRANGE: Exhaust port 90 ATDC, transfer ports 118 ATDC

MIDRANGE AND HIGH RPM: Exhaust port 84 ATDC, transfer ports 116 ATDC

COMPONENT: Reeds

LOW TO MIDRANGE: Dual-stage or 0.4-mm fiberglass petals

COMPROMISE: Thick carbon fiber petals

MIDRANGE AND HIGH RPM: Large area 30-degree valve

COMPONENT: Carburetor

LOW TO MIDRANGE: Smaller diameter or sleeved down carb (26 mm for 80 cc, 34 mm for 125 cc, 36 mm 250 cc)

MIDRANGE AND HIGH RPM: Larger carb (28 mm for 80 cc, 38 mm for 125 cc, 39.5 mm for 250 cc)

COMPONENT: Pipe

LOW TO MIDRANGE: Fatty or Torque

MIDRANGE AND HIGH RPM: Desert or rpm

COMPONENT: Silencer or Spark Arrestor

LOW TO MIDRANGE: Short, small diameter

MIDRANGE AND HIGH RPM: Long, large diameter

COMPONENT: Ignition Timing or Advance Timing

LOW TO MIDRANGE: Stock timing

MIDRANGE AND HIGH RPM: Retard timing

COMPONENT: Flywheel

LOW TO MIDRANGE: Add weight

COMPROMISE: Stock flywheel

MIDRANGE AND HIGH RPM: PVL internal flywheel

COMPONENT: Fuel

LOW TO MIDRANGE: Super-unleaded 93-octane

MIDRANGE AND HIGH RPM: Racing fuel 105-octane

for high rpm. High-rpm powerbands usually require frequent use of the clutch to get the engine up into the rev range where the powerband is most effective. An engine that sustains high rpm requires more frequent replacement of parts such as piston and rings, reeds, crankshaft bearings, and clutch plates. Also, the carb jetting becomes more critical. If the main jet is one size too lean, the piston can seize. High-rpm powerbands have high compression ratios and fuel selection is critical. Most tuners recommend racing fuel because the specific gravity of these fuels doesn't vary with the season like super-unleaded pump fuel.

TUNING GUIDE TO PERFORMANCE MODIFICATIONS

Before you begin modifications, you need to decide what you want from your engine. What kind of riding do you do? What level of rider are you? How much money do you have to

The cylinder on the left is ported and the cylinder on the right is stock. Porting is a metal machining operation that includes general smoothing and matching of the ports with port timing changes made at the intersection of the port windows and the cylinder bore.

and transfers) that alters the timing, area size, and angles of the ports to adjust the powerband to better suit the rider's demands. For example, a veteran trail rider riding an RM250 in the Rocky Mountain region of the United States will need to adjust the powerband for more low-end power because of the steep hillclimbs and the low air density of higher altitudes. The only way to determine what changes to the engine will be necessary is to measure and calculate the stock engine's specifications.

The most critical measurement is the port time-area, the calculation of a port opening's area and timing in relation to the displacement of the engine and the rpm. Experienced tuners know what exhaust and transfer port time-area values work best for different purposes (motocross versus enduro, for example).

In general, if a tuner wants to adjust the engine's powerband for more low to midrange, he will do the following two things.

1. Turn down the cylinder base on a lathe to increase the effective stroke (distance from TDC to exhaust port opening). This also retards the exhaust port timing, shortens the exhaust port duration, and increases the compression ratio.

2. Narrow the transfer ports and reangle them with epoxy to reduce the port

spend? Remember that you need to bring the bike to peak stock condition before you add aftermarket equipment.

This section lists each performance mod and describes how to modify each system for the performance you want.

CYLINDER PORTING

The cylinder ports are designed to produce a certain power characteristic over a fairly narrow rpm band. Porting or tuning is a metal machining process performed to the cylinder ports (exhaust

These are silicon molds of popular combustion chamber designs starting from the left: flat top, domed, and hemispherical designs. Flat-top chambers are good for motocross and off-road because of their quick throttle response and use of lightweight flat-top pistons. Domed chambers are better for thermally loaded, high-rpm engines. Most factory 125s use domed pistons. Hemi chambers are used for road racing and shifter kart applications.

The latest performance trend in cylinder head design is the two-piece head. The water jacket housing and combustion chamber are separate pieces bolted together on the cylinder. Bronze combustion chambers are used because the material transfers heat efficiently and is more resistant to detonation damage. Chamber designs and compression ratios can be quickly changed for different applications.

can be stroked or de-stroked. Generally speaking, stroking refers to increasing the distance between the big end and crank center, and de-stroking refers to reducing the distance. Stroking increases the displacement of the engine, and de-stroking reduces the displacement.

PLAYING THE NUMBERS GAME

Certain combinations of cylinder bore size, crankshaft stroke, and connecting rod length produce ideal powerbands for certain applications. In 125-cc motocross, the accepted standard is a bore of 54 mm, a stroke of 54.5 mm, and a connecting rod length of 105 mm. In road race it's 56x50 and 110. A short stroke enables a higher rpm before critical piston speed is attained (4,500 feet per minute); that's why a shorter stroke is used for road racers. These engine configurations are termed "over-square" because the bore is greater

time-area for an rpm peak of 7,000. The rear transfer ports need to be reangled to oppose each other rather than pointing forward to the exhaust port. This changes the flow pattern of the transfer ports to improve scavenging efficiency from 2,000 to 5,000 rpm.

For both of these types of cylinder porting changes to be effective, other engine components need to be changed as well.

CYLINDER HEAD MODIFICATION

Cylinder head shape also affects the powerband. Generally speaking, a cylinder head with a deep, small-diameter combustion chamber and a wide squish band combined with a high compression ratio is suited for low-end and midrange power. A cylinder head with a wide, shallow chamber and a narrow squish band and a lower compression ratio is suited for high-rpm power.

Cylinder heads with wide squish bands and high compression ratios will generate high turbulence in the combustion chamber. This turbulence is termed maximum squish velocity (MSV) and is

rated in meters per second (m/s). A cylinder head designed for supercross should have an MSV rating of 35 m/s, whereas a head designed for motocross should have an MSV rating of 25 m/s. The only way to accurately determine the MSV rating of a head is by measuring some basic engine dimensions and inputting the numbers into a TSR computer program called SQUISH. In the model tuning tips chapters, the SQUISH program was used to calculate the modified head dimensions.

Aftermarket companies such as Cool Head also offer cylinder heads that have different cartridges to give different cylinder head shapes. The various head cartridges have different combustion bowl shapes, compression ratios, and MSV ratings. The head cartridges are incrementally different, corresponding to powerbands ranging from extreme low end to high rpm.

CRANKSHAFT STROKING

Stroking refers to a combination of metal machining processes that relocates the center of the rod's big end in relation to the crankshaft center. A crank

This is a Wiseco GP piston, designed for ported cylinders. It is a high-performance piston for a 125-cc engine. Unlike a stock piston, the Wiseco GP uses a nickel crown coating that reduces detonation, a moly coating on the skirt that is a dry film lubricant, lightening cutouts inside the piston for wider exhaust porting, and 50 percent of its mass is centered in the piston crown for better thermal efficiency. The ring is pinned on center to allow for wider transfer ports.

than the stroke. Conversely, the popular MX configuration is termed "under-square" or "long stroke." Long connecting rods are commonly thought to produce more leverage, but the real advantage of a high-revving engine is that the piston dwells longer at TDC and allows for a greater pressure rise and hopefully more brake mean effective pressure (BMEP), or the average pressure per square inch in the cylinder from TDC to BDC.

The manufacturers fiddle around with bore, stroke, and rod combos all the time. The latest rage for the amateur class for 125s where the 80-over rule applies is a 55.5-mm bore and a 55.2-mm stroke with a 109-mm rod. Suzuki has determined that to be the winning combo and requires its support riders to have their engines modified to that spec. For the Kawasaki KX80, the magic numbers are 48.5x53x92. Kudos to Pro-Circuit for doing the legwork on that one!

So how does one find that magic combo? You could spend loads of time and money to try every possible combination, or you could use a simulation program such as Virtual Two-Stroke or Dynomation. There are a lot of things going on in a two-stroke engine. When you change one thing like the stroke, several other things change too, for better or worse.

WHAT HAPPENS WHEN?

These are the things that are affected when the stroke is changed.

1. The displacement increases.
2. The port timing advances.
3. The ignition timing advances.
4. The compression ratio of the combustion chamber and crankcase increase.
5. The reed valve timing advances and the reed lift increases.
6. The piston speed is greater at any given rpm.
7. The maximum piston speed is reached at a lower rpm.
8. The rod bearing wear accelerates.
9. The rod ratio decreases.
10. The bore-to-stroke ratio is altered.

WHAT THINGS MUST BE ACCOUNTED FOR?

The cylinder must be shimmed up or the head's squish band must be machined to compensate for the increase in stroke.

1. The port time-area must be increased to compensate for the stroke and displacement change.
2. The ignition timing may need to be retarded.
3. The combustion chamber in the head must be enlarged for greater volume.
4. The connecting rod bearing and piston pin bearing must be changed more often.
5. The crankcase diameter may need to be increased for rod clearance due to the greater offset of the rod.

FOUR WAYS TO STROKE A CRANK

There are four popular ways to change the stroke of a crank:

1. Manufacture new crank halves with the dimensions built in.
2. TIG weld the big end pin holes and drill new holes farther from the crank center.
3. Bore the big end holes larger and TIG weld eccentric flanges.
4. Precision grind an eccentric crankpin.

Manufacturing new stroked crankshafts is the most expensive choice and currently there are no aftermarket products of this type for modern dirt bikes.

Relocating the big end pin holes is the most logical and reliable choice. The crank is disassembled, the holes are TIG welded with stainless-steel filler rod, and the holes are rough-bored and finish-honed with the crank halves jigged together to ensure accuracy.

Eccentric flanges are manufactured by gun-drilling rod stock off center, and then turning the rod on a lathe into a flange shape. The crank's big end holes are bored oversize and the flanges are installed, indexed, and TIG welded to the crank halves.

Eccentric big end pins were popularized in Germany 20 years ago. The German logic is to avoid heating/welding material to the crank halves so as to minimize stress and distortion. Oversize rod stock is OD (outside diameter) ground to

Cylinder base shims are used for three reasons: to accommodate stroker cranks and long-rod kits or to advance the port timing.

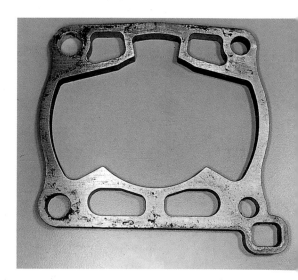

This spacer plate was custom-made by Cometic Gasket Co. Average cost is $50.

This is a view of the head, cylinder, and piston on an engine where the crank has been stroked. Notice how the piston crown extends over the top of the cylinder. The head's squish band recess gap has been increased so the piston doesn't contact the head.

form the three surfaces. However, the crank cannot be rebuilt by traditional means because of the difficulty with indexing the crank halves for the proper stroke dimension.

BALANCE FACTORS—THE MAGIC BULLET

Truing and balancing are often confused. Truing the crank refers to the process of aligning the crank halves about the big end pin, making the halves parallel to each other. Balancing refers to changing the balance factor, which is the ratio of the reciprocating mass to the rotational mass. The reciprocating mass consists of most of the connecting rod and the piston assembly. The rotational mass consists of the crank halves. Crankshafts are lightened at the top near the big end pin using a number of different methods. Sometimes there are holes drilled in the crank halves or lighter materials are substituted.

Crankshaft balance is important because excess vibration is converted to friction and heat, which spread throughout the crankcases and reduce the charge density. And that directly affects the peak power.

Altering the balance factor may

include adding weight of a denser mass to the bottom of the crank halves or lightening the halves at the top. Substitute materials for adding weight include Mallory, lead, and osmium.

FAQ: LONG ROD KITS AND SPACER PLATES

The terms "long rod kit" and "spacer plates" were popularized by the motorcycle press. Here are some frequently asked questions on these items and their effects on engine performance.

What is a long rod kit?
A long rod kit consists of a longer connecting rod and all the special parts that must be used with it. A longer connecting rod only changes the rod ratio between the stroke length and the rod's center-to-center length. Long rod kits do not change the displacement of the cylinder, only the crankcase.

How does a long rod kit improve the powerband?
The longer rod allows the piston to dwell at TDC longer for a greater pressure rise. Before the piston opens the exhaust in the middle of the stroke, the longer rod will have greater leverage. Near BDC,

the piston travels faster, causing greater intake velocity on piston port engines and greater reed petal lift and mass flow on reed valve intake systems.

How would the porting change with a longer dwell time?
The operating speed is about 8,000 to 11,000 rpm. The timing of the intake, transfers, and exhaust will change, even if the cylinder is spaced at the same distance difference as the longer rod.

Why don't all bikes in stock form have long rods? Do they work on all 125-cc bikes?
Two-stroke engine designers have to balance a number of factors when making an engine for a particular application. For example, a rod ratio of 4:1 is considered ideal for a road racer, while 3.75:1 is better for MX. On small engines, the greater the rod ratio, the lower the primary compression ratio. MX engines need a primary compression ratio of about 1.8:1 in order to have strong throttle response to clear obstacles.

Is there an ideal length or is longer better?
For a typical 54.5-mm stroke, the rod can range from 102 to 112 mm.

Why use a spacer plate and is there an alternative?
A spacer plate is like a thick base gasket, usually made of aluminum with a standard gasket on each side to provide some sealing means. The spacer plate serves to compensate for the difference in the extra rod length. In order to use a spacer plate, the cylinder base studs and the power valve linkage rod must be longer. The head-stay brackets must also be slotted, and the exhaust system brackets will need to be repositioned. The use of spacer plates enables the port timing to remain close to stock, which will help the midrange to top-end power. The alternative to a spacer plate is to machine the cylinder head's squish band and combustion chamber to accommodate the piston travel. This would also serve to retard the port timing due to the relative position of the piston.

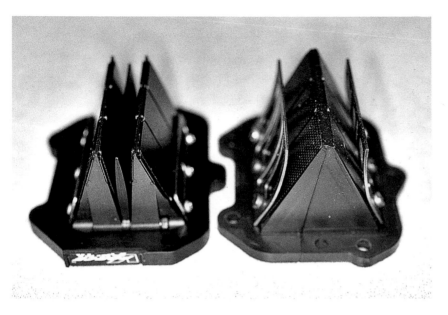

Here is a comparison between a V-Force (left) and conventional stock reed cage (right). The V-Force has double the reed area but also double the angle. V-Force reed valves generally improve the low-end to midrange power.

CARBURETOR MODIFICATION

In general, a small-diameter carburetor will provide high air-mass velocity and good flow characteristics for a low- to mid-rpm powerband. A large-diameter carburetor works better for high-rpm powerbands. For 125-cc engines, a 34-mm carburetor works well for supercross and enduro, and a 36- to 38-mm carburetor works best for fast motocross tracks. For 250-cc engines, a 36-mm carburetor works best for low- to mid-rpm powerbands, and a 39.5-mm carburetor works best for high-rpm powerbands.

Recently, there has been an increase in the use of air foils and rifle boring for carburetors. These innovations are designed to improve airflow at low throttle openings. Some companies, such as Performance Engineering in Florida, offer a service to overbore the carb and include inserts to reduce the diameter of the carburetor. For example, a 38-mm carb for a 250-cc bike will be bored to 39.5 mm and two inserts will be supplied. The carb can then be restricted to a diameter of 36 or 38 mm.

Not every carb can be overbored. The maximum diameter of the carburetor cannot exceed the width of the slide or air will bypass the venturi and the engine will run too lean. There are two ways to overbore a carb: by stripping it down and turning it on a lathe (Keihin PWK and Mikuni round slide), or by milling it on a vertical mill using a rotary table. The rotary table method is necessary for carburetors where the needle jet cannot be removed (Keihin PJ and Mikuni TMX). Whenever a carb is overbored, the jetting must be richened to compensate for the loss of intake velocity.

AFTERMARKET REED VALVES

Like large-bore carburetors, bigger reed valves with large flow area work best for high-rpm powerbands. In general, reed valves with six or more petals are used for high-rpm engines. Reed valves with four petals are used for dirt bikes that need strong low-end and midrange power. Three other factors must be considered when choosing a reed valve: the angle of the reed valve, the type of reed material, and the petal thickness. The two common reed valve angles are 30 and 45 degrees. The 30-degree valve is designed for low-end to midrange power, and the 45-degree valve is designed for high-rpm power. Two types of reed-petal materials are commonly used: carbon fiber and fiberglass. Carbon fiber reeds are light-weight but relatively stiff (spring tension) and are designed to resist fluttering at high rpm. Fiberglass reeds have relatively low spring tension to instantly respond to pressure changes in the crankcase; however, the low spring tension makes them flutter at high rpm, thereby limiting the amount of power. Fiberglass reed petals are good for low-end to midrange powerbands, and carbon fiber reeds are better for high-rpm engines. Regarding longevity, fiberglass reeds tend to split whereas carbon fiber reeds tend to chip.

Some aftermarket reeds, such as the Boyesen dual-stage reeds, have a large, thick base reed with a smaller, thinner reed mounted on top. This setup widens the rpm range where the reed valve flows best. The thin reeds respond to low rpm and low-frequency pressure pulses. The thick reeds respond to higher pressure pulses and resist fluttering at high rpm. The Boyesen RAD valve is different than a traditional reed valve. Bikes with single rear shocks have offset carbs. The RAD valve is designed to evenly redistribute the gas flow from the offset carb to the crankcases. A RAD valve will give an overall improvement to the powerband. Polini of Italy makes a reed valve called the Supervalve. It features several mini sets of reeds positioned vertically instead of horizontally (as on conventional reed valves). These valves are excellent for enduro riding because they improve throttle response. Tests on an inertia chassis dyno show the Supervalve to be superior when power shifting. However, the valves do not generate greater peak power than conventional reed valves.

THE SECRET LIFE OF A TWO-STROKE EXHAUST PIPE

A pipe's job is to draw out the burnt gases from combustion along with some unburned gases, and then reflect a wave that plugs the unburned gases back into the cylinder before the piston closes off the exhaust port. The pipe is comprised of five distinct sections: header, diffuser, center dwell, convergence cone, and stinger. There are algebraic formulas for

FMF makes tailpipe silencers in three basic variations: short for low end, long for top end, and a spark arrestor for sound and fire safety.

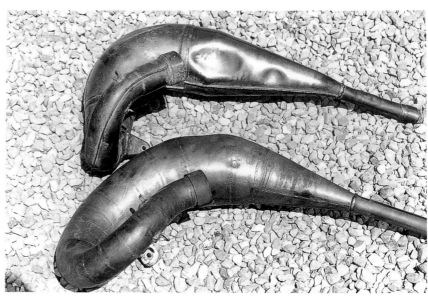

This is a comparison between two pipes for a 125-cc engine. The pipe on top is designed for a high-rpm powerband. It has a short tuned length and steep cone angles. The other pipe is designed for a low- to mid-rpm powerband. A long, tapered head pipe and shallow cone angles highlight the difference from the rev pipe.

the dimensions of each section of the pipe, but they are only a baseline for designers. The problem is that exhaust gas and outside skin temperature are variables to consider. Getting the temperature correct inside the pipe provides a greater tuning advantage than just swapping to a different hop-up company's pipe. The temperature inside the pipe is affected by the carb jetting, fuel formulation, and ignition timing curve. Cylinders with exhaust valve systems that employ large cavities or venting can also dramatically affect how the pipe works. Some of these things you can control, others you can't.

How Aftermarket Companies Design Pipes
You're fooling yourself if you think that the pipe manufacturers run comprehensive R&D programs on every model of

dirt bike that they make a pipe for. They are challenged with bringing a large variety of pipes to market quickly and the way that they do it is simple. They start by doing a dyno run on the stock pipe. Then they decide which area of the powerband they want to improve. Next, they cut the front and rear cones off the pipe and weld spring loops. Then they interchange a selection of angled cones and make dyno runs. Some companies use the same cones on all their 125s or 250s since the Japanese manufacturers use nearly identical bore, stroke, rod length, and port timing. Once they are satisfied with the cone choices, they weld the cones permanently into place. Finally, they cut and rotate all the cones so the pipe forms a "C" shape. Then they cut off the header flange and the stinger. From there, the pipe goes to the die maker, who makes the aluminum casting of the pipe that becomes the press-die.

Torque and Rev Pipes
Pipes are stamped from sheet metal into a C-shaped pattern. Press-dies have a limited life span rated in the number of parts stamped. It isn't that they crumble

to pieces, but they do slowly wear. When the press-die wears, it changes the dimensions of a part. Dies start out larger than the target size and wear. The parts at the beginning and end of the die's life are different sizes. Pipes are fabricated by welding two C-shaped pipe shells together; then the sections are cut, rotated, and welded again. Every time the pipe is cut on the band saw, the length is reduced by the width of the saw blade and the amount of material that is sanded off the cut edges. Multiply that by the number of cuts and a pipe can shift its tuning range pretty quickly, especially if an overzealous worker sands too much here and there.

Manufacturers rate pipes by their length. A long pipe is a "torque" and a short pipe is a "rev." The engine manufacturers do the same thing with pistons and cylinders with the markings "A" and "B." The label is a dimensional representation of a finished manufactured part. Some manufacturers, like FMF, don't rate their pipes, but the pipes are still different dimensions. That's why you can buy two of the same model pipes from one manufacturer and they will perform slightly differently.

What's a Rocket Engine Doing in the Pipe?
When FMF introduced its SST pipe the manufacturer described it as a rocket engine in the pipe. Actually, it's a rapid convergence cone and it is shaped like the business end of a rocket engine. By constricting the outlet of the stinger before the silencer, it serves to raise the pressure in the pipe and the piston crown temperature. It has the greatest effect at high rpm. In shifter kart racing, RCE markets a pipe with a selection of tuning cones that feature different angles and diameters to adjust the tuning effect for different rpm ranges.

The opposite of a rapid convergence cone is a rapid diffuser. A bulge in the junction between the convergence cone and the stinger was used on the Yamaha IT and YZ490 models of the mid-1980s. That shape prevents a backup of pressure in the stinger, mainly because those old bikes had a sharp bend in the pipe to compensate for. FMF uses a rapid diffuser in its four-stroke header pipes and calls it a "Power Bomb." A multi-phase resonator is commonly used on snowmobiles and it works differently on a two-stroke engine. (A rapid diffuser allows for less loss of energy when waves moving in opposite directions pass through each other. In the field of unsteady gas dynamics, that is called "super-position." A multi-phase resonator has a specific volume, length, and orifice size that allow the resonator to have an effect based on rpm and its position in the expansion chamber.)

What's a Titty Pipe?
I'm waiting to flip open a dirt bike magazine someday to read about "The Titty Pipe." I think the average teenager who reads these magazines could embrace the concept. Randy Nouis, an engineer at GM Racing, invented the multi-phase resonator, nicknamed the titty pipe. It looks like a bulging chamber that fastens to the pipe. Some modern Canadian snowmobiles and Italian trials motorcycles use them in production. Basically, the multi-phase resonator consists of an oval flask with an orifice that intersects with the edge of the pipe. It serves to add

volume and length to a particular section of the pipe. The orifice size determines the rpm at which the resonator will function. Honda used a similar device on CR125 and 250s on the 1985 and 1986 models. The concept was abandoned because the butterfly valve used to control the orifice of the chamber frequently clogged with carbon.

How the Ignition Changes the Pipe
Though it doesn't actually have anything to do with the pipe, an adjustable ignition can have a great effect. The ignition boxes have two timing circuits built in. A switch is provided to go from one circuit to the other. One timing curve has a steep advance for good low-end power and quick throttle response. The other circuit has a shallow advance curve with a high-speed retard circuit that times the spark close to TDC. This is called the top-end or hole shot switch. Essentially, combustion takes about 55 degrees of crank duration to occur. Retarding the spark causes more heat

from combustion to shift into the pipe and out of the cylinder. Raising the temperature in the pipe raises the rpm peak in accordance with piston speed.

FLYWHEEL WEIGHTS
A heavier flywheel will smooth out power delivery. The flywheel is weighted to improve the engine's tractability at low- to mid-rpm. Flywheel weights are best for powerful bikes with decent low end and an explosive hit. The weight smooths out the hit and reduces wheel-spin, which will improve the drive out of corners. One common misconception of flywheel weights is that they increase low-end power. If an engine doesn't have enough low-end torque in the first place, it will actually be worse with the extra flywheel weight.

Steahly manufactures thread-on flywheel weights that thread on to the fine left-hand threads on the center hub of most Japanese magneto rotors. Thread-on flywheel weights can only be used if the threads on the flywheel are in perfect condition.

This flywheel has been modified for a longer stroke length. The stock big-end pin is bored off center and a steel slug is welded in place and bored to size.

A centered spark plug head is threaded to a Goodson Automotive mandrel and installed in the three-jaw chuck of a lathe to facilitate tuning changes.

Modern bikes use external rotor flywheels. They have a larger diameter than internal rotor flywheels so they have greater flywheel inertia. PVL makes an internal rotor flywheel that gives quicker throttle response.

IGNITION TIMING

The ignition timing has a minimal effect on the powerband. Retarding the timing has the effect of reducing the hit of the powerband in the midrange and extending the top-end over-rev. "Over-rev" is a slang term that describes the useable length of the powerband at high rpm.

The scientific reason for the shift of the powerband to extremely high rpm is that the temperature in the pipe increases with the retarded timing because the burn cycle takes about 55 degrees of crankshaft rotation. When the timing is retarded, the burn cycle starts later and continues into the pipe. Raising the exhaust gas temperature raises the velocity of the waves, making them more synchronous with the piston speed and port timing of the cylinder.

Advancing the timing increases the midrange hit of the powerband but makes the power flatten out at high rpm. The relatively long spark lead time enables for a greater pressure rise in the cylinder before the piston reaches TDC. This produces more torque in the midrange, but the high pressure contributes to pumping losses at extremely high rpm.

ENGINE MANAGEMENT SYSTEMS

Motorcycle engines have always been at the forefront of engine design. The next leap will come in the form of engine management systems that control the ignition system, power jet, exhaust valves, and resonator temperature and pressure. Right now, we're seeing new products such as programmable or switchable ignition boxes. In the near future, we'll see a continual stream of products that will culminate in a direct-injected, two-stroke engine with a management system that coordinates the ignition, intake, exhaust, and ultimately the powerband with just a tweak of the thumb.

The Optimum GP Control package for the Suzuki RM250 is a kit that includes a handlebar switch, KX250 carburetor with pumper and throttle position sensor, and a computer that fits under the seat on a hinged plate. The unit coordinates the ignition system with the carb's fuel pump. The handlebar switch offers 42 positions, and the jetting and ignition can be adjusted on the fly. There is also a separate hole shot switch that provides smooth power delivery and better trac-

This cylinder is fastened on an expanding mandrel and mounted in a lathe. The cylinder base is being turned down to reduce the ports' duration, retard the timing, and increase the compression ratio. This machining operation serves to improve the low to midrange power of a dirt bike.

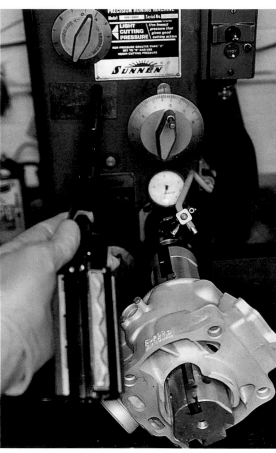

Honing machines are either portable or stationary. The hone on the left is a portable tool that can be driven with a drill. Sunnen makes stationary honing machines with a wide variety of mandrels and stones. Diamond stones are required to hone modern plated cylinders.

tion. You can program the control package with a PDA and change things such as the engine's ability to perform on less-expensive fuel. The Kawasaki Keihin electronic carburetor with throttle position sensor is ideal for computer control and coordination with things such as exhaust valve systems.

There are less-expensive aftermarket parts such as igniter boxes. FMF sells the Wolf brand igniter box that features adjust-on-the-fly timing. Products such as these offer a choice of an advanced curve for better midrange or one with a retarded curve for better over-rev. Normally, these products sell for about the same price as the OEM igniter box.

PERFORMANCE MACHINING TOOLS AND TECHNIQUES
MACHINE TOOLS

There are four different machine tools used for performance machining of motorcycle parts: lathe, vertical mill, horizontal or portable hone, and grinding or polishing tools.

Lathing

A bench lathe can be a handy machine in a motorcycle workshop. A 9x20-in.

bench lathe costs as little as $995 new from mail-order companies such as ENCO and Harbor Freight. This simple lathe can handle most of the tasks needed to maintain dirt bikes. Common uses for a lathe include resurfacing two-stroke cylinder heads, boring cylinders and carbs, machining circular-ring grooves, turning cylinder bases, polishing axles, and checking the trueness of a crankshaft.

Tooling for lathing includes the cutting tools and the mandrels or fixtures needed to mount a work piece. For centered two-stroke heads, a threaded mandrel can be purchased from Goodson for $25. For offset heads, you'll need to fasten and space the heads on bolts and pins on a face-plate.

To turn cylinders, expanding mandrels are the best setup. The mandrel's adjustable sleeve clamps on the cylinder bore. Precision Devices has the biggest selection of expanding mandrels, but mandrel kits can cost $200 to $1,000.

The most cost-effective way to buy cutting tools is to purchase a kit with five tool bit holders and replaceable tips. Considering that most machining tasks on dirt bikes will be performed on

aluminum parts, the TiN-coated tips work best because they resist buildup of aluminum on the cutting tip.

Milling

A vertical mill is like a lathe turned up on end. The main difference is that on a lathe the cutting tool is stationary and a mill spins the tool with the work piece mounted stationary. The uses for a mill include installing flywheel weights that use three Allen bolts, boring crankcases, removing broken bolts, resurfacing gasket surfaces such as crankcases, boring cylinders, and back-cutting tranny gears.

For my business, I chose a combination machine that enables lathing and

This crankcase is being bored on a milling machine. Because the crankshaft was stroked for a 2-mm offset, the area where the connecting rod swings past the crankcase must be bored 4 mm larger for the proper clearance.

Cylinder heads with offset spark plug holes must be mounted to a face-plate for machining in a lathe. Three of the bolt holes are tapped to a 3/8-NC thread and spaced from the plate with wrist pins and washers.

milling tasks. It's made by Smithy and is called Granite 1324. This machine sells for $3,700 with a package of accessories, including lathe tool bits, end mills, collets, live center, boring/facing head, and a rotary table.

Honing

Honing is considered a finish machining process. The two types of hones used in the motorcycle business are a horizontal machine with a stationary mandrel and a drill-operated, portable honing mandrel. Common applications for honing include the cylinder bore, connecting rod, a cylinder head's cam and tappet bore surfaces, crankshaft big end bores, and valve guides.

The biggest supplier in the world for motorcycle honing machines and supplies is Sunnen, headquartered in St. Louis, Missouri.

Grinding and Polishing

The two types of grinding tools are bench and cable-driven. Both a 6-in. bench grinder and a hand-operated setup like a Dremel can accept a variety of media ranging from rough stones to fine, rubberized abrasives.

In my porting business, I use a Dremel model 732. It has changeable tool handles in straight and right-angle configurations. There are hundreds of tool bits, varying in shape, size, grit, and material from felt to diamond.

The popular uses of grinding and polishing include cylinder porting, cleaning carbon from manifolds and pipes, leveling the wear grooves on clutch baskets, slicing the rusted bearing cages of swingarms and linkage, polishing carbon from power valves, and removing the molded rubber ears of two-stroke intake manifolds for V-Force reed cage installation.

Cylinder porting tool bits differ greatly for uses on nickel-plated and cast-iron-lined cylinders. Plated cylinders are harder and more brittle. It is a common mistake to chip the plating at a port's edge, which can lead to ring snagging and bore failure. Stones or diamond tooling cut through the hard nickel-plating, where traditional fluted carbide tool bits can take over the porting tasks. Virtually any tool bits can be used on cast-iron-lined cylinders because the material is much softer.

The biggest supplier of porting tools in the motorcycle industry is CC

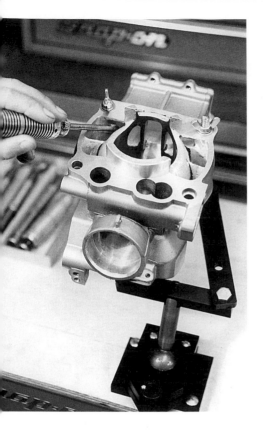

Portable grinding tools have cable-driven and foot-operated electric motors with quick-change tool capability. They are used most often for cylinder and head porting tasks.

These are tool handles, straight and right-angle designs. These tools hold tool bits of different shapes, materials, and textures. Tool handles plug into cable drives. CC Specialty in Lawrenceburg, Tennessee, is the biggest supply company for porting tools, bits, and polishing supplies.

Specialty in Lawrenceburg, Tennessee. They sell everything from electric and air-driven tools to tool bits and polishing supplies. They even sell measuring tools and flow benches.

VALVE SEAT MACHINE TOOLS

The latest trend in performance machining is the multi-angle carbide cutter that floats in the valve pocket holding a concentric path. Serdi and Newen sell complete machines from bench-top micro to heavy-duty production machine tools. Goodson Automotive, a mail-order supply company, markets an exclusive line of multi-angle cutters from famous tuners such as Tony Mondello. On four-stroke heads, much of the porting is accomplished by getting the right carbide cutter profile for the application and valve size. Goodson also sells a floating tool holder designed for the R-8 collets used in most vertical milling machines. The tool holder sells for $900 and the carbide cutters for $40 each.

There is hardly a need to resurface a valve because most of the hard coatings are applied during manufacturing.

This is a Serdi Micro multi-angle valve seat refacing tool. Multi-angle seats offer improved flow and longer valvetrain life.

CHAPTER NINE

FOUR-STROKE ENGINES

Four-stroke engines are very reliable, but when they finally break down, there are so many engine components that problems can be hard to diagnose. A four-stroke engine has more moving parts than a two-stroke engine, especially in the top end of the engine. Components such as the valves, guides, piston, and rings wear at different rates

If you ride a four-stroke, you need an hour meter. Modern racing four-stroke engines are more maintenance-intensive than two-strokes. Considering that a CRF is 1/8 of a Formula 1 engine, valves need to be adjusted every 10 hours. Complete top-end service intervals range from 25 to 75 hours. Yamaha sells hour meters for about $40 with an alarm set for 10-hour intervals.

based on service intervals and riding use. For example, if you run the engine with a dirty air filter, the piston and rings will wear faster than the valves. Conversely, if the valve-to-tappet clearance is too tight and the valves hang slightly open from the valve seats, the valves are subject to overheating from the high combustion temperature and pressure. So how are you supposed to diagnose top-end engine components without totally disassembling the engine?

A simple diagnostic test—the leak-down test—can be performed on any four-stroke engine. The test enables you to determine the condition of the top-end components.

LEAK-DOWN TESTING

A leak-down tester provides regulated, pressurized air to the cylinder through a hose threaded into the spark plug hole. A leak-down tester has two pressure gauges, one to control the test pressure and one to monitor the percent of airflow that leaks past the worn engine components. These types of testers are available from Snap-on tool dealers or auto parts stores. You will also need an air tank with 100 psi or an air compressor. Leak-down testers come with a variety of adapters that thread into any size of spark plug hole. Leak-down testers sell for $50 to $150.

HOW TO TEST

First, attach the compressed air source to the tester and set the regulator control so the gauge needle reads 100 percent. Thread the adapter hose into the spark plug hole. Turn the crankshaft so the piston is at TDC on the compression stroke. Attach the adapter hose to the leak-down tester. The

Leak-down testers are available from auto parts stores or Snap-on dealers. The tester consists of two pressure gauges, an air pressure regulator, and connection hoses to a compressor and the spark plug hole. Because modern four-strokes have automatic decompressors, leak-down testing is the only way to check the condition of the valves and piston rings.

compressed air will fill the combustion chamber. If there is a pressure leak, the leak-down tester's gauge will show the percentage of loss.

The normal amount of pressure leakage is 1 to 8 percent. If the leakage exceeds 10 percent, you need to find and repair the leak. The most apparent

All four-strokes have top dead center (TDC) marks stamped in the flywheel, positioned behind access covers. The marks are convenient but difficult to see. Try removing the left-side engine cover. You can easily see the marks, turn the flywheel with a wrench, and check for trapped metal from worn parts that accumulate in crevices at the bottom of the cover.

This is the intake valve. There are excessive carbon deposits that cause a flow problem at low valve lifts. The deposits may have a number of causes. The crankcase oil level may be too high. The valve stem seal could be leaking. The rings might be worn, and blowby pressure might be pumping oil through the vent tube and into the air box.

places to track down a leak are at the crankcase breather, the carburetor, and the exhaust pipe. The following are some tips on diagnosing leaks for the top-end engine components.

Piston Rings

If the piston and rings are worn, pressure will seep past the rings and into the crankcases. When the pressure is too great, it pushes crankcase oil out at the rubber crank seal and the breather hose that connects to the air box. An oil leak at the crankshaft seal (behind the ignition rotor) is a telltale sign of worn rings. Excessive oil in the air box is another sign of worn rings. Check the air box and filter for oil residue. With the leak-down tester installed and pressure in the cylinder, remove the breather vent hose from the air box. Cap your thumb over the end of the hose and feel for leaking air pressure.

Valve-to-Seat Leaks

Most pressure leaks are the result of carbon buildup on the valves, which occurs when oil leaks past the valve-stem seals, burns, and accumulates on the valve seat. The buildup wedges the valve open slightly, causing the leak. When this happens to the intake valves, the engine may make a coughing sound at idle. The coughing noise indicates that a small amount of combustion gases are flowing backward in the intake port and into the carburetor. The back-flow of gases causes a surge in the carb and momentarily stops the fuel from flowing. Remove the air box and the exhaust pipes, and then connect the leak-down tester to the engine and pressurize the cylinder. Cup your hand over the end of the carburetor or exhaust port and feel for leaking air. You will probably be able to hear the sound of the leaking air.

FIXING THE LEAKS

Piston, Rings, and Cylinder Bore

The average service interval for a dirt bike's piston and rings is about 3,000 miles. After 3,000 miles, you probably will need to overbore the cylinder for an

oversize piston because cylinder bores wear in a tapered, or slightly out-of-round, pattern. Some tuners prefer to overbore cylinders to boost the engine's displacement or compression ratio. If the rings are leaking on a relatively new bike (less than 1,000 miles), it's probably due to an improper break-in procedure. If an engine isn't broken in properly, oil will burn into the crosshatch grooves in the cylinder walls, forming a glaze that prevents the rings from sealing properly. The best fix for this problem is to replace the rings and hone the cylinder bore with a Flex-Hone. Flex-Hones are made by Brush Research in Los Angeles. Flex-Hones are made of hundreds of silicone-carbide balls mounted to plastic stems and fastened to a center shaft. They don't remove metal like a mandrel hone, but Flex-Hones remove the burned-oil glaze and polish down the surface of the bore so the rings can seal properly.

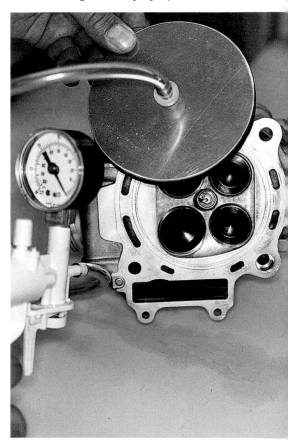

Goodson Automotive makes this vacuum tester to test the leakage of the valves and seats.

147

This is a CRF450. The intake valve clearance is measured by inserting a feeler gauge between the shim cup and the camshaft lobe. The exhaust side can be checked at the rocker arm. Whenever the exhaust shims are changed, the decompressor clearance must be adjusted with the screw and nut. If the decompressor adjustment becomes too loose, the bike will be hard to kick start.

Valves and Seats

Fixing leaking valves and seats can be as easy as replacing the stem seals and cleaning the valves with a wire brush. However, if the valve has been wedged open by the carbon for many engine-running hours, the valve and seat surfaces are probably burned and pitted. In this case, the valve-seat angles will need to be refaced and the valves replaced. Whenever the valves are removed, I recommend lapping the valve to the valve seat with fine lapping compound. Auto parts stores sell kits with fine lapping compound and a suction-type valve-lapping tool. The tool looks like a round rubber tentacle. Place a dab of lapping compound on the valve seat and squish the lapping tool onto the valve face. Then turn the tool back and forth for about two minutes until the lapping compound polishes the valve-to-seat interface.

This valve is being lapped for better valve and seat contact with a fine abrasive compound. Only steel or stainless valves can be lapped. Titanium valves cannot be lapped because the abrasives will remove the protective oxide finish and cause premature wear to the valve.

Get Help Fast!

If you don't have the knowledge or the specialized tools to perform a leak-down test on your bike, bring it to a motorcycle shop. A leak-down test takes about an hour and shops charge between $30 and $60. A leak-down test is much less expensive to do during a tune-up because the technician will already have the valve cover removed to set the tappet clearance. Perform a leak-down test once a year to stay informed on the condition of your bike's engine.

COMMON PROBLEMS

A word of caution to all of you slackers who refuse to work on your bikes until they break down. Here are some examples of what can happen when simple mechanical problems manifest into catastrophic engine damage.

TIGHT VALVES

If the tappet clearance is inadequate, the valves may hang open when the engine is running at peak temperatures. The exhaust valves may get so hot that they break apart, causing catastrophic engine damage. Leaky intake valves may cause a backfire that ignites unburned gas mixtures in the air boot and air box, thereby starting a fire.

WORN SPARK PLUG

Over time, the spark plug gap will increase due to erosion of the electrode and ground arm. The greater the spark plug gap, the greater the voltage required to arc across the gap. This raises the temperature of the electrode and ground arm, eventually causing the metal to fracture. If the spark plug's tiny ground arm breaks off, it could wedge itself between the valve and valve seat, causing the valve to break apart. Spark plugs last as long as 60,000 miles on some automobiles but only a fraction of that time in a motorcycle. Modern motorcycle engines have high-compression, high-turbulence combustion chambers that produce spark plug temperatures between 1,800 and 2,300 degrees Fahrenheit. Most manufacturers recommend changing the plugs every 1,000 miles.

WORN PISTON

A worn piston has excessive clearance to the cylinder wall, which causes an increase in crankcase pressure, in turn forcing some oil out the breather vent. When too much oil is lost, the remaining oil's temperature rises, causing a breakdown in lubrication. Eventually, the piston will shatter from the vibration. The shattered fragments of the piston fall into the crankcase and can damage the crankshaft and gearbox.

This is a view of a YZF head. Most pistons have part numbers engraved in the crowns. Notice the piston number stamped in the head near the edge. This engine had a worn connecting rod and main bearings, allowing the piston to contact the head. The engine ran hot and warped the head. When most single-cylinder engines overheat and warp, the deepest spot is usually on the exhaust side. This head and cylinder were repaired with minor lapping using fine emery cloth on a granite surface block.

This is a left-side view of a Honda CRF. The cam sprocket bolts are being removed, and the cam is held still by a wrench on the crankshaft bolt.

Whenever you do a top-end rebuild on a YZF, always replace the cam chain. Make sure to check the condition of the sprockets on the cams and crankshaft. This sprocket is chipped, and the journal surface has chatter marks from bouncing around in the main bearings. This crank needed replacement.

FOUR-STROKE TOP-END REBUILDING

A four-stroke engine is more difficult to rebuild than a two-stroke engine because there are more moving parts in the engine's top end. Here is a guide to rebuilding the top ends of single-cylinder four-stroke engines.

Before you disassemble the engine, you need to do a pressure leak-down test to determine which top-end parts are worn. See the leak-down section for detailed instructions on performing a leak-down test.

Before you attempt to disassemble the engine, you should remove the fuel tank and pressure-wash the engine and upper frame. This will help prevent dirt from falling into the disassembled engine. The following section details the procedures for rebuilding the top end of a single-cylinder four-stroke engine.

TOOLS AND MATERIALS

You should have the following tools and materials before you begin: new top-end gasket kit, service manual, torque wrench, oil drain pan, spray penetrating oil, spray cleaner, plastic mallet, assorted wrenches and sockets, parts bins, clean towels, measuring caliper, Flex-Hone, and drill.

TEAR DOWN

Start the engine disassembly by removing the inspection caps from the left-side

The KTM engines have a manual cam-chain adjuster, so the chain links must be removed and re-fitted whenever the cylinder head is removed. KTM makes a special tool to press a new master link on to the cam chain. The old link cannot be reused. This procedure is performed at TDC; it's easy to hold the KTM crank because there is a special bolt on the front of the engine for that purpose. Unthread the bolt, remove the two copper washers, and rethread it into the case.

engine cover. One is located in the middle of the cover to allow access to the crankshaft bolt. This bolt retains the flywheel and will be used to rotate the crankshaft to get the piston in the proper positions while rebuilding the top end and timing the camshaft. The crankshaft should only be turned in the normal direction of rotation; otherwise, the cam-chain tensioner could be damaged. The other inspection cap is mounted in the front of the engine cover, and it allows you to see the TDC stamping mark on the side of the flywheel. This is an important reference mark when timing the camshaft during top-end assembly. Remove the spark plug, exhaust pipe, carburetor, cam cover, and oil lines.

CAMSHAFT REMOVAL AND REFERENCE MARKS

After removing the cam cover, rotate the crankshaft so the TDC mark on the flywheel aligns in the center of the inspection window. The camshaft should not depress the valves; if it does, rotate the crankshaft another revolution and the piston will be at TDC on the compression stroke. All Japanese single-cylinder four-stroke engines are designed for camshaft installation at this crankshaft position. Look at the reference marks on the right side of the camshaft drive

sprocket. Compare the marks with the ones in the service manual or make a drawing for your own reference. Normally, there is a straight line on the sprocket that aligns with the gasket surface of the cam cover. Pay close attention to these marks—you will have to align the camshaft upon assembly and synchronize the crankshaft to the camshaft. Failure to do this properly will cause engine damage. To remove the camshaft, you may have to remove the sprocket from the camshaft, depending on your model engine. If you do remove the sprocket, take care not to drop the sprocket alignment pin into the crankcases.

HEAD REMOVAL

Now, you can remove the cam-chain tensioner, head, and cylinder. The head and cylinder are fitted with alignment pins, so it may be difficult to remove these parts. Never use a screwdriver or chisel to split the head and cylinder apart because that will damage the gasket surfaces. Instead, use a dead-shot plastic mallet to split the engine components apart. The cam-chain guides are plastic bars that either fasten or are wedged into place. Tie a piece of wire around the cam chain to prevent it from falling into the crankcases.

Inserting a small, straight-blade screwdriver down the center passage and turning the worn gear-driven plunger clockwise will release an automatic cam-chain tensioner.

Always stuff clean rags in the crankcases when attempting to remove or install circlips. If anything falls into the open crankcase, you may need to disassemble the engine unless you get lucky fishing it out with a telescopic magnet.

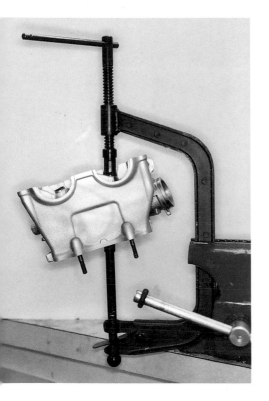

On all four-stroke dirt bikes, you need a special tool to remove the valve springs. Automotive tools are too big and won't fit. Kiowa makes kits with a G-clamp and several sizes of tips to fit the wide range of dirt bikes. They can be easily mounted in a bench vise to give you more control when trying to compress the spring and remove the keepers.

CLEANING AND INSPECTION

Clean the engine parts in mineral spirits solvent to remove the oil. Carbon buildup can be removed with spray oven cleaner. After cleaning, rinse the parts with detergent and water. If you don't have the proper tool to compress the valve springs, bring the head to a franchised dealer and pay them to remove the valve springs. Warning: Automotive valve spring compressors may not fit the tiny valve retainers of motorcycle engines and may damage the cylinder head. Take care to keep the sets of valve springs and retainers together, matched to the sides they were removed from. To check the valve-to-guide clearance, extend the valve from the seat 10 mm, grasp the valve head, and try to move it side to side. If you feel excessive movement and the back side of the valve is covered with carbon deposits, the valve guide and seal are worn and must be replaced.

Next, clean the valve with a wire brush and check the valve seat for pitting, cupping, or a sharp edge. The pitting indicates that the hard coating on the valve is destroyed, and a sharp edge indicates that the engine was over-revved and the valve springs floated, causing the valve to hammer up against the seat. Valves cannot be repaired because of the hard coating. The only option is to replace the valve. Kibblewhite stainless-steel valves are the most reliable aftermarket valves. Kibblewhite also sells high-performance spring kits that prevent valve floating at high rpm.

MEASURING THE PISTON AND CYLINDER

An easy way to measure the piston and bore diameters is with a digital caliper. Calipers cost about $125 and are very accurate. Measure the piston at its widest point, near the bottom of the skirt, and compare the measurement to the minimum diameter spec listed in the service manual. Measure the bore at the bottom of the cylinder because bores tend to wear fastest at that point. Some mechanics prefer to measure the cylinder bore with a dial-bore gauge, a precision measurement device that enables you to check the out-of-round and taper of the cylinder. Most motorcycle machine shops will do this service for free in an effort to get your business for overboring. If you have the tool, it only takes 10 seconds to check the size. Measure the piston rings by inserting them into the cylinder bore evenly, then measuring the end gap with a feeler gauge. If you go to the trouble to disassemble your engine, you may as well replace the rings.

Check the piston pin and small end of the connecting rod for scouring. Four-stroke engines do not use needle bearings like two-stroke engines. The pins ride on the polished steel surface of the rod or on a bronze bushing pressed in the rod. You can see tiny bits of bronze seized to the pin between the scour marks.

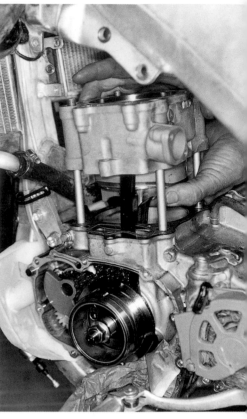

If you don't have a ring compressor, you can use this simple method. Turn the cylinder upside down. Use your thumbs to squeeze the rings into the grooves and into the bore. For the older YZF and KTM cylinders that do not have skirt cutaways, grind and polish two small U shapes in the bottom of the skirt in line with the piston pin. This will make it easier to install the rings and allow room for the piston pin to protrude for easy installation.

There are two ways to install the piston assembly in the cylinder. The first is to pin the piston to the rod and lower the cylinder onto the rod. You'll need a good ring compressor for the KTM and Yamaha YZF engines. However, with the Honda CRF you can squeeze the rings like a two-stroke and slide the cylinder down on the piston. Make sure none of the piston ring gaps overlap. Position them 90 to 120 degrees apart. All markings on the compression rings should face up.

Single overhead cam engines such as the CRF and KTM are easy to align. Make sure you apply a locking agent like Loctite Red on the threads of the two retaining bolts.

CYLINDER HONING

If the cylinder does not require boring, you should hone it before reassembling the engine. The best tool for deglazing a cylinder bore is a ball hone. The flexible aluminum-oxide balls remove burnt oil and refinish the crosshatch marks that are so important for proper ring sealing. Ball hones are available from Brush Research Co. under the product name Flex-Hone. The hones work great for both two- and four-stroke engines. Cylinder honing is performed by chucking the hone in a drill, coating the cylinder with oil, and spinning the hone

When performing a valve adjustment on a double overhead cam engine such as the YZF, KXF, and RMZ, set the crankshaft at TDC and use a yellow grease pen to mark the top alignment dots and the cam chain. Consult your factory service manual for the number of chain link pins between the dots. This is the critical overlap phase on the cams. Install the exhaust cam first upon reassembly. Check the crank TDC and exhaust cam marks for proper alignment before installing the intake cam.

in the cylinder while rapidly moving it up and down in the cylinder for 30 seconds. Clean the cylinder in detergent and water, dry it, and spray it with penetrating oil.

READY FOR ASSEMBLY

There are several methods for installing the piston and rings in the cylinder. The Japanese motorcycle manufacturers make a special tool for squeezing the rings, but it is expensive and cumbersome. My method is as follows: Install the piston on the connecting rod and lock in the circlips. Align the end gaps of the rings so they don't overlap each other and cause a loss of compression or oil. Buy a hose clamp that is slightly larger than the piston diameter from an auto parts store. Clamp it snugly around the piston rings. Make sure that

Automatic cam-chain tensioning devices can wear out from vibration and heat cycles. Test the tensioner by pushing and wiggling the device in your hand. If the plunger slips, replace it with a new part. The KTM uses a manual tensioner and requires frequent adjustment, about every 25 to 50 hours.

To check the valve-to-guide clearance, extend the valve out of the seat about 10 mm and try to wiggle it in any direction. Excessive movement means that the guides need to be replaced.

When the shims need to be changed in the valvetrain, stuff some clean rags down into the cam-chain galley so shims, clips, and alignment pins don't fall into the crankcase.

some part of the piston is exposed above the hose clamp. This will act as a pilot to guide the piston into the bottom of the cylinder evenly so the rings don't break upon installation. Grasp the cylinder with one hand and center it above the piston. Use your other hand to support the underside of the piston. Push the cylinder down onto the piston until the hose clamp slides down past the rings. Now, remove the hose clamp. Bolt down the cylinder head and install the cam-chain guides.

TIMING THE CAMSHAFT AND CRANKSHAFT

The cam chain may have some slacking links below the sprocket on the crankshaft, so grasp the chain and pull it taut while turning the crankshaft until the TDC mark on the flywheel is centered in the inspection window of the left-side engine cover. Install the cam, paying attention to the alignment marks. The cam shouldn't depress the valves. Install the sprocket, but don't lock the tabs on the bolts yet. Install the cam-chain tensioner and release it so it tensions the chain. Now, rotate the crankshaft two revolutions and check the alignment marks. You may find that

the marks are slightly off, indicating that the cam sprocket must be moved one tooth on the cam chain. The cam-chain tension was likely loose when the cam sprocket was installed because the tensioner wasn't installed yet (it is impossible to get the cam sprocket onto the cam with the tensioner installed). To realign the cam chain to the sprocket in the proper position, you must remove the cam-chain tensioner and repeat the process. After the camshaft and crankshaft are aligned properly, apply a locking agent to the threads of the bolts that fasten the sprocket to the camshaft, and then lock the tabs over the bolts.

CHECKING THE VALVE CLEARANCE

There are two types of valvetrains on modern four-stroke dirt bikes. The most basic is a rocker arm with a threaded adjuster bolt and nut; the more advanced high-performance system uses a shim cup arrangement. A small steel shim with a precise thickness is positioned between the valve and the cup. The cup rides against the cam.

Measure the valve clearance when the engine is cold and the cam lobe is facing away from the actuator (rocker arm or shim cup). The exhaust valves require more clearance to compensate for heat expansion since they run at a higher operating temperature than the intake valves. To measure the valve clearance, rotate the crankshaft to the TDC position on the compression stroke so both valves are closed, and then measure the clearance with a feeler gauge. Modern 250- and 400–450-cc engines that use shim cups require a special narrow feeler gauge set to fit in the space between cam lobes. Generally speaking, you can expect the rocker arm valvetrains to increase in valve clearance over time and the shim cup valvetrains to decrease valve clearance over time. The reason for this is simple: the rocker arm systems wear and the shim cup systems stay constant in dimension. The valve slowly wears and moves

When the top end is rebuilt and new rings are installed, the end gap must be set to a general specification of 0.003 inch per 1 inch of bore size. That is 0.009 inch on the average 250-cc cylinder and 0.012 inch on a 450 cc. This tool is called a ring grinder and is available from Goodson Automotive for under $100. It has a hand-operated ceramic abrasive wheel to grind the ring ends evenly.

deeper into its seat, which causes the valve clearance to decrease. When an engine is constantly over-revved, the valve bounces off the seat and clearance decreases quickly. Engines with worn valve seats tend to pop on idle because gases escape past the valve seat.

Adjusting the rocker arm systems is easily accomplished using a feeler gauge and a set of wrenches. Adjusting the shim cup systems is much more difficult and requires removal of the camshaft to gain access to the shim, which is placed under the cup. Manufacturers offer a narrow range of shims of varying thickness. The original shims are on the thick side of the range to allow adjustment. When the clearance requires extremely thin shims, it is an indication that the valve is worn from bouncing. In that case, the valve will need to be replaced and the seat refinished. One caution when attempting to adjust the valve clearance of the shim cup style systems: your local dealer probably won't have the shims in stock and will need to special order the parts. I suggest that you first measure the clearance and

then remove the cams to access the shims. The shims are marked with a size number; write down the number corresponding to the valve for future reference. That way, when you periodically check the clearance, if it's tight or loose, you'll have an indication of what shim to order in advance.

BREAK-IN PROCEDURE

If you ball-honed the cylinder, no special ring break-in procedure is necessary. Just go easy on the throttle for the first ride. If the cylinder was over-bored, you will need to apply a high-detergent, straight-weight, non-synthetic, break-in oil. Break in the engine in three separate sessions of 20 minutes each, with a 20-minute rest period between each session. In the first session, never exceed 1/2 throttle and third gear. In the second and third sessions, never exceed 3/4 throttle and fourth gear. Rev the engine up and down while shifting gears. Ride the bike on flat, hard ground (mud and sand exert too much of a load on the engine and can make it overheat easily). After an hour of running, change the crankcase oil.

CHAPTER TEN

WHEELS, TIRES, AND BRAKES

Wheels, tires, and brakes make our bikes roll, stick, and stop. How effectively these things happen depends on how true you keep the wheels, the types of tires you choose, and how often you service the brakes. This chapter provides tips that will save you the expense of catastrophic failures and reduce the time spent working on your bike so you can spend more time riding it.

HOW TO FIX WHEELS

Your bike's wheels are your safety net. When you land from a big jump and the suspension bottoms, the wheels are the only things that keep you and your bike from smashing into the ground, yet hardly anyone checks the spoke tension between rides. That is the only way you can prevent catastrophic damage to the wheels. This section is a comprehensive wheel maintenance guide that covers the spectrum from routine spoke tensioning to total lacing and truing. The information presented is applicable to the older-style, angle-head spokes as well as to the modern straight-pull spokes.

RIGHT AND WRONG TOOLS

Tools such as vise grips and adjustable wrenches are the wrong tools to use on spokes because they deform the flats on the spoke. Spoke wrenches are the right tools to use; they are designed to tightly fit the spoke flats so you can tighten the spoke without the chance of stripping the flats. A new tool hit the market in 1999—a spoke torque wrench. It's a good tool for people who have difficulty judging spoke tension. However, if the spoke threads start to corrode, you'll have to apply much more torque at the nipple in order to get the same spoke tension.

White Bros. distributes a wide range of wheels, discs, and brakes for all facets of motorcycle racing. This is a supermoto setup with Excel rims and hubs, a Braking oversize disc, and Brembo six-piston calipers.

BASIC TENSIONING TIPS

If you overtighten the spokes, the rim could crack at the weld line. Take care when tensioning spokes; a little loose is better than too tight.

Apply penetrating oil to the threads of the spoke before attempting to tighten the spokes. Power-washing a bike can cause the threads to corrode. The penetrating oil breaks down the corrosion on the threads.

Tighten every third spoke 1/4 turn, starting with the spoke nearest the air valve. After three revolutions, you will have tensioned the spokes equally. The spoke threads on from the inner-tube side of the tire, so when you look at the spokes from the rim center, you need to turn the spoke nipple counterclockwise to tighten it.

LACING AND TRUING WHEELS

The following wheel lacing procedure is for wheels with inner and outer spokes. Wheels with inner and outer spokes are more difficult to service than the straight-pull spokes. The inner/outer spoked wheels require you to remove four spokes just to install one new one. Inner/outer spoked wheels have two different styles of angled heads: one for the inner spokes and one for the outer spokes. Straight-pull spokes do not have angled heads, so they are easy to remove and replace individually. The truing process is the same for either type of wheel.

1. Wrap a piece of masking tape around the crossed spokes before you remove the spoke nipples. This will make it easier to relace the spokes in

This rim is being trued with the help of a stand and a dial indicator to monitor rim deflection.

When lacing a new rim, start by lacing all the inner spokes first.

4. Mount the wheel in a truing stand, and then fix a dial indicator stand onto the truing stand and against one side of the rim. Tighten the spokes 1/4 turn, alternating every third spoke, until all the spokes are tight. Use the dial indicator to check for runout; adjust the spoke tension so the rim has no more than 0.020 to 0.050 in. runout.

DENTED RIMS

There is no way for you to remove the dents from your rims; you will have to replace them. Excel rims are much stronger than OEM rims.

I use a Rowe spoke wrench that has wide, casehardened flats. Tallon Engineering in England and Buchanan Wheel in California (626-969-4655) offer stainless-steel spoke nipples for all popular brands. Buchanan also makes custom spokes to fit applications such as smaller rims for dirt track racing.

WHEEL BEARING REPAIR

Top Grand Prix mechanics replace the wheel bearings after every race. In racing, you need every small advantage. Less demanding riders might only need to replace their bikes' wheel bearings once each race season. This section's tips show you how to check and change your wheel bearings the easy way.

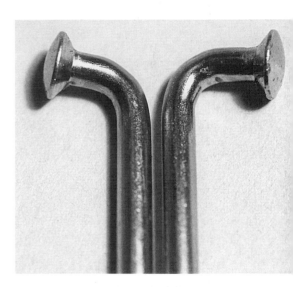

Although most modern wheels use straight-pull spokes, the old-style spokes were designed for inner and outer hub lacing. The inner spoke on the right has a tighter radius than the outer spoke on the left.

BASIC CLEANING AND INSPECTION

1. The seals in the hubs can be removed, cleaned, and greased many times before replacement is needed. You should also clean out the area between the seal and the sealed bearing. Now you can check the condition of the bearing.

2. Place your finger on the inside race and try to spin it. If the bearing is worn out, it will be hard to turn.

the proper rim holes. The spoke with the 110-degree bend is an inner spoke. The spoke with the tighter, 90-degree bend is an outer spoke. Wheels with straight-pull spokes have only one type of spoke.

2. Place the spokes in the hub and swing them into position. Spokes next to each other cross four other spokes. This is called a "cross-four" pattern and is the standard spoke pattern for dirt bike wheels.

3. Place the rim over the top of the hub and spokes. Start by installing one inner spoke in position and lace all the inner spokes around the rim. Take care that you lace the spoke through the spoke hole on the correct side of the rim. Do the initial spoke tightening with a screwdriver. Thread all the nipples onto the spokes an equal number of threads. Repeat the process for the outer spokes.

This is the inner assembly of the hubs. Seals on the end, a double set of bearings, and a center spacer comprise the inside of the typical dirt bike hub.

Check for excessive movement in the race. A wheel bearing should never have any movement.

3. Wheel bearings fit into the hubs with an interference fit. That means that the bearing is larger than the hole it fits into in the hub. The hub must be heated with a propane torch in the area around the bearing so that the hub expands enough to allow the race to be removed.

4. After the hub has been heated with a propane torch for about three minutes, use the following procedure to remove the bearings. From the back side, position a long drift rod onto the inner race of the bearing and strike it with a hammer; rotate the position of the drift rod around the circumference of the race to push the bearing out of the hub evenly.

5. The wheel bearing assembly consists of two seals on each end, two wheel bearings, and one axle spacer. After removing one bearing, pull out the axle spacer. Then remove the second

bearing. Notice how dirty and corroded the bearings and spacer become when the seals fail.

6. Clean the inside of the hub, and then heat it with a propane torch for about three minutes just prior to installing the bearing.

7. One side of each bearing is sealed (the side that faces out). Before installing the bearings, pack the open side with white-lithe or moly grease.

8. Use a hammer and a bearing driver to install one bearing. Universal bearing/seal driver kits are available from auto parts or industrial supply stores. Drive the bearing until it's completely bottomed into the hub. Now install the seal with a dab of grease to prevent water from penetrating the bearing. Install the axle spacer, and then install the second bearing until it is fully seated. Install the second bearing's seal with a dab of grease and you're done.

TIRES

The tires of a dirt bike are important because of the terrain that we ride upon. You can have a bike with the most expensive suspension revalving and a powerful engine, but if the knobs are all rounded off, you'll still end up on your butt. In the European motocross GPs, riders and mechanics regard tires as a suspension component. They are constantly fiddling with different tire patterns, compounds, and hybrid mousse inserts just to get a slight competitive edge. I try not to let

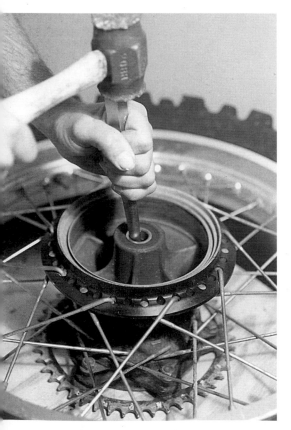

The rear wheel bearings can be removed with an offset drift punch and a hammer.

This is a close-up view of the offset drift punch. This was custom-ground on a bench grinding wheel.

tires dominate too much of my mechanic duties, but this section includes information that will make tire selection and tire changing a lot less stressful.

TOOLS FOR HOME AND TRAIL

You will need the following tools to change a tire: a 12-mm wrench for the rim lock and the Schrader valve, a valve stem tool, an air pressure gauge, a set of short and long tire irons, a compressed air source, and a bottle of spray detergent. If you want to put together a collection of tools that fit into your trail-riding tool kit, get two short tire irons, a valve stem tool, a pressure gauge, a bar of soap, and Moose Racing's compressed air cartridges.

Once you break the bead away from the rim, insert one iron in the tire at a time, folding the tire over the rim, alternating every few inches until the tire is two-thirds of the way off.

Use a plastic bowl to cover the sprocket so it doesn't get damaged while changing the tire.

CHANGING TIRES

Changing tires without tearing the bead or pinching the inner tube is just a matter of technique. You can struggle with the task, or you can stay patient and use your head. Here are some tips that I've picked up over the years.

You will need the following tools: a 12-mm wrench, valve stem tool, air pressure gauge, long and short tire irons, and spray detergent (warm, soapy water in a spray bottle works just fine).

First, loosen the rim lock and remove the valve stem nut. Then, break the bead using the following technique: Place the wheel on a flat surface and put one foot on the rim while using the

Grab the tire with one hand while holding the spokes with your other hand. Slip the tire off the rest of the way and remove the rim lock and inner tube.

other foot to press down on the sidewall of the tire. Remember to protect the disc rotor with a piece of cardboard so the ground doesn't scratch it.

The proper technique for removing one side of the tire goes like this: Insert the curved end of the tire iron between the tire and rim, pulled back at a 45-degree angle to the rim while inserting another iron about 3 in. away. Then, pull back the first iron to the rim while setting the second iron at a 45-degree angle. Remove the first iron and insert it again, 3 in. away from the second iron, and repeat the process. At some point, you will be able to use your

When installing the tire, start by putting the tire on the rim and then insert the lock and the inner tube. It helps to lube the tire with soap to prevent the tire iron from pinching the tube.

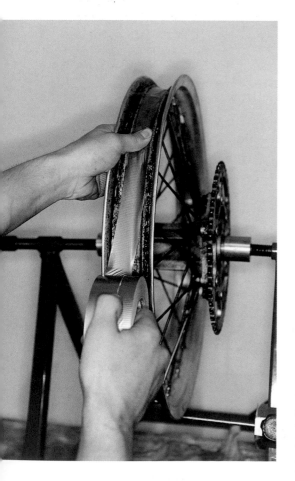

Original wheels come with rubber rim bands. Some mechanics like to replace the rim band with duct tape to prevent water from seeping into the tire.

hands to remove the tire. The fewer times you insert the tire irons, the less the chance of pinching the tube. I prefer to use the shorter tire irons for the front tire because the sidewall of the tire is thinner and requires less force to lift it off the rim.

After you have lifted one side of the tire over the rim, reach inside the tire and remove the tube and rim lock. Then, you can use the long tire irons to remove the tire. This is the proper technique: Grasp the rim with one hand and cross your other hand over and insert the flat side of the iron between the tire and rim. Once you bend the iron over as far as it will go, you can usually grasp the tire with your hand and push it downward to remove the tire all at once.

Before you try to install the tire, elevate the wheel by putting it on top of a rigid plastic or steel bucket. To install the tire, first put the rim lock into the rim and the rim band over the lock to hold it in position. Spray detergent on the inner side of the tube to prevent it from being pinched by the rim and irons. Spray some detergent on the inside of the tire's bead to help the tire slide onto the rim. Use the short irons to carefully install the tire over the rim. Then, rest both irons on each side of the rim lock and push the rim lock up into the tire past the bead. Remember to thread the lock nut on a few threads to the rim lock before popping the rim lock past the bead. Otherwise, the rim lock could fall into the tire, making it difficult to install in the hole of the rim. Start at the rim lock and work over to the air valve, then around the rest of the tire. Try to roll the tire's bead on with your hand before using the tire irons. Every time you use the tire irons, you run the risk of puncturing the inner tube. When I first started working in motorcycle shops in the early 1970s, motorcycle tire machines had not yet been invented and the service manager wouldn't let the mechanics use tire irons to install tires. We had to roll the entire bead of a street tire or knobby with our hands. It's possible, but only with the right technique.

TREAD PATTERNS, COMPOUNDS, AND PRESSURE

There are many different tread patterns and compounds for off-road tires. In general, hard compounds are better for soft terrain such as mud and sand, and soft compounds are better for hard terrain such as clay. Regarding tire patterns, the best patterns for hard-packed surfaces are those with tightly spaced, low profile knobs. The soft-compound, short knobs can conform to the terrain surface without breaking loose. In the 1995 supercross season, Jeremy McGrath had great success using Dunlop's dual-sport tire (K940) on the tracks with hard-packed clay surfaces. The best tire patterns for soft terrain are those with tall knobs that are widely spaced. The hard compound knobs can penetrate the terrain surface and resist becoming clogged up, thanks to the open area between the knobs. The latest

These are the two basic types of front tire tread patterns. Soft terrain tires (left) have widely spaced, tall, pointy knobs. Tires designed for hard-packed terrain have closely spaced, low-profile knobs with more surface area.

These are three rear tire tread patterns. On the right is a paddle tire designed for sand. The tire in the center has widely spaced knobs, which work best in mud. The tire on the left is a Pirelli bi-directional type. The bi-directional can be installed so the tread pattern's direction of rotation suits either intermediate or hard-packed terrain.

trend in tires is a reversible type to cover intermediate and soft terrain. Pirelli was the first to offer this type of tire.

A tire's air pressure can be adjusted to take advantage of the tire's tread pattern and compound. In general, lower pressure is used for soft terrain because it allows the tire to conform to the ground for maximum traction. On a muddy surface, there aren't as many sharp-edged bumps and it's difficult to get big air over jumps, so it isn't necessary to use high air pressure to prevent the tube from being punctured. However, on hard-packed or rocky surfaces, it's necessary to run higher pressure for three reasons: to resist punctures from hard landings, to keep the tire from spinning on the rim lock, and to make the soft-compound tire conform to proper profile.

Here are some guidelines for selecting the proper models of the three most popular brands of tires—Pirelli, Dunlop, and Bridgestone—along with some recommendations on air pressure.

PUNCTURE PROTECTION

There are some precautions that you can take to ensure against punctures. Heavy-duty inner tubes should be used on every bike except minis and 125s that are raced competitively in motocross. The reason is that the tubes are heavy and pose a bit of drag on small engines. In some forms of racing, such as desert events held in rocky terrain, the risk of puncture is great, even with heavy-duty tubes. For this situation, you may want to use either a mousse tube or a combination mousse and inflatable tube like the Dunlop Crescent mousse. Mousse is a dense, closed-cell foam tube that does not deflate when punctured. Many off-road racers riding large-displacement bikes choose to install mousse in the tires. Mousse also gives the tire some extra protection from rock impacts. The mousse enables the tire to absorb the impacts of rocks instead of bottoming and deflecting in a random manner. Mousse tubes do have some disadvantages, however. They are prone to shrinkage, and they have a high cost per usage ($175 each for about 1,000 miles). The Dunlop Crescent mousse product sells for about $120 and is available for both front and rear tires.

SNOW AND ICE TIRES

Riding in snow and ice can be as much (if not more) fun than riding typical terrain. It also can be a way for riders in northern climates to stay sane during the winter. With good tires, the effect is not all that different from riding on loose sand.

TIRE CHART

HARD	INTERMEDIATE	SOFT
Clay, Churt, Dry Dirt	Loamy Soil, Some Rocks	Sand, Mud, Rocks
DUNLOP K490/K695	K755/K737	K752/K752 DUNLOP
BRIDGESTONE M23/M22	M57/M58	M25/M26
PIRELLI MT460	MT32	MT320
14–12 psi	12–10 psi	10-8 psi

The first set of numbers is for the front tire and the second set is for the rear tire. The same follows for the recommended tire pressure.

Winter conditions can vary drastically. Off-road bikes can't handle extremely deep snow, but studded tires allow the bike to navigate 12 in. of snow or less with ease (not to mention throwing huge amounts of roost). Also, ice riding and racing are generally good as long as the ice is safe and basically flat-tracking (although you can find heaved ice to jump under the right conditions).

Ice Studs

There are several ways to get good traction in frozen conditions. The most common is to screw ice studs into your tires. The aftermarket studs are better than regular sheetmetal screws for several reasons. For one, they are actually unfinished sheetmetal screws. The finishing process smoothes the surface of the screws, which reduces their traction. Also, the aftermarket screws are coated, making them more durable than regular sheetmetal screws. Use the pattern shown in the photos to install the screws.

Keep in mind that screws will eventually round off and may pull out of the tire on occasion. Replace the screws regularly as you ride.

Trelleborg Ice Tires

Former national enduro champ Kevin Hines recommends Trelleborg tires for winter trail riding. He says Trellys have the best compound and stud arrangement. The studs are carbide-tipped points molded into the knobs. Trellys are very durable and cost about the same as a tire and liner with 800 screws (under $200 each).

Ice Racing Tires

Jeff Fredette is an avid ice racer, besides being the "King of KDXs." Fredette was one of the first racers to use a 21-in. front wheel for ice racing. I remember when he showed up for a race at a popular circuit outside the Chicago area back in 1980. That circuit attracted the local hard-core dirt track racers. People thought Fredette was lazy because he just studded up the stock tires of his Suzuki PE175. He left the lights on the bike and everything, but people weren't

Trelleborg tires are mud knobbies with molded-in spikes for snow and ice trail riding.

This is an ice tire custom-modified by Jeff Fredette. He is the ice racing god. Jeff double-lines the tire and installs 800 sheetmetal screws into the knobs. This tire produces more traction on ice than a sharp knobby does in dirt.

laughing much when he kicked their asses by holding the inside line!

Fredette reasoned that the wide-spaced knobs of the 21-in. tire were ideal for penetrating the top layer of snow and

ice debris that covers the corners of an ice racing track. Since then, he has become a well-known ice tire expert.

Fredette sets up his own tires for oval-track ice racing. He lines his tires with old street tires. He first strips the sidewalls and bead off the street tires with a carpet knife. He lines the rear with an 18-in. street tire and uses a 21-in. Harley-Davidson tire to line the tire up front. The lining keeps the points of the screws from rupturing the tube.

He places only the tread of the street tire into the Kenda Ice Master trials tire. The tread pattern and compound of the Kenda tire are excellent for holding the 800 5/8-in. Kold Kutter screws that provide the traction on ice and fasten the Kenda and street tire liner together.

You might think, "Hey, what's the big deal? You just get a screw gun and jam a bunch of sheetmetal screws into a set of tires." You might be able to get away with that for riding around the cow pasture, but to be competitive in ice racing, you'll need to do more. The alignment of the screw heads is critical because it is the edges and corners of the screws that help the tire gain traction on the ice. The edges of the screw are used for a paddle effect, and the corners are positioned to bite when the tire is leaned over in a turn. Each of the 800-odd screws must be threaded into the tire perpendicular to the knob with a screw gun (see photograph).

BRAKE SYSTEMS

The elements and the laws of physics punish the brakes of a dirt bike. The disc brake pads push against a disc that is sometimes covered with water, mud, and sand. Consequently, dirt bike brake systems wear much faster and need much more maintenance than the brake systems on cars or street bikes.

In racing, the front brake is primarily used to slow the motorcycle. The rear brake is used to change a bike's attitude over jumps by creating a torque reaction. The rear brakes can also be applied lightly to keep the rear end of the bike tracking straight through

If a log or rock dings the front disc, you can fix minor deflections by clamping the disc with a crescent wrench and straightening it.

whoops sections. Dragging the brakes quickly wears out the pads, so you should check them often. The friction from dragging the brakes also creates a lot of heat, and that heat transfers through the caliper piston and into the brake fluid. This heat rapidly breaks down the fluid, so it too, must be checked often.

In addition to normal maintenance, you can tune your brakes in a number of ways. Manufacturers make different pad material to improve longevity in various riding conditions. Metallic pads work best in sandy conditions, and composite pads offer superior braking power. There are different types of discs too. This section gives you all the basics of brake-system repair, maintenance, and tuning, along with some tips on troubleshooting braking problems.

BRAKE FAQs

WEAK FRONT BRAKES

QUESTION: The front brake on my KX250 is weak. I change the fluid often and have tried different types of pads. Nothing helps much. I power-wash the brakes after I ride to keep out the dirt. What do I need to do to fix this bike's brakes?

ANSWER: *Power-washing the brakes with soap is a bad thing. The soap film attacks the adhesive in the pad and bonds to the ridges in the disc. Soap can also glaze the disc. You can deglaze the disc with medium-grit sandpaper or there are companies that can resurface the disc. The best cure is to install a braking stainless-steel disc and a set of composite or metallic pads.*

BRAKES GET HOT AND LOCK UP

QUESTION: The disc brakes on my bike start to get hot and lock up. The pads get wedged against the disc and I can't even turn the wheel until the brakes cool down. I have to bleed out some brake fluid when it gets really bad. What do you think is wrong with my bike's brakes?

ANSWER: *This is a common problem. The two brake pins that the pads slide on become grooved and prevent the pads from moving away from the disc when the brake lever is released. Try replacing the pads and pins and changing the brake fluid to a DOT 4. The best fix for preventing the problem of grooved brake pins is to use stainless-steel pins made by WER (Works Enduro Rider). WER makes the pins with hex heads, too, so they are easy to remove when changing brake pads.*

KEVLAR BRAKE PADS WEAR TOO QUICKLY

QUESTION: I put a set of expensive Kevlar brake pads on my bike and they are shot after only a few rides. The material is still on the pad, but I have to pull in the lever really hard just to get them to lock up. What gives?

ANSWER: *I'm guessing that you are a power-washing freak. That is a sure way to damage Kevlar pads. The strong detergents that commercial power-washing systems use can damage the Kevlar material used on the pads. The detergent bonds to the pads and causes them to form a low-friction glaze. That is why the pad material has not worn down but the pad won't grip the disc. Don't try to file or sand the pad; just get a new set, and wash your bike with water only!*

Remove the calipers to change the pads. Take care not to lose the carrier clips.

This is a worn set of pads and pins. The pins have wear divots, and the backing has fallen off the pad. The pads are scoured and worn past the service limit line.

BASIC CLEANING AND PAD REPLACEMENT

The following are some basic tips on checking and changing brake pads. If you are having a specific problem with your brakes, see the troubleshooting guide at the end of this chapter. Always review the factory service manual for your model bike before attempting any service procedures.

1. Before you attempt to change the brake pads, first power-wash the brakes clean with water (no soap). The high-strength detergents used in power washers can damage the caliper seals, disc surface, and even attack the bond used on the pad, so avoid spraying the brakes when you wash your bike. Next, clean the dirt from the inside of the Allen-head caliper screws with a pick or brake cleaner. This ensures that the Allen wrench gets a rigid grip and doesn't strip the screw when you remove it.

2. Remove the brake pins and check the pins' surfaces for divots, dents, and corrosion. These surface blemishes can cause the pads to drag when the brakes get hot. Replace the pins at least once a year, and never apply grease to the pins.

3. After you have removed the brake pins, you can remove the caliper and pull out the pads. Check the pads for glazing or wear. If the pads are worn out, replace them.

4. Reinstall the pads, calipers, and pins, and tighten all the screws. Always depress the brake lever several times after you have installed the wheels to enable the brake pistons to pump up to the pads.

FLUID REPLACEMENT

The brake fluid should be changed at least two times a year. Race mechanics change the fluid on their bikes every two races. There are two methods for replacing the brake fluid and bleeding the brakes: pump-and-purge or with a hand-operated vacuum pump.

The Pump-and-Purge Method
If you don't have a brake bleeder tool, this is the best method to change brake fluid.

1. Remove the master cylinder cap, and top the cylinder with brake fluid.

2. Put a six-point box-end wrench on the bleeder valve located on the caliper. Slip a 10-in.-long piece of

Perhaps in the next edition of this performance handbook we'll be explaining how two-wheel fluid drive systems work. This system, partner-pioneered by Ohlins and Yamaha, uses a vane hub and hydraulic feed lines to drive the front wheel of this YZ250.

clear plastic tubing over the end of the bleeder valve.

3. Slowly pump the brake lever and hold it fully engaged; then loosen the bleeder valve a quarter of a turn for one second before tightening the valve.

A jackshaft chain drive transfers power from the countershaft sprocket to drive a fluid pump to produce a two-wheel-drive dirt bike.

4. While frequently checking fluid level in the master cylinder and topping it off as necessary, repeat Step 3 until the fluid coming out of the tube is clean and clear and without bubbles.
5. Remove the hose, snug down the bleeder valve, top off the master cylinder, and replace the master cylinder cap.

The Hand-Pump Method
A brake bleeder tool will speed up your brake fluid change. Use the following method to change your oil with the tool.
1. Connect a collection tank between the pump and a hose attached to the bleeder valve.
2. Remove the master cylinder cap. Be prepared to constantly replenish the master cylinder with brake fluid during the bleeding process.
3. Loosen the bleeder valve a half turn and use the vacuum pump to slowly pump the fluid through the brake system. Don't forget to replenish the master cylinder.
4. When the fluid coming out of the bleeder valve looks clean, clear, and free of bubbles, stop pumping and snug down the bleeder valve.
5. Detach the pump from the bleeder valve, replenish the master cylinder, and replace the master cylinder cap.

TROUBLESHOOTING

PROBLEM: The brakes drag when they get hot.

SOLUTION: The brake fluid could be saturated with water. It's best to change the brake fluid twice a year.

PROBLEM: After only 15 minutes of riding, the rear brake pedal has no free movement and the brakes are very sensitive.

SOLUTION: The brake pins could be bent or have divots that cause the pads to drag against the disc. The heat is transferred through the caliper piston and into the brake fluid. The water in the fluid boils and expands, and that causes a lack of free movement at the brake pedal. Check the brake pins and change the fluid.

PROBLEM: The brake lever or pedal pulsates when the brakes are applied.

SOLUTION: The disc is bent and is pushing the piston back into the caliper. This force is transferred into the pedal/lever, making a pulsation for every revolution of the wheel. Replace the disc because it cannot be repaired.

PROBLEM: The front brake pads wear on an angle.

SOLUTION: The front caliper carrier bracket is bent; replace it.

PROBLEM: The brakes make a squealing noise.

SOLUTION: The discs and pads have a thin film of glazing on their surfaces. The glazing could have occurred from leaking fork seals, power-wash detergent, or chain lube accidentally sprayed on the disc. Medium-grit sandpaper can remove the glazing from the surface of the discs and pads. Afterward, clean the discs with brake cleaner—never with a detergent.

CHAPTER ELEVEN

TUNING TIPS FOR HONDA DIRT BIKES

1990–2004 HONDA CR80/85

FLAWS: fork damping

FIXES: Emulator valve

This bike hardly changed between 1987 and 1995. The engine is excellent, a design far ahead of its time, but the chassis and the suspension are archaic. The swingarm on the early models was stamped sheet metal that was clipped together. Later, Honda changed to a conventional, welded design. The forks are simple oil-orifice, damper rod type. This suspension setup is the single biggest hindrance to an aspiring mini racer. The biggest problem with the CR is the spring rate of the forks and shock. Pro-Action makes a selection of aftermarket springs, calibrated accurately. Ask a suspension tuner for recommendations on both front and rear spring choices based on the rider's weight, height, and ability. Heavier or taller riders will need stiffer springs, for obvious reasons.

FORKS

Riders who use the front brakes hard will need stiffer fork springs to prevent the front end from diving abruptly in braking bumps. These are damper rod, not cartridge, forks. There are two ways to change the damping rate: either change the viscosity of the oil (SAE 10 weight) or vary the diameter of the hole in the damping rod. Changing the oil level will change the bottoming characteristics of the fork but not the damping. In 1994, a new product became available for CR forks called the Emulator valve, made by Race Tech. The valve improves the damping of the compression and rebound circuits, emulating the effect of cartridge forks.

MX World of Great Britain pioneered the "supermini" concept, developing and marketing products for Honda CR80s with the help of legions of British schoolboy racers.

The valve costs just over $100 and is easy to install. The Emulator valve fits between the fork spring and the damper rod of each fork leg.

SHOCK

When the low-speed compression damping is too soft, try adjusting the clicker to between four and six clicks out.

BIG WHEEL SUSPENSION

Most riders will benefit from stiffer springs on both ends. Companies such as Race Spec and Pro-Action specialize in hard-to-get springs for minis. The rear shock needs more compression damping because the longer swingarm causes the shock's shaft speed to be slower. Also, the rebound damping is too stiff. Try adjusting the clickers to remedy these problems.

CYLINDER

The port timing of the stock cylinder is okay for most riders. For expert riders, I suggest widening the right rear transfer port to 17 mm, the same width as the corresponding left rear transfer. The exhaust port can be raised to a maximum height of 25 mm, measured from the top of the cylinder. The boost ports that connect the intake to the transfer ports can be enlarged to 12 mm. These mods will help top-end power. Chronic head gasket leaks are common on all CR80s. The problem is not the head or gasket, it's the top of the cylinder. The surface has imperfections all around the stud holes and the water ports. Fix this problem by removing the studs, and then lap the top surface of the cylinder on a flat surface using medium-grit sandpaper.

Always use a gasket sealer on steel Honda head gaskets.

BUILDING A SUPERMINI FROM A CR EXPERT

The CR80/85 Expert was introduced in 2001. It features bigger wheels and extended wheelbase to make the bike competitive in the supermini and 125-cc classes. The maximum displacement limit set by the AMA for the supermini class is 105 cc, achievable only with changes in the bore size, not crankshaft stroking. Wiseco makes a 101.5-cc piston and gasket kit. This kit requires boring, porting head mods, and electro-plating. If you're strictly looking for more low-end power for women racers or trail riding, then simply boring and plating the cylinder will be ideal, but you still have to modify the head for piston clearance. For expert riders, the porting changes have to be extreme to take advantage of the top end. I suggest widening the exhaust port to a chordal width of 49 mm, raising the exhaust to 24.7 mm, raising the center transfer to the same height as the other transfers, and opening up the boost ports to 12 mm. The head must be modified as follows: enlarge the diameter to 52.5 mm and set the squish band angle to 10 degrees with a recess depth of 1 mm.

2000–2003 HONDA CR125

FLAWS: weak powerband
FIXES: V-Force reed valve, exhaust valve modification

After being accused of having an anti-quated engine with a high-maintenance exhaust valve system, Honda made a bold change in the top end of the CR125. The cylinder is nearly identical to the RS250 road racer design. There is a new exhaust valve that has only three main parts. The valve varies the effective stroke, port time-area, and duration. Overall, Honda made a good decision to update this model. The new top end has a lot of potential. Many of the parts from the 2000–2002 models interchange. The crankcases and cylinder were changed in 2003, and that engine is very peaky with hardly any low-end power.

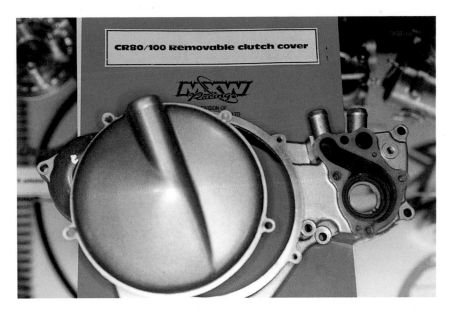

MX World clutch with easy access cover.

BEST VALUE MODS

ENGINE: V-Force reed valve, porting, 12-tooth sprocket, steel clutch plates, exhaust valve mods

SUSPENSION: springs for your geared weight

CYLINDER MODS

The 2000 and 2001 cylinders have a lot of potential. The exhaust port and valve can be modified in a number of different configurations. For more top-end power, raise the exhaust port to 28 mm from the top of the cylinder. Also drop the outer edges of the exhaust port 5 mm. The ports on the 2002 and 2003 models are actually too big. If you're looking for more low to midrange power, switch to the Wiseco 755MO5400 piston kit from an RM125. The timing height is higher, which retards and reduces the timing and duration of the ports. The cylinder head will need to be modified for piston clear-ance. On a lathe, cut the squish band to a recess gap of 0.060 in./1.5 mm. Use a blend angle of 20 degrees and narrow the squish band to 0.0235 in./6 mm.

EXHAUST VALVES

There is a new exhaust valve with only three main parts. The valve varies the effective stroke, port time-area, and

duration. It's a great design except for the shape, which is easily tuned. Honda did tuners a favor by making the valve halves so large and restrictive. The valves can be ground to different profiles. In stock form, the valves don't allow for enough blow-down timing from 4,500 to 8,000 rpm, prior to when the valves flip wide open. A simple way to advance the exhaust valves is to make a bushing for the stop pin to limit how far the valves close. A bushing with a 5-mm diameter, placed over the top of the original stop pin, is ideal for most riders.

The 2002 and later exhaust valves have blow-down ports that achieve the same thing as the bushing on the stop pin. The valves also have labyrinth channels for better sealing at low rpm. The 2002 valves fit into the 2000–2001 cylinders.

CRANKCASE MODS

The 2000 CR cylinder has a gross mismatch with the crankcases. The cylinder hangs over into the cases, partially blocking the flow. If you're looking for more top-end power, the cylinder ports should be ground larger to fit the cases. If you're looking for strictly low-end power, apply epoxy to the cases to blend into the cylinder ports.

REED VALVE

The V-Force 3 brand of reed valve gives a big gain in low to midrange power. Modifying the intake manifold for use with a V-Force reed valve is a fairly difficult task. You have to remove the two rubber wings that normally extend into the stock reed valve. The Honda manifold doesn't use a gasket because it has a molded O-ring instead. I use a two-step process to remove the rubber wings. Start by clamping the manifold in a vise but not on the O-ring surface. Use a hacksaw to saw off the wings within 1/8 in. of the base. Then use a Moto-Tool with a sanding drum to polish off the remaining material.

GEARING

Install a 12-tooth countershaft sprocket with a stock rear sprocket to make second gear more useable and virtually eliminate the need for first gear.

EXHAUST MANIFOLDS

Honda changed the exhaust manifold and exhaust port duct shape on every model of CR125 from 2000 to 2003. All the manifolds interchange, but the 2002 stands out as the best design for getting more low to midrange response. The main differences are the length and D-shape to the inside diameter.

1998–1999 HONDA CR125

FLAWS: weak top-end power
FIXES: Cometic base gasket and head mod
The 1998 CR125 was a great evolutionary design leap. With an aluminum frame, five-speed gearbox, and a new exhaust valve system, Honda came under criticism from the motorcycle press for switching from a six-speed to five-speed. The frame follows the same concept as the CR250, and has proven reliable and rigid. The five-speed gearbox enabled Honda engineers to widen the gears, making the tranny more reliable. Earlier models tend to break first gear, which is part of the main shaft. This failure occurs most often when aftermarket clutch plates are installed with stiffer springs. The new HPP exhaust valve system cures a

The Honda CR125 carries on the spirit of the old Elsinore and has become the reliable workhorse of the 125 class.

SRS is an Italian hop-up shop that makes the world's best trick parts for CR125s.

twofold problem related to performance and reliability. The new HPP eliminates blowby over the valves and prevents a worn valve from contacting the piston.

BEST VALUE MODS

ENGINE: Cometic gasket, bigger carb, CR250 air boot
SUSPENSION: Pro-Action revalving

NEW HPP

The new exhaust valve system solves a number of maintenance and performance problems. The new valves feature an L-shaped guide rail that prevents the valve from contacting the piston after it wears. The new design seals properly in the closed position for more compression and better low-end power. Some of the magazines claim that the bike doesn't have enough top-end power, which is due to the lower exhaust port height of the new HPP valves. The effective stroke is longer and the compression ratio is lower so that the engine can run on pump gas.

CYLINDER

The cylinder porting and casting quality are excellent. All you need to do is experiment with the cylinder height. That involves swapping base gaskets with different thicknesses. Cometic makes base gaskets in the sizes of 0.010, 0.020 (stock), and 0.039 in. If the thinnest gasket is installed, the engine's powerband will shift down the rpm scale—good for tight stadium racing. There is no head modification needed. However, if you install the thickest gasket, you'll need to modify the head. If you really want to get the cylinder ported, here are some guidelines. Widening the exhaust port will only cause the valves to snag the ring. The transfer ports can be raised to 41.25 mm for the front set and 42 mm for the rear set for more top-end power. Grind the valve guides on an angle so the port height measures 28.5 mm from the top of the cylinder to effectively raise the exhaust port.

HEAD

The head's gasket surface can be turned down as much as 0.024 in. (0.6 mm) to raise the compression ratio to compensate for the Cometic 0.039 base gasket.

EXHAUST PLUGS OR VALVES?

The HPP valve system maximizes the powerband by adjusting the time-area of the exhaust port to the engine's rpm. If an engine is to be tuned for maximum top-end power and the application can sacrifice some low-end power, exhaust valve plugs are the best choice. On dirt track motorcycles and shifter karts, I install plugs because the engine is used in a narrow, high-rev range. Boyesen Performance manufactures the aluminum exhaust plugs. The plugs are installed in place of HPP valves. The exhaust port height can be raised to 28 mm, measured from the

top of the cylinder. That will really make the engine rev. By removing the exhaust valves, you can also remove the power valve governor that drives off the crankshaft to reduce drag and friction on the crank and yield extra horsepower.

CARBURETOR AND AIR BOOT

The 1998 CR can gain more top end by installing the intake setup from a CR250. A Keihin PJ38 carburetor with the air boot from a 1998 CR250 will boost maximum airflow through the engine. A carb from a 1990–1996 CR250 will fit the best. The baseline jet settings for that carb are 58 Slow jet, 1468 Needle P-2, 170 Main jet. The Honda part number for the needle is 16012-KS6-004. The 1999 CR125 already uses the larger air boot but still needs the larger carburetor.

1990–1997 HONDA CR125

FLAWS: carb jetting off, clutch fades, rims dent easily

FIXES: richen jetting, install steel clutch plates, lace-up Excel rims

The CR is regarded as the best 125 of the early to mid-1990s. These models have had their share of problems, but overall this is the most reliable 125 cc motocross bike. Simple problems such as carb jetting can be adjusted with just a needle and main jet change. The clutch performs better with steel plates and frequent oil changes. The stock rims are very soft and dent easily when riding in rocky conditions. It's best to replace them once they are dented with Excel rims.

The CR engine can be modified to be a better enduro bike or have the raging top-end power for GP motocross. Whatever type of dirt riding you do, the CR125 can be modified to suit your riding demands.

BEST VALUE MODS

ENGINE: 1468 needle for carb, RAD valve, 53-tooth rear sprocket

SUSPENSION: stiffer fork springs

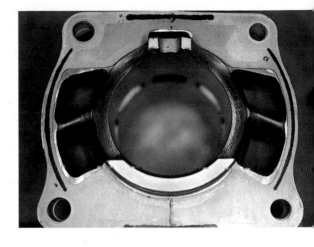

This 2000 CR125 has a mismatch between the cylinder and crankcases. Check out the overlap between the cylinder base and gasket.

Thick putty epoxy, marketed as a gas tank repair kit in auto parts stores, is the most reliable filler material for cylinder ports. For this application, a 1997 CR250 that is woods-ridden gets this "twin spin" treatment to boost the low-speed throttle response.

SUPERCROSS OR ENDURO POWERBAND

If you want to increase the low-end and midrange power of your CR125, these modifications are the hot ticket. These are great for supercross, where you need quick bursts of power, or enduro riding, where mellow power is better for navigating snotty trails. These modifications are also well suited to lower level riders. The bike will be easier to ride with the sacrifice of some top-end power.

Aluminum CR frames need wide glide plate protection for the bottom frame tubes.

HPP VALVES

The exhaust valve guides of the 1993 to 1997 models are manufactured with such a high opening that, when the valves are closed, the exhaust gases can pass over the top of the valves. For more low-end to midrange power, install the exhaust valve assemblies from the 1999 CR125. These parts are very expensive at about $150, but they really help the low-end power. Honda part numbers: left, 14700-KZ4-000; right, 14600-KZ4-000.

HEAD MOD

The 1990 and 1991 models have domed pistons and hemi-shaped combustion chambers. The 1992 model was the first year of the flat-top piston design. Never mix heads and pistons on the earlier and later CRs or you may damage the engine. The 1990 and 1991 cylinder head can be improved by turning down the face of the head 0.028 in. or 0.7 mm. Then the squish angle must be cut at a 10-degree angle with a deck height of 0.020 in. or 0.5 mm. On the 1992 and later models, the spark plug doesn't thread in flush to the combustion chamber. The top of the spark plug lug should be turned down on a lathe 1 mm. The compression ratio and squish band width are good, so no other modifications are necessary.

REED VALVE

The Boyesen RAD Valve makes a tremendous difference in the low and midrange of the powerband and is a must for enduro riding.

EXHAUST PIPE

The best pipe for these engine mods is a Dyno-Port low-end pipe.

HIGH-REV POWERBAND

The stock engine peaks at about 10,500 rpm. To be competitive in the national championships or GPs, the engine must have a powerband that starts at 9,500 and peaks at 12,500 rpm. Modifying the CR for that extra elusive 2,000 rpm is very expensive and requires total engine disassembly and special machining. This is a parts list of the engine components and an explanation of how they are tuned to work together: 1992 CR125 cylinder 12110-KZ4-860; 1991 head 12200-KZ4-730; 38-mm PJ Keihin carb; aftermarket pipe and silencer; and carbon fiber reeds.

The 1992 CR125 cylinder has more aggressive exhaust and transfer port timing than the 1993 and 1994 models. You can use the 1993–1996 HPP valves, but you need to switch to the domed piston and head. The domed setup enables more efficient cylinder scavenging at high rpm. The carbon fiber reeds are less prone to fluttering, and the larger carb is needed to boost the rpm peak of the engine.

CRANKCASE MODS

The cases must be machined for a larger intake port with better flow up to the transfer ports.

REEDS

Use carbon fiber reeds instead of the stock reeds, which start to flutter at about 10,700 rpm. The carbon fiber reeds produce excellent top-end power without fluttering at high rpm.

PISTON AND HEAD

The domed piston has a slight advantage at extremely high rpm. Use a Wiseco Pro-Lite and the 1991 head.

CR125 CARBURETOR JETTING

Here are some specs on a starting point for carb jetting. The specific gravity is different between North America and Europe, so European jetting specs need to be slightly richer. American carb jetting for 36-mm PJ Keihin using 93-octane pump gas with a pre-mix ratio of 40 to 1; air screw 1.5 turns; slow jet 58; needle 1468; main jet 168. European specs for unleaded premium petrol with a 40 to 1 pre-mix: air screw 1.5 turns; slow jet 62; needle 1468; main jet 178.

Baseline carb specs for a 38-mm PJ Keihin are one step richer on the slow and main jets using the 1468 needle.

CR CLUTCH TIPS

Never install stiffer clutch springs in a CR125. The clutch is designed to slip when the gears engage on upshifting. This helps reduce the impact on the transmission. Stiffer clutch springs could accelerate wear on the transmission because of the increased load. Steel clutch plates wear slower and don't contaminate the gear oil. However, they do increase the drivetrain inertia, just like a flywheel weight. The heavier steel clutch plates will help you hook and stay in control on slippery, hard-packed tracks, but the bike will feel a bit slow to respond in deep sand or where you have good traction. The additional weight of steel clutch plates can make the bike a bit easier to ride as well. When the stock clutch basket wears out, replace it with a Hinson racing clutch. The Hinson clutch basket is made of better material and hard-anodized with Teflon.

1985–1989 HONDA CR125

FLAWS: left-side crankshaft seal leaks, clutch plates wear out

FIXES: replace seal often, install Barnett steel plates

Honda perfected the 125 in the late 1980s. Here are some general things to pay close attention to or modify for better performance.

BEST VALUE MODS

ENGINE: 53-tooth sprocket, 1468 carb needle

SUSPENSION: shock revalving, stiffer fork springs

GEARING

A good baseline for gearing on all models should be 13/53 for motocross and 12/52 for supercross and enduro. Adjust by single teeth on the rear for slightly different tracks and conditions.

CARBURETOR

A 36-mm carburetor works best using these jetting specs: 58 slow jet; 6 slide; 1468 needle; and 168 main jet (vary slightly according to elevation and extreme air temperature differences).

CRANKSHAFT

The left-side crankshaft seals wear out quickly because the left-side cover is flimsy. Replace the seal often; otherwise, the piston could overheat and seize on the exhaust skirt. The 1987 model's crankshaft was updated to a stronger design. The new connecting rod uses a 15-mm pin, so you must change the piston with the crankshaft. Both parts are standard on the 1988 model.

CYLINDER INTERCHANGE

The 1989 cylinder is Nikasil-plated and it will fit the 1987 and 1988 models (which are not plated).

CLUTCH

Replacing the aluminum clutch plates with steel plates makes the clutch last longer and doesn't hurt performance. Never install stiffer springs in the clutch of a CR125 because it will cause the first gear drive to fail. First gear wears quickly on these bikes normally, and it is part of the clutch shaft, so it is expensive to replace.

REEDS

Honda doesn't make replacement reeds for its bikes; use Boyesen reeds.

ATAC SYSTEM

The exhaust valve on the 1987 to 1997 models can be damaged on installation. The right-side valve end has a flat machined on it, and if you tighten the actuator lever too much, it can round the flat edge. This causes the valve to hang open and raise the exhaust-gas temperature at high rpm, eventually causing the piston to seize.

SHOCK

The rear shock can be modified for better handling on the 1985 to 1988 models. These types of shocks use straight shims. The rebound valve stack has two transition shims, one in the middle and one closest to the piston. Put both transition shims between the number 26 and 27 shim from the piston. After this, the shock will handle square-edged bumps much better.

2002–2004 HONDA CR250

FLAWS: reeds chip, powerband short
FIXES: V-Force reed valve, porting for midrange and top end

Back to the future—that's the theme of the 2002 and later CR250 engine. This case reed design traces its roots to the late 1980s, when it was used in a dual-sport bike for the Japanese market. Many people think that the 1992 to 2001 engine was a superior design, including factory rider Mike LaRocco, who continued to use the old engine for two seasons after the new engine was released. The biggest innovation on the 2002 model was the electronically controlled RC power valve system. The 2002 and later models suffer from a narrow powerband concentrated in the center of the rev range. Installing a top-end pipe helps the over-rev, but the main problem with the powerband is in the cylinder porting.

CYLINDER

The RC valve design changed in 2003 because the original valves had gaping pockets on the sides and roof of the exhaust port duct. The 2002 to 2004 cylinder's exhaust port can be raised 0.060 in./1.5 mm. In order to get the widest powerband, the cylinder needs to be turned down by 0.030 in./0.75 mm and the cylinder head's recess squish gap needs to be machined by the same amount to ensure the proper piston-to-head clearance.

REED VALVE

The stock reeds are prone to chipping. The V-Force reed valve is much more reliable because it distributes the load to double the sets of reed petals.

1997–2001 HONDA CR250

FLAWS: piston and ring design, secondary coil
FIXES: Wiseco piston, replace coil when misfire starts

The 1997 model was the first generation of advanced ignition systems. The traction control concept of monitoring rpm changes versus time is good, but Honda missed the mark on the 1997 model. It needs a steeper advance curve in order to give the powerband a hard-hitting midrange, for which previous models were famous. The 1998 model has a slight change in the cylinder head and the ignition. The 1999 model has a different cylinder with porting that is a bit too mellow for most riders.

A few mechanical problems have surfaced with time, including failure of the ignition coil and the piston ring. When the top coil fails, the engine starts misfiring and then loses spark completely. The piston ring tends to spin around the ring groove after the centering pin works loose from the piston. The best solution to these problems is to keep a spare top coil in your toolbox and replace the stock piston often or switch to a more durable Wiseco piston.

The 1997 model was the first year to use the aluminum frame. By 2000, Honda changed the frame at the front down tube and lengthened the swingarm. Some of the problems on early models involved clearances at the motor mounts and head-stays. That could easily be fixed with shim washers to take up the gap. Lengthening the swingarm helps the handling on the 2000 models. Handling on earlier models can be improved with revalving.

The 2001 model has the best 250-cc engine built by any motorcycle manufacturer—a strong lower end and tranny with a new cylinder casting featuring reinforcements in critical areas such as the intake skirt. The port timing is on the radical side and the bike is faster than most riders need. Honda switched to a Mikuni carburetor for the 2001 model. The jetting is extremely rich and requires leaner jets on the pilot, needle, and main jet. For more information on engine mods, check out the next section on the 1992 to 1996 models.

BEST VALUE MODS

ENGINE: Wiseco Extreme Lite piston, Cometic thin base gasket

SUSPENSION: revalving

SECONDARY COIL

The 1997 CR250 has a problem with a bad batch of secondary coils mounted on the left side of the frame that connect to the spark plug. High-rpm misfire and hard starting are clear symptoms of a faulty coil. Eventually, the coil fails completely and the engine loses spark. In 1998, Honda cured the problem with a better quality coil.

CARBURETOR

In 1997 and 1998, Honda used an electronic carb that monitored rpm with a black box; the system was sensitive to a couple of problems. The wire connector was located on the outside of the frame and was prone to water seepage. The black box was sensitive to electrical noise; it's important to use a resistor spark plug to reduce the interference. Lean bogging in the midrange during hard acceleration is a symptom of a faulty solenoid. If this is happening, disconnect the wire connector and install a richer jet needle, such as a 1368.

1992–1996 HONDA CR250

FLAWS: chain and sprockets wear, cylinders break, rear suspension kicks

FIXES: loosen chain tension, install 1999 cylinder, revalve shock

There is hardly any difference among the engines used from 1992 to 1996, and the modifications listed will apply to the previous models. The focus of the engine mods is to make the CR easier to ride for motocross riders and even better for enduro riders.

Sometimes, the CR250 engines shift in the frame, making a gap at the head-stay. Rather than squeezing the bracket together, shim washers can be added to reduce the compression load on the cylinder head.

BEST VALUE MODS

ENGINE: carb jetting, flywheel weight

SUSPENSION: revalving

CRANKCASE MODS

The 1992 CR250 has poor oil flow between the transmission and clutch cavity. On any dirt bike, when the clutch spins, it forces oil into the transmission. Passageways link the trans and clutch cavities so the oil can circulate and cool the clutch. Starting in 1993, Honda bored two additional oil flow passages in the right-side crankcase, linking the two cavities. If your 1992 CR burns up clutch plates frequently, drill two 8-mm holes in the crankcase as shown in the photo.

CARBURETOR

The jetting needs to be richened to a 1368 needle and a 185 main jet.

CYLINDER HEAD MODIFICATION

Index the spark plug depth by turning it down on a lathe. The spark plug lug must be turned down 0.040 in. If the cylinder base hasn't yet been turned, then 0.5 mm can be turned off the

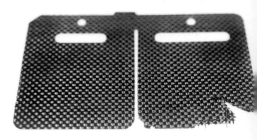

The new series of 2002 CR250 case reed has some issues with chipped reeds. The V-Force reed valve is more reliable.

cylinder head gasket surface to reduce the minimum clearance space between the piston and head, increase the compression ratio, and give a stronger pulling powerband for more torque.

CYLINDER TUNING

The original Honda castings are excellent, and the port timing is consistent. However, you can gain a big increase in low-end torque with the proper use of epoxy and a right-angle, hand-grinding tool. This work is better left to professional tuners. The cylinders are

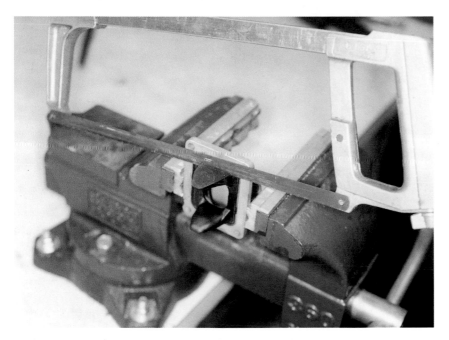

Honda CRs need the intake manifold modified by having the stuffers hacksawed off.

Take care not to strike the molded O-ring surface with the saw. It's best to leave a little material to finish with a sanding roll and a Moto-tool.

interchangeable among the 1992 to 2000 models. The 1995, 1996, and 1999 cylinders are the best because of their smaller exhaust and intake ports. These cylinders have the best timing combination and the most sealing surface area for the rings. The 1999 cylinder has extremely small exhaust ports and smooth power delivery; it works great to tame down the 1997 and 1998 models. However, many people complain that the 1999 model is flat on the top end. For the 1999 model, I recommend raising only the sub-exhaust ports to 39 mm, measured from the top of the cylinder. The smaller intake port doesn't hinder performance and is stronger to reduce piston skirt wear. The cylinders with the smaller intake port are easier to install because the rings are less likely to pop out of the grooves when sliding the cylinder down on the piston. Apply epoxy on alternate sides of the separating bridge for more crankcase compression. This also changes the flow pattern up through the transfer ports and into the cylinder bore. Flow shaping is also performed on the rear transfer port window exit angles. This cylinder will peak at 7,500 rpm and works great with the stock pipe, stock or spark arrestor silencer, and intake system. To attain the optimum compression ratio and

exhaust port time-area on the 1992 to 1994 model cylinders, the cylinder base must be turned down (0.5 mm) on a lathe. The transfer ports must be raised to 58 mm, measured from the top of the cylinder.

FLYWHEEL WEIGHT
The flywheel weight is the final component to tune. Tuners normally overlook this component. Dave Watson, who teaches riding schools in England, thinks that flywheel weights make the power delivery easier for most riders to handle, especially junior and vet motocross riders or trail riders.

SWINGARM
The 1992 CR250 has a problem with cracks forming in the swingarm. You can gusset the swingarm for additional strength. The biggest cause for a cracked swingarm is too little chain slack. Take care when adjusting the chain; it's better to be a bit loose than tight.

1990–1991 HONDA CR250
FLAWS: leaky air boot, carbon-seized HPP valves, fork debris
FIXES: seal boot, chamfer HPP valves, Eibach springs and Pro-Action preload cones

These bikes are very reliable but have some handling problems that are easily fixed. The engines produce good torque, but the exhaust valve system is difficult to service. Here are some fix-it and tuning tips for these models of CR250s.

BEST VALUE MODS
ENGINE: carb jetting, flywheel weight
SUSPENSION: aftermarket springs, Pro-Action cones

HPP VALVE MODS
The HPP valves are prone to carbon seizing. See the recommendations on exhaust valve servicing in Chapter 6.

CARBURETOR JETTING
Here are some jetting specs when using a 40-to-1 pre-mix ratio with 93-octane unleaded fuels and an NGK BP7ES spark plug: 55 slow jet; 1369 needle in the third position; and a 175 main jet.

AIR BOX SEALING
The air boot-to-air box flange must be sealed on the older CRs. The best sealer to use is weather stripping adhesive because it isn't fuel-soluble. Never use silicone sealer because the fuel will deteriorate the sealer and allow water and dirt to enter the air box.

To install a new Hot Cam on a CRF450, you have to use internal snap ring pliers to remove this retaining clip. Next, the cam and bearings must be shifted sideways out of the Unicam carrier.

CYLINDER TUNING

There are some simple modifications you can perform to the cylinder with just a file. Remove the casting flaws around the boost ports for smoother flow through the intake, and match the HPP valve guides to the exhaust port. This is a critical area of the cylinder because even a small mismatch can cause a shock wave that effectively blocks the exhaust port. Other more difficult mods include raising the transfer ports to 58 mm from the top of the cylinder, turning down the cylinder base 0.5 mm, and narrowing the rear transfer ports as listed in the paragraph for the late-model CRs.

HEAD MODS

The top of the spark plug lug must be turned down on a lathe 3 mm to allow the spark plug to thread down flush into the combustion chamber. This modification improves throttle response and reduces spark plug cold-fouling.

FLYWHEEL WEIGHT

The CRs benefit from a flywheel weight. Sixteen ounces is the standard size that companies such as A-Loop or Steahly use for their products, although they will have several options available. In general, heavier weights are better for enduro and off-road, while lighter weights are geared toward motocross or supercross. For novice and intermediate riders, the heavier weights can work very well. Power delivery is a bit more manageable and low end is greatly improved. The bike will be easier to control, yet deliver the same amount of horsepower.

Steahly makes thread-on flywheel weights. This product threads onto the fine left-hand threads on the center hub of most Japanese magneto rotors. Normally, the threads are used for the flywheel remover tool. Thread-on flywheel weights can only be used if the threads on the flywheel are in perfect condition.

BIG DISPLACEMENT KITS

If your cylinder's plating is worn and needs to be repaired, consider a Wiseco oversize piston kit. Wiseco offers 265-cc pistons. The kit requires modifications to the exhaust valves.

IGNITION TIMING

Advancing the ignition timing gives the CR more midrange hit in the power-band. Normally, Honda stator plates aren't adjustable. To make the plate adjustable, you need to file the plate 1 mm at the lower bolt hole. This will enable you to rotate the stator plate clockwise to advance the ignition timing.

CRANKSHAFT SEAL

The left-side crankshaft seal is prone to failure. Honda redesigned the seal in 1992. The seal fails because dirt and water enter the ignition cover. Boyesen

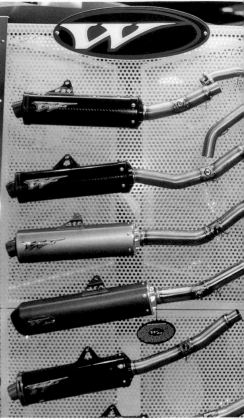

White Bros. makes a variety of high-end exhaust systems for the CRF line of Hondas.

Engineering makes an aluminum cover that seals properly. If your CR bogs at low rpm, the seal is probably blown and needs to be replaced.

FUEL TANK INSERT NUTS

The fuel tank insert nuts are square-shaped and pressed into reliefs in the plastic fuel tank. When the scoop bolts are overtightened, the insert nuts tend to spin in the tank when the bolt is removed, making it impossible to remove the radiator scoop. The solution is to remove the insert nut and bond it back in place with epoxy. Removing the nut will be difficult. I use an air impact wrench to spin the bolt while using a large flat screwdriver to pry off the scoop just behind the insert nut. Take care not to puncture the fuel tank. Once you remove the scoop and insert nut, grasp the square insert nut with a wrench or channel lock pliers and remove the bolt.

This is a comparison view of the stock (top) and the low-boy header pipe. A longer header pipe like this one should give better low to midrange power.

Apply a dab of Duro Master-Mend epoxy to the insert nut and the relief in the fuel tank. Press the insert nut in place for about 15 minutes.

FORKS

These cartridge forks have the early model valve design with a small-diameter piston. They are prone to clogging with metal debris. The forks have to be disassembled and cleaned often. The main sources for the metal debris are the springs and the spring preload cones. The springs have a coating that flakes off. The preload cones are made of steel with sharp-machined edges. The cone fits into the spring and aggravates the flaking problem. Use Eibach fork springs, which are powder-coated with a flexible material that doesn't flake off. Pro-Action makes an aluminum preload cone that doesn't wear or vibrate like the stock steel cone. Performing these two modifications will save you money in fork oil changes and improve the bike's handling.

Some suspension companies offer hard anodizing for fork parts. On bikes produced after 1989, most fork parts come hard-anodized from the manufacturer. Hard anodizing prevents the aluminum parts from wearing prematurely. This service is to repair slider tubes on the 1990 and later CR250 models.

Many companies make aftermarket base valve kits for cartridge forks. These products improve performance through changes to the piston design and the valve shim stacks. If you are going to the expense of installing a base valve kit, make sure that the fork springs are matched to your riding weight, skill level, and the base valve kit. Race Tech provides a tuning manual with its Gold Valve products. The tuning manual provides guidelines on spring rates and valving changes for a variety of rider profiles.

2002–2004 HONDA CRF450

FLAWS: weak valvetrain, suspension valving
FIXES: Kibblewhite Black Diamond stainless-steel and titanium valvetrain kit, suspension revalving

Building a 450-cc four-stroke for motocross was a brilliant first effort for Honda. This bike is a careful blend of traditional XR reliability with a Formula 1 edge. Innovations such as separate oil cavities, automatic decompression, and low-cost, modular replacement parts are the benchmarks that Honda challenged its competitors with. Overall, the CRF450 is a great bike with tons of aftermarket accessory choices. In 2002, the bike needed aftermarket triple clamps with more offset, so Honda incorporated the design changes for the 2003 model. As with most Honda models, the engine parts interchange easily.

Considering that the 450 is 1/10 of a Formula 1 auto racing engine, it's pretty reliable for a dirt bike. Some minor problems have nagged this engine with valvetrain issues. Here are some of the details about OEM parts and the best choices of aftermarket accessories for this popular bike.

VALVETRAIN

The valvetrain on a four-stroke dirt bike engine consists of the intake and exhaust valves, springs, collets, retaining clips, tappets, shims, camshaft, and cam chain. The CRF450 requires frequent maintenance of the titanium intake valves. The valve seat area tends to form a cup shape when the valve springs sack out with use. The valves bounce off the valve seat, causing the hard oxide protective coating on the valve to wear off. The solution is to install stainless-steel valves with dual-rate springs.

The new trend of flame-retardant foam air filters advocates the removal of the suppression screen of the filter cage. Clips are used to hold the screen. Removing the screen also produces more intake noise.

Kibblewhite makes a complete replacement kit with valves, springs, collets, and retainers for stock and high-rev engines. The parts sell for about $375 and require valve-lapping during installation, which gives a performance advantage because you can hand fit the valve to the seat for an excellent seal. The hard materials of the valve guides and seats ensure high quality.

DECOMPRESSION ADJUSTMENTS

The automatic decompression mechanism is located on the right side of the camshaft. The lash adjustment to the right-side exhaust valve is accomplished with a screw and nut adjuster mounted to the end of a rocker arm. The adjustment tends to become looser with use, which makes the engine harder to kick start. The decompressor needs to be adjusted every time the exhaust valves are re-shimmed.

HIGH-COMPRESSION BIG BORES

The piston needs to be replaced between 50 and 100 hours of use. Wiseco makes high-compression piston kits for the stock bore and 3 mm over stock.

CAMSHAFTS

The 2002 camshaft is considered a peaky cam for a high-rpm powerband. The 2003 is a torque cam. Hot Cams makes aftermarket cams of similar high- and low-rpm choices.

These Summers Racing Concepts fork braces improve the stability for the traditional line of XRs, which use conventional forks.

AIR BOX MODS

The factory recalled the original 2002 air boxes for sealing problems. PC Racing makes a positive seal kit for the air box and filter. It's intended for use on the 2002 model and can be applied to the later models.

CHAIN TENSIONER TESTING

The 2002 and 2003 cam chain tensioners are prone to failure. Replace them with a 2004 tensioner. Test an old tensioner by squeezing it in your hand. Try to make the plunger retract by wiggling and squeezing it together. If you can make the plunger retract, the tensioner needs to be replaced.

WATER PUMP

Water pump leaks are common with the 450. Always replace the shaft and bearings along with the two seals. Make sure that the seal spring faces out toward the impellor; it's a common mistake to install it flush and backward. Take care when installing the right-side engine cover. The water pump drive lub is rectangular and must fit precisely in the crankshaft.

1990–2001 HONDA CR500

FLAWS: abrupt powerband, headshaking
FIXES: lower compression ratio, stiffer fork springs

The CR500 hasn't changed much in the past five years, and there is a lot you can do to this bike. The engine hits abruptly and riders complain that it is hard to ride on slippery surfaces. Here are some mods that will help the engine pull smoothly from low-end and rev out further.

BEST VALUE MODS

ENGINE: DEP sport pipe and silencer
SUSPENSION: fork springs

CARBURETOR

A 39.5-mm Keihin PWK carb will add 3 horsepower to the top end and make the engine pull cleanly off the low end. Sudco sells an aftermarket PWK or you can use a carb from a 1992 and later KX500.

CYLINDER HEAD

You can turn the head on a lathe to reshape the transition between the combustion chamber and the squish band. Set the tool angle to 25 degrees and cut into the squish band, starting 15 mm from the edge of the chamber. Install a projected nose spark plug such as an NGK BP6ES.

CYLINDER

The hook angles of the rear transfer ports should be filled with epoxy so the transfers are aimed at each other instead of toward the exhaust port. The narrower the port, the smoother the low-end power. The minimum chordal width of each rear transfer port is 10 mm. Raise the exhaust port 1.5 mm and widen the two ports 4 mm on each outer edge. The steel sleeve will be rough from the original manufacturing process and should be matched to the aluminum casting. Polish the port edges with fine-grit sandpaper to improve piston and ring life.

Monitor the bore of the cylinder for out-of-round wear and taper wear. I have had the best luck running oversize Wiseco pistons, set to 0.004-in. piston-to-bore clearance.

EXHAUST SYSTEM

Pro-Circuit, FMF, and DEP Sport make excellent pipe and silencer combinations for the CR500.

The XR400 has some issues with loose head studs, especially when a 440 big bore kit is installed. This heavy-duty stud kit improves the longevity of the air-cooled XR.

FORK SPRINGS

Riders who weigh over 170 pounds may want to switch to a stiffer spring rate (23–25 pounds). If bottoming and head-shake occurs frequently, that is a sign that you need stiffer fork springs and to raise the fork oil level. The highest fork oil level is 120 mm, for the minimum air space and highest pressure.

1985–1989 HONDA CR250 AND CR500

FLAWS: soft fork springs, magneto covers leak, air boot leaks
FIXES: stiffer fork springs, Boyesen magneto cover, seal air boot

The big CRs went through an amazing design evolution in the late 1980s. The suspension went from drilled passageways and squirting fork oil to upside-down cartridge forks and a rear shock with technology rivaling an Ohlins. The CRs changed more in five years than they had in the 12 years since their inception. There are many innovative products built by European and American companies that bring the mid-1980s CRs into the 1990s. The 1986 and 1987 models share the same exhaust valve system and are easy to control. However, the HPP system requires frequent service. Here is a survey of the products and mods for these timeless motorcycles.

BEST VALUE MODS

ENGINE: 1369 carb needle, chamfer HPP valves, T-vents in carburetor

SUSPENSION: fork springs, check linkage bolts

CR250 EXHAUST VALVES

The earlier models (1984–1985) have a butterfly valve linked to a can at the exhaust manifold to increase the volume of the header pipe at low rpm and boost the low-end power. The butterfly valves are prone to carbon buildup, which locks the valve in the open position and reduces the top-end power of the engine.

SUSPENSION

Honda had problems determining the proper fork-spring preload on the early cartridge forks. The proper amount is 5 to 15 mm, although Honda used as much as 30 mm on production bikes. The best fork spring rates to use are 0.40–0.41 kilogram for the CR250 and 0.44 kilogram for the CR500. The Race Tech Emulator valve is about the only aftermarket accessory that you can use to improve the handling of the older CRs. It's the closest thing to a cartridge fork.

LINKAGE

The suspension linkage and the floating rear drum brakes of the 1985 and 1986 models are also trouble points. The 1988 CR250 had chronic problems with bent rear-shock-linkage bolts until Honda redesigned the parts and added flanges to the heads of the bolts. The part numbers for the new bolts are H/C 2976678 and H/C 2976686. The CR linkage requires careful attention and frequent lubing. A seized linkage can put an enormous strain on the frame, causing everything from cracks in the frame to leaks at the head gasket.

REAR WHEEL

In 1989, Honda redesigned the rear hub to be lighter. It was too weak and often shattered. Honda had a recall campaign in Europe but not in America. The 1990 hubs look similar to the 1987 hubs with a conical taper, compared to the straight diameter hub of the 1989 model. Tallon makes an excellent replacement hub that is far stronger than the stock hub.

ERGONOMIC CHANGES

Bolt-on parts for the rest of the chassis include wider foot pegs, stiffer seat foam, a skid plate to protect the frame, and a cable to prevent the rear brake lever from tearing off in berms.

ENGINE

The only real change to the CR500 in the late 1980s was the switch to water cooling. The air-cooled models suffered from detonation, and the cylinder head had to be modified to lower the compression ratio and narrow the width of the squish band.

SPARK PLUG

The best spark plug heat range is an NGK BP7ES.

CARBURETOR PROBLEMS

The carb's fuel-inlet needle and seat wear out quickly because of the vibration, causing the engine to flood when the bike is dropped. Change them every season.

SILENCER

The later model CR500s suffer from chronic breakage of the silencer core. The silencer needs to be packed often; otherwise, there is nothing to protect the core tube from vibration.

Muzzy Performance makes lightweight, effective, and inexpensive titanium exhaust systems for the CRF line.

REED VALVE

In 1986, Honda put a plastic insert in the reed valve to stuff the dead air space and boost the velocity. FMF sells aftermarket "reed stuffers." Boyesen reeds are a good investment because the reed stop plates block the cylinder's rear boost port. Boyesen reeds are more responsive than original Honda reeds and they don't require the stop plates.

CARBURETOR

Jetting for the 1986 to 1991 models burning 93-octane pump gas with a premix ratio of 40 to 1 should be 55 slow jet, 1369 needle, and 172 main jet. Take care setting the float level and replace the inlet needle and seat every year. Changing to a modern T-vent system for the carb is also beneficial. In this way, if you ride through mud, your bike won't vapor lock (mud splattered up under the bike blocks the carb's float bowl vents).

IGNITION SYSTEM

The ignition systems require frequent maintenance in the form of cleaning the inside of the flywheel. The dirt and water that get drawn in from the plastic side cover break down the coils, corrode the flywheel, and wear down the left-side crankshaft seal. Boyesen Engineering makes aluminum side covers that seal better than the stock plastic covers. They also function as a heat sink to transfer damaging engine heat away from the ignition. Ignition coils and spark plug caps tend to break down on the CRs.

AIR BOX

The air boot flanges on the CRs tend to leak after you pressure-wash the bike with strong detergents. Reseal the air boot with weather stripping adhesive, available from auto parts stores.

HONDA XR TUNING
WITH SCOTT SUMMERS AND FRED BRAMBLETT

Honda XRs are used for everything from play riding to hare scrambles to desert racing. They are perhaps the most bulletproof and widely used dirt bikes on the planet. Although enduro and trail riders have been using XRs for decades, Scott Summers, one of the best off-road riders in the sport, put a No. 1 plate on the flanks of an XR600 several times in the 1990s and has demonstrated that XRs are capable of much more than just plunking down trails or crawling through the woods. He and his mechanic, Fred Bramblett, are not the typical rider–mechanic duo. They are motorcycle innovators. They've devised some interesting innovations for the XR line of Hondas. They've tested just about everything possible for XRs. Whether racing the Baja 1000, the ISDE, or cow trailing through the deep woods of Kentucky, they know the setup that works best.

ENGINE
Air Filter

Clean the air filter and the air box after every ride. Check the filter for excess oil buildup near the point where the crankcase vent enters the air box. If the

This is a Fastway clutch cable bracket for a CRF450. It offers better clutch feel at the hand lever by reducing the flex of the bracket point.

rings are worn, crankcase oil will flow up the vent and into the air box and coat the filter. This can cause a rich fuel jetting condition.

Oil and Filter

Change the crankcase oil after every two rides and the filter on every other oil change (four rides). Check the wire mesh screens that are mounted in the bottom of the frame and in the crankcase. If you ride a mud race and have to fan the clutch often, the fiber clutch plates can start to disintegrate and pollute the crankcase oil. The particles will become trapped in the wire mesh filters. You should clean the filters at least twice each year.

Lube the Cables

Lube and adjust the clutch and throttle cables. Remember that the clutch cable free-play will be reduced as the clutch plates wear.

Valve Adjustment

The XRs don't need frequent valve adjustment, but keep in mind that the valve lash will be reduced as the valve and seat wear. Check and adjust the valve lash every 200 miles or after every fifth riding weekend.

CHASSIS
Chain and Sprockets

Clean the chain and sprockets after every ride, and lube the chain and check the free-play. Inspect the sprockets for chipped teeth, caused by rocks. Check the alignment of the rear chain guide. Sometimes rocks or ruts can bend the guide, causing it to push the chain out of alignment with the rear sprocket, which can cause the chain to derail.

Keep It Greased

The XRs have grease zerks mounted in the swingarm and linkage pivots. You should grease the zerks after every other ride for two reasons: to force water and dirt from the bearing cavity and to lube the bearing. Fred Bramblett fits grease zerks to the neck of the XR frame to provide grease to the steering head bear-

ings. The zerks are mounted to the frame and the races are notched to allow the grease to enter the bearing. Grease the steering head bearings every four rides. That may seem frequent, but consider that the XR holds the crankcase oil in the frame. When the oil gets hot, the frame temperature rises and the grease in the steering head bearings can melt and disperse from the bearing.

Spokes

Because the XR is a fairly heavy dirt bike, the spokes require frequent attention. Check them after every ride and don't be tempted to overtighten the spokes. That can crack the rims.

Brake Fluid

Change the brake fluid after every four rides. Use DOT 4 fluid.

DAMAGE CONTROL

The XR models are well-developed bikes that are extremely reliable. Crashing is one thing that all dirt bikers do from time to time. The rider–mechanic team of Summers and Bramblett have come up with a line of products that help make the XR more resistant to crash damage. Their products are available through Summers Racing Concept (800-221-9752).

Foot Levers

The shift and brake levers are reinforced to prevent them from bending but are also designed to break off clean in a crash to minimize damage to more expensive components. For example, the shift lever is designed to break clean at the shift shaft during really hard impacts. That way, the shift shaft doesn't bend or damage the crankcases. A stainless-steel cable wraps around the end of the levers and connects to the frame to prevent tree branches from wedging between the side covers and levers. The cables also serve to prevent the levers from snaring in deep ruts.

Wire Protectors

The Summers team noticed a common problem with XRs—the wires and rubber plug that exit from the right-side engine cover get snared by branches and yanked out of the side cover. This allows the crankcase oil to leak out of the side cover and eventually cause catastrophic engine damage. The guys developed an aluminum guard to protect the wires from tree branches. The guard just bolts on to a few of the side cover's mounting screws, and silicone seal is applied to further insulate the wires.

Chain Guard

The original chain guard should be modified to allow the chain to derail downward if the chain is forced off the sprockets or breaks. It is possible for the chain to bunch up and break the crankcases with the original guard design.

Fork Brace

A special fork brace was developed for the conventional cartridge forks used on the XR650L, XR600, and the new XR400. The brace reduces the front wheel deflection when riding over ruts or over large rocks.

XR PERFORMANCE OPTIONS

If you are considering bolt-on performance parts or high-performance services for your XR, consider your riding demands and the type of terrain that you ride on. There are a myriad of products available for the XR designed to suit a wide variety of applications.

Cooling Systems

There are two ways to improve the cooling systems of air-cooled engines: welding additional fins to the head and cylinder or installing an oil cooler. The oil cooler is the most efficient setup for reducing the engine temperature. The weld-on fin setup is commonly used on desert racers that run at high speeds where there is more free air available to take advantage of the additional fins. XRs Only and Ballard Cycles sell the weld-on fin kits. Lockhart makes an aftermarket oil cooler, or you can adapt the OEM oil cooler from the XR250 to the XR600.

High-Compression Piston

Wiseco makes an optional high-compression piston for the XR600. Higher compression pistons are generally more beneficial for slow-speed woods riding or high-altitude riding.

Carburetor

The stock carb works great for woods riding, and many riders prefer a larger 41-mm carb for desert racing. The White Bros. 41-mm carb kit gives an increase of about 4 horsepower and 6 miles per hour. However, the larger carb sacrifices the slow-speed throttle response that is important for woods riding over muddy or rocky terrain.

Head Pipe

There are three types of head pipes: straight, tapered, and oversize. All OEM head pipes are straight. The XR head pipes are available in two different lengths that effectively widen the powerband at low rpm with a sacrifice in peak power. The Summers team uses the tapered head pipe marketed by Yoshimura. A tapered head pipe improves scavenging efficiency and reduces pumping losses because the pipe draws out the exhaust gases rather than relying on the piston to pump out the cylinder. Typically, tapered head pipes can cause odd jetting problems, but Fred Bramblett says that he hasn't experienced any jetting problems with the Yoshimura pipe. Tapered head pipes work best with OEM cams or those with slightly retarded exhaust timing. Oversize head pipes are generally used in conjunction with big bore kits or for high-rpm applications such as desert racing or DTX.

Tailpipe

There are two types of tailpipes: straight-through silencers and spark arrestors. Some riding areas and racing organizations require the use of spark arrestors on

The CRF sump screen is located under the left-side cover. You have to clean this at least once a year. If the screen gets clogged, a bypass reed valve opens to allow oil but doesn't filter out metal chunks. You will need to remove the flywheel to gain access to the sump screen, which simply unplugs. Honda dealers can get you the special flywheel puller with protective end cap.

off-road motorcycles. Check the rules before you purchase an expensive aftermarket tailpipe. Straight-through silencers provide the right flow characteristic and resultant back pressure to produce maximum power over a wide rpm band. Spark arrestors have a series of baffles that prevent particles of combustible gases from exiting the tailpipe. The Summers team uses the Yoshimura tailpipe for closed-course racing.

Camshaft

The Summers team uses the stock XR cam for hare scrambles and enduro racing and the HRC cam for desert racing. The HRC cam has a higher lift and longer duration. Most aftermarket cams offer 2 to 4 degrees of duration over OEM cams. Increasing the duration generally improves peak power, but changing the overlap of the intake and exhaust has a more dramatic effect on the powerband. Decreasing the overlap improves low-end torque with a sacrifice of peak power, while increasing the overlap improves peak power with a sacrifice of low-end power.

CHAPTER TWELVE

TUNING TIPS FOR KAWASAKI DIRT BIKES

2000–2004 KAWASAKI KX65

FLAWS: poor powerband

FIXES: porting and head modifications

Kawasaki revamped the KX65 in 2000, changing the chassis and the engine from the old KX60. The new chassis is a scaled-down version of the KX80. This model has much better handling and braking. Unfortunately, the 2000 engine isn't on par with the chassis. For model year 2001, Kawasaki incorporated new cylinder porting and an exhaust system for a powerband competitive with the KTM65.

BEST VALUE MODS

ENGINE: turn down cylinder base, raise exhaust port, and re-cut the recess in the head 1 mm

SUSPENSION: Ohlins shock

CYLINDER AND HEAD MODS

The basic problem with the KX65 is that the exhaust port is too small and low and the transfers are too high. That means that the blow-down timing is too short, causing burned and unburned gases to mix in the cylinder, in turn causing the engine to bog in the midrange and misfire on top end. A simple way to fix the problem is to turn down the cylinder base 1 mm, raise the exhaust port to 22 mm from the top of the cylinder, and recess the squish band in the cylinder head 1 mm at a 10-degree angle. You can also turn down the top of the spark plug hole 1 mm to enable the plug to thread flush to the combustion chamber.

1990–2000 KAWASAKI KX60

FLAWS: cylinder ports vary, crankcase plugs leak, forks too soft

FIXES: adjust cylinder ports, epoxy plugs, install Terry fork kit

The only significant changes to this engine have been igniter boxes with different ignition curves. In the past, I've recommended mods such as raising and widening the exhaust ports and grinding bypass ports in the intake sleeve of the cylinder. Those modifications still work well, along with other updates that include raising the crankcase compression ratio. In the United States, the latest rage is to over-bore the cylinder 2 mm and plate the cylinder to fit the Wiseco Pro-Lite piston 648P8. The AMA rules allow cylinders to be over-bored up to 2 mm. In England, it's now possible to boost the displacement of the 1999 and older KX60s to 65 cc. This requires cylinder boring and plating to fit the 2000 KX65 piston. Also in England, it's possible to fit a centrifugal clutch to a KX60 to help a rider make the transition from auto to shifting on a larger bike. The kit is available from Moto X Rivara.

BEST VALUE MODS

ENGINE: cylinder porting, Boyesen reeds

SUSPENSION: Terry fork kit and stiffer springs

REEDS

There are some simple things you can do to boost the midrange power. One is to install a set of Boyesen dual-stage reeds to help the low- to mid-throttle response.

CYLINDER PORTING

The KX60 cylinder can be modified to suit a wide variety of riders. The following are some setups for beginner and expert riders. If you have a good set of files, you can match the exhaust ports to 0.845 in. or 21.5 mm, measured

This photo shows the channel that can be ground into the intake skirt of any KX60 and KX65. This bypass channel improves the midrange throttle response.

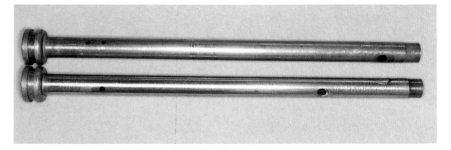

Terry Cable makes a long travel fork kit for KX60s.

from the top of the cylinder. Each exhaust port should be 21 mm wide, measured on the circumference of the bore. To change the heights of the transfer ports, you'll need a right-angle die grinder. Set the transfer port heights to 1.265 in. or 32 mm, measured from the top of the cylinder. To make crankcase boost ports, use a round file to grind channels in the intake side of the cylinder sleeve. These ports (5 mm wide and 3 mm deep) will enable gases to flow directly through the transfer ports for more midrange power. This procedure is applicable for all model years of KX60s.

The setup for low-end porting is more difficult than for top-end porting. The cylinder base must be turned down 0.010 in. or 0.25 mm to retard and reduce the exhaust timing and duration. Also, the transfer ports must be modified for lower time-area. Apply epoxy to the rear transfer ports and narrow them 3 mm, measured on the circumference of the bore.

PIPES

For more top-end over-rev, use a tuned pipe such as those from FMF or Pro-Circuit.

CARBURETOR

The stock carb is too small for expert riders who need top-end power. The KX80 carb (26 mm on 1990 to 1996 models) fits into the intake and air boots of the KX60. This carb needs only minor jetting changes to adapt to the KX60.

CRANKCASES

The crankcases have three casting plugs positioned around the main bearings. Occasionally, these plugs leak, so it's best to smear some epoxy over the plugs from the outside of the crankcases. Photos in an earlier section demonstrate how to apply epoxy to the casting plugs.

FORKS

If you are a relatively large rider or are aggressive with the front brake, you should switch to the optional stiff fork springs (Kawasaki part number 44026-1175) to reduce front-end diving. Terry

All Kawasaki KXs have oval plugs positioned around the main bearing cavities of the crankcases. Over time, they may cause leaks. To fix them, clean the affected area and apply a dab of JB Weld epoxy for a fuel-resistant sealer.

Kit, in the United States, makes an aftermarket fork kit that increases the forks' travel by 20 mm and offers better damping characteristics. The kit includes damper rods with different-sized holes for the rebound and compression damping. It's possible to improve the damping with the stock fork parts. This mod involves welding three holes closed in the damper rod and relocating the compression holes. Braze up both compression holes (holes located near the bottom of the damper rod). Drill one 5-mm hole positioned 46 mm from the bottom of the damper rod, and one 5-mm hole opposite of the first hole and 66 mm from the bottom of the rod. This mod gives the forks more low-speed compression. To improve the rebound damping, braze up one of the rebound holes (closest to the top of the damper rod). Use 10-weight fork oil after performing these mods.

SHOCK

The stock shock design doesn't allow for maintenance or valving. Companies such as WP, Ohlins, Works Performance, and Pro-Racing make aftermarket shocks that can be serviced and revalved. Switch to one of those brands if you are interested in enhancing the rear suspension.

SWINGARM

Novation Racing makes an aluminum swingarm that eliminates the linkage system and saves 4 pounds.

1998–2004 KAWASAKI KX100

FLAWS: sluggish powerband
FIXES: porting, bigger carb

This latest generation of KX100 features a new exhaust valve system. That feature wasn't well received because it doesn't provide significant performance gains. The system is also plagued with design problems that include frequent breakage of the flapper part of the valve.

BEST VALUE MODS

ENGINE: porting, 28-mm flat slide PWK Keihin carb, FMF pipe
SUSPENSION: springs

CYLINDER PORTING AND HEAD MODS

Since the 100's cylinder is just a bored-out 82-cc cylinder, the ports are too small for such a large piston. Key areas such as the transfer ports and exhaust outlet and bridge must be machined to let the gases flow through the cylinder. When I port a KX mini cylinder, I use an old exhaust pipe flange fitted to the

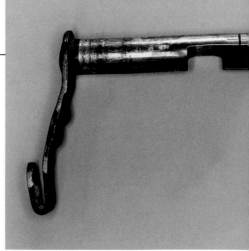

This is a typical KX clutch actuating rod. You can improve the clutch lever feel by polishing the corner of the rod. Also, a 1/2-inch section of metal can be splice-welded to improve the leverage.

exhaust outlet. This helps me cut the appropriate material out of the cylinder. The exhaust bridge can be narrowed to 2 mm wide, and the outer top corners of the port can be blended for better flow and less chance of ring scuffing. The exhaust port height can be raised to 25 mm and the transfers to 35 mm. The rear transfer ports can also be widened 1.5 mm toward the front transfers. The head doesn't need any modifications unless you build the engine for strictly low-end power.

ALTERNATIVE BIG BORES
The KX is a prime platform for a big bore because the crankshaft can be stroked easily and Wiseco makes piston kits 2 mm larger than stock. Big-bore strokers reduce the reliability on engine parts because of the material removed from key structural areas of the cylinder and crankshaft. It's possible to increase the displacement of KX80/85/100 to 112 cc.

AFTERMARKET CARB
The best choice of an aftermarket carb is the Keihin PWK 28-mm.

1994–1997 KAWASAKI KX100
FLAWS: mismatched ports, soft forks, under-carbureted
FIXES: port cylinder, stiffer springs and base-valve kit, 28-mm carb
The KX100 cylinder can be improved greatly. Kawasaki used the stock 80 cc cylinder casting and bored

and plated it for a larger piston. The problem is, they used a pipe designed for an 80-cc engine and the ports aren't corrected to suit the flow of a larger piston. One simple cylinder modification can improve throttle response. Drill two 6-mm holes on each side of the intake port into the transfer ports. These are called Boyesen ports, named after the prolific inventor. The KX80 already has them. Use a file to widen each exhaust port to a total of 27 mm wide (measured with a thin plastic ruler conformed to the bore). Set the height of the exhaust to 25 mm from the top of the cylinder. A simple bolt-on, 28-mm carburetor will provide smoother power with more top end. Both Mikuni and Keihin have carb kits available.

BEST VALUE MODS
ENGINE: 28-mm carb
SUSPENSION: base valve kit

PORTED PISTON
A boost port can be added to the intake side of the piston; use a KX80 piston as a model for duplication.

HOT SUSPENSION MODS
The big-wheel KX100, introduced to the United States in 1994, has upside-down cartridge forks. Installing the compression base valve from the 1992 Yamaha YZ125 will improve the compression damping of these forks. Pro-Racing makes a tuned aftermarket base valve for the KX big-wheel forks.

1998–2004 KAWASAKI KX80/85
FLAWS: sluggish power
FIXES: porting
The new exhaust valve system was designed to make the KX mini more competitive with the RM but it takes too much energy to drive the power valve governor mechanism so it slows the engine down. Porting for more top-end power helps overcome the drag from the governor. Overall, this bike has better suspension than previous models. There are more springs available for the forks and shocks, and the forks have modern valving that can be tuned.

BEST VALUE MODS
ENGINE: porting
SUSPENSION: springs

CYLINDER MODS
Porting this cylinder is a bit tricky and should be left to professionals. Like the 100 cylinder, I use an old exhaust pipe flange to carefully match the junction of the exhaust port and the pipe. Then I raise the exhaust port to 24.5 mm, widen each exhaust port 1 mm, and narrow the bridge 1 mm. The intake and exhaust bridges are very critical because the edges need to be deburred to minimize the wear on the piston and rings. The transfer ports should be matched for a height of 35.5 mm.

IGNITION CHANGES
Just rotating the stator plate to Kawasaki's

prescribed marks will have a slight effect on the power. Advancing the timing will benefit most riders. FMF and Mimic make switchable CDI boxes that enable a big change in the powerband.

1990–1997 KAWASAKI KX80

FLAWS: air leaks, connecting rod bearings, lacks low-end power

FIXES: seal casting plugs and lap crankcases, pre-mix ratio 20 to 1, cylinder and head machining

The KX performs consistently, handles well, and is reliable. However, many riders complain that the KX80 can't run with an RM80 from corner to corner. That is because the RM has power valves that give the RM80 more low-end torque. The following are some tips on making the KX more competitive with the RM's engine.

BEST VALUE MODS

ENGINE: 28-mm carb
SUSPENSION: Eibach fork springs

CYLINDER AND HEAD MODS

The KX80 can be given more low-end and midrange bursting power by turning down the cylinder base on a lathe. This retards the port timing. The stock port timing is too radical for the loamy technical tracks of the Midwest and eastern United States. Turn 0.028 in. or 0.7 mm from the base. The cylinder head must also be turned so the deck height from the gasket surface to the start of the squish band is 1 mm. The squish angle should be 10 degrees and 5 mm wide.

CARBURETOR

For more top-end power, install a 28-mm Keihin PWK carburetor, available from Carb Parts Warehouse.

CRANKCASES

The crankcase halves are sealed on Kawasakis with a non-drying sealer rather than a paper gasket. As the bike gets older, forces acting on the frame strain the engine mounts and the crankcases, and the crankcases sometimes begin to leak. I recommend lapping the crankcase halves whenever the main bearings are replaced. Kawasaki dealers sell a non-drying gasket sealer called Three Bond #4. It's the same substance as Yamabond, sold at Yamaha dealers. Apply a thin, even coating of the sealer on both sides of the case halves. A business card is a good tool for spreading the sealer evenly across the gasket surface. Let it air dry at 70 degrees Fahrenheit for 10 minutes before assembling the engine.

Another problem affecting the crankcases of KX80s is that the casting plugs vibrate loose. The plugs are positioned around the outside of the main bearing race. Spread a thin, even layer of epoxy over the plugs to seal them from leaking. Use Duro Master Mend epoxy.

CONNECTING ROD BEARINGS

The connecting rod bearing is prone to failure from lack of lubrication. Run a pre-mix ratio of 20 to 1 and jet the carb accordingly (richer).

SUSPENSION

The 1990s line of KX80s was steadily improved. The forks use a Travel Control Valve, which is similar to Race Tech's Emulator Valve, so there is no need for any expensive mods. Just spring the bike for the rider and change the suspension fluids every 10 races or 20 running hours.

FORKS

The forks need stiffer damping for aggressive riders. Switch to 15-weight fork oil and tighten the preload spring on the travel control valve one turn clockwise. Riders who weigh more than 120 pounds should change to a stiffer spring rate.

SHOCK

The shock suffers from too-soft, low-speed compression and rebound. Try setting the race sag to 75 mm, the compression adjuster to five clicks out, and the rebound adjuster to six clicks out.

1985–1990 KAWASAKI KX80 AND KX100

FLAWS: crankcase air leaks, cylinder wears quickly

FIXES: epoxy and lap cases, electroplate cylinder

Kawasaki struggled for years developing its KX80 into the excellent bike that it became in 1990. Problems with design and materials plagued this model. Common problems include broken frames, crankcase air leaks, and scored cylinders. The frame can be gusseted with mild steel plates at the bottom motor mounts and the steering head. The crankcases can be lapped on a surface lapping plate. It's best to lap the cylinder base surface and the crankcase mating surface. Use Yamabond as a sealer between the crankcases. The cylinders of the older KX80 have a problem of the rings rotating past the ring centering pins and snagging on the rear transfer port edge. The ring centering pins are positioned incorrectly on the piston, too close to the port edge. Wiseco pistons have the pins centered on the bridge between the ports.

The standard Kawasaki electrofusion plating wears out quickly. It's best to replate the cylinder with Nikasil or ceramasil. If you're looking for more performance from the engine, Boyesen reeds make a big improvement over the stock fiberglass reeds. Also, there is a big mismatch between the exhaust port and the exhaust pipe. I use an old pipe flange as a guide for the grinding tool. This mod works on all KX80s and KX100s through present-day models.

BEST VALUE MODS

ENGINE: Boyesen reeds, cylinder plating
SUSPENSION: suspension service

2001–2004 KAWASAKI KX125

FLAWS: too much pipe

FIXES: cylinder base and head machining

Kawasaki replicated the YZ porting and, in 2003, changed to plunger-type exhaust valves. In 2002, Kawasaki switched from its traditional bore coating electrofusion to ceramachrome. The new coating is nickel-based, not hard chrome. New bore coating will provide a big improvement in top-end reliability.

BEST VALUE MODS

Pro-Circuit pipe and silencer

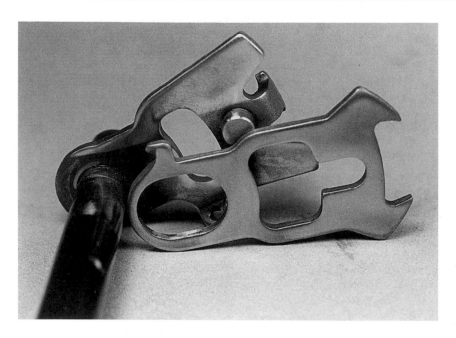

KX250 shift shafts can be polished for smoother shifting.

TOP END

The cylinder port timing is a bit more aggressive than the YZ, making this bike pipey. The easiest way to get the KX power closer to the YZ is to turn down the base of the cylinder 0.030 in. or 0.75 mm. Then, re-machine the cylinder head squish band and equal depth change at the same angle as stock, 10 degrees.

1998–2000 KAWASAKI KX125

FLAWS: too-high compression, exhaust valve sticks open

FIXES: head mods, Pro-Circuit valve cover, stiffer springs

Although it has some minor problems, the 1998 model is a significant improvement over the previous generation. The 1998 model started with problems such as being sluggish and sprung soft, but by the time the 2000 model was released, the magazines were praising it as the best bike of the class.

BEST VALUE MODS

ENGINE: head mods, Pro-Circuit pipe, silencer, and valve cover

SUSPENSION: stiffer springs, Pro-Action Incremental Valving

NEW KIPS SYSTEM

The 1998 model used the new exhaust valve system. Initially, Kawasaki had a recall on the valves because they would seat deep into the valve cavity and eventually contact the piston. Another common problem is breakage of the pin that the flapper valve pivots on. The most chronic problem is sticking wide open. Pro-Circuit makes a replacement valve cover that includes a stopper to prevent the valves from opening too far and jamming. The 1999 model features a thicker, heavy-duty exhaust valve for improved low-end power. Unfortunately, the new valve doesn't fit in the older 1998 cylinder, but the entire 1999 cylinder and valve will fit on the 1998 crankcases.

HEAD MODS

The compression ratio on the 1998 and 1999 models is good for a typical MX or enduro engine but makes the powerband run flat at high rpm. Modifying the head for greater chamber volume will improve the top-end power but reduce the low-end power. Normally, I narrow the squish band by 2 mm on a lathe by setting the tool angle to 22 degrees and cutting into the bowl. Afterward, polish the head with

medium-grit sandpaper to remove the tool marks.

CYLINDER PORTING

With the 1998 cylinders, tuners tried all sorts of things, including lowering the transfers by turning down the cylinder base, widening the exhaust port, narrowing the exhaust bridge, and even grinding the exhaust valve cavity deeper near the bore so the flapper valve would open the port completely. On the 2000 model, Kawasaki seems to have gotten the porting right. They dropped the transfer ports and raised the exhaust. If you're looking for more low-end power, you can have the cylinder turned down 0.75 mm and the head's squish band machined for a 1-mm recess. For more top-end power, just experiment with layering base gaskets.

FORKS

Kawasaki changed the forks on the 2000 model in a subtle way. In an effort to make the forks more like twin-chamber designs, they added a rubber gas bladder to separate the air space from the oil to prevent mixing, or aeration, of the oil. In the summer of 1999, Ricky Carmichael's factory bike ran with hose connections to the fork caps. The fork caps were plumbed with hoses that attached to a central gas accumulator. That way, the forks were more balanced. It was a new use for a tried-and-true idea.

1997 KAWASAKI KX125

FLAWS: sluggish acceleration, soft front end

FIXES: igniter box, stiffer fork springs

Just when the 1996 model was starting to perform as well as the 1994 model, Kawasaki took a step back with the 1997 bike. Overall, it's a reliable bike and performs well as a trail bike. But for MX, it doesn't accelerate as quickly as some of the other bikes and the suspension is too soft because Kawasaki chose to use progressive-rate fork and shock springs. Early and late models used straight-rate springs. The acceleration shortcoming is due to a combination of things such as the cylinder, ignition, and crankshaft.

This is a view of the right side of the engine. This is the shift detent, a spring-loaded lever and roller that applies tension to the shift star to prevent the tranny from slipping in and out of gear. Sometimes, the detent can bind up from clutch debris. For best shifting, polish the shift star, detent, and mounting bushing.

BEST VALUE MODS

ENGINE: 1996 ignition box, porting for low end

SUSPENSION: straight-rate fork springs

IGNITION

The black box on the 1997 model is programmed for a conservative advance curve. That hurts the midrange hit that is so critical on technical tracks. The 1996 model black box works much better (21119-1453). When switching to the 1996 black box, for best results, advance the ignition timing to the far mark stamped on the stator plate.

CYLINDER AND HEAD MODS

The 1997 cylinder is nearly identical to the previous models of 1995 and 1996. These models suffer the same problem—the transfer ports open too soon. In order to lower or retard the transfer ports' timing, the cylinder base must be turned down on a lathe by 0.6 mm. The exhaust ports must be raised to 28 mm, measured from the top of the cylinder. The cylinder head's squish band must be relieved by 0.5 mm. The angle of the cut on the squish band is 7 degrees.

CRANKSHAFT

Although Team Green recommends installing the 1996 model crankshaft when the 1997 crank wears out, I don't think the difference in weight is worth the expense. The lighter 1996 crank (13031-1407) makes the engine rev quicker but lacks the ability to control wheelspin in slippery track conditions.

FORKS

The forks work well for most riders. Use Team Green's recommendations on determining which spring rate is best for you.

SHOCK

There are two ways to make a bike turn tighter: use different pull rods in the linkage or extend the shock travel. Both methods enable the rear end to ride higher and transfer more weight to the front end. Pro-Circuit and DeVol Racing offer aftermarket pull rods. The simplest way to lengthen the shock travel is to install two 18x0.3-mm shims between the top-out plate and the shock shaft.

LINK BOLT

Check the torque of the linkage bolts, which is the only chronic problem with the KX. Otherwise, the bike is extremely reliable and inexpensive to maintain. Check the entire bike's bolts between races, and use non-permanent locking agent on the threads of the bolts and screws.

1993–1996 KAWASAKI KX125

FLAWS: stiff rear suspension
FIXES: revalve softer

The KX125 peaked in 1994. The 1996 model uses the same linkage ratio and power valve governor. The 1996 model was the first to use the new Keihin carb with air foils. The 1993 model has the best top-end power, but the later models have much wider powerbands. The good thing about a Kawasaki is that you can mix and match OEM engine components to change your bike's powerband. For example, when converting a 1993 model for enduro riding, use the 1995 cylinder, head, piston, and wedge valves. The following are some tips on changing the KX125's engine for different types of powerbands.

BEST VALUE MODS

ENGINE: cylinder porting
SUSPENSION: Pro-Circuit link rods, shock revalving

SUPERCROSS/ENDURO POWERBAND

The stock 1994-and-newer intake parts and pipe are ideal for supercross, enduro riding, or novice motocross. These tuning components have a peak of about 9,600 rpm. The 1993-and-older intakes were designed for a 13,000-rpm peak. However, the 1993 cylinder and head can be greatly improved. Using TSR design software, I examined the 1993 cylinder and found that the rear transfer ports are too big. Also, the exhaust port timing is very radical. The solution is to turn down 0.7 mm from the base of the cylinder to retard the port timing and boost the compression ratio. Then, remove the same amount of metal from the cylinder head's squish band to maintain the proper piston-to-head clearance of 1 mm.

Next, use epoxy to reshape and narrow the two rear transfer ports. The width of each rear transfer port should be 14 mm, and they should be aimed directly at each other. This will improve the gas flow between 3,000 and 8,000 rpm and make the engine pull strong in the midrange. You won't have to fan the clutch with this little tractor.

This photo from the Indy Motorcycle Show highlights a cutaway of an SFB billet side cover and DeVol water pump to reveal a Rekluse Z-Start auto clutch for a KXF250.

CYLINDER INTERCHANGE

The cylinders of the 1993 and 1994 models interchange. The 1993 cylinder is best for high rpm because of the size of the transfer and exhaust ports. The exhaust duct on 1993 cylinders is round as opposed to the smaller, oval diameter of the 1994 cylinders. The 1994 cylinder is best for low-range to midrange, plus there is greater sealing surface for the piston and rings so they last longer. The cylinder heads do not interchange because flat pistons, domed pistons, and different water spigot positions were used in the model years of KX125s. The 1995 KX125 cylinder will not interchange with earlier models because the center wedge exhaust valves are thicker.

HI-RPM MX POWERBAND 1994–1996 KX125

The biggest improvement you can make in the top-end power of the 1994 to 1996 KX125 is to switch to some engine parts from the 1993 KX. Parts such as the intake system enable the 1994 to 1996 models to rev to 12,500 rpm. The 1995 model needs different power valve governor parts because that year's design was faulty and prevented the KIPS valves from opening fully.

CARBURETOR

Use a 38-mm Keihin PWK. The carb's air boot spigot will need to be turned down and cut shorter to fit into the 1994 to 1996 air boot. The 1994 model uses a small-body (35-mm) Keihin PWK carb, and it can be bored to a maximum of 37 mm.

INTAKE SYSTEM

The reed valve from the 1993 KX is designed for better flow at high rpm, much better than the four-petal reed valve introduced in 1994. Install the 1993 reed valve and intake manifold (Kawasaki part numbers 12021-1085 and 16065-1246) in late-model KXs. The crankcases will need to be modified to accept the larger reed valve.

CRANKCASE MODS

In order to install the bigger reed valve from the 1993 model, the engine must be disassembled to modify the crankcases. Remove about 0.080 in. or 2 mm from the top and bottom of the reed valve cavity in the crankcases.

AIR BOX

The side panel ducts must be cut away with a hacksaw to enlarge the air ducts to the air box. You can remove the clear plastic splash shield from the front, top edge of the air box; this will also improve airflow.

CYLINDER HEAD MODS

The squish band in the cylinder head is too wide to be revved to 12,800 rpm. Narrow the squish band's width to 5 mm using a lathe.

IGNITION

The igniter box from the 1996 model should be installed on earlier models because the timing curve is better suited to a high-revved engine.

POWER VALVE GOVERNOR

The governor is a spring-loaded centrifugal device that controls the KIPS exhaust valve position in relation to engine rpm. When the engine gets to 8,000 rpm, the power valve governor's steel balls develop enough centrifugal force to overcome the tension of the spring. The 1995 model had a two-stage ramp cup designed to widen the powerband. Unfortunately, the second angle of the ramp cup was too steep, so the governor never fully shifted, preventing the exhaust valves from opening fully. The 1994 and 1996 models use ramp cup 49111-1051; it's best to switch to that part on the 1995 KX125.

LINK STAY BARS

Pro-Circuit makes link stay bars for the 1993 to 1996 bikes. This changes the rear ride height and transfers the weight differently, so the bike turns tighter. Caution: Because of the wide production tolerances on Japanese dirt bikes, you need to check the clearance between the aftermarket stay bars and the swingarm through the total rear wheel travel. You have to do this with the shock removed and file the stay bars or swingarm if either part contacts the other.

REAR SHOCK

The original shock compression valving is too stiff. It must be revalved softer. Not only does this mod improve the bike's handling, but it also reduces shock fade. Shock fade is less likely because revalving the shock for softer/faster compression damping lowers the velocity of the shock fluid. Enzo Racing sells a thick foam bottoming cone and an extended reservoir cap for Kayaba shocks. The foam cone helps prevent the shock from bottoming hard and causing damage to the shock's internal parts. The reservoir cap allows for more oil volume, which will extend the amount of time before the shock fades.

1992 KAWASAKI KX125

FLAWS: chronic connecting rod failure, carb bogging, shattered pistons
FIXES: install a Hot Rod kit, change carb jetting, fix crankshaft problem

This model features a redesigned engine and chassis. As with most first-year bikes, it is plagued with mechanical problems.

BEST VALUE MODS

ENGINE: 1990 igniter, porting
SUSPENSION: fork springs, better fork bushings

CARB JETTING

Team Green recommends switching to a 162 main jet and a NORH needle (16009-1707).

CRANKSHAFT

The original connecting rods are sensitive to breakage if the engine is over-revved. The original rods don't have enough torsional stiffness. Kawasaki later produced a better-quality connecting rod and bearing, but the Hot Rod kit is a better design.

CYLINDER AND HEAD

The 1992 model cylinder and head won't interchange with any other models. The best tuning mods are to turn down 0.5 mm from the cylinder base and narrow the width of the rear transfer ports with epoxy to a total width of 16 mm. This gives more low-end power and reduces the need to over-rev the engine.

GEARING

Gear up to a 51-tooth sprocket.

FORKS

The fork spring rate should be at least 0.38 kilogram. The bushings in the forks that support the piston rod in the top of the damping rod wear out fast and cause a loss of rebound damping. The forks top out fast and hard, often making a clunking noise. The bushings can be replaced with accessory parts. See the cartridge fork section for information on how to change the bushings.

1990–1991 KAWASAKI KX125

FLAWS: water and air leaks, frame breakage, rough acceleration
FIXES: lap crankcases and epoxy casting imperfections, gusset frame, jet carb

If you could combine the best parts of each of these models you'd have a great bike. The following are some tips on how to prevent mechanical failures and improve performance with Kawasaki parts.

BEST VALUE MODS

ENGINE: Boyesen RAD valve, carb jetting
SUSPENSION: frame gusseting

CARB JETTING

Stock pilot jet, 1.5 turns out on the airscrew, CA6 slide (16025-1164), an N84C needle (16025-1164), stock or one size larger main jet.

IGNITION

The igniter box from the 1990 KX125 has a timing curve designed for high rpm, while the 1991 model is designed for an enduro-type of powerband. If your 1991 KX coughs and sputters when you accelerate out of a turn or pops at high rpm, the 1990 igniter will work best for you. The Mitsubishi stator plate coils suffer from moisture buildup and break down. Look to a service company to repair the coils. The best method for insulating the wires to protect them from moisture damage is a process called wet wrapping. The copper wire is fed

through a bath of resin and then wrapped onto the coil. Companies that offer stator plate rebuilding do this type of service. Electrex makes aftermarket coil kits that you can install yourself with the help of a soldering iron and rosin core silver solder.

IGNITION TIMING

Here is a simple way to fine-tune your ignition timing without buying expensive measuring gauges: Remove the magneto cover from the left side of the engine. Looking directly at the stator plate from the left side of the bike, imagine that the stator plate is a clock. If you turn the stator plate clockwise, you will advance the ignition timing. This makes the engine hit hard in the midrange but fall flat on the top end. If you turn the stator plate counterclockwise, you retard the ignition timing. This makes the bike smoother in the midrange and rev higher before falling flat. Kawasaki has provided reference marks on the crankcases and the stator plate to gauge how far to rotate the stator plate without damaging the engine. Normally, enduro and supercross riders prefer to advance the ignition timing, and motocross, grass track, and kart racers prefer to retard the ignition timing.

INTERCHANGING TOP-END PARTS

The major difference between the KX125 models from year to year is the piston and head design. Never mismatch pistons and cylinder heads from 1990 and 1991 models. The concave design of the 1990 model offers better performance but suffers from head gasket leaks. The 1991 model uses an alignment pin between the cylinder and head. All the 1991 KX parts will fit the 1990 model and offer greatly improved reliability.

REED VALVE

Boyesen's RAD valve makes a big difference on these models because the stock reed valve has too much flow area and a high-rpm peak. The RAD valve gives more torque before coming on the pipe, so the bike gets better traction out of corners. It will also save you money in clutch plates.

CLUTCH TIPS

For best longevity, use steel clutch plates and springs from the KDX-200. EBC and Barnett make accessory clutch kits with excellent materials and stiffer springs. Barnett plates have wider tabs on the fiber plates, so they resist grooving the clutch basket.

CYLINDER MODS

The weakness of the 1990 and 1991 cylinders is the timing of the exhaust and transfer ports. There isn't enough time for the exhaust gases to depressurize the cylinder before unburned mixture gases flow from the transfer ports. Turn down 0.5 mm from the cylinder base, raise the exhaust port to 26 mm from the top of the cylinder, and install a (046) head gasket from Kawasaki.

CRANKCASE MODS

The 1990 and 1991 models suffer from casting flaws in the front corners of the crankcase ports. The casting holes can be plugged by applying epoxy to the area affected. Also, take care when tightening the oil drain plug. The casting on the crankcase for the drain bolt hole is very thin. It's easy to crack the plug hole from overtightening the bolt.

CLUTCH AND SHIFTING PROBLEMS 1990–1996 (ALL MODELS)

The following are some ways to improve the clutch performance and ease shifting:

1. Drill two small-diameter holes into the female splines of the clutch hub, and then chamfer the holes with a triangular file. This will improve the oil flow to the metal clutch plates and reduce the galling to the clutch hub. This mod also gives you a better feel when fanning the clutch through the turns.
2. The stamped-steel plates attached to the shift shaft should be thoroughly chamfered and polished. This reduces the friction on the plates so they can

Pro-Circuit makes this special linkage for KXF250s.

slide together easier, making for quicker shifts.
3. File and polish the edges of the shift star that is bolted to the end of the shift drum. The shift star relies on a spring-loaded roller to keep the transmission in gear.

1985–1989 KAWASAKI KX125

FLAWS: lack of low-end power, clutch problems

FIXES: Boyesen reeds, lap crankcases, Barnett plates and springs

The late-1980s KX125s are great bikes, real workhorses. Sure, they have some problems, but what bike doesn't? Here are some tips for improving the longevity of these bikes.

BEST VALUE MODS

ENGINE: Boyesen reeds, carb jetting
SUSPENSION: Race Tech Emulator Valve, Excel rims

AIR LEAKS

Like all Kawasakis, they have characteristic air leaks at the crankcases because Kawasakis don't use center gaskets; instead, they use a non-drying sealer. Lapping the crankcases makes a big difference in low-end power and engine longevity.

CYLINDER MODS

The 1986 model was the slowest 125 of that year. The best modifications include turning down 1 mm from the cylinder base and machining the head 1 mm at the squish band.

SILENCER

The silencer core from the 1985 model should also be used on the 1986 model (order Kawasaki part number 49099-1113).

SOFT RIMS

The 1986 and 1987 models have problems with the front rims cracking at the weld. Replace the stock piece with a Tallon or Excel rim.

1988–1989 KAWASAKI KX125

The 1988 and 1989 models have an engine design that features the concave piston design and multiple transfer ports, along with a new triple exhaust valve system. This is a great engine design with loads of potential. The 1988 and 1989 models can be improved in the following ways.

CARBURETOR

The carb's needle-jet primary hood (the half-cylinder-shaped piece sticking up into the venturi) should be filed down 1.5 mm. This will make the engine run leaner in the midrange.

HEAD GASKET LEAKS

The cylinder head on the 1988 model has chronic head gasket leaks that eventually cause the piston to crack off at the top ring groove. The solution is to fit the head and cylinder with alignment pins, which came standard on the 1989 model. Another way to fix the head gasket problem is to drill out the head-stay bolt hole larger and install a Nylok nut and two large-diameter washers. The Nylok nut allows you to tighten the head-stay bolt to a lower torque value without the bolt falling out. This enables the bolt to flex from the top shock mount forces but not affect the cylinder head.

2004 KAWASAKI KXF250

FLAWS: overheats, clutch slips, sticky shifting, valvetrain problems
FIXES: Boyesen water pump kit, stiffer clutch springs, shift plate kit, stainless valvetrain parts

The 2004 KXF250 is an excellent first-year effort for Kawasaki's entry into the four-stroke 250-cc category. Owners of this first model year bike discovered some problems that were redesigned for the 2005 bike. The problems encountered ranged from overheating due to a combination of too small a radiator and slow recirculation rate of the coolant. Pro-Circuit sells a larger set of radiators, and Boyesen makes a twin access cover water pump with a high-flow impellor. The clutch slippage can raise the rpm and produce more heat. Switching to stiffer clutch springs will help, but they are noticeably stiffer in lever feel. The sticky shifting is traced to the lack of alignment points on the shift plate. The 2005 model shift plate uses tapered panhead screws for stability and alignment. The valvetrain problems can be traced to riders who chronically over-rev the engine. The stock valve springs aren't well suited for high rpm. Kibblewhite makes dual spring kits with titanium collets and retainers, along with stainless-steel valves.

BEST VALUE MODS

Boyesen twin cover water pump kit, Barnett clutch springs, Varner Racing shift plate kit, Kibblewhite valve and spring kit.

2001–2004 KAWASAKI KX250

FLAWS: midrange-only powerband
FIXES: porting for more exhaust timing, Pro-Circuit pipe and silencer

This generation of KX250s suffers from stagnant design and development. Minor changes were made to the cylinder and KIPS system to improve reliability. The cylinder exhaust ports and intake boost ports were reduced in size, which makes this bike fall flat on top end. Porting like the previous model year's works well. Adding a Pro-Circuit pipe is much easier.

BEST VALUE MODS

Pro-Circuit pipe and silencer

1997–2000 KAWASAKI KX250

FLAWS: power hits hard, sticky shifting, soft forks
FIXES: porting, updated detent spring, stiffer fork springs

The KX has a hard-hitting midrange with weak over-rev. That, combined with the new close-ratio gearbox, makes a rider short-shift too much. By duplicating the exhaust porting of the 1997 CR250, the KX can be made to rev more like the Honda. That is exactly what Kawasaki changed on the 2000 model.

BEST VALUE MODS

ENGINE: porting
SUSPENSION: fork springs

CYLINDER PORTING

There are two distinctively different porting jobs that I perform on the KX250. The most popular porting gives a powerband that starts pulling early and transitions smoothly into the midrange. The other porting gives more top-end over-rev.

Smoother, Broader Powerband
These porting modifications include extensive use of epoxy in the rear

transfer ports to redirect the flow and raise the crankcase compression ratio. None of the port heights change, just balance them from side to side.

More Over-Rev Powerband
These porting mods involve some critical machine work that requires a right-angle porting tool. The sub-exhaust ports must be widened and raised 2 mm. The main exhaust port must be ported to an oval shape. The transfer ports need to be ported to heights of 58 mm for the front ports and 58.5 mm for the rear ports.

PISTON AND HEAD MOD

The stock piston and head offer a high compression ratio so there are no modifications needed. However, if you want a quicker revving engine, consider the new lightweight flat-top piston from Wiseco. The piston kit is designed to combine a flat-top crown with super-lightened skirts (Wiseco 704PS). Wiseco originally designed this piston for Team Kawasaki. The new piston is designed for high-maintenance racing use and is much lighter than the standard domed piston. The flat-top design has greater mechanical efficiency than the standard dome design. The flat-top crown makes it necessary to adjust the cylinder head's combustion chamber and squish band to suit. The gasket surface of the head must be turned down on a lathe by 2.5 mm. Then the squish band must be re-cut at a 4-degree angle. The depth of the squish band, measured from the gasket surface, is 0.25 mm. Switching to a projected insulator spark plug (NGK BP7EV) will improve throttle response between 1/4 and 1/2 throttle.

SHIFTING WOES

For the 1997 model, if you're having problems shifting from first to second, or if the tranny pops out of gear often, replace the shift detent spring with Kawasaki part number 92145-1063. For any other year KX, the problem could be as simple as clutch debris collecting in the cases near the shift drum or shift linkage. You can simply remove the right-side engine cover and spray some brake cleaner at the shift drum to flush out the debris. Changing the tranny oil more often will help too.

SUSPENSION

Forks

The fork springs are too soft for most riders who weigh more than 160 pounds. Change to a set of 0.41-kilogram springs.

Shock

Set the race sag to 95 mm. The valving is good, and lengthening the shock's travel will improve the front end. The simplest way to lengthen the shock travel is to install two 18x0.3-mm shims between the top-out plate and the shock shaft.

1993–1996 KAWASAKI KX250

FLAWS: frame breakage, poor low-end power, weak front brake

FIXES: gusset frame, cylinder porting, Braking front disc

The 1993 KX was the first year of the new engine. The main difference was the KIPS valve system. A more efficient wedge valve design was adapted because the old system was prone to mechanical failure and excess noise. The KIPS system has problems of its own, but it is still the best exhaust valve design for two-stroke engines. The new chassis is narrower and the top shock mount was made integral to the frame. In 1994, Kawasaki changed the steering head angle of the KX250. They changed the rake angle so the bike would turn better at slow speeds. The rear shock valving is generally stiff while the spring is soft for riders over 175 pounds. Here are some of the mods that I recommend for the KX250.

BEST VALUE MODS

ENGINE: cylinder porting, Boyesen RAD valve

SUSPENSION: Braking oversize front disc kit, aftermarket brake hose

CYLINDER

I recommend raising the sub-exhaust ports to 40 mm from the top of the cylinder and transfer port heights to 58 mm. The rear transfers will need to be narrowed with epoxy (4 mm) and re-angled so they are aimed toward each other. If you are really after the maximum power, consider having the cylinder plated to a tighter piston-to-cylinder wall clearance of 0.0025 in. The stock clearance runs between 0.004 and 0.006 in. The cylinders for the different years of KXs don't interchange. The 1993 and 1994 are similar and the 1995-and-newer models are similar. The intake tract is shorter on the 1995 cylinder. The exhaust duct is a smaller diameter and won't fit with the earlier model pipes.

The 1995 cylinder is great for enduro and supercross, but the small exhaust duct limits its top-end potential. All these cylinders have casting slag in the Boyesen ports (located between the intake and transfer ports). You can use a rasp file to remove the slag and enlarge the port to the standard casting lines. Enlarging the port too much doesn't improve performance.

The best option for an oversized piston is the Wiseco 74-mm kit, which increases engine displacement to 310 cc. The kit fits the 1993 to 2000 KX250s and requires modifications to the exhaust valves and cylinder head. Cometic makes a special head gasket for this kit.

CYLINDER HEAD

There is no need to turn down the cylinder head of the 1994 model for more compression; you can just use the optional thinner head gasket available from Kawasaki (11004-1240).

KIPS VALVES

Previous model KX250s had a two-piece KIPS actuating rod. The fit between the two pieces was loose and that caused a variance in the KIPS valve range of movement. In 1994, Kawasaki redesigned the rod as one piece. Kawasaki recalled early production models in the United States and installed an upgraded rod. This part fits KX250s from 1992 and 1993. Because the KX250 uses a relatively stiff power valve governor spring, the link plate tends to

crack. If your older KX has sluggish performance, check the link plate. It is located under the right-side engine.

Burred corners are also a common problem with the KIPS wedge valve. The exposed corners of the wedge valve get heated from the exhaust gases while striking the flapper plate. This causes the ends of the wedge valve to develop burrs. The burrs limit the travel of the wedge valve. The wedge valve is prevented from closing to the stop so the powerband feels weak on the low end. At high rpm, the wedge valve is prevented from opening fully. That makes the engine run flat at high rpm because the flapper is hanging out in the exhaust gas stream. The wedge valve should be checked when servicing the top end. Grasp the KIPS rack and move it through its travel, opening and closing the exhaust valves.

FRAME BREAKAGE

The 1994 model has characteristic frame breakage on the gusset plate for the rear shock mount. That is due to stiff high-speed compression valving in the shock. The frame absorbs the energy rather than the shock. The valving on the 1995 model was softened to fix this problem. To improve the frame, I suggest adding gusset plates to key areas such as the foot peg brackets and the top shock mount.

CHAIN ROLLER PROBLEM

The 1994 KX250 has a design flaw in the placement of the upper chain roller. The roller is mounted too close to the air boot. The roller doesn't freewheel evenly, and when the chain contacts the roller, it spins it, causing it to wear away the air boot. Eventually, the air boot develops a hole and debris is drawn into the engine, causing a seizure. Turn down the chain roller's outer diameter on a lathe so it can freewheel.

BIG BRAKES

Braking offers a special front brake kit for the KXs. The kit was developed for Mike Kiedrowski and Mike LaRocco when they were teammates for Kawasaki. Many other factory race teams use oversize front and rear Braking disc kits. The KX disc is 20 mm larger, making it 260 mm in diameter. The kit includes a caliper mounting bracket, the disc, and a set of pads. Braking discs are laser cut from stainless steel and textured for a consistent finish.

If you want to improve the front braking power of your old KX and don't want to spend much money, try a WP replacement brake line. These hard plastic lines don't expand like the stock brake line so the brakes feel less spongy and more like a Honda's brakes. Another simple mod to the brakes is stainless-steel hex bolt pins for the brake pads. Moose Racing and WER offer aftermarket brake pins. These items resist forming divots as the brake pads are engaged and released. Stock Kawasaki brake pins tend to form divots that prevent the brake pads from sliding away from the disc. Typical symptoms of this problem are stuck brakes.

GEARING

Switch to a 50-tooth rear sprocket and this bike will pull stronger through the loamy bends and steep uphills. This works on KX250s from 1990 to 1995.

REAR SUSPENSION

The rear shock spring is too soft for riders who weigh more than 170 pounds. A 5.2-kilogram spring is the best choice. The compression valving should be changed for softer high-speed compression when you switch to the stiffer spring.

1991–1992 KAWASAKI KX250

FLAWS: cylinder wears fast, front end steers slow

FIXES: replate the cylinder, Terry triple clamps

These bikes have much-improved frames but different cylinders. The 1991 cylinder needs Boyesen boost ports added to the intake port for more midrange power. Both cylinders have large intake ports that cause the piston skirts to wear and crack prematurely. Later models have bridged intake ports that solve the piston wear problem. KXs

are noted as bikes that handle well at high speeds. However, this makes the bike steer wide in tight, slow turns.

BEST VALUE MODS

ENGINE: Boyesen RAD Valve, KIPS valve mods

SUSPENSION: revalve shock, Terry triple clamp

STEERING

The KX fork rake angle is greater than that of a Honda CR. This makes the bike stable at speed but difficult to turn tightly. Terry Products developed a triple clamp set for the KX that has a rake angle 2 degrees less than stock. This product works on 1991 to 1993 KX250s. Terry even makes a kit for 1994 and 1995 models, but Kawasaki reduced the rake angle on those frames in production. The Terry triple clamp kit requires you to press out the original stem into the Terry bottom clamp. This task requires straight jig fixtures and a 20-ton press—better to trust this job to a professional who has the tools and knowledge. The Terry clamps sell for $250 and the labor is about $50.

CYLINDER

I recommend getting the cylinder nickel-silicon-carbide plated (Max Power, US Chrome, or Aptec). There are some options for oversize piston kits. La Sleeve makes a 295-cc piston kit and Klemm makes a 310-cc kit that includes a sleeve. The 295-cc piston can be used in a plated cylinder, but the 310 cc requires the use of a special sleeve that can only be installed by Klemm.

1990 KAWASAKI KX250

FLAWS: abrupt powerband, frame breakage

FIXES: lower compression ratio, use shims on engine and shock mounts

This bike is a hard-hitting screamer with an abrupt powerband. To tame it down and get some traction, clean up the jetting and install a flywheel weight. This was the first model with the upside-down forks and perimeter frame. These frames are notorious for

cracking near the top shock mounts and the steering head bearing cup.

BEST VALUE MODS

ENGINE: carb jetting, flywheel weight
SUSPENSION: gusset frame

CARB JETTING

Install the jets in the carb: 6.0 slide and a N87C jet needle. The Boyesen RAD Valve is designed to improve the low-end and midrange power. The compression ratio of the stock engine is too high. Installing the optional thick head gasket available from Kawasaki or a Cometic fiber gasket can lower the compression ratio.

KIPS VALVES

Add two shims next to the spring to increase the power valve governor spring tension. Kawasaki part number 92026-1238 will stall the KIPS valves from opening until a higher rpm. Adding a flywheel weight will reduce wheelspin and soften the hit in the midrange.

FLYWHEEL WEIGHT

If you use a KX250 for DTX or micro sprint racing, don't use a flywheel weight. Flywheel weight puts a greater strain on the main bearings on engines that are over-revved.

IGNITION TIMING

Try retarding the ignition timing to reduce the hit in the powerband and make the engine run cooler. Kawasaki makes it easy to change the timing. There are marks in the stator plate and a reference mark on the crankcase. Loosen the stator plate mounting bolts and rotate the stator plate counterclockwise to the far mark (about 1 mm).

FRAME BREAKAGE

The frame on this bike is prone to breaking because the top shock mounts were put under a compression load when the top shock bolt was tightened. Space the shock mounting plate away from the frame with washers to reduce the compression load on the shock bolt. The frames usually break at the shock mounting plates, bottom motor mounts, and top steering race in the neck. Add gussets to the frame to strengthen it and a weld-on skid plate to hold the frames together. Refer to Chapter 4 for more information on strengthening frames with gussets.

1985–1989 KAWASAKI KX250 AND KX500

FLAWS: frame breakage, KIPS valve wear, shock absorber wear
FIXES: gusset frame, replace KIPS valves, replace shock bushings
BEST VALUE MODS
ENGINE: thick head gasket, carb T-vents
SUSPENSION: Braking oversize disc brakes, gusset frame

FRAME BREAKAGE

Tabs and mounting brackets tend to break away from the frame tubes because the parts were MIG-welded on the assembly line. Always have the parts TIG-welded and gusseted. Reinforcing the foot peg brackets, engine mounts, top shock mount, and neck are very important. Welding a

sheet of 0.6-mm stainless steel to the bottom of the frame will act as both a gusset and a skid plate to strengthen and protect the frame.

SHOCK PROBLEMS

Because of strong demand, companies are making seal and bushing kits for the rear shocks. If the shock body has worn out, the best option is to buy a reconditioned Ohlins shock. These shocks are totally rebuildable and have better damping than stock shocks.

FRONT FORKS

Non-cartridge forks can work similarly to modern forks with a Race Tech Emulator Valve.

BRAKES

The bolts that support the brake pads tend to develop divot marks with prolonged use. Replace them with WER or Moose Off-Road stainless-steel hex-head bolts. To eliminate the spongy feel of the brakes, use a White Power hard plastic brake hose. If the discs are glazed, they will make a squealing noise when the brakes are applied. The discs

can be resurfaced on a surface-grinding machine. Look to a machine shop for this service. Change the brake fluid every three months for best results. Use Motul 300C brake fluid.

CARBURETOR

If your KX bogs when riding over whoops or landing from big jumps, fit double vents to the carb, as on the 1995 models. There are aftermarket kits or you can get two 1/8-in.-diameter brass T-fittings and hoses from a pet shop. (They sell them for aquariums.) Route one set of hoses down and one set up under the fuel tank or into the air box. You can improve the low-end power of the 1990 KX250 by installing an N87C needle and a number 6 slide.

KIPS VALVES

The two drum valves of the KIPS system tend to wear at the drive channels for the center valve. The center valve is steel, and the drum valves are hard-anodized aluminum, so the drum valves wear quicker. When the drum valves wear too much, the center valve remains in the closed position all the time, and that can reduce top-end power.

Check and clean your exhaust valves frequently (see section on exhaust valves for specific instructions), and replace the drum valves periodically.

CRANKCASE MAIN BEARINGS

If your bike has a lot of vibration, the crankshaft's main bearings may be worn, or worse yet, the crankcase races may be oblong-shaped. If you disassemble the engine and the main bearings just fall out of the cases, the races are worn. The bearing races are made of cast iron and tend to wear into an oblong shape. It is possible for a machine shop to fit steel races to the crankcases, and this is usually less expensive than buying new crankcases. The problem is common on KX500s.

GEARBOX PROBLEMS

KX500s that are raced for two or more seasons tend to develop transmission problems. It is characteristic for them to

Bubba has a styling pit bike.

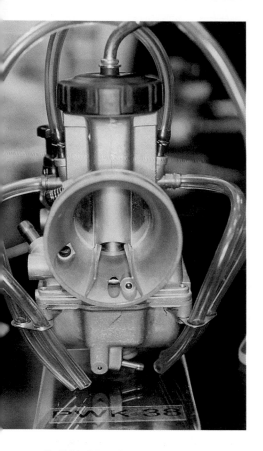

The Keihin PWK Air-Strike is a great replacement carburetor for older KX250 and 500s.

jump out of third gear. Rounded engagement dogs on the third gear drive and bent shift forks usually cause the problem.

PISTON CRACKING

The KX500s have problems with pistons cracking at the intake skirt because the stock cylinders wear quickly. This problem is eliminated when the cylinder is plated with Nikasil.

KX250 COMPRESSION RATIO

The KX250s have a very high compression ratio, which can lead to a variety of problems, among them, head gasket leaks. Use two head gaskets to reduce the compression ratio and the possibility of head gasket leaks.

REED PETAL BREAKAGE

The big-bore KXs tend to chip the stock carbon-fiber reed petals at the outer corners. The problem can make the engine hard to start, bog at low rpm, and pop at high rpm. Replace the stock reeds with Boyesen Dual-Stage or Aktive reed petals. They are more durable and increase low-end power.

CLUTCH LURCHING

Kawasaki clutches need stiffer clutch springs. Look to aftermarket companies such as Barnett or EBC for springs. One way to reduce clutch lurching is to radius the edge of the clutch actuator rod with a file. This will make it engage smoother. Switching to automatic transmission fluid will help the clutch work better because these types of oils are designed to work with fiber-to-steel clutch plates.

1990–2004 KAWASAKI KX500

FLAWS: third gear engagement dogs wear, powerband flattens out

FIXES: replace third gear, install a thicker head gasket

The only way to improve this near-perfect bike is too focus on suspension tuning and regular maintenance. Make sure the fork and shock springs are matched to your weight. Use guidelines for setting race sag and determining the proper spring rates as listed in the "Baseline Settings" section of Chapter 4. If you want to make your KX500 turn tighter for tracks with many off-camber turns or for enduro riding, a Terry triple clamp kit will do the job. This triple clamp kit will reduce the steering head angle 2 degrees. Ty Davis, the famous off-road racer, developed the triple clamp kit.

BEST VALUE MODS

ENGINE: thicker head gasket
SUSPENSION: proper springs

TRANSMISSION

The KX500s have a characteristic problem of developing worn engagement dogs on third gear. This occurs because riders often load the engine the hardest while riding in third gear.

ENGINE MODS

If you want to get a smoother low-end pulling powerband with more over-rev, install two thick head gaskets (11004-1186) and an aftermarket exhaust pipe.

1983–1996 KAWASAKI KDX200
WITH JEFF FREDETTE

Author's note: Jeff Fredette is a veteran enduro rider who has raced the International Six Days Enduro (ISDE) 16 times. He's finished all 16 times and scored 10 gold medals, 5 silver medals, and 1 bronze medal. Jeff's company, Fredette Racing Products, specializes in Kawasaki KDX200 models. Fredette offers a wide range of parts, accessories, and high-performance services. Jeff answers technical questions over the phone on the most popular topics. He also has a two-hour video on KDX repair and tuning, and he answers questions on an online forum at www.dirtrider.net.

FRONT SUSPENSION
1983–1985
Use the stock fork springs for riders up to 180 pounds. Over that weight, use 0.32-kilogram springs with 5-weight oil and a fork oil level of 5.5 in., measured with the springs out and the forks bottomed.

1986–1988
The best fork oil weight to run is 7.5 (mix 5 and 10 Wt. 50/50). Run an oil level of between 4.75 and 5.5 in. The forks are characteristically harsh on small rocks and need to be revalved for the best performance. Use progressive-rate fork springs on all models for heavier riders (over 170 pounds). The stock fork springs sag over time. The maximum distance that the forks should sag under the bike's own weight is 3/4 in.

1989–1993
These forks are a little soft. Switching to stiffer springs makes a big improvement. For riders who weigh up to 170 pounds, we recommend 0.33-kilogram springs from the 1988 KDX. For heavier riders, we recommend progressive, 18- to 26-pound springs. Try setting the compression adjusters 6 to 11 clickers out. If that still isn't to your liking, I offer revalving for the forks.

1995–1996

The stock forks are sprung and valved for a 130-pound rider. For riders between 140 and 190 pounds, switch to 21-pound springs; riders over 200 pounds should use 23-pound springs. Set the oil level to 100 mm and the compression adjuster 10 to 18 clicks out. The Race-Tech Gold Valve kit works well with my shim placement specs.

REAR SUSPENSION

1983–1985 KDX

I use the stock spring and set the damper to position 2 for fast riding (whoops) and position 3 for slower riding (rocks). I set the sag to 1/2 in. unladen (the bike's own weight only) for riders under 175 pounds and 1/4 in. for riders over 175 pounds.

1986-1988

I use the stock shock valving with good results. The settings that work best are: 1/2 in. unladen sag for most riders and no sag for riders over 200 pounds. Compression damping settings are best at 3 clicks out for fast, whooped-out courses and 12 clicks out for tight woods and slow riding over rocks. Run the rebound adjuster at 2.5 turns out. Have the shock oil changed frequently (every 1,000 miles) to prevent shock shaft wear.

1989–1993

The stock spring and shock valving are good if dialed in properly. Start with a fresh oil change. Set the sag to 3.75 in. (with rider and full fuel tank). Set the compression clicker to 6 for fast terrain and 10 for slow terrain. Set the rebound clicker to 8 for fast terrain and 12 for slow terrain.

1994–1996

The stock spring and shock valving work well for riders who weigh 170 to 200 pounds. If you are lighter or heavier than that, you would benefit from a different spring. Lighter riders should use 4.8-kilogram springs and heavier riders should use 5.2-kilogram springs. When you ride on fast terrain,

Factory Connection makes trick suspension products for the Kayaba suspension components used on all KX models.

set the compression adjuster to 8 clicks out; set it to 16 clicks for slow terrain. Set the rebound adjuster in the same way, more damping at higher speeds.

ENGINE PERFORMANCE

1983–1985

The stock pipe works best with an Answer Products SA silencer. Clean and match the cylinder ports and jet the carburetor as follows: 1983, 150 main jet; 1984 and 1985, 35 pilot jet and a 280 main jet. Changing the silencer on the 1986 to 1988 KDX makes the biggest improvement in performance. The Answer SA Pro works well with an FMF pipe. Cylinder porting (clean casting and match port heights) will tame the hard-hitting powerband and give more low and top end. Carburetor jetting is as follows: 1986 and 1987 models, 30 pilot jet, p-2 needle clip position, 330 main jet; 1988 model, 48 pilot jet, p-3 needle clip position, 155 main jet. When performing a top-end rebuild, the factory service manual doesn't explain the KIPS valve timing procedure. The dot marks on the drum valves align with the ring mark on the actuator rod (rack). When the actuator rod is pulled out to the stop, the valves should be open, and when pushed in, the valves should be closed.

1989–1994

These modifications work best to improve the powerband over the entire rev range: FMF pipe, straight-through silencer, Boyesen RAD Valve, cylinder porting. Carburetor jetting: 48 pilot jet, 1173 needle in the middle clip position, 158 main jet, and turn the air screw to 1.5 turns out.

1995–1996

The 1995 model was the first year for the new KX-style exhaust valve system. The design utilizes a wedge valve for the main exhaust port and enables better control of the effective stroke and compression ratio over a wider rpm band. The best mod is an FMF pipe. A silencer would be the next best choice. If you can run a straight-through silencer, use the FMF. If you need to run a spark arrestor, use an FMF or an Acerbis 035.

The next modification to consider is cylinder porting. The cylinder needs the casting marks smoothed and polished for more power throughout the band, especially on top end. A Boyesen RAD valve gives a modest gain in performance. If you are having problems with clutch slippage, switch to stiffer clutch springs: Kawasaki 92144-1484. Run the trans oil level on the high side of the sight window to help reduce the noise from the clutch side of the engine.

GENERAL TIPS

1983–1985

The clutch basket nut and crank gear nut are likely to come loose. It is best to apply a thread-locking agent such as Red Loctite to the threads and check them periodically. Keep the ignition clean and dry. Condensation can cause the coil to break down. Ricky Stator in Santee, California, can rewind the Mitsubishi stator plates for a fraction of the cost of a replacement. Make sure you use Loctite on the kickstand bolt. The rock screen on the headlight makes a great headlight lens cover. Just bend the tabs to remount over the lens.

1986–1988

The rear brakes need more return spring action. Attach a conduit connector to the brake cam bolt with the "C" of the conduit connector facing the rear. Make some rubber bands from an old inner tube and run them toward the swingarm. Tap a bolt in the swingarm to anchor the rubber bands. Kawasaki brake shoes last the longest. Disc brake conversion kits can be purchased for about $400 from Fredette Racing.

1989–1994

Use Loctite on the left foot peg, kickstand, kick starter nuts, and the odometer reset knob screw. These are costly parts to replace if you lose them. Use a pipe cutter to cut the handlebars down so you can remove the end plugs easier. Flush and replace the brake fluid monthly with Dot 4 brake fluid to prevent brake fade.

CHAPTER THIRTEEN

TUNING TIPS FOR SUZUKI DIRT BIKES

2002–2004 SUZUKI RM85

FLAWS: shock oil wears out fast, flat top-end power

FIXES: change shock oil frequently, bigger carb, high-flow impellor

The 85 introduced an engine with a revised top end with plating rather than the old iron sleeve. The bore size was increased to the class limit, and a new rigid exhaust valve system was added.

Suzuki used a cheap replacement carb, but a Keihin flat slide 28 mm carb gives this bike more over-rev. Because the cooling system is challenged, a Boyesen water pump kit is needed for aggressive riders.

BEST VALUE MODS

Keihin 28-mm carb, Boyesen water pump kit

SUPERMINI KIT

The RM85L is the alternative big-wheel model that can be raced in the supermini or 125-cc classes. However, the stock 85 cc is not competitive. Most riders push the displacement to the maximum class limit of 105 cc. Wiseco makes a 100-cc piston kit. The kit installation requires boring, porting, plating, head and valve mods, and crankcase grinding.

1990–2001 SUZUKI RM80

FLAWS: magneto cover leaks, pistons wear fast

FIXES: Boyesen magneto cover, Wiseco Pro-Lite piston

This bike is a great design that suffers from one big problem—poor-quality materials were used in the engine components. The forks are a little soft too. Here are some tips on improving the longevity of the RM80.

The Suzuki RM125 has a reputation as a quick, maneuverable bike.

BEST VALUE MODS

ENGINE: Boyesen magneto cover

SUSPENSION: Emulator valve, fork spring preload

ENGINE

The cylinder bore and the crankshaft bearings wear out quicker than other Japanese dirt bikes. The cylinder uses a steel sleeve that can be bored to accept an oversize piston and rings. Wiseco Pro-Lite forged pistons are much better quality than the original cast Suzuki pistons. The cylinder can only be over-bored twice; any larger and the liner can't transfer out the heat and the engine will lose power. The cylinder has rough transitions between the liner and the ports. Remove the burrs from the ports and turn down the head 0.010 in. to broaden the powerband. Don't waste a lot of money on porting because the cylinder won't last forever.

The connecting rod and main crankshaft bearings need to be changed at least once a racing season. The plastic water pump impellor tends to melt when the engine gets really hot. Boyesen Engineering makes an aluminum impellor that pumps more water and won't melt.

MAGNETO LEAKS

Replace the magneto cover with one made of aluminum to seal water out from the generating coils, a common cause of ignition failure. Boyesen Engineering sells aluminum magneto covers for RM80s.

FORKS

The forks need stiffer springs, but no manufacturer makes springs for the RM80. Most tuners add 10-mm-long aluminum spacers between the fork caps and the springs. Race Tech's

196

Emulator Valve significantly improves the fork damping. Change the fork oil to 10-weight for Emulator valves and 15-weight for the stock forks.

1997–2004 SUZUKI RM125

FLAWS: 1997 to 1999: piston and cylinder breakage

FIXES: weld-narrow exhaust port and replate

In 1997, Suzuki made its latest generation of the RM125. With conventional twin-chamber forks and revised frame geometry, the bikes have excellent turning and handling characteristics. The bottom end of the engine is essentially the same as previous models. The cylinder is similar to the design from the early 1990s. By 2000, Suzuki had managed to perfect the cylinder for a wide powerband and great longevity. More recent models have the new generation of electronic carbs that pump fuel into the venturi during the midrange.

After making slight changes to the connecting rod length and rod ratio, Suzuki finally made a significant design step forward with the 2004 engine. The new engine was inspired by KTM's newfound success as the horsepower king of the 125 class. Suzuki switched to a longer connecting rod, flat top piston, and triple exhaust port, but with milder port timing than the KTM.

BEST VALUE MODS

ENGINE: cylinder plating, Wiseco piston

SUSPENSION: revalve shock for more rebound, stiffer fork springs

CYLINDER MODS

The new 125s have a redesigned cylinder that is a hybrid, retro design with a new exhaust valve and a 1992 cylinder port design. The extra set of sub-exhaust ports was eliminated because of chronic problems with the plating flaking off between the exhaust ports.

The 1997 and 1998 models have their own flaws. In an effort to get enough exhaust area to compensate for the sub-exhaust ports, the main exhaust ports were widened to 95 percent of the bore's total width. If the piston and ring are not changed often enough, the ring will eventually break and tear up the bore.

The maximum chordal width of the exhaust ports for reliable running is 51.5 mm, measured from widest outer edges of the exhaust ports. That is the same spec as the 2000 cylinders. In the United States, many of the big tuning shops widen the ports too far. Caution: Don't exceed the maximum chordal width spec or the rings could be prone to accelerated wear. If you have a 1997 RM125 cylinder that was modified by a tuner for a wider exhaust port, it's possible to repair the cylinder by welding the corners of the exhaust port, thereby narrowing the port. Max Power and Aptec offer this service along with their replating services.

If you want to get more midrange and top-end power from the 1997 through 1999 cylinders, simply raise the exhaust ports. The highest that you can raise the exhaust ports is 28 mm, measured from the top of the cylinder.

HEAD MODS

When you raise the exhaust port, you have to turn down the sealing surface of the head. In this way, you can compensate the compression ratio in accordance with the change's effective stroke. When you raise the exhaust port to 28 mm, turn down the head 0.6 mm.

CLUTCH

Never use aftermarket clutch plates and springs in this bike. I tested two popular kits and the springs were either too stiff or the plate thickness was incorrect. When the stock basket wears out, replace it with a Hinson Racing clutch.

FORKS

Set the oil level to 210 mm and install stiffer fork springs if your weight is a factor (over 160 pounds in riding gear).

SHOCK

The stock shock has too much low-speed rebound (LSR). To compensate, set the race sag to 95 mm and the

Multi-time GNCC champ Rodney Smith proved the reliability of the RM250 and inspired a line of heavy-duty off-road parts marketed by Moose Off-Road.

rebound adjuster to six clicks out. If you have to switch to a stiffer spring because of your weight, you'll definitely have to get the shock revalved for more rebound damping. Consider frequent oil changes—every 20 riding hours. The bushings are very soft on these shocks and wear quickly.

1990–1996 SUZUKI RM125

FLAWS: nylon reeds crack, air box leaks

FIXES: carbon-fiber reeds, seal the air box

The RM125 went through some big changes in the early 1990s. The 1989 to 1992 models are similar in that they have the same generation engine and chassis. The 1993 model features the redesigned frame, inspired by the testing done by Donnie Schmit and Stefan Everts when they won world championships in the early 1990s. The 1993 model handles better through whoops sections, and when the twin chamber forks were introduced in 1994, it made the Suzuki the best-handling 125. The 1993 cylinder features new sub-exhaust ports. The port timing on these new cylinders has too much transfer port time-area, so the powerband is flat in the low end and hits hard when the exhaust valves open at 8,000 rpm.

BEST VALUE MODS

ENGINE: carbon-fiber reeds, cylinder mods

SUSPENSION: shock revalving

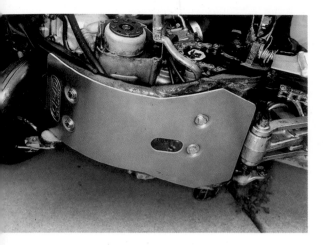

RM125s have drain plugs that are easily damaged from casing the bike into whoops and jumps. By installing a glide plate, you'll protect the drain plug and slide with less resistance when casing obstacles.

SUSPENSION

The suspension on the RMs is very good. The rear shock, however, needs more rebound damping. This can be improved with revalving or with an aftermarket piston and valve kit such as one from Pro-Action.

IGNITION

The new digital ignition system on the 1994 to 1996 models will fit on the 1991 to 1993 models. It must be used as a set (stator and igniter box). The old ignition style suffers from high-rpm misfiring over 12,000 rpm, which builds heat and eventually overheats the igniter box.

INTAKE SYSTEM

The old-style nylon reeds are prone to cracking and need to be checked. The new carbon-fiber reeds help the top-end over-rev. Aftermarket carbon-fiber reeds are good replacements for the 1990 to 1993 reed valves. The air box doesn't seal very well at the junction of the boot and the box. Reseal this junction with weather stripping adhesive.

CYLINDER AND HEAD MODS

The engine has a similar powerband to the other 125s. It can be modified for more low end with a hard midrange

burst from 3,000 to 9,800 rpm or for a strong-pulling upper midrange with more peak horsepower from 8,800 to 12,500 rpm. The first powerband is ideally suited for supercross, intermediate motocross, or enduro racing. The second powerband is for top experts only.

CLUTCH PROBLEMS WITH 1993–1996 RM125

Heavy clutch action with a low trans oil level will make the clutch cover wear out at the bushing where the actuating lever seats. This allows the actuating lever to wobble, causing poor clutch action. The symptoms of a worn cover are dragging, slipping, and difficulties adjusting the lever play. It's impossible to fit a needle bearing to the cover because there isn't enough cover material to fit the bearing. Replace the cover when it wears out.

LOW/MID POWERBAND

The cylinder base must be turned down 0.032 in. or 0.8 mm on a lathe to reduce the exhaust port duration. Then the transfer ports must be raised to 42 mm from the top of the cylinder. The rear transfer ports should be redirected to oppose each other rather than hooking toward the exhaust port.

Hooked ports waste fuel by short-circuiting the fuel out the exhaust port before the engine comes on the pipe. Because the cylinder base was turned down, the cylinder head's squish band must be remachined so the piston doesn't contact the head. The distance from the gasket surface to the squish band should be 1.2 mm and the squish-band angle (10 degrees) should be matched. Boyesen reeds or a RAD valve will match the intake system to the new powerband. For a final modification, set the power valve spring tension to one turn clockwise from zero.

TOP-END POWERBAND

The main exhaust port must be raised to 28 mm from the top of the cylinder.

PJ1 Coatings makes OEM-colored frame paint to keep your RM looking new.

The two sub-exhaust ports must be widened 1 mm each. Turn down the cylinder head 0.5 mm at the gasket surface. Install a 38-mm PJ Keihin carb and start with these jets: 60 slow jet, 5 slide, 1469 needle-middle position, and 175 main jet. The Messico GP pipe makes 2 horsepower more than the next-best pipe. Messico pipes are made in Italy. All these mods will help the RM produce an honest 36 horsepower at the rear wheel. That is about 6 horsepower more than original.

ATEV

The 1995 RM125 has a new-generation exhaust valve system that features bypass ports that vent gas pressure waves out the exhaust valve chamber. I recommend installing an automotive PCV check valve to prevent water from being drawn up the vent hose. The vent hose is mounted to the upper left side of the cylinder. Insert the PCV valve halfway up the vent hose to prevent any debris from being drawn into the cylinder. The new exhaust valves will interchange with older models but they don't offer any advantage.

A NOTE ON THE 1996 RM125

The 1996 model uses the bypass ports in the exhaust valves just like the 1995 model. The main difference is in the shape of the exhaust valves. In an effort to improve the low-end power of the RM125 cylinder, the new exhaust valves are oval in shape and have a flat edge that makes them seal closer to the piston. This lengthens the effective stroke and gives the engine better low to midrange power with a slight sacrifice of top-end power. The cylinder and head mods listed for the 1995 and earlier models work well on the 1996 model too. However, it isn't possible to interchange the 1996 and later cylinders with the 1995 and earlier models.

1985–1989 SUZUKI RM125

FLAWS: chronic piston seizures, ATEV breaks, linkage seizes
FIXES: thick sleeve and Wiseco piston, 1990 valves in 1989 RM125s, grease bearings

These bikes are plagued with all sorts of problems ranging from chronic piston seizures to broken exhaust valves and corroded swingarm and linkage bearings.

BEST VALUE MODS
ENGINE: Wiseco piston and cylinder sleeve
SUSPENSION: grease linkage frequently

TOP END

The cylinders can't be bored past 0.5 mm or 0.020 in.; otherwise, the cylinder sleeve becomes too thin and can't transfer out the heat properly. You must have the cylinder sleeved if you need to bore beyond 0.5 mm. The aftermarket sleeves are much thicker than the one in the stock cylinder. Aftermarket sleeves can be overbored as much as 2 mm when using Wiseco pistons. RM125s suffer from exhaust

RM125s and RM250s have some clutch issues. The baskets are made of soft material, the springs are too soft, and aluminum plates tend to look charred. Wiseco clutch baskets are forged tough and come as a complete kit with bolts, socket, and new rubber dampers. Moose Off-Road sells steel clutch plates that last longer.

valve problems. The old-style drum valves become carbon-seized, so they must be cleaned often. The 1989 and 1990 models crack at the stems, causing them to fall into the cylinder bore and crash into the piston.

CRANKSHAFT SEAL

The left-side crankcase seals are prone to failure and should be replaced every 10 engine running hours.

SWINGARM

The swingarm bearings and linkage are prone to corrosion, so grease them often.

2001–2004 SUZUKI RM250

FLAWS: top-end failures from intake port design, weak clutch components
FIXES: TIG-weld intake bridges, Hinson Pro clutch kit

Suzuki fluctuated between adapting designs from the KX250 and later YZ250. Each year, they changed the exhaust valve system giving it more moving parts and complexity.

BEST VALUE MOD

Boyesen RAD valve, Hinson clutch

CYLINDER

The 2000-2002 models suffer from top-end failures traced to the design of the intake port, which uses two vertical bridges. The bridges are too narrow with a tight radius at the top. The bridges tend to crack and scour the

piston and eventually crack off the intake skirt. The only way to fix the problem is to strip the plating off the cylinder, TIG-weld the bridges wider with large corner radii, and replate the cylinder. The 2003-and-later cylinders use a design like a YZ. It has a large, smooth oval intake port that works well. The 2003 cylinder needs a higher exhaust port for more top end. The 2004 cylinder was refined and the RM250 was heralded as the best engine in class in the dirt bike press.

REED VALVE

A Boyesen RAD valve works much better than stock and gives a boost to top-end power.

CLUTCH

The stock clutch components are weak. The basket material is soft and grooves fast, the hub gets notched from the steel plates, and the pressure plate isn't very stiff. Hinson Racing makes a Pro kit that includes the basket, hub, and pressure plate. These parts offer better clutch feel and improve reliability.

1996–2000 SUZUKI RM250

FLAWS: weak suspension linkage, exhaust valve system problems
FIXES: monitor linkage for cracks and lubrication, polish exhaust valves

In 1996, the RM250 was *Motocross Action's* Bike of the Year. It was the most improved bike of its class, but every

Former World Champion Kevin Schwantz races supermoto with the Yoshimura Suzuki DRZ440.

new generation model has its share of problems. The 1996 RMs were delayed because the top shock mounts were welded onto the frames in the wrong position. Soon after the bikes were released, the shock linkage was recalled. Suzuki replaced the original linkage with a new-and-improved unit. The new unit still requires frequent maintenance and should be inspected for cracks near the pivot holes. The 1996 engine is a close copy of the Honda CR250 engine, with a 66.4x72 bore and stroke and a cylinder reed valve. Some riders complain that the model doesn't have enough top-end power, but woods riders favor the excellent low-end to midrange power.

BEST VALUE MODS
  ENGINE: cylinder porting
  SUSPENSION: shock revalving

EXHAUST VALVE SYSTEM
Although Suzuki copied Honda's cylinder design, it couldn't infringe on the patents of Honda's HPP system. The one thing Suzuki couldn't copy was Honda's excellent exhaust valve system. The 1996, and 1998 to 2000 center exhaust valve is made of aluminum that causes a shock wave in the exhaust port when the valve is in the high-rpm position. The design is also prone to carbon buildup and erratic operation. The center valve doesn't fully recede into the roof of the port, leaving the flat edge of the valve exposed to the exhaust stream. It is possible to radius the bottom edge of

the valve to improve the top-end power but with a sacrifice of low-end power. Another common problem is carbon buildup on the actuating rod that links the side drum valves to the center valve. The rod is exposed to the exhaust stream on each side of the center valve.

This exhaust valve system requires frequent cleaning. You can polish the sharp edges of the valves to reduce the friction, but take care not to remove the brown hard-anodized coating that protects the valves. Over time, the center valve will become so worn at opposing corners that it will be prone to jamming in one position. Suzuki designed a stiff return spring for the new valve system. The spring, located behind the indexing knob on the right side of the cylinder, should be set to one turn clockwise past zero tension.

The articulated steel exhaust valve of the 1997 RM is a better design than the single-stage aluminum valve. Unfortunately, Suzuki only used it for one model year. The steel valve has two stages, like the RMX design, intended to give the engine a smoother powerband. But there are some simple mods to perform before this system works as well as the system on the CR. For the biggest improvement in top-end power, grind the minor center valve smooth so it conforms to the exhaust port roof. The stock design allows the valve to protrude out into the airstream and impede the outflow of the exhaust. It's easy to polish down the sharp edge with a round file. Remove the cylinder, turn it upside

down on a bench top, and open the exhaust valves to the max. File down the portion of the minor exhaust valve that extends into the port. Take care not to let the file touch the plated cylinder bore; that could cause the plating to chip and damage the bore. After you've finished, disassemble the exhaust valve system and clean out all the metal particles. The exhaust valve spring tension is critical. Set the minor valve spring tension (upper knob) to 3/4-turn clockwise. Set the major valve spring tension to 1/2-turn clockwise. If the spring tension is too tight, the valve's opening timing will be retarded, causing a detonation noise while accelerating through the midrange. Sometimes, excess spring tension can prevent the valves from opening, depending on the amount of carbon buildup on the valves.

CYLINDER
The cylinder porting is very good, a close copy of the CR. However, if you want more top-end power, raise the sub-exhaust ports to 39 mm, measured from the top of the cylinder. The 1998 model has a very small main exhaust port. It can be widened and raised to the same height as the sub-exhaust ports. On the 1999 and 2000 models, Suzuki copied the KX250 cylinder design. Unfortunately, the bridges that support the intake port tend to cause piston seizures. You can fix that problem by gusseting the bridges to increase rigidity and prevent them from flexing into the piston. However, the cylinder needs to be replated in order to repair the weak intake bridges. The modified height of the transfer ports should be 58 mm, measured from the top of the cylinder.

HEAD MODS
In 1998, Suzuki switched from a dome-shaped piston to a flat top design. The flat top design works well. Wiseco makes a flat-top piston (part number 705PS) for the 1996 to 2000 RM250. When this piston is used on domed heads, it requires that the head is modified in the following manner: turn

down 2.5 mm from the sealing surface; set the tool angle to 4 degrees; set the squish recess depth to 1 mm; and cut the squish angle until the tool blends into the chamber bowl.

CARBURETOR

Riders at high altitude or in warm climates complain of rough running when accelerating out of turns. The reason is that the carb's slide cutaway is too rich. Modify the cutaway by filing and polishing for a finished depth of 7 mm. Take care when performing this mod because a rough edge can cause the throttle to stick open.

CLUTCH

Most pros switch to a Hinson Racing clutch basket and pressure plate, combined with KX250 plates and springs (Kawasaki fiber plates: 13088-1105; metal plates: 13089-1066; springs: 92144-1351). This setup resists lurching and slippage better than the original clutch parts.

SUSPENSION

Forks
Set the oil height to 210 mm and adjust the clickers for conditions.

Shock
Set the sag to 95 mm, and set the rebound adjuster to six clicks out.

1993–1995 SUZUKI RM250

FLAWS: rich carb jetting, front end dives, clutch plates break
FIXES: lean jetting, revalve rear shock and shorten, install Barnett or 1996 KX250 clutch plates and FMF aftermarket pressure plate

In 1993, Suzuki changed the crankcases and added more flywheel weight in an effort to reduce the hard-hitting midrange. The cylinder hasn't changed since 1992. This cylinder has such large transfer ports that it can't pull the extra flywheel weight, which makes the bike seem as if it has no low-end power. In 1995, Suzuki redesigned the

exhaust valve system to use bypass ports in an effort to regain low-end power. In 1996, Suzuki changed the entire engine design to one that was very close to the current Honda CR250. The bore and stroke was changed to 66.4x72 mm. The cylinder was changed to the old reed valve in the cylinder design used in 1988. A new exhaust valve system was employed, but it is prone to carbon seizing. Also, this exhaust valve design hinders the top-end power potential of the model. Here are some things you can do to tune the RM.

BEST VALUE MODS

ENGINE: aftermarket silencer, cylinder porting
SUSPENSION: revalve and shorten shock, stiffer fork springs

INTAKE SYSTEM

Because of the angle of the stock reed valve, the reed petals tend to flutter at about 7,000 rpm. Replacing the petals with those made of carbon fiber will help. The carb jetting is a bit too rich. I've had the best luck with a Honda CR needle R1368N with the clip in the middle position and a 185 main jet. The needle is leaner than stock and the main jet is richer. Combined with an NGK BP7EV spark plug, your RM will run smoother and crisper through the rev range. The stock air box is prone to water seepage. The air box should be sealed at the seams with duct tape.

SILENCER

The original Suzuki silencer is poorly designed. Changing to an aftermarket silencer will dramatically improve the power over the full rev range.

CYLINDER PORTING

If you want a strong pulling powerband with more low end and a smoother midrange with loads more top-end over-rev, the cylinder has to be ported. The exhaust port must be raised to 37 mm from the top of the cylinder and widened 2 mm on the outer edge of each exhaust port. The transfer ports are

SFB makes color-anodized aftermarket engine covers and thread-on flywheel weights for most late-model dirt bikes.

too large, making the stock RM flat at low rpm (under 4,000 rpm). Narrow the set of rear transfers 6 mm (each port) at the back corner angles, and direct the ports to flow straight across at each other. This procedure must be done with epoxy since it is nearly impossible to fill the ports with molten aluminum during TIG-welding.

EXHAUST VALVE PRECAUTIONS

The two most common mistakes made with Suzuki's ATEV exhaust valve system are: turning the spring preload knob too far clockwise, which puts too much tension on the valves and then they won't open at all (maximum preload is 1.5 turns clockwise from zero preload); and installing the right-side shaft spring in a crisscross position (that spring is designed so the spring tabs are parallel to each other).

1995 EXHAUST VALVE SYSTEM

This system features bypass holes drilled in the exhaust valves. The exhaust gases are allowed to enter the chamber cover and provide resonance. However, there is a serious design flaw—this chamber is vented to the atmosphere, allowing hot exhaust gases to escape out the black rubber vent hose fastened to the left side of the cylinder. The pressure waves present in the exhaust gases travel to the

This Synergy carbon-fiber supermoto bike costs $20,000!

The RMZ250 is a popular bike supported by hundreds of aftermarket products to improve performance and reliability.

into the crankcases through the right-side crankshaft seal and combusts in the engine. You can tell when the seal is blown because the exhaust pipe billows out white smoke, spark plugs foul, and oil drips from the pipe. Install 1,000 cc of oil in the transmission and change it every 10 engine running hours.

REAR FRAME SUPPORT

The support bar that bridges the rear frame tubes is vulnerable to being dented by the seat base when a rider lands hard from a jump. Reinforce the frame support bar by welding a piece of steel flat stock on top of the existing support.

REAR SUSPENSION

The rear shock has too much travel, which causes the weight bias to transfer forward. The common solution employed by suspension tuners is to shorten the shock travel. Insert shims (8 mm in total thickness) between the shock seal assembly and the bottoming plate to shorten the shock travel. Of course, the shock must be disassembled to do this modification and you should entrust the work to a skilled suspension tuner.

GEARING

Change the rear sprocket to a 50-tooth. Check the sprocket bolts frequently because they are prone to vibrating loose.

1990–1992 SUZUKI RM250

FLAWS: clutch problems, rich jetting, loose primary gear bolt

FIXES: replace needle bearing, leaner slide, replace bolt

These were fairly reliable bikes in their time. They have good suspension components that can be greatly improved with revalving. The forks need stiffer springs, and the compression valving must be softened. The rear shock needs more rebound damping, but that has always been a characteristic problem with Suzukis. The engines had some chronic problems such as clutch failures, leaky seals, and piston failures. Suzuki has redesigned these OEM parts for better reliability.

end of the tube and reflect back into the cylinder, drawing cold air and debris into the cylinder. It's best to block the vent tube with a bolt tapped into the cylinder casting. There is a tube on the right side of the cylinder to vent excess transmission oil gases and water condensation. I recommend installing an automotive PCV valve. Make sure the PCV valve has hose ends of 1/4 in. Connect the PCV

valve in the middle of the left-side vent hose. The PCV valve is a one-way valve—position the PCV valve so it flows outward. This will prevent debris from being drawn up the hose and into the engine.

TRANS OIL FILLING

Suzukis tend to lose transmission oil from the countershaft seal, or it leaks

BEST VALUE MODS

ENGINE: install a 4.5 slide in the carb, Boyesen RAD valve

SUSPENSION: soften fork compression, install 0.41-kilogram fork springs

CARB JETTING

The carb jetting is too rich. I recommend using a 40 pilot jet, 4.5 slide, position three on the needle, and a 320 main jet. Install an NGK BP7ES spark plug or the equivalent heat range in another brand of plug.

SILENCER MODS

Shorten the silencer 50 mm to improve the power throughout the rev range. This is easy to do on RMs because they use a straight silencer. Mark 50 mm from the end of the silencer body (not the end cap). With the silencer assembled, use a hacksaw to cut the silencer. Then, grind off the rivets from the end cap. Pack the silencer with new packing material (Silent Sport packing), and put the end cap on the body. Mark the holes for the rivets, and drill three new rivet holes in the silencer body. Then, install new rivets.

CHRONIC CLUTCH PROBLEMS

If your RM has chronic problems with breaking clutch plates, the problem might be that the center bushing and needle bearing is worn. This causes the clutch basket to wobble and puts a strain on the steel plates. Barnett clutch kits have wider tabs on the fiber plates and reduce the gouging that occurs in the fingers of the clutch basket.

CYLINDER AND HEAD MODS

The main difference between the early- and late-model RM250 cylinders is the size of the exhaust port outlet, which is larger on the early models. Suzuki wanted to boost the midrange torque of the later models to reduce the size of the port, thereby boosting the exhaust gas velocity. That mod is nearly impossible to do on the early-model cylinders. However, turning down the cylinder base 1 mm will improve power throughout the rev range. The exhaust and transfer ports have the same dimensions as the late-model cylin-ders, so modify the ports as listed in the 1993 to 1995 RM recommendations.

LOOSE PRIMARY BOLTS

The bolt that retains the primary gear on the crankshaft tends to come loose. If the bolt ever comes loose, replace it with one from a 1995 model, apply a thread-locking agent to the bolt, and torque it to factory specs.

REED VALVE

A Boyesen RAD valve improves the low to midrange power of the RM250 and is one bolt-on item that is really worth the money.

1985–1989 SUZUKI RM250

FLAWS: cylinder plating chips, ATEV spring fails, bushings wear

FIXES: electroplate cylinder, replace spring, service bushings

During the late 1980s, the RM250 was transformed from a wide, top-heavy trail bike to a sleek racer that carves a tight line. The 1987 and 1988 models were very similar and represented a major design change over the 1985 and 1986 models. *Dirt Rider* magazine rated the 1987 RM250 as the best bike of the class. These bikes have conventional cartridge forks and a modern, tapered-shim shock-valve design. If you are currently riding a 1987 or 1988 RM250, your bike may have some of these symptoms: front forks rebound too quickly, exhaust smoke is excessive, powerband is flat, and spark plugs foul easily.

The 1989 and 1990 models are narrow bikes with low centers of gravity. They featured the original inverted cartridge forks, a case-reed-valve engine, and the TMX Mikuni carb. These models have a hard-hitting powerband, and the suspension works well for aggressive riders. Characteristic problems include: clutch plate breakage, the transmission pops out of second and third gear, spark plug fouling at low speeds, and rear shock kicking.

BEST VALUE MODS

ENGINE: cylinder plating

SUSPENSION: Braking oversize disc

Athena makes these big bore kits for the RMZ250, boosting the total displacement to 290 cc for less than $900.

This is a comparison of worn and new RMZ shim cups. Worn valve springs allow bounce, and eventually the shim breaks through the top of the cup. If you see any marks on the top like on the left, replace the shim cup.

The left cam lobe reveals a wear pattern from valve bounce and the shim cup, making a double imprint on the hard face of the back side of the lobe.

CYLINDER PLATING

The boron-composite cylinder plating material tends to flake on the 1987 to 1989 models. Examine the intake side of the cylinders for wear. The cylinders

If the cam lobes look oddly uneven when set to the TDC mark of the crankshaft, the cam may have slipped on the sprocket hub. The cams need to be replaced.

Fastway adjustable foot pegs vary the offset forward, backward, up, and down.

can be repaired with nickel-silicon-carbide plating from companies such as US Chrome.

EXHAUST VALVE SYSTEM

The exhaust valves tend to accumulate thick oil deposits that eventually lock the valves in the closed position. When this happens, the engine runs flat at high rpm. Remove the cylinder and clean the valves with oven cleaner, detergent, and water. Manually operate the exhaust valve control lever and make sure the valves move with the lever. There is a spring on the lever, so it can move even if the valves are seized. If the exhaust valve spring tensioner (located on the upper left corner of the cylinder) is turned too far clockwise, the valves will be sprung in the closed position. If your RM has been overbored and has an aftermarket steel sleeve installed in the cylinder, the exhaust valves must be filed for adequate clearance.

LOOSE PRIMARY BOLTS

The bolt that holds the gear on the right side of the crankshaft tends to vibrate loose. When it backs off the threads, it prevents the exhaust valve governor control from operating the exhaust valves. The best fix is to remove the bolt and clean the bolt and crankshaft threads. Then apply a thread-locking agent such as red Loctite, and torque the bolt to factory specs.

EXCESSIVE SPARK PLUG FOULING

If your RM pumps out exhaust smoke like mosquito abatement trucks and fouls spark plugs, the right-side crankshaft seal is probably blown. This is a common problem that is cheap and easy to fix. The seal costs about $10. The right-side engine cover and clutch must be removed to access the primary gear.

The seal is under the primary gear. If you do not have a clutch-holding tool or access to pneumatic impact wrenches, bring your bike to a mechanic. This is a simple mechanical procedure, but it is dependent on the right tools.

CLUTCH PLATE BREAKAGE

If your RM breaks clutch plates periodically, the bushing and needle bearing for the clutch basket may be worn, allowing for excessive axial movement of the clutch. The bushing and bearing should be replaced every two riding seasons. Another cause of clutch plate breakage is a clutch basket with deep groove marks from the fiber plates. When the clutch is disengaged, the plates just stick in the grooves, causing the clutch action to be "grabby." Sometimes, you can fix the problem by filing down the edges of the grooves in the clutch basket. In most cases, you should replace the worn clutch basket as a set with a new bushing and bearing.

MISSED SHIFTS

The 1989 to 1992 RM250s sometimes develop shifting problems from downshifting too often with too great of an engine load. Worn or bent shift forks cause the problem. The shift forks should be replaced every time the lower end of the engine is rebuilt or every two riding seasons.

SUSPENSION REBOUNDS TOO QUICKLY

The forks and the shock can slowly develop too fast of rebound damping for the same reason: the bushings are worn out. If the forks make a clanking sound on the upstroke or cause your forearms to pump up severely, the bushings on the piston rod are so worn that the oil bypasses the piston, thereby reducing the damping effect. The piston rod seal band and bushing are only available with the repair service from companies such as Pro-Action, White Bros., Race-Tech, and Scott's.

BIGGER BRAKES

Oversize brake discs can give a boost in braking power. The front end especially

Pro-Circuit makes aftermarket high-capacity radiators for RMZ and KXF250s.

benefits from this modification. A company called Braking makes oversize disc and caliper bracket kits for the front end of the 1989 to 1995 RMs.

MIKUNI CARBURETOR UPDATE

The 1985 to 1988 RM250s have the Mikuni TM carb. Later models have TMX carbs. These carburetors do not have an idle adjustment. If you are trail riding and would like the convenience of a bike that idles, you need a Mikuni TMS carb, available from White Bros. If your RM bogs when landing from big jumps, add a Boyesen Super Bowl and T-vent kit.

1989–1999 SUZUKI RMX250

FLAWS: weak power, chain guides bend, brakes weak

FIXES: gusset chain guide brackets, Braking disc

The RMX hasn't changed much over the years. The chassis and suspension have evolved slower than the RM. The main difference between the engine of the RM and RMX is the top end and transmission. The RMX has a superior exhaust valve design, but the RM has a better cylinder and head design. The RMX has lower gear ratios for first and second and a higher ratio for fifth gear.

BEST VALUE MODS

ENGINE: Head mod, Cometic gaskets, FMF Fat Boy pipe

SUSPENSION: steering damper

TOP END

The RMX cylinder needs a wider exhaust port and smaller transfer ports. The compression ratio is very low. There is a simple solution: Advance the port timing with a thicker base gasket (1 mm or 0.039 in.) and a thinner head gasket (0.25 mm or 0.010 in.). Cometic sells these gaskets individually. If you want to have the cylinder and head machined, widen the exhaust ports (2 mm or 0.080 in.) on each outer edge. The rear transfers can be epoxied in the back corners. The head can be turned down (0.75 mm or 0.030 in.). These modifications are for a stock base gasket and a 1989 RM250 head gasket or the Cometic equivalent. The exhaust valve system on the RMX uses a dual-stage valve design. It's great for smooth power delivery but requires frequent cleaning. There are two long coil springs that exert tension on the secondary valves. Those springs get clogged with carbon. Clean those springs well when servicing the exhaust valve system.

CARBURETOR

A 39.5-mm Keihin PWK is the best-performing carb for the RMX. It has an idle circuit that makes it more controllable at low-throttle openings, and the throttle response is smoother.

PIPE

FMF Fatty or Gnarley pipe and silencer.

KICK STARTER

The kick starter knuckle joint tends to wear prematurely, allowing the kick starter lever to flop around. Unfortunately, there is no aftermarket replacement part. You have to keep the knuckle joint clean and oiled with chain lube.

BRAKES

I recommend a Braking oversize disc for the front end. Braking discs are laser cut from stainless steel and offer better longevity and stopping power than OEM discs. Moose Off-Road hex-head brake pins are more durable than the OEM pins, and they are easier to remove.

CHAIN GUIDE MODS

The chain guide is mounted to the swingarm with straight tabs. There is no support to prevent the tabs from bending inward and guiding the chain off-center. Butt-weld triangular tabs on the chain guide tabs and the swingarm. Aluminum covers for the guide aren't really effective until the mounting tabs are improved.

CHAPTER FOURTEEN

TUNING TIPS FOR YAMAHA DIRT BIKES

2002–2004 YAMAHA YZ85

FLAWS: weak low-end power, hard on clutches

FIXES: machine cylinder base and head, use steel clutch plates and stronger Hinson basket

When Yamaha bumped the displacement for the class limit, the exhaust port was raised too. Some riders complain that this bike doesn't accelerate out of the turns like the KX or RM. Those models use power valves, so the YZ is at a disadvantage. By turning down the cylinder base (0.030 in. or 0.75 mm) and the head correspondingly, you can raise the compression and retard the port timing for better midrange hit.

BEST VALUE MODS

Hinson clutch with steel plates

1993–2004 YAMAHA YZ100 CONVERSION

It is possible to convert a YZ80 into a big-wheel 100 with a combination of aftermarket engine and OEM parts.

ENGINE MODS

Two big bore piston kits on the market have displacement sizes suited to different racing associations. The biggest displacement kit is made by LA Sleeve. It starts at 103.5 cc to 108 cc on the maximum oversize. The other kit is made by Wiseco and uses stock gaskets. The Wiseco kit requires the cylinder to be bored, ported, and electroplated. The head must be enlarged to accept the 52.5-mm piston. The crankcases must also be modified because the piston skirt contacts the exhaust side of the cases. It's acceptable to mask off the crankshaft and grind away the minor areas of the cases for adequate piston clearance. Other additions to the 100-cc conversion include a flat slide Keihin 28-mm carb and an R&D pipe and silencer.

CHASSIS AND SUSPENSION

Yamaha's accessory division, YZR, offers an extended swingarm and wheel kits that include rims and spokes. In order for the YZ to be legal for racing in the supermini class, it needs a longer wheelbase and bigger wheels. Normally, when you switch to a longer swingarm, you'll need to switch to stiffer springs front and rear.

1993–2001 YAMAHA YZ80

FLAWS: poor low-end power, non-adjustable forks

FIXES: cylinder and head mods, adjustable base valve

Although the YZ80 is a good bike for expert mini riders due to an abundance of high-rpm power and good suspension, it has too little low end and midrange for most riders. The problem is a combination of radical port timing and high gearing. Like most of the minis, the YZ doesn't have the quick response to keep up with the RMs out of turns.

BEST VALUE MODS

ENGINE: cylinder and head mods
SUSPENSION: base valve kit

CYLINDER MODS

To get more midrange from the YZ80, turn down the base of the cylinder 0.028 in. or 0.7 mm and remove the same amount from the squish band of the cylinder head. This retards the port

The world's first Yamaha YZ was raced by 1973 AMA National Champion Pierre Karsmakers. Karsmakers has a motocross museum in the mezzanine of his motorcycle dealership in Eindoven, Netherlands.

timing and reduces the port duration, plus increases the compression ratio.

INTAKE
Install a set of Boyesen dual-stage reeds.

GEARING
The stock gearing is too high and should be changed to 12/52 for quicker acceleration. Expert riders prefer changing to a larger carb (28-mm flat slide Keihin) for more over-rev.

GEARBOX
Earlier models had problems with wear on the teeth of second gear. Yamaha has since improved the gear and pulled all the old parts from stock. If you ever have to split the cases for engine rebuilding, check the gear teeth for wear. The wear pattern looks like corrosion.

CLUTCH
Yamaha recommends switching to stiffer clutch springs. The part number is 90501-216A6.

FORKS
The forks can be improved by installing an adjustable base valve kit to make the forks plusher. There are two options for base valves: 1992 YZ125 OEM base valve or a tuned valve from Pro Racing or Race-Tech. The stock fork and shock springs are too soft for most riders. The way to check the spring rate is to set the race sag to 75 mm in the rear and check the unladen sag (bike's weight without rider). If the unladen sag is under 10 mm, you need to install a stiffer shock spring. The front fork sag should be between 20 and 30 mm. If the forks sag more than 30 mm, you need to install stiffer springs.

1997–2004 YAMAHA YZ125
FLAWS: requires frequent top-end service, forks bottom
FIXES: replace the piston kit every 15 hours of running, stiffer fork springs, and hydraulic anti-bottoming device

This bike is widely considered to have the best engine in its class, but it sacrifices some reliability. A couple of key

areas to pay attention to are the top end, connecting rod, and frame. The 1999 cylinder has the best performance but is the most prone to failure. The 2000 model cylinder is the best overall design and includes a new exhaust valve design. The frames are prone to cracking when the bikes are jumped too hard and key bolts are left loose like the engine mounts and swingarm pivot. Refer to Chapter 4 for tips on inspecting and strengthening frames.

BEST VALUE MODS
ENGINE: Wiseco Pro-Lite piston kit, weld cylinder exhaust bridge
SUSPENSION: Magnum anti-bottoming fork accessory, weld frame cracks

CYLINDER
The cylinder's exhaust port is very wide. The exhaust port bridge has a weak spot, about 10 mm down from the top of the port. The problem is that the exhaust valve pockets are machined too deep and intersect the bridge, reducing its thickness at a critical point. The bridge is prone to cracking at this point if the piston seizes. It's best to replace the piston rings every five hours of engine time. If the exhaust bridge cracks, have it repaired by a company that specializes in electroplating. The bridge needs to be welded and made wider (3 mm). This modification will require you to fit the exhaust valves. You'll have to chamfer the corner of the valves that butt the exhaust port bridge. If you don't grind the valves properly, they won't close all the way.

CRANKSHAFT
Another significant design error lies in the crankshaft. A two-stroke crankshaft has less mass on top near the pin hole to compensate the balance factor of the reciprocating mass of the connecting rod and piston assembly. Manufacturers use different designs to fill in the void around the pin hole. Honda fits sheetmetal covers around the crank. Kawasaki and Suzuki use lightweight aluminum slugs. Yamaha uses plastic slugs. The problem seems to be that the plastic slugs are fitted

Check the tranny gears of the YZ80s. Stiffer aftermarket clutch springs can make the gears wear faster.

so closely around the pin hole that they shroud the big end bearing from getting enough lubrication. The crank gets hot around the big end and the plastic starts to swell up, thus compounding the problem. Eventually, the plastic melts and flows into the big end bearing, causing the bearing to fail. Disassemble the crank to replace the rod assembly. Remove the melted plastic with a die grinder and a large fluted tool bit. Bevel the plastic slug at a 45-degree angle all around the pin hole, so as to allow more area for the pre-mix to lubricate the big end bearing. Removing plastic from the slug does lower the crankcase compression ratio and that causes a slight loss of low-end power, but reliability is worth the sacrifice in performance.

CARBURETOR
The carb jetting on the 1999 model has too rich of a slide. Switch to a 7.0 slide if your bike bogs when fluctuating the throttle over whoops and through turns.

FORKS
The YZ125 has the best performing fork for a 125. However, some riders complain about the metallic clunking noise when the forks bottom out. Yamaha switched to an elastomer foam bumper for the anti-bottoming device. Hydraulic products work much better. Devol Racing has a product called the Magnum. It is an anti-bottoming device

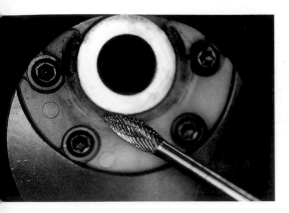

The late-model YZ125s use plastic inserts to stuff the crankshaft and maximize throttle response. When the rod wears and produces more friction, the heat melts the edges of the insert. Here, a porting tool is used to grind away the burnt material prior to installation of a new connecting rod kit. If the plastic is melted, it's cheaper to buy a new Hot Rod crankshaft rather than repair the stock crank.

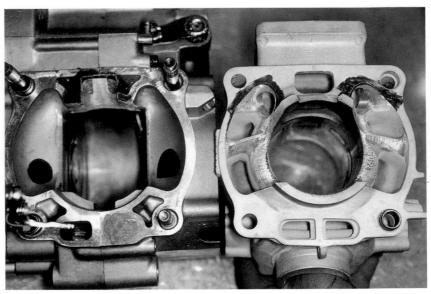

This is a cylinder and crankcase set for 1994 to 98 YZ250s, modified for a rear boost port. This offers a midrange to top-end powerband.

that fits inside the cartridge. It requires specialized knowledge of cartridge forks to install the device so it's best to rely on a suspension technician who has the proper tools. Take care to use the correct spring rate for your geared weight and riding style. If the front fork race sag is less than 30 mm, switch to a softer spring rate. If the race sag is more than 55 mm, switch to a stiffer spring rate.

SHOCK
The stock shock valving is very good and it's not likely that you'll need to have it revalved.

FRAME
The frame is especially prone to cracking at the foot peg mounts. The best preventive maintenance is to reinforce the foot pegs with gusset plates welded under the foot pegs and along the frame tubes. Another trouble spot is the lower engine mounts. They are only spot-welded on one side of the plate. Find a skilled fabricator in your local area to reinforce the foot peg and engine mounts.

1994–1996 YAMAHA YZ125
FLAWS: frame tabs crack, chronic coolant leaks

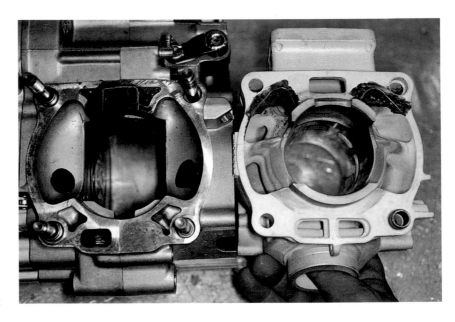

This is a cylinder and crankcase set before the modifications, showing the new ports marked in blue ink.

FIXES: gusset frame, install head alignment pins

This bike is a good design. The exhaust valve system is similar to the RM in that it reduces the volume of the exhaust port and boosts the port velocity at low rpm. The system was refined each model year to improve performance and reduce the need for maintenance. The

1994 model has some teething problems. Yamaha redesigned the connecting rod and bearing to reduce premature failure. The problem of second gear seizures was remedied in the 1995 model. The frame on the 1995 model was gusseted in several places because the 1994 model develops cracks at the radiator mounts, top shock mount, and foot pegs. That problem can

BBR makes these trick aluminum frame kits for YZFs and other brands of dirt bikes.

be easily corrected with frame gusseting. The YZ cylinder and head need alignment pins because the forces from the head-stay can cause chronic coolant leaks. This problem manifests into erosion at the top edge of the cylinder, damaging the Nikasil plating.

The powerband is similar to that of the other 125s—good midrange but falls flat at 10,600 rpm, making 29 horsepower at the rear wheel. Don't believe the exaggerated horsepower claims of some Japanese manufacturers. They all make this same peak power at nearly the same rpm. The YZ has great low to midrange power, making it an ideal trail bike. If you want to make your YZ competitive in motocross, you have to modify the cylinder and head, plus add a pipe and silencer.

BEST VALUE MODS
ENGINE: FMF pipe and silencer
SUSPENSION: Eibach fork springs

SHIFTER MODS
Over the years, Yamahas have been criticized as being hard to shift. Polishing the shifting mechanism and drilling oil holes in the clutch hub will help, but the best product on the market is Race-Tech's external shifter mechanism. It's fairly expensive, but many riders swear by it. This product enhances the leverage ratio of the shift lever.

FORKS
The Kayaba forks have great damping, but the spring rate is set for a fairly light rider (160 pounds). If you have any problems with head shaking or front-end diving when braking for turns, consider stiffer fork springs.

HIGH-RPM POWERBAND
The setup for producing top-end power from the YZ is similar to the other 125s but much less expensive than the Honda.

CYLINDER AND HEAD
The cylinder and head designs of the 1994 to 1996 models are similar. The cylinder transfer ports have the right profile, but the exhaust port needs to be raised and widened for a 12,500-rpm peak. The exhaust port must be raised to 28 mm from the top of the cylinder and enlarged 1 mm on each side. The head should be machined for a higher compression ratio. If your YZ125 suffers from chronic coolant loss, machine the squish band's recess in the head to 0.75 to 1.0 mm. This helps keep the engine from developing coolant leaks because it reduces the pressure on the O-ring in the cylinder. Also, you should elongate the head-stay bolt hole to allow for a bit of movement in that area of the motor mount. Older bikes especially need more clearance at the head-stay because the frames tend to get deformed from too many hard landings.

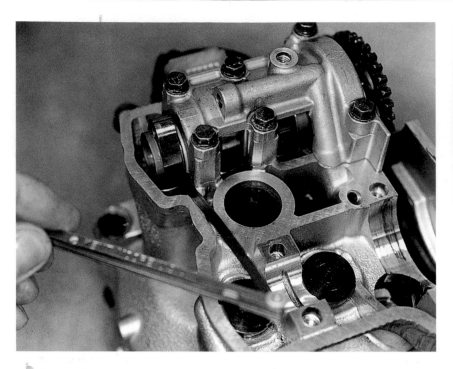

In order to check the valve clearance on a YZF, you'll need this special Yamaha tool—a thin-blade feeler gauge set.

Check the small end of the connecting rod on YZF250s. If scouring occurs, replace the crankshaft.

PISTON INTERCHANGE

The 1998 model piston has a boost port in the intake side that improves top-end over-rev and helps the piston run cooler. The 1998-and-newer pistons use a smaller pin and a bearing with thicker needle bearings. The pin is lighter, and the bearing will take a higher load than the old-style bearing. These parts can only be used as a set. The Wiseco order numbers are a 726P8 piston kit and a B1038 needle bearing.

EXHAUST SYSTEM

The stock silencer is too restrictive for a high-revving engine. In 1994, World Champ Bob Moore and Motocross des Nations Champion Paul Malin used FMF pipes and silencers.

INTAKE SYSTEM

The intake system is the next component to be modified. You'll need to upgrade to a 38-mm carb (Mikuni Jetting: 20 pilot, 4 slide, 63 needle, 360 main jet).

Install carbon-fiber reeds (0.5 mm thick) or a RAD valve because the stock reeds start to flutter and restrict the intake flow at 11,200 rpm.

CRANKCASE PORTING

This final mod is optional, but it makes a significant difference. The crankcases are slightly mismatched to the cylinder, and the transition between the intake port and the crankcase ports can be improved with filing and polishing.

1992–1993 YAMAHA YZ125

FLAWS: flat power, ring pins vibrate out
FIXES: match power valves, Wiseco Pro-Lite

The 1992 and 1993 model cylinders are similar to the 1990 model.

BEST VALUE MODS

ENGINE: power valve matching, carb jetting
SUSPENSION: basic servicing

POWER VALVE MODS

Matching the power valve to the exhaust port can provide big gains in performance when the valve is fully open. The power valve governor control is located under the right-side engine cover. Installing a ramp cup and spring (90501-30742-00 ramp cup; 3XJ-11912-00 spring) from earlier YZs can help the midrange power.

PISTON

Install a Wiseco piston because the piston ring alignment pins tend to fall out of the OEM pistons after sustained over-revving of the engine.

HEAD MOD

The squish band of the cylinder head needs to be narrowed to 6 mm, measured from one side of the chamber. The work can be performed on a metal lathe. If you raise the exhaust port, you'll have to reduce the volume of the cylinder head to a total of 9 cc.

CYLINDER MODS

Recommended cylinder mods include turning down the cylinder base 0.5 mm and raising the exhaust port to 26 mm from the top of the cylinder. Apply epoxy to the hook angles of the rear transfer ports. These mods reduce the time-area of the transfer ports and increase the exhaust port. This will help the bike accelerate harder in the midrange with more top-end over-rev.

CARB JETTING

Recommended baseline jetting for the 36-mm Mikuni carb: 20 pilot jet, 4.5 slide, 56 needle, and a 310 main jet.

REED VALVE

The Boyesen RAD valve works well for overall power gains, and Carbontech carbon-fiber reeds work well for high-rpm powerbands.

1990–1991 YAMAHA YZ125

FLAWS: weak low-end power (1991 model)

FIXES: change gearing, reeds, and 1990 power valve parts

The 1990 top-end parts are regarded as the best-tuned components Yamaha ever designed for the YZ125, and the 1991 model is notorious as the worst. Where the 1990 engine is great for motocross, the 1991 has a narrow, hard-to-use powerband. The weak low end made 1991 YZ125s slow out of turns. Changing to a lower final-drive ratio and installing Boyesen reeds helps a lot. On the 1991 model, it's best to switch to the ramp cup and spring from the 1990 power valve governor. The 1991 model uses a two-angle ramp cup that actually works well on the 1992 and 1993 models.

BEST VALUE MODS

ENGINE: 1991 model: Boyesen reeds,

Moose Off-Road makes these crankcase vent filters to prevent dirt from entering the crankcase.

1990 power valve parts, 11-tooth countershaft sprocket

SUSPENSION: basic servicing

CYLINDER INTERCHANGE

If you have a 1991 model and need to replace the cylinder, consider switching to the 1990 model parts. You'll need to change the cylinder and power valve as a set.

GEARING

Use a front sprocket that is one tooth smaller to get more low-end to midrange power from either of these models.

REEDS

Boyesen Dual-Stage reeds will dramatically improve the YZ's low-end power.

1985–1989 YAMAHA YZ125

FLAWS: weak clutch, engine bogs

FIXES: Barnett clutch, carb jets

The 125s from the late 1980s suffer from drivetrain problems. The clutches don't get enough oil flow, the clutch springs are too soft, and second gear is prone to breakage. In addition, the Mikuni carb has bogging problems when landing from jumps.

Mike Brown's YZF250.

BEST VALUE MODS

ENGINE: T-vents for carburetor

SUSPENSION: regular service

CLUTCH

The clutch is easy to fix. Stiffer clutch springs and better-quality plates such as those found in Barnett clutch kits will fix the slipping problem. Polishing the clutch actuating rod helps, too. Yamaha recommends drilling two oil holes (1/16-in. diameter) in each of the female splines of the inner clutch hub. This helps the oil flow, keeping the clutch plates cooler.

Second gear drive and driven gears are prone to breakage. The best precaution is to use the clutch when downshifting and change the transmission oil often. The gear ratios are very wide between first and second gear and the engines don't have much low-end power. If you are having problems bogging the engine out of turns, switch to a 12-tooth countershaft sprocket.

CARBURETOR

The carb on the 1986 to 1988 models is prone to bogging and starvation. Make sure the float level is set parallel to the

This 41-mm Keihin FCR carburetor gives big bore YZFs more top end.

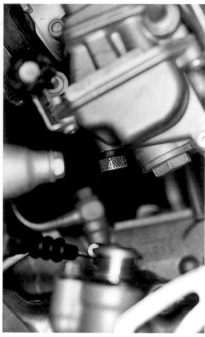

Zip-Ty makes this trick fuel adjuster for the YZFs.

float bowl base, and use these jets as a starting point: 45 pilot, 4 slide, Q-0 needle jet, 290 main jet, and a 3.5 inlet needle and seat. Install the modern T-vent setup.

REED VALVES

The FMF RAM valve works well on YZ125s. Use the short rev plates for more low-end power.

2001–2004 YAMAHA YZF250

FLAWS: no auto-decompressor on older models, crank and valvetrain prone to wear
FIXES: 2004 Hot Cam for exhaust auto-decompressor, replace crankshaft, stainless-steel valves

The 2001 YZF250 started out with some chronic crankshaft problems, which

were traced to undersized crankshaft journals and too much clearance. As described in Chapter 9, four-stroke crankshafts should be replaced for the main reason of cam chain sprocket wear. The lightweight titanium valves have a limited part life, and if allowed to tighten in clearance, could fail by cracking the heads off. Stainless-steel valves suit the maintenance habits of even a lackadaisical owner, and are far less expensive than stock replacement parts.

In 2003, Yamaha included an automatic decompressor in the exhaust cam. The 2003 OEM or aftermarket Hot Cams fit in the older models of YZF250.

BEST VALUE MODS

Hot Cam, Wiseco high-compression piston, Kibblewhite stainless valves and spring kit

EASY POWER

The two best products that give the biggest difference in power and reliability are the high-compression Wiseco Pro-Lite piston kit and Hot Cams with the auto-decompressor on the exhaust cam. The stock piston kit will last for a maximum of

100 hours before it's prone to cracking. Yamaha recommends 15-hour service intervals. When the top end is being rebuilt, always get a new cam chain and check the rear chain guide for wear.

VALVETRAIN

The titanium valves are for racing only. If you ride a lot and want a more reliable alternative, consider stainless-steel valves. They're more durable and the service intervals are longer.

CRANKSHAFTS

Always replace the crankshaft when the rod wears out. The price is under $200. On four-stroke engines, the journal ends and the cam chain sprocket get worn beyond repair.

FUEL MIXTURE NEEDLE

The stock fuel mixture screw tends to vibrate and fall out. The mixture screw is located under the front and center of the carburetor. It can be adjusted with a short, narrow, straight-blade screwdriver. There is a better aftermarket product made by Ty Davis. The accessory mixture screw is much longer so you can adjust it without a special tool, and it is red-and-white anodized so you can easily see the setting.

BIG BORE KITS

Wiseco makes a 2-mm oversize high-compression kit that boosts the displacement to 262 cc. Athena and RPM make 290-cc replacement cylinder and piston kits for about $900 complete.

1999–2004 YAMAHA YZ250

FLAWS: wheelspin, flat top end
FIXES: flywheel weight, raise exhaust port to 39 mm

Yamaha introduced a new 250-cc engine in 1999. The bore and stroke were changed to the same as all other 250s. The old engine was a square bore and stroke and the new engine is over-square, meaning that the stroke is longer. The new exhaust valve system is similar to the CR and RM designs, with the exception that the sub-exhaust ports open at a higher rpm than the center valve.

Wrapping "header tape" around the pipe as it snakes past the carburetor could prevent fuel boiling and vapor lock.

The old YZF400 has a smaller small end pin diameter than current YZFs. When the connecting rods are pushed past their normal service limit, they tend to snap like this one.

BEST VALUE MODS
ENGINE: flywheel weight
SUSPENSION: springs for your weight

CYLINDER AND HEAD MODS
The sub-exhaust ports can be raised to 38 mm from the top of the cylinder for more top end, and the head can be turned down at the gasket surface 0.5 mm. The setup requires race gas to run properly. The engine tends to be explosive in the midrange. A flywheel weight will make the power more tractable.

1997–1998 YAMAHA YZ250
FLAWS: soft top end, wheelspin
FIXES: port cylinder, raise compression, flywheel weight

Yamaha redesigned this engine, particularly the cylinder and head. The new cylinder has transfer ports similar to a Honda, the most copied design on the market. The new reed valve is excellent and you won't have to worry about it protruding into the rear boost port like previous models. However, Yamaha chose very conservative transfer port timing.

BEST VALUE MODS
ENGINE: Cometic thick base gasket 0.039, flywheel weight
SUSPENSION: set sag and clickers, stiffer fork springs for riders over 180 pounds

CYLINDER
Raise the transfer ports 1 mm or use the optional thick base plate marketed by Yamaha. The plate requires you to turn down the head 1 mm. The sub-exhaust ports have been raised, but the power valve's sub-exhaust channels have been altered to retard the port's opening timing. You can use a round file to adjust the sub-exhaust channels on the power valve for more top-end power. Modify the channels to open sooner by filing the leading edge of the power valve 4 mm at a 45-degree angle. Don't be tempted to raise the main exhaust port as Yamaha recommends in its published *Wrench Reports*. That modification will only make the plating peel from the port, causing cylinder failure.

HEAD MODS
If you are using just the stock Yamaha base gasket, the most you can turn down the head is 0.5 mm. No adjustments to the squish band depth or angle are necessary. If you want to install the Wiseco flat-top piston (#706PS), turn down the head 2 mm, set the squish band depth to 1 mm, and set the squish band angle to 4 degrees.

FORKS
The fork valving is good in stock form. Heavier riders will need to change to a stiffer spring rate like a 0.41 kilogram. The fork oil level works best at 90 mm. Set the compression clicker from four to eight clicks out.

SHOCK
Set the race sag to 95 mm for best results. The rebound adjuster is very sensitive to

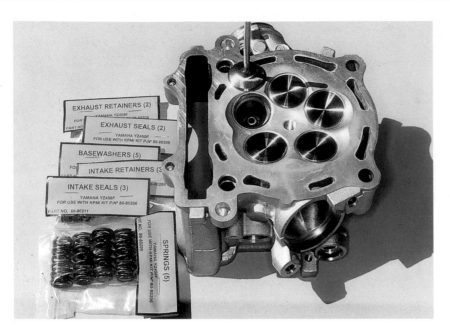

Kibblewhite makes high-performance stainless-steel valves that last much longer than the OEM titanium valves.

changes. The rebound adjuster works best in the range of four to eight clicks out. Set the compression adjuster to 12 clicks and experiment from there.

1994 YAMAHA YZ250 CYLINDER AND LONG-ROD KIT

There's been a lot of hoopla in the magazines about things like "long rod" kits and the 1994 YZ250 cylinder. In 1997, Yamaha riders Kevin Wyndam and Ezra Lusk used long-rod kits and 1994 cylinders on their factory bikes. The magazines never explained what the individual parts do and how they affect performance. The 1994 YZ250 cylinder doesn't utilize a resonator like the newer models. The resonator improves the low end of the powerband before the power valve opens (6,000 to 8,000 rpm). The 1994 YZ has a powerband with a hard midrange hit. It also has a lack of low-end power—great for pro riders but bad for trail riders. The 1994 YZ cylinder has larger transfer ports and an additional boost port linking the crankcase to the intake side of the cylinder. When combined with the 1989 YZ250 connecting rod and crankcase mods to feed the boost port, the 1994 cylinder conversion can make the 1997 and 1998 YZ250s into powerful midrange performers.

Building a factory replica YZ like this isn't cheap. The average price is about $1,600. It requires total engine disassembly and a new exhaust system. Here is a short explanation of the key components to this expensive conversion and how to get the most from the investment in parts.

ROD RATIOS

Connecting rods are all about time and leverage. On a two-stroke engine, changing the connecting rod length affects a number of other components. The rod ratio is the connecting rod length (center to center) versus the length of the stroke. Generally speaking, the higher the rod ratio (longer connecting rod), the better suited the engine will be for more high-rpm power.

When the piston reaches bottom dead center of the stroke (BDC), the longer connecting rod will cause the piston to accelerate faster on the upstroke. The rapid changes in crankcase volume cause the reeds to open to their maximum flow area. When the piston rises to top dead center (TDC), the long rod will dwell the piston at TDC for a longer period of time than a shorter rod. By dwelling the piston at TDC, a greater pressure rise could occur inside the combustion chamber before the piston starts on its down-stroke.

WHAT CHANGES WHAT?

Using a longer connecting rod makes it necessary to install a spacer plate under the cylinder with a thickness equal to the difference between the stock and longer connecting rods. The common misconception is that a longer rod gives the engine more displacement. It doesn't increase the displacement because the stroke length can only be changed at the crankshaft flyweights. That is called stroking a crankshaft because the distance from the center of the crank to the big-end pin is relocated farther away from the center. The biggest change in the engine comes from the increase in crankcase volume and the resultant decrease in the primary compression ratio. This may cause a loss of throttle response and low-end power. Some tuners use epoxy to line the walls of the transfer ports in an effort to decrease the crankcase volume and raise the primary compression ratio.

CYLINDER INTERCHANGE

Although the cylinders are the same height, the power valve, ports, and exhaust spigot are all different. In order to install a 1994 YZ250 cylinder on a later model, you have to swap the exhaust pipe flange or buy a pipe from Pro-Circuit. Check on availability of the pipe first. The transfer ports at the crankcase side are much different, requiring both the 1994 cylinder and the later model cases to be matched as a set. The power valve and head from a 1994 cylinder must also be installed. Regarding reed valves, the Boyesen or the V-Force is a better choice over stock valves.

1992–1996 YAMAHA YZ250

FLAWS: shock linkage, reeds, detonation, lean jetting (Mikuni carbs)

FIXES: DeVol linkage, Boyesen reeds, 59 needle and 400 main jet for Mikuni only.

This engine and chassis have great potential for improvement. The stock

When a YZF overheats, it may suffer from chronic head gasket leakage due to warping of the head.

engine has a hard midrange hit but falls flat at high rpm. The stock chassis has a shock linkage system with a high rising rate ratio. This makes the rear end handle harshly when accelerating out of turns. The carb jetting on the models with Mikuni carbs (1994 and earlier) were jetted too lean. The Keihin carburetor was introduced in 1995, and the standard jetting is very close to optimum. The 1995 model features an updated exhaust valve system. The new system uses a surge chamber for low rpm. This helps soften the midrange hit but the power valve is still susceptible to wearing, as were the earlier models. The 1996 model features a new chassis with a shock linkage system similar to the DeVol design. The top end was changed too. Yamaha changed the cylinder head design to one with greater piston-to-head clearance. This modification reduces the need for race gas.

BEST VALUE MODS

ENGINE: Boyesen reeds, head mod
SUSPENSION: DeVol linkage

SHOCK LINKAGE

DeVol Engineering has developed a rear suspension linkage kit. The kit improves the rear suspension by eliminating the mid-speed damping spike caused when going in and out of turns. DeVol changed the linkage ratio curve to be more linear. This reduces the shock shaft speed to a range where the stock shock can be adjusted to handle the braking and acceleration bumps that lurk in the bends of a racecourse.

INTAKE AND CARBURETOR

The best products for better engine performance are the Boyesen Superbowl and RAD valve. The original reed valve peaks and starts to flutter at only about 7,000 rpm. The RAD valve has a wider flow range so it extends the top end. The new float bowl design prevents the fuel from foaming and starving the engine.

CYLINDER AND HEAD MODS

The port timing of the original cylinder makes the powerband come on abruptly and fall flat early. Careful use of epoxy and a grinding tool can transform the cylinder into a wide, strong pulling engine with more top-end potential than any of the other bikes. An easy way to extract more top end from the YZ250 is to grind round the lower side of the oval exhaust port outlet. This will reduce the

exhaust gas velocity and improve flow at high rpm. Regarding the porting, the best mod for gaining top end is to raise the sub-exhaust ports to 38 mm, measured from the top of the cylinder. The squish velocity rating of the stock head is very high—too high for premium-unleaded fuel. The stock engine detonates in the midrange due to the high compression ratio and squish velocity. The solution is to narrow the cylinder head's squish band 9 mm, measured from one side of the chamber.

IGNITION TIMING

Set the ignition timing to 0.8 mm BTDC. This will eliminate any chance of pinging but unfortunately reduces the midrange hit in the powerband.

CYLINDER AND HEAD MODS 1996

The 1996 cylinder and head have less transfer time area than the previous models. You can adjust the ports to the same specs as the earlier models by raising the transfer ports 1 mm. The cylinder head can be turned down 0.020 in. or 0.5 mm on the face.

POWER VALVE MOD FOR WR250

Many riders complain that the powerband on the WR is difficult to manage on slippery off-cambers because the power hits too hard because the power valve snaps open in a narrow rpm band. The power valve timing can be changed using a file. To mellow the WR's powerband, file open the sub-exhaust ports on the power valve. This will enable those ports to open sooner and slowly bleed off some of the combustion pressure before the big exhaust port opens. This is the same principle that the 1995 YZ YPVS is based on.

CARB JETTING

The carb jetting for the Mikuni is too lean. The needle and main jet can be richened to a 59 needle and a 400 main jet. This makes the engine rev higher with more power. The Keihin carb used on the 1995-and-later models is jetted very close and only needs changes to suit local conditions.

REEDS

The next time you remove the cylinder from your YZ or WR, turn it upside down and look up the rear crankcase boost port. You'll notice that the reed stop plates block the upper and lower ports. Install a set of Boyesen reeds because they don't require the use of the reed stop plates and that will enable the boost ports to flow as they were intended to.

CLUTCH MODS

You can make the clutch easier to pull by rounding the edge on the actuating lever. Oil circulation holes can be drilled in each female spline on the clutch hub. I recommend using Cratex rubberized abrasives and an electric drill to polish the splines on the clutch hub. This will make the clutch plates react quicker without generating excess friction. The 1994 Yamaha *Wrench Report* recommends replacing the thrust washer that fits between the crankcase and the clutch basket with part number 2K7-16154-00-00. This thrust washer is 1 mm thinner and will improve the leverage at the handlebar.

POWER VALVE GOVERNOR

In 1994, Yamaha switched to a five-ball ramp from a four-ball ramp in the power valve governor mechanism. The mechanism is located under the right-side engine cover. Yamaha recommends switching back to the four-ball ramp because the extra ball makes the power valve open too soon. This effect is beneficial to enduro riders, but motocross riders will notice that the engine is sluggish when shifting from third to fourth gear on uphills. The balls are the same dimension for 1990 to 1994, so all you need to change is the ramp and discard one of the ball bearings. The Yamaha part number is 5X5-11911-01-00 (retainer).

YZR LONG-ROD KIT

Yamaha markets a kit that includes a longer connecting rod, a spacer plate for the cylinder, and longer power valve linkage. The long rod yields benefits for engines designed for high rpm. With a longer connecting rod, the piston will

accelerate quicker from BDC, causing the reeds to open farther. The rod spends more time at TDC, which enables the flame front to spread across the chamber before the piston moves on the downstroke. The spacer plate raises the cylinder to lower the primary compression ratio (increase in the volume of the crankcase) and positions the cylinder for the proper port timing. This kit is intended for expert-level motocross and DTX racing. This mod works well with other components such as aggressive porting, a 39.5-mm carb, and a high-revving pipe.

1991–1992 YAMAHA YZ250

FLAWS: forks rebound fast, rear end kicks, engine pings and detonates
FIXES: replace fork bushings, install DeVol linkage, richen jetting and modify cylinder head

These models don't handle as well as the next generation of YZ, but they have good engines with strong low-end power. The bikes are excellent second-hand bikes and can be bought for bargain prices.

The WR250 used engine designs that were a generation behind the YZs (until 1994). Many of the mods and accessory parts recommended for the YZ250 will work well on the WR250.

BEST VALUE MODS

ENGINE: Boyesen RAD valve
SUSPENSION: stiffer fork springs

EXHAUST SYSTEM

The stock exhaust system doesn't work very well. Pro-Circuit makes an excellent pipe and silencer for this bike that improves the power all throughout the rev range.

INTAKE SYSTEM

Replace the stock reeds with Boyesen dual-stage reeds and discard the stock reed stops. The reed stops block the rear boost ports.

FORKS

Change to a set of 0.41-kilogram Eibach forks springs. If the forks rebound too quickly and make a clanking noise, the piston rod bushings are worn out. That

is a common problem. The oil bypasses the rebound piston and flows past the bushing, thereby eliminating most of the damping effect. The bushings must be replaced as a set, and they are available from aftermarket companies such as Pro-Action, Race-Tech, and Pro-Circuit.

REAR SUSPENSION

DeVol makes a linkage kit for this bike that will make the older YZs handle almost as well as the 1996 YZ. The rear shock should be revalved in conjunction with the DeVol linkage kit. Check the chrome finish on the shock shaft because it is prone to peeling. Check the bottom of the shock linkage because the links hang so low on the YZ and are prone to cracking when the bike bottoms out.

CYLINDER HEAD MOD

The squish band of the cylinder head is too wide and causes the engine to ping in the midrange. Using a lathe, narrow the squish band to a width of 9 mm, measured from one side of the chamber. This mod also helps top-end power and makes it possible for the engine to burn super-unleaded premium fuel.

POWER VALVE PROBLEMS

The power valve has a stop tab on the left side that controls the full-open and closed positions of the power valve. The power valve is made of aluminum, and the stop plate is made of steel. The aluminum tab wears, allowing the power valve to rotate open and closed too far. When the valve closes too far, it contacts the piston and could cause the piston rings to break. Inspect the tab of the power valve. If it has worn more than 1 mm, replace it.

SLEEVE NUT

The aluminum sleeve nut that retains the top tapered bearing on the steering stem tends to seize to either the stem or the top clamp. Remove the sleeve nut and apply anti-seize or moly paste to the inside and outside of the nut. If the nut seizes on your bike, apply heat with a propane torch and spray penetrating oil on the nut. Caution: Never spray the penetrating oil at the torch because it is a flammable liquid.

1985–1990 YAMAHA YZ250

FLAWS: rod breakage, shift centering gets loose

FIXES: monitor rod clearance, epoxy pin

Yamaha has always had a great 250. Every year, the development team focuses its attention on making the bike perform better and last longer. Overall, the YZs are durable bikes. The following is a list of some areas to pay careful attention to.

BEST VALUE MODS

ENGINE: Boyesen boost ports, Boyesen reeds

SUSPENSION: Emulator valve, chain buffer

CRANKSHAFT CONNECTING RODS

Before 1990, the YZ250 had a 130-mm-long connecting rod that was prone to breaking 10 mm below the small end. This happens when the connecting rod's side clearance is allowed to wear past the manufacturer's service limit. In 1990, Yamaha shortened the rod to 125 mm, which fixed the problem. Unfortunately,

you can't interchange the rods. Just monitor the rod's side clearance and replace it when it becomes worn.

BOYESEN PORTS

On the 1985 to 1990 models, there is only one port linking the intake to the transfer ports. On these models, drill an additional hole (1/2-in. diameter) on the opposite side of the existing hole and install Boyesen reeds. The midrange power will be greatly improved.

SHIFT CENTERING PIN

On the right side of the crankcase behind the shift lever, there is a steel pin that is used as a pivot for the shift-shaft spring. The fit of the pin in the cases is loose, and it can fall out, causing the shift lever to flop around. Smear a dab of epoxy on the pin to hold it into the case. Be sure to clean the surfaces first or the epoxy won't adhere.

NOISY CHAIN BUFFERS

The chain buffer blocks on the 1988 YZs are made of a hard, durable material. Unfortunately, the chain makes a horrible slapping noise when it hits the

buffer block. Switch to the block from the 1989 model, which is made from a softer material.

CLUTCHES

The 1988 YZ has an inferior clutch pressure plate design. Switch to the 1989 part. It has stronger ribs on the back side. The 1989 part makes it easier to adjust the clutch to prevent dragging and slipping. Stiffer clutch springs will also help.

FORKS

The best mod for the damper rod forks (before 1989) is a Race-Tech Emulator valve.

REAR SHOCK

In the mid-1980s, YZ250s used a component called a B.A.S.S. system. The device was activated by the foot brake through a cable. The cable operated the compression valve of the rear shock. It was designed to adjust the shock damping when riding through whooped-out straights while dragging the rear brake. The B.A.S.S. system requires constant adjusting, cleaning, and servicing, and the cable adjuster is prone to corrosion failure. Most suspension technicians disable the B.A.S.S. system when servicing the shocks.

Another characteristic problem with the YZ shocks is shock shaft corrosion. This problem is aggravated by lack of oil changing. The shaft starts to turn blue and the chrome peels off the shaft, eventually causing seal failure. Change your shock oil often.

TRANSMISSION PROBLEMS

Put your YZ up on a stand. With the engine off and the transmission in neutral, try to rotate the rear wheel. If it is very difficult and there is a lot of drag, the bearing that supports the left side of the clutch shaft could be working its way out of the crankcases and rubbing up against the second-gear drive. Eventually, the bronze bushing inside the gear will seize to the shaft. Whenever you have the engine apart for new bearings, replace the left-side clutch-shaft bearing and use a sharp drift rod to stake it to the cases.

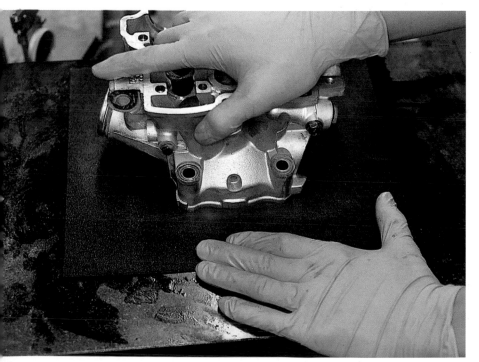

The head can be lapped flat using sandpaper and a surface plate.

Falicon makes this knife-shaped connecting rod for the YZF450. It's a stronger design than stock, and the shape reduces oil windage.

This will prevent it from sliding out toward the gear.

ELECTRICAL PROBLEMS

The biggest cause of hard starting is a poor ground at the secondary coil (top coil under the fuel tank). Remove the coil and file the frame tabs where the coil mounts. Another common problem is high resistance in the generating coils (the coils behind the flywheel). The coils can be repaired for half the price of a new stator plate assembly.

2003–2004 YAMAHA YZF450
FLAWS: weak crankshaft, too hard hitting
FIXES: install Falicon connecting rod kit, oversize header pipe

Yamaha built the YZF450 to compete with Honda's big bore entry. Redesigning the 426 engines, making the castings and steel parts thinner and lighter, may lead to future reliability issues. Riders complain that the power hits hard like a two-stroke.

Installing an oversize header pipe or a heavier flywheel weight will tame the hit in the 450 and make it more like the old 426. There have been some connecting rod failures and Falicon responded by making a knife-shaped connecting rod that reduces windage and is much stronger than stock connecting rods.

BEST VALUE MODS
Oversized header pipe

2000–2002 YAMAHA YZF426
FLAWS: hard to start
FIXES: auto-decompressor cam

The YZF426 is one of the best-built dirt bikes of all time. There are some characteristic Yamaha items to pay attention to: monitoring the valve clearance, taking care to torque the cam cap bolts to only 60 in./pounds, replacing the cam chain and head bolts at every top-end job, and changing the oil frequently. Some other problems are common to YZFs raced on hard-pack terrain such as clay, pavement, or ice—fifth gear tends to disengage in a high-load situation. The problem is the engagement dogs wear rounded and won't hold engagement with the opposing gear. In most cases, if the 426 suffers from a slipping tranny, there are several gears in matching pairs that need to be changed all at once.

BEST VALUE MODS
Hot Cams

1998–1999 YZF400
FLAWS: Too-lean jetting
FIXES: Carb jetting

BEST VALUE MOD
ENGINE: Hot Start Button, jetting
SUSPENSION: springs

The best-selling MX bike has had thousands of magazine pages written about every aspect of its maintenance and performance. With the huge range of accessories available, you can get carried away buying things for this bike. So rather than focus on particular accessories, let's look at the basics affecting reliability.

CARB JETTING
The stock jetting on the 1998 is a bit lean, especially for loamy terrain and cold climates. Good baseline settings are a 50 pilot jet, a 185 main jet, and adjust the air and fuel screw to tune it in. The accelerator pump needs periodic cleaning; dirt and water seep past the rubber boot and slow down the action of the pump. For more information about this high-maintenance carb, look to Chapter 5.

HOT START BUTTON
The Hot Start Button from Terry Products is a handlebar control for the carb's air bypass system. The Hot Start Button makes it easier to restart the bike in a hurry and can be used to lean the jetting. The button has a wide range of incremental movement. If you're riding at a steadily increasing altitude, you can adjust the carb jetting for the less dense air by cracking the button open.

FLYWHEEL WEIGHT
In rocky or slippery terrain, the YZ may be prone to stalling or quick wheelspin. You can buy flywheel weights that bolt on to the perimeter of the stock flywheel.

CLUTCH BREAKAGE
Riders with tendencies to fan the clutch frequently should change the aluminum clutch plates for steel ones. If the plates shatter, the debris tends to flow to the oil sump screen, causing it to clog and reduce lubrication.

CRANKCASE BREATHER
The crankcase vent hose exits from the top of the engine. That hose needs a filter at the end to reduce the dust that collects in the hose. K&N makes a stainless-steel filter, marketed mainly for sport riders. Look to a road bike shop for the crankcase vent filters.

BIG BORE KITS
The 1998 and 1999 YZ400 cylinders can be overbored 2 mm to 94 mm for a total displacement of 420 cc. The 2000 YZ426 cylinder casting is much thicker than the earlier models. Wiseco makes a

97-mm piston kit for the YZ426 that boosts the displacement to 450 cc. It is possible to install the 2000 cylinder on the previous models of YZ400, but in order to use the Wiseco 97-mm piston you have to install a rod kit from a YZ426 because the small-end pin size is larger. The part number for the 97-mm Wiseco kit is 4698P8. Cometic makes a corresponding gasket kit.

PISTONS

Wiseco makes the oversize piston kits in the stock and high-compression models. The sizes range from 94 to 97. The compression ratios are 12.5 to 1 (part 4649) and 13.5 to 1 (part 4650). High-compression pistons are good for high-altitude correction and give more low-end to midrange torque. The 13.5 to 1 pistons perform best using VP C-18 fuel. That fuel is blended for pro-stock drag racing and improves the throttle response.

AFTERMARKET ENGINE MANAGEMENT KITS

Optimum Power Technologies offers an engine management solution for the YZ400/426. The system includes a generator, DC power system, complete ignition system, throttle body, and fuel pump. The unit features total control of the ignition and fuel system via a handlebar switch.

A laptop or PDA can diagnose system errors and make programming changes. You can even download ignition and fuel maps from Optimum's website, www.optimum-power.com

That way, you can customize the fuel and ignition systems to suit a variety of aftermarket components or displacement sizes.

GEARING

Most riders increase the size of the rear sprocket as much as 54 teeth, depending on the local riding conditions.

SUSPENSION

Overall, the shock spring and valving are stiff and the forks are soft. This bike needs balanced springs front to back. A simple rule of thumb is riders with geared weight under 165 pounds need softer fork springs and riders with geared weight over 175 pounds need stiffer fork springs and revalving.

For heavier riders, the bike may seem to ride pitched forward. If the front race sag is 2 in. or greater, the springs are either sacked out or too soft for your weight.

TECHNOGEEK'S LIBRARY

If you are looking for the highest level of technical information about racing motorcycle engine and chassis design, these six books and related software programs are the best to get you started. Most of these books are written for college-level readers enrolled in mechanical engineering programs. With the exception of Kevin Cameron's sportbike book, all of these books may seem shockingly expensive and you can't just run down to the local bookstore to find them. Once you obtain some of these books and software, I encourage you to seek out other related works by these talented authors. In my own library, I have copies of SAE papers, patents, and notes from seminars led by some of these men.

Design and Tuning of Four-Stroke Engines, $90

Design and Tuning of Two-Stroke Engines, $90
   By Gordon P. Blair
   www.sae.org
   www.professorblair.com

Professor Gordon P. Blair was the Pro Vice Chancellor of the Queen's University of Belfast. He is a motorcycle racing enthusiast and was the driving force in combining the power of the digital computer with the disciplines of unsteady gas dynamics and thermodynamics to produce a line of programs and books. The Prof's books are threaded with math equations, and his lively writing style gives the reader a sense of history and the insight gained from simulations that debunk many of the performance myths that plague the motorcycle industry. Professor Blair sells a line of high-end software with his partner Hans Herman and they work as consultants to many of the Nextel Cup teams.

Motorcycle Constructor's Handbook, volumes 1 and 2, $100 each
   By John Bradley
   www.eurospares.com

In my opinion, John Bradley is the most talented and well-rounded motorcycle engineer alive today. His two-volume set of books thoroughly covers the theory of how motorcycle systems work, the design of components, selection of materials, and a wide array of practical manufacturing and fabrication methods. John's books are written to teach you how to design and build a motorcycle from the ground up.

Motorcycle Handling and Chassis Design, $50
   By Tony Foale
   www.tonyfoale.com

Tony started his career as a nuclear scientist, but his love of racing motorcycles directed him to dedicate his life to discovering and explaining the theory of how these wonderful machines work. His books, CDs, and software focus on improving motorcycle handling. Although the material is geared toward road racing bikes, it's all relative and excellent reading, especially for mechanical engineers. Tony also runs a series of technical seminars based on his book.

Sportbike Performance Handbook, $25
   By Kevin Cameron
   www.motorbooks.com

Kevin is the technical editor for *Cycle World* magazine and the most prolific writer in the history of the sport. Kevin's book covers all the major systems of a sportbike, starting with design theory, history of development, and practical modification techniques.

Precision Auto Research Software, $400
   By David Redzus, Ph.D.
   www.precisionautoresearch.com

This software set features over 200 Excel macro programs related to the design and reference of automotive and motorcycle engineering topics. These programs are thought provoking and have proven in practice to help solve inherent maladies with component designs. The web site features many demos of the individual programs.

Two-Stroke Racing Software, $60–$300
   By Tom Turner
   www.tsrsoftware.com

Tom Turner had a great career as a tuner and drag racer, building engines for legendary racers in the sports of dirt track, drag racing, and motocross. Tom channeled his efforts into writing over 100 software programs to help amateur tuners with the math and layout of things like cylinder ports, heads, and expansion chambers. Most of the two-stroke porting and cylinder head specifications listed in this book were developed using PORT 2000 software.

INDEX

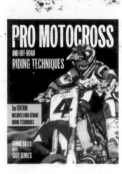
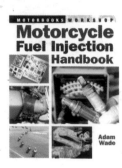

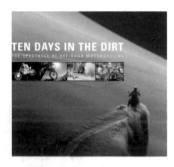

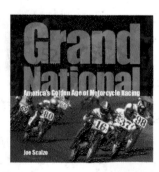
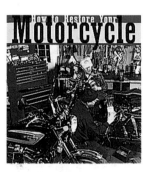
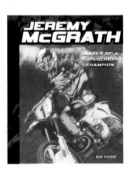